Voices of the Heart

D0890867

VOICES
of the HEART
Asian American Women on Immigration, Work, and Family

●·•● ●●● • ●●,●•● ●●●● •● ●●,●● ● ● •

HUPING LING

Truman State University Press

Cover design: Teresa Wheeler

Type: Text is Minion, © Adobe Systems Inc.
Printed by: Thomson-Shore, Dexter, Michigan USA

Library of Congress Cataloging-in-Publication Data

Linghu, Ping, 1956–
Voices of the heart : Asian American women on immigration, work, and family / Huping
Ling.
p. cm.
Includes bibliographical references and index.
ISBN 978-1-931112-68-0 (pbk. : alk. paper)
1. Asian American women—Middle West—Social conditions—Anecdotes. 2. Asian Ameri-
can women—Middle West—Biography—Anecdotes. 3. Women immigrants—Middle
West—Biography—Anecdotes. 4. Asian American women—Employment—Middle West—
Aanecdotes. 5. Acculturation—Middle West—Anecdotes. 6. Family—Middle West—
Anecdotes. 7. Middle West—Ethnic relations—Anecdotes. 8. Middle West—Biography—
Anecdotes. 9. Middle West—Social conditions—Anecdotes. 10. Oral history. I. Title.
F358.2.A75L56 2008
305.48'8950092277—dc22

                                                                    2007029143

The paper in this publication meets the minimum requirements of the American National
Standard for Information Sciences—Permanence of Paper for Printed Library Materials,
ANSI Z39.48-1992.

To my family, my students, and the Asian American community.

Contents

Illustrations

Preface

This volume contains fifty-four interviews selected from over three hundred interviews conducted by me during the 1990s and 2000s and by students under my supervision between 1993 and 1996. The interviewees were identified through public and private directories and personal contacts, and were selected to represent the broad and diverse aspects of Asian American women's lives. A standard questionnaire was used to ensure a uniform and consistent methodology in order to make meaningful comparisons. The questionnaire covers various dimensions of Asian American women's life including immigration or ethnic background, education, settlement choice, employment, discrimination, marriage, dating, family life, child rearing, community service, assimilation, cultural preservation, political participation, and religious practice. Most interviews consisted of two-hour long tape-recorded interviews, and many had follow-up interviews. My assistant team and I carefully read transcripts of each interview, highlighted the information reflecting the above-mentioned aspects, and selected cases that best represent each ethnic group. We then converted all interviews into narratives. I reorganized each by topic and chronology. To protect the privacy of the interviewees, the individual names have been altered. The women's original language and speech patterns have been retained as much as possible to maintain the originality and authenticity of the oral history interviews; however, they have been lightly edited for clarity. The varied length, intensity, and articulation of the interviews cordially reflects the diverse educational, socioeconomic, and ethnic backgrounds as well as the individual personalities and temperaments of these women.

The volume is organized first by ethnicity, then by topic to allow each group to maintain their coherence and interconnections, and to facilitate dealing with each ethnic group's experiences as compared to other ethnic groups. It includes the larger and earlier groups of Asian

American women—the Chinese, Japanese, Filipinas, Koreans, and Asian Indians—as well as the newer groups of Asian Americans who have arrived since the 1970s—the Vietnamese, Laotians, Hmong, Thais, and Pakistanis. The women interviewed reveal the social and economic conditions in their countries of origin, their aspirations and expectations prior to immigration, their frustrations and difficulties in the initial years of their American life, their joys and successes in their education and occupation, and their efforts in preserving their ethnic heritage while assimilating into American society. The women interviewed include those with a single ethnic heritage and many with mixed ethnicity who make up a growing segment of the Asian American population, but are often omitted from literature focusing on single ethnic groups. The interviews also include students, both native-born or naturalized Americans and international students, some of whom may eventually settle in the United States, while others may return to their homelands.

Each chapter begins with an introduction to highlight interview cases in the chapter and significant themes for that ethnic group. Some themes are common to all the women interviewed (immigration, work, interracial marriage, and cultural identity), but the interviews also revealed topics unique to each group. For the Chinese women, a section is devoted to the native-born and foreign-born students in higher education. For the Filipinas, it includes a topic on Filipinas in the health industry. For the Japanese women, it is a reflection on the internment experience. For Korean women, the issue of adoption is addressed. For the South Asian women, there is coverage of the management of hotels and motels, and for the Southeast Asian women, attention is given to the refugee experience and the status of Vietnamese adoptees.

The majority of interviewees are from the midwestern region of the United States, as reflected in its title *Voices of the Heart*. The "heart" here implies not only the deep personal feelings of Asian American women, but also the heartland of the United States. As Asian American studies have been heavily concentrated on the West and East Coasts and Hawaii, the Midwest has been a frontier in the field and awaits further scholarly investigation.

Acknowledgments

I have had the great fortune to have the assistance of many individuals and institutions over the past decade and a half as I worked to produce this volume about Asian American women. I am deeply indebted to the individuals who have generously shared their valuable time and life experiences with me during the 1990s and 2000s and with my students from classes on Asian American women. My heartfelt thanks go to the fifty-four interviewees included in this volume, whose names have been changed to protect their privacy.

Between 1993 and 1996, students from my classes on Asian American women conducted oral history interviews under my supervision. They conducted and transcribed interviews, and wrote analytical papers based on interviews and other primary and secondary sources. I am most grateful to the following former students, who allowed me to publish their interviews: Christopher Ahrens, Trish Aumann, Tina Beyene, Claralyn P. Bollinger, Jayson Campbell, Colin W. Cross, Kim Dickmann, Raymond Flojo, Gwen Garthe, Nikki Griep, Heather Hagedorn, Melissa Blagg Holcomb, Misato Ito, Kimberly Kerlin, Shawnna Matteson, Kym Miller, Kimberly Oelschlaeger McElwain, Courtney L. McKenny, Jennifer J. Orey, Hina Patel, Tyson A. Riemann, Laura Rodey, Maggie Roth, Nicole Schmitz, Greg Smith, and David Spight.

A number of students from Truman State University have helped me with the project as my student assistants during the 1990s and 2000s. Devon Bireta, Christie Boyle, Claire Grothe, Crystal Morgan, Janet Noll, Jennifer VanHuton, and Catherine Webster converted the original interviews into narratives and/or typed them. Eric Roger read and highlighted the crucial information of each interview. Their assistance was invaluable and indispensable to the completion of the volume.

Colleagues in Asian American studies have served as incessant sources of inspiration, encouragement, and consultation. I am very grateful to the two anonymous reviewers who enthusiastically endorsed the manuscript and offered invaluable suggestions, which have been incorporated into the book. I am especially thankful to the most respected specialists on specific groups of Asian Americans, who have generously taken time from their busy schedules to review and critique the respective chapters of the manuscript: Yen Le Espiritu (Filipina and Vietnamese), Gary Y. Okihiro (Japanese), Todd LeRoy Perreira (Thai), Min Hyoung Song (Korean), Rajini Srikanth (South Asian), and Kou Yang (Laotian, Hmong, Vietnamese). Their careful editing and judicious and insightful comments have ensured the quality and credibility of the volume; however, I am responsible for any spelling or factual errors that may remain.

Anna Crosslin, president of the International Institute of Metro Saint Louis, generously provided me with the Directory of the International/ Intercultural Resources in St. Louis and allowed me to interview her and a number of staff members. I am also grateful to Kit Hadwiger, Kazuko Miller, Zakira Nayeem, Bella Shao, and Grace Chen Yin for sharing personal photos with me; to Ann Rynearson of the International Institute of St. Louis for generously allowing me to use photos from her collection; to Huang-Suk Harrington for permitting me to use her personal photo; to James Harrington for reproducing the photo; and to Ha, Pai Yen Lin Lu, and Dara Phannarath for granting me permission to use their photos. Kit Hadwiger also carefully reviewed the chapter on Filipinas for spelling and factual errors. I am grateful to Tim Barcus, the photographer at Truman State University, who provided vital assistance in reproducing the images for the book.

Truman State University, my home institute, has been most generous in supporting my research and writing. My colleagues in the history discipline have served as the most enthusiastic supporters of my professional undertakings by wholeheartedly supporting my proposals to offer undergraduate and graduate courses on Asian Americans and to establish an interdisciplinary minor with a concentration on Asian and Asian American studies. The Division of Social Science and the Office of Academic Affairs at Truman have generously funded research trips for this project. The staff members of Pickler Memorial Library at Truman have tirelessly processed my numerous requests for materials through inter-library loan.

The Truman State University Press has been the most wonderful home of the book. Its staff members have been extremely enthusiastic and supportive of the project, editing the manuscript with a high level of thoroughness and intelligence, designing the book with grace and sensitivity, and skillfully guiding it through every stage of production.

My family has gone through all the troubles and joys of my academic endeavors with me in the past decade and a half. My husband, Dr. Mohammad Samiullah, has been a critique, consultant, and technical support of the project (and all my other undertakings as well). In addition, he assisted me with numerous technical details on special names and terms concerning South Asian cultures. My sons, William and Isaac, are the most candid critiques of my work, never failing to express their opinions. My family has sustained my professional and personal life. Without their loving support, this book would not exist.

A Historical Review and Synthesis of Asian American Women

To better understand Asian American women, one needs to first look at their cultural and historical background. Asian American women can trace their diverse cultural and religious background to the lands of their ancestors. Over the past millennia, the landmass of Asia and the neighboring islands have embraced the rich and diverse cultural and religious institutions of Confucianism, Daoism, Hinduism, Buddhism, Sikhism, Islam, Shintoism, and Christianity. Of these ideologies, Confucian restrictions had the greatest impact on women's thoughts and actions, but other religions' values also profoundly affected their personal behavior.

Confucian Dominance in East Asia

The bend of the Yellow River in northern China has been known as the cradle of Chinese civilization; here the earliest Chinese dynasty, Xia (2205–1766 BCE), arose. The succeeding Shang dynasty (1766–1122 BCE) has been credited with the invention of the writing system in China, the *jiagu wen*, with characters inscribed on turtle shells and animal bones. The Zhou dynasty (1122–221 BCE) that replaced Shang contributed greatly to the contending schools of philosophy in ancient China, among which Confucianism and Daoism have been the most enduring.

Confucianism is named for its originator, *Kong Fuzi* (Latinized as Confucius). Confucian ideology has strongly influenced spiritual and political life in East Asia. Rules of successive dynasties found it a most effective governing ideology; consequently it became entrenched in Chinese society and was introduced to its neighboring countries of Korea, Japan, and Vietnam. Throughout history, generations of Chinese scholars have interpreted and elaborated Confucian teachings in numerous volumes; however, the essential ideas of Confucianism are centered around basic concepts of virtue and individual behavior. In terms of governing, the Confucian ideology stresses the moral ethic of the ruler and his government. Individuals maintain their proper places in the hierarchical society by obeying central, local, and familial authorities in their roles as subjects, wives, sons, and daughters.

For Chinese women, the multilayered hierarchical structure is encapsulated in the Three Obediences and Four Virtues. A Chinese woman is expected to obey her father before marriage, her husband after marriage, and her son when widowed. She is also expected to possess virtues of obedience, reticence, pleasing manners, and domestic skills. These rigid ideological constraints were reinforced by a physical torment known as foot binding that instilled the concept of women as weaker and, therefore, inferior creatures. The practice of foot binding may have begun with dancers at the imperial court during the Tang dynasty (618–907 CE). By the Song dynasty (960–1279 CE), the custom had been introduced among upper-class women. During the Qing dynasty (1644–1911 CE), the custom became common throughout Chinese society. At the age of three to five, girls had their feet tightly wrapped and gradually bent until the arch was broken and the toes, except for the big one, tuned under. The "lily foot" produced by such practice crippled women to the extent that they could barely walk without support.[1]

The origins of Korea are related to the movement of people from the Manchurian area of China into the Korean peninsula. Tan'gun, supposedly a scion of the Shang royal line of China, founded the Korean state in 2333 BCE. The area came under China's direct rule when Wudi of the Han dynasty (206 BCE–220 CE) conquered Chosŏn (the ancient name of Korea) in 109/8 BCE and set up four commanderies in the peninsula. When the Chinese colonies in Korea dwindled in the fourth century, three native Korean kingdoms emerged and divided the peninsula among themselves: Koguryŏ in the north, Paekche in the southwest, and Silla in the southeast. By the late seventh century, the peninsula was unified by Silla. During the Silla period (668–935 CE), Korean society was greatly influenced by the Chinese ideals of the Tang dynasty; the sinicization of the peninsula was so profound the state was nicknamed Little Tang. Yet, it was the Yi dynasty (1392–1910) that was seen as a model Confucian society.[2] The Koreans in

---

[1]Ko, *Cinderella's Sisters*; Fairbank, *East Asia, Tradition and Transformation*, 142–43; Ling, *Surviving on the Gold Mountain*, 19; and Xu, "Sancun LinLian" [Bound Feet].
[2]Fairbank, *East Asia*, 300–2.

the Yi dynasty adopted Confucianism with great enthusiasm and restructured their government, value system, and society strictly along Chinese lines, revering and observing Confucian principles as dogmatic rituals. Koreans faithfully practiced filial piety and dutifully observed the three-year period of mourning for parents. Women were restricted and the remarriage of widows was severely condemned.

The Vietnamese people can be traced back to Mongoloid groups who, in prehistoric times, migrated from South China into the Southeast Asian peninsula. China extended control over this region by the end of the third century BCE and called it Nam Viet, meaning "South Yue," referring to the southern frontier of the Chinese civilization. The Han dynasty annexed the region and established a Chinese government, along with the Chinese writing system, Confucian classic learning, and a Chinese official-dom. Chinese domination continued until late in the Tang dynasty (about 939 CE), when disorder in South China encouraged the Vietnamese upper class to develop a sense of national identity. They established the Vietnamese dynasties of Later Li (1010–1225), Tran (1225–1400), Later Le (1428–1789), and Nguyen (1802–1945). Though purely Vietnamese regimes, these dynasties continued the early imitation of Chinese government, high culture, literature, dress, and codes of conduct.[3]

The Japanese, like their neighbors in Korea and China, are a homogeneous Mongoloid people. But unlike Korea and Vietnam, Japan was never invaded by Chinese armies; however, Chinese culture and ideologies influenced Japanese society and government. While the natural boundary of water protected Japan from continental invasion, it also made the Japanese more aware of their cultural isolation and more conscious of borrowing from the outside. The Japanese state, which dates back to the first emperor, Jimmu, in the seventh century BCE, had regular contact with the continent, especially Korea. This contact strengthened the Yamato government culturally and economically. In the sixth century, Buddhism was introduced to Japan through Korea. The introduction of Buddhism ushered in a series of cultural and institutional changes including the establishment of the Chinese type of central government, nationalization of land, taxation, adoption of the Chinese writing system and Chinese calendar, and regular trade with China. The process of sinicization came to a halt during the Heian period (794–1185 CE), when the Tang dynasty in China began to decline and the Japanese had been so immersed in many aspects of Chinese culture

[3]Fairbank, *East Asia*, 268.

that further borrowing became less relevant. The decline of the central government in Japan resulted in the rise of a feudal system dominated by a ruling class of warriors (samurai) that lasted for seven centuries. The Confucian ideologies associated with bureaucratic skills were valued again during the Tokugawa shogunate (1600–1868) when prolonged peace meant the government was more in need of Confucian scholar-bureaucrats than warriors. Consequently, Confucian codes of conduct were reinstated and a substantial portion of the samurai transformed themselves from rough warriors into refined Confucian scholars. As a result, the status of Japanese women declined to conform to the Confucian restrictions.

During the Meiji period (1868–1912), the Meiji government abandoned feudalism and encouraged economic growth and industrialization to modernize Japan and enable it to meet challenges from the West. The entire country was mobilized to realize the patriotic dream, with the women's role defined as ensuring the smooth operation of a male-centered, authoritarian, traditional family.[4] The Meiji government's slogan "Good Wife, Wise Mother" promoted Japanese state policy that emphasized a woman's responsibilities in the domestic sphere. The Meiji Civil Code of 1898 established the samurai ideal of the *ie* (house) as the legal unit of society and the national standard for the family. The code legally subordinated women to men in several ways: a wife needed her husband's consent before entering a legal contract; a husband could divorce his wife on the ground of adultery; and a woman under age twenty-five could not marry without the permission of the household head.[5] These Confucian-centered and authoritarian restrictions placed women in a disadvantageous position within their own societies. They also helped form the perception among outsiders that Asian women were more family-oriented and were docile, submissive creatures.

Religious Traditions

Confucianism, though not a religion, has been revered as such by many in East Asian countries. Other religions, including Hinduism, Buddhism, Sikhism, Islam, Shintoism, and Christianity, have also contributed to the cultural traditions of Asian American women.

The term Hindu is derived from the Sanskrit *Sindhu*, referring to the River Indus. The Aryan invaders who arrived in the Indus Valley region in

[4]Bernstein, *Recreating Japanese Women,* 8.
[5]Bernstein, *Recreating Japanese Women,* 8.

the second millennium BCE (and from whose language Sanskrit is derived) practiced the Vedic religion, which was based on the worship of deities related to natural phenomena with rituals centered on animal sacrifices and the use of soma to enter a trancelike state. Modern Hinduism evolved from the ancient Vedic religion, with the development of philosophical concepts of ethics and duties (*dharma*), the cycle of birth, life, death, and rebirth (*samsara*), action and subsequent reaction (*karma*), and liberation from the cycle of *samsara* (*moksha*). According to Hindu doctrines, the ideal life for a Hindu man consists of four stages: *brahmacarya*, a period of discipline and education; *vanaprasthya*, the retirement stage, a time of retreat for loosening bonds to the material world; and *sannyasa*, the ascetic stage, a time of renouncing worldly attachments and preparing to shed the body for the next life. Thus, the Hindu system of values emphasizes the attainment of knowledge, active work, sacrifice and service to others, and renunciation of earthly pleasures.

An important component of Hinduism is its caste system, which divides people into social groups depending on descent, marriage, and occupation. There are about three thousand castes, divided into four major groups: Brahmans (priests and religious teachers), Kshatriyas (kings, warriors, and aristocrats), Vaisyas (those engaged in commerce and trades), and Sudras (farmers, servants, and laborers). Over time, the hereditary caste system has maintained a uniform division of labor, class stratification, and stable social interactions, and has therefore been mostly preserved by Indian society. The caste system also prohibits intercaste marriage, although anuloma marriage (in which the bridegroom is of a higher caste than the bride) has been acceptable and children of such marriages belong to the caste of their father.[6] Muslims, Christians, and Sikhs in India also have castes, although they are usually more fluid than Hindu castes. The Hindu religious ceremonies generally can be classified into several categories of daily meditations, prayers, and rituals; weekly religious observances such as fasting on a certain day of the week; prayers and penances performed according to the lunar calendar; and the annual festivals connected with the worship of particular gods and goddess of the Hindu pantheon.

Buddhism, which also originated in India, follows the teachings of Siddhartha Gautama (563–483 BCE), prince of a small kingdom on the south edge of Nepal who renounced his princely life to seek enlightenment.

---

[6]Molly, *Experiencing the World's Religions*.

He left his home at age twenty-nine, attained enlightenment, and became known as Buddha (enlightened one) when he was thirty-five, after developing a philosophy centered around the Four Noble Truths: 1) life is painful; 2) the origin of pain is desire; 3) the cessation of pain is to be sought by ending desire; and 4) the way to this goal is through the Noble Eightfold Path of right understanding, right motives, right speech, right action, right livelihood, right effort, right mindfulness, and right meditation. Buddhism is divided into the schools of Mahayana (great vehicle) and Hinayana (lesser vehicle) or Theravada (doctrine of the Elders). Hinayana, which developed distinctive practices, is mainly practiced in Sri Lanka, Myanmar (Burma), Thailand, and Cambodia; Mahayana has spread to China, Korea, Japan, and Vietnam.[7]

Sikhism originated in the sixteenth century in northern India. The term "Sikh," deriving from the Sanskrit, means "disciple," "learner," or "instruction." Sikhism is based on the teachings of Guru Nannak Dev (1469–1538) and his nine successors (Angad Dev, Amar Das, Ram Das, Arjan Dev, Har Gobind, Har Rai, Har Krishan, Teg Bahadur, and Gobind Singh) and a collection of writings called the *Gurū Granth Sāhib*. Sikhism's primary concepts include the belief in one god, disciplined meditation on God, hard work, service to others, and charity. The traditions and teachings of Sikhism are closely associated with the history and culture of the Punjab province of India, where most of the world's 23 million Sikhs live.[8] The strong military and political organization of the Sikh made it a powerful force in medieval India and a large number of Sikhs served in the military under British rule or in police forces in various parts of the British Empire, which made them more worldly and susceptible to migration. Among the near 7,000 Indians who immigrated to the United States between 1899 and 1914, most were farmers from Punjab province, men from martial castes, and landowning families.[9]

Islam, like the other two primary monotheistic religions in the world, Judaism and Christianity, emerged from Southwest Asia and is based on the belief in one god as creator of the universe and humankind, and accepts Abraham and Moses as important teachers and prophets. Under the leadership of Muhammad and his successors, Islam rapidly spread by religious conversion and military conquest and has become one of the primary

[7]Humphreys, *Buddhism.*
[8]Singh, *Illustrated History of the Sikhs.*
[9]Leonard, *South Asian Americans,* 24.

religions in South and Southeast Asian countries. Of the estimated 1.4 billion Muslims in the world, 60 percent live in Asia,[10] and almost one third in South Asia.[11] The four nations with the largest Muslim populations—Indonesia (194 million), India (150 million), Pakistan (145 million), and Bangladesh (130 million)—are all in Asia. In addition, China has 39 million Muslims.

Shintoism, the indigenous Japanese religion that originated around the seventh century BCE, combines shamanism, hero and ancestor worship, nature worship, and fertility worship. It does not have a fully organized theology, canon of scripture, or defined set of prayers, but is based on a belief that *kami* (gods or spirits) exist everywhere and that people can mediate their relations with the spirits through certain rituals. According to Shinto mythology, a divine pair of *kami* named Izanagi and Izanami gave birth to the Japanese islands, and their children became the deities of various clans. One of their children, Amaterasu (Sun Goddess), was the ancestor of the Japanese imperial family.

Shinto also emphasizes the notions of pollution and purity. The purification ritual is not only important in spiritual life but also penetrates various aspects of daily life; Japanese people traditionally take baths, wash their hands, and rinse out their mouths often. In Shintoism, death, injury, disease, menstrual blood, and childbirth are considered pollution and should be avoided. Shinto also places a high value on family and tradition; the family is the main mechanism by which traditions are preserved, and morality is based upon what is beneficial to the group.[12]

Christian influence in Asia in the first millennium, though less known, has been documented by scholars.[13] After European traders reached Japan in the sixteenth century, Jesuit missionaries followed. Francis Xavier (1506–1552) initiated the Christian missionary movement in Japan in 1549, and Matteo Ricci (1552–1610) was sent to China in 1582. The evangelical missions since then have converted millions in East, South, and Southeast Asian countries and impacted Asian immigration to America, with Korean immigrants as the most illuminating example, consisting of 40 percent Christians around the beginning of the twentieth century.

[10]"Islam"; and Hefner, "Islam and Asian Security"; and Armstrong, *Islam*.
[11]Gregorian, *Islam*.
[12]Hendry, *Understanding Japanese*, 116–19.
[13]Gillman and Klimkeit, *Christians in Asia Before 1500*.

Thus, Asian women emigrating to America bring rich and varied cultural and religious traditions that have significant effects on their assumptions and actions.

———————————◆◆◆◆◆———————————

In addition to their cultural and historical roots, Asian American women are also affected by the conditions of their migration, both in their ancestral lands and in the host country. Upon landing on American soil, the immigrant women's most urgent need is survival and possibly success through hard work, whether at home, at a garment workshop, at a family business, at a factory, or at a professional job. While consciously preserving their cultural heritage, Asian American women also deliberately assimilate into the host society, as demonstrated by interracial marriage and other aspects of their lives.

Patterns of Immigration

Immigrant women from Asia share common traits and the push and pull paradigm is applicable to most Asian immigrant groups. The ratio of men to women among immigrant groups in the late nineteenth and early twentieth centuries had usually been uneven, as a result of American immigration restrictions and the socioeconomic conditions of the countries of origin. The majority of Asian immigrants to the United States before World War II were men not accompanied by families. Most were laborers rather than professionals, seeking employment in menial jobs. Those who were successful in finding jobs often sent for their families or brought over a wife. However, the post–World War II and particularly the post-1965 Asian immigrants were more likely to arrive in family groups and included a higher percentage of professionals than their earlier counterparts.

CHINA

In the mid-nineteenth century, Chinese immigrant women were pushed by forces in China and pulled by attractions in the United States. The push mainly came from natural disasters and internal upheavals in China during the 1840s and 1850s. The pull resulted from a strong desire for family reunion, economic pursuits, and personal fulfillment.[14]

During the 1840s, China experienced a number of natural calamities. In 1847, there was a severe drought in Henan province; in 1849, there was a

---

[14]Ling, *Surviving on the Gold Mountain*, 20.

famine in Guangxi province; the Yangtze River flooded in the provinces of Hubei, Anhui, Jiangsu, and Zhejiang. Flood and famine gave way to the catastrophic Taiping Rebellion (1850–64), which devastated the land, uprooted the peasantry, and disrupted the economy and polity.

Moreover, the importance of opium deepened the social and economic crisis. As a result of the Opium War of 1840 through 1842, opium traffic practically became unrestrained. The volume of opium imported rose from 33,000 chests in 1842 to 46,000 chests in 1848, and to 52,929 chests in 1850. The year 1848 alone witnessed the outflow of more than 10 million taels of silver, which exacerbated the already grave economic dislocation and copper-silver exchange rate. The disruptive economic consequences of opium importation were further compounded by the general influx of foreign goods in the open ports. Canton was particularly hard hit due to its long history of foreign trade and the wide foreign contact. Local household industries collapsed and the previously self-sufficient economy suffered. Those who were adversely affected became potential emigrants.

Among the pulling factors, the desire for family reunion played an important role from the beginning of Chinese women's immigration. According to immigration records, of the thousands of women who were admitted to the United States between 1898 and 1908, more than 90 percent were joining their husbands or fathers in America.[15]

Some Chinese women sailed the Pacific Ocean for their own personal fulfillment. A few Chinese female students arrived in the United States as early as 1881.[16] According to a survey conducted by the China Institute in America in 1954, the number of these students continued to increase after the turn of the century. Between 1910 and 1930, the number increased sixfold in direct proportion to the overall increase in the Chinese student population as a whole. Since the survey probably did not include all Chinese students in the United States, the actual number of Chinese female students in America was likely even higher.[17]

After World War II, more Chinese women came as alien wives of veterans and American citizens under the War Bride Act of December 28, 1945, and the G.I. Fiancées Act of June 29, 1946. During the three-year operation of the War Bride Act, approximately six thousand Chinese war

[15]Entry 132, "Chinese General Correspondence, 1898–1908," RG 85. National Archives, Washington DC.

[16]Wang, *Chinese Intellectuals and the West*, 49; Ling, "History of Chinese Female Students in the United States," 81–109.

[17]China Institute in America, *Survey of Chinese Students*, 26–27.

brides were admitted. The Displaced Persons Act of 1948 and the Refugee Relief Act of 1953 allowed several thousand Chinese women to immigrate to America. The former gave those with the status of "displaced" (Chinese students, visitors, and others who had temporary status in the United States) the opportunity to adjust their status to that of a permanent resident. The latter allotted three thousand visas to refugees from Asia and two thousand visas to Chinese whose passports had been issued by the Nationalist China government that had lost power in mainland China in 1949.[18] Thus, by 1960, the number of Chinese in the United States, as reported by the 1960 census, had reached 237,292 (135,549 males and 101,743 females).[19] The gender ratio among the Chinese in America was finally almost even.

PHILIPPINES

Although Filipinos have been immigrating to the United States since the 1700s, the majority came following the Immigration Act in 1965. Since passage of the law, the number of Filipinos entering the United States has increased annually. In 1973, the United states admitted 30,000 Filipinos; by the end of the 1980s, over 50,000 Filipinos were entering the United States each year.[20] In 1990, the Filipino population in the United States was 1.5 million.[21] According to the 2000 census, there were 1.8 million Filipinos in the United States, making them the second largest Asian group (behind Chinese) in the United States.[22]

The 1965 Immigration Act alone does not explain the influx of Filipino immigration. The United States' presence in the Philippines has also propelled and shaped this migration. Prior to the 1965 Immigration Act, most Filipinos came to America as laborers or *pensionados* (students). Many Filipino men were also recruited by the U.S. Navy to fight during the two world wars. Two of the largest American military installations overseas are located in the Philippines—Clark Air Base and Subic Bay Naval Base—and most of the services needed by military personnel on those bases are provided by Filipinos.[23] In addition, the United States serves as

[18]Ling, *Surviving on the Gold Mountain*, 114.
[19]Ling, *Surviving on the Gold Mountain*, 114.
[20]Agbayani-Siewert and Revilla, "Filipino Americans," 142.
[21]Agbayani-Siewert and Revilla, "Filipino Americans," 142.
[22]The U.S. Census, 2000.
[23]Chan, *Asian Americans*, 149.

the Philippines' major trading partner and American investment accounts for half of the country's foreign investment.[24]

The military and socioeconomic ties between the United States and the Philippines have profoundly affected Filipino society in many ways, resulting in an Americanization of Filipino culture; this is embodied in the government structure, educational system, language, customs, and values. The post-World War II Filipino government and educational systems are based on the American model. English is used in public and private schools, and Filipino television is inundated with American movies and soap operas. Some academics assert that Filipino immigration to the United States has been a result of the Americanization of Filipino culture through American colonization.[25]

Many Filipinos were pushed out of the country by its grave political, economic, and social conditions. Although Ferdinand Marcos' military dictatorship was ousted in 1986, the new democratic government under President Corazon Aquino was plagued with political instability. Because the Philippines' economic policy rested completely on the U.S. involvement in the Vietnam War, the country's economy went bankrupt in the 1980s. Problems of inflation and foreign debt were compounded by widespread unemployment, dependency on agricultural exports, and inequality in the distribution of income and wealth.[26]

The over-supply of educated people in the Philippines since the 1960s also contributed to the Filipino exodus. In 1970, 25 percent of college-age Filipinos were enrolled in colleges and universities; only the United States had a higher percentage.[27] However, the country could not provide its educated people with adequate employment and pay. For instance, nurses in the United States could earn twenty times more than their counterparts in the Philippines.[28]

Because of this imbalance, many Filipino professionals have migrated to the United States since the 1960. The majority are physicians, nurses, and other health practitioners, in part due to the aggressive recruitment policy of the United States aimed at filling the shortage of trained personnel in the health industry. Two-thirds of the Filipino immigrants to the

[24]Chan, *Asian Americans*, 149.
[25]Agbayani-Siewert and Revilla, "Filipino Americans," 143.
[26]Espiritu, *Home Bound*, 11; and Chan, *Asian Americans*, 149.
[27]Espiritu, *Home Bound*, 32.
[28]Chan, *Asian Americans*, 150.

United States in the 1960s were women, many of whom were nurses. By the late 1980s, there were 50,000 Filipino nurses working in the United States.[29]

JAPAN

Japanese immigration to America was a direct result of the Meiji Restoration in 1868, which toppled Japan's century-long feudalism and attempted to industrialize the country in order to meet the challenges of competition with Western imperialist countries. The dismantling of feudalism eliminated the samurai class's monopoly on the privilege of serving in the military, and the establishment of a new national army based on conscription in 1873 made all adult males eligible for military service. To finance its industrialization, the Meiji oligarchs instituted a new land tax under which farmers were taxed based on the assessed value of their land rather than on the value of their harvest. This meant regardless of their harvests, the farmers had to pay a fixed tax. Consequently, immigration became an attractive alternative to conscription and land taxes. However, unlike their Chinese counterparts who came to the United States as contract laborers and whose passages were paid for by future employers, most Japanese immigrants were not from the poorest segment of the population, but free immigrants who paid for their own passages.[30]

Between 1869 and 1894 when Japanese immigration was handled by an individual American—Robert Walker Irwin, a friend of the Japanese foreign minister, Inoue Kaoru—about 29,000 Japanese and women went to work on the sugar plantations in Hawaii under a three-year contract.[31] Between 1894 and 1908, when Japanese immigration was handled by private companies, approximately 125,000 Japanese, 15 percent of whom were women, went to Hawaii through these companies.[32] However, most Japanese women immigrants arrived after this peak period for male entry. Although their socioeconomic background resembled that of their male counterparts, their status of entry differed as they came as dependents of the Japanese male immigrants, as wives, brides, or daughters. The majority of Japanese immigrant women before 1924 came as brides of Japanese male immigrants who had been in the United States for years. Some women came to the United states with husbands who had returned to

[29]Chan, *Asian Americans*, 150.
[30]Glenn, *Issei, Nisei, War Bride*, 26.
[31]Chan, *Asian Americans*, 12.
[32]Chan, *Asian Americans*, 12.

Japan for the marriage. Many, however, were picture brides, who accepted marriage proposals based on pictures of their prospective husbands, were married in Japan without the presence of the grooms, and came to America to join them.[33] These immigrant women, or *issei*, came from farming and small entrepreneurial families in southern Japan. They followed the traditional pattern of marriage arranged through a *baishakunin* (go-between).

Nisei, the second-generation Japanese women, were mostly born between 1910 and 1940. Many grew up in moderate circumstances and were immersed in a mixture of Japanese and American cultures. One scholar wrote that, "They spoke both Japanese and English, or often a combination of both, at home; ate corned beef and vegetables with rice; studied flower arrangement and piano; toasted *mochi* at the New Year and roasted the turkey at Thanksgiving; attended American school all day and trudged off to Japanese school in the afternoon."[34]

Post-war Japanese immigrant women came from diverse backgrounds. They had been brought up in families that were well-to-do, middleclass, or poor workingclass. They came from all areas of Japan, both provincial towns or major cities. However, they shared one common trait: the economic deprivation and social dislocation of World War II and the years following had resulted in their employment in jobs that brought them into contact with American servicemen. Their marriage to American servicemen and consequent immigration to America brought them greater economic stability, but also brought cultural and social difficulties that forced them to make adjustments to survive in the new environment.[35]

KOREA

Like early Chinese and Japanese immigrants, the bulk of early Korean immigrants, about 7,000 between 1902 and 1905, also came to work on Hawaiian sugar plantations. However, early Korean immigration differed in several ways. While most Chinese and Japanese immigrants came from certain geographical areas (Guangdong province in China and southwest Japan), Koreans came from all parts of the country, especially from port cities and their vicinities. Most Chinese and Japanese immigrants were farmers, while Korean immigrants were mostly laborers, former soldiers,

[33]Ichihashi, *Japanese in the United States*, 10; and Chan, *Asian Americans*, 107.
[34]Glenn, *Issei, Nisei, War Bride*, 51.
[35]Glenn, *Issei, Nisei, War Bride*, 59.

and artisans. Many Korean immigrants went to Hawaii not in response to labor recruiters but because Christian missionaries encouraged and assisted members of their congregations to move to Hawaii. As a result, 40 percent of the 7,000 Korean immigrants were Christians.[36] Because of church sponsorship, many Korean immigrants could come as families, so that nearly 2,000 of early Korean immigrants were women, proportionally more than any other immigrant group from Asia at the time.[37] During the Japanese colonial rule of Korea (1910–45), only approximately 1,000 picture brides were allowed to leave for the United States; most joined husbands in Hawaii.[38]

In the post-war era, new waves of Korean immigrants came to the United States. From 1951 to 1964, there were 14,027 Koreans who entered, mostly related to the post-Korean War immigration.[39] The majority of post-war immigrants were war orphans being adopted by Americans, wives and children of American servicemen stationed in Korea, or relatives or Korean women who had married American servicemen.[40] By 1980, approximately 50,000 Korean women who had married Americans were living in the United States.[41]

The liberalization of national quotas under the 1965 Immigration Act ushered in a third wave of Korean immigration, characterized by a significant shift in the immigrant profile in which both families and individuals immigrated.[42] Most of the new immigrants had been middle-class professionals in Korea. They were attracted to America because of its economic promises and the strong dollar against Korean *wôn*. In addition, the oppressive regimes in Korea during the 1970s and 1980s and the acute tension between North and South Korea during the late 1970s compelled many Koreans to consider America as a refuge from political instability.[43]

INDIA

Most Indian immigrants to North America came from the Punjab region of northwestern India, an area known as India's breadbasket. Despite the region's rich agricultural resources, the 1849 annexation of the Punjab by

[36]Chan, *Asian Americans*, 15.
[37]Yang, "Korean Women in America," 167–81.
[38]Lee, *Quiet Odyssey*, xliii.
[39]U.S. Immigration and Naturalization Service, *Annual Report*, 1995.
[40]Park, *Korean American Dream*, 9.
[41]Barringer and Cho, *Koreans in the United States*.
[42]Noland, "Impact of Korean Immigration on the U.S. Economy."
[43]Park, *Korean American Dream*, 12.

the British colonial government produced circumstances conducive to emigration. The colonial administration decided to collect land taxes in cash instead of in kind, the system previously practiced. This new policy affected farmers negatively; many had to mortgage their lots to ensure cash for tax payments and eventually lost their land. Some of these landless farmers became migrant workers; others joined the British colonial army or police force and were dispatched to various parts of the vast British Empire. The overseas experiences made Punjabi Sikhs into daring fortune seekers in other countries including the United States.[44]

The passage from Punjab to North America was long, difficult, and expensive. The Punjabi emigrants had to take a train first to New Delhi, then to Calcutta, where they could board steamers to Hong Kong and then to many major ports of the world, including San Francisco. The early Sikh migrants to California numbered around 5,000, most of whom were employed by lumbering and railroad companies. However, the Sikh migrants later turned to agriculture, mainly concentrated in two areas: the Imperial Valley in the south and the Sacramento Valley in the north. In agriculture, the Sikhs were initially farm laborers, but many later purchased or leased their own land to farm. They suffered similar legal and extralegal discriminations as did other Asians, such as the 1924 Immigration Act that denied entry to virtually all Asians, the anti-immigrant sentiment on the West Coast at the time, and the alien land laws, which prohibited aliens (mainly Asians) from owning land in many states on the West Coast and in the Midwest.

A small number of women came with their husbands. According to immigration records, of the 5,800 East Indian immigrants entering the United States between 1901 and 1911, there were only 109 women.[45] The prevalence of the anti-miscegenation laws (then in thirty-eight states), which outlawed marriage between a white and a colored person,[46] coupled with the shortage of Asian Indian women, resulted in interracial marriages between Sikhs and Mexican women. In the Imperial Valley area, the Sikh husband and Mexican wife was a persistent marital pattern for at least a generation.[47] Smaller Asian Indian communities were also established in New York and other eastern and midwestern cities. Most members of these

[44]Chan, *Asian Americans*, 20.
[45]Kitano and Daniels, *Asian Americans*, 104.
[46]Ling, *Surviving on the Gold Mountain*, 88–89.
[47]Leonard, *Making Ethnic Choices.*

communities were merchants and middle-class professionals from Hindu backgrounds.

The major transformation of the Indian community in the United States occurred after 1965 with the overhaul of the Immigration Act, which allowed immigrants with professional and technical training to enter the country. By 1970, there were about 75,000 Asian Indians in the United States, two-thirds of whom were foreign-born and 47 percent of the foreign-born Asian Indians were managers, professionals, and executives. This trend continued and by 1985, more than 500,000 Asian Indians had entered the United States.[48] The gender ratio among Asian Indians also grew more balanced; in 1990, there were 117 males to every 100 females.[49]

Most Indian women who entered the United States after 1970 came as young brides of Indian students or professionals. They were sponsored by their husbands or close relatives and belonged to middle- and upper-class groups. Although they came as dependents of their husbands, many Indian women with advanced education and professional training found jobs in the United States. According to the 1990 census, more than 55 percent of South Asian women had at least a bachelor's degree and 59 percent of them were working in the country.[50]

VIETNAM, LAOS, CAMBODIA, AND THE HMONG

Among Asian Americans, the Indochinese constitute the most recently formed ethnic group. Unlike the earlier Asian American groups, Vietnamese, Laotian, Hmong, and Cambodian Americans were refugees and their children were American-born. Their immigration patterns and their lives in America thus are inevitably intertwined with the refugee experience.

Since the end of the Indochina Wars in 1975, over one million refugees and immigrants from Vietnam, Cambodia, and Laos have arrived in the United States. These refugees are a product of the longest war in modern history, beginning in 1945 and ending in 1975. The First Indochina War (the French Indochina War) ended when Vietnamese forces defeated French colonial authorities and gained independence. Although the conflict was centered in northern Vietnam, fighting also spread to Laos and Cambodia. After the French withdrew, conflict soon broke out between the newly-created North and South Vietnam and spread into Cambodia and

---

[48]Jensen, *Passage from India,* 280–82.
[49]1990 U.S. Census.
[50]Dasgupta, *A Patchwork Shawl,* 3.

Laos. The Second Indochina War (the Vietnam War) involved efforts of South Vietnam and its ally, the United States, to prevent North and South Vietnam from being united under communist leadership. The Vietnam War became the single most divisive event in U.S. history since the Civil War, defining an entire generation of young people in the 1960s and polarizing the American electorate. The war cost the United States 58,000 lives; over 300,000 Americans were wounded and more than 2,000 were missing in action.

The war divided America, but it devastated Vietnam, Laos, and Cambodia. During the period of U.S. involvement, starting from the French withdrawal from Vietnam in 1954 and ending in 1975 when the last U.S. troops retreated, an estimated four million Vietnamese soldiers and civilians on both sides were killed or wounded. In South Vietnam, a third of the total population was displaced during the war and over half of the total forestland and 10 percent of the agricultural land was laid waste by aerial bombardment, tractor cleaning, and chemical defoliation (Agent Orange). In Laos, the Hmong, an ethnic minority of the mountainous highlands who originally migrated from southwest China, fought on the U.S. side against the Pathet Lao (over 80 percent of the Hmong males were recruited by the CIA in the so-called secret war) and bore the brunt of the war casualties, with 400,000 Hmong killed, thousands more injured and disabled, and countless men missing. By 1975, the war had uprooted about a third of the Hmong population; they lost their homes and fled the country. In the late 1970s, a quarter of the Cambodian population was killed in the political crackdown after the war.

Since 1975, when South Vietnam fell to the Communists, over 2 million refugees have fled Vietnam, Laos, and Cambodia. These waves of refugees were shaped by complex political and socioeconomic factors. The first wave of Vietnamese refugees was primarily from an elite class who left Vietnam due to the Communist takeover. These included army officers and their families, government bureaucrats, teachers, doctors, engineers, lawyers, students, businessmen, and Catholic priests and nuns. The later waves of refugees came from more modest backgrounds, including farmers and fishermen fleeing continuing regional military conflicts and deteriorating economic conditions.[51] While Vietnamese elites and professionals were joined and outnumbered by the later waves of refugees who were

---

[51]Rumbaut, "Structure of Refugee," 97–129.

relocated to American bases in Guam and Philippines under emergency conditions after the fall of Saigon, the elites from Laos and Cambodia were more likely to be settled in France.

The Indochinese refugee women, like their male counterparts, fled their home countries by planes or boats, or crossed the border on foot. They experienced the terror of pirates on the high sea, the brutality in refugee camps in Thailand, and the anxious waiting in refugee camps in Guam and the Wake Islands before traveling on to meet their sponsors. The intense emotional trauma haunted many refugees for a prolonged period of time after they settled in the United States. Elderly women, many of whom had difficulty learning English and were reluctant to reach out for federal assistance, suffered the highest level of mental stress.[52]

Employment Patterns

The primary goal of most immigrants has been to improve their economic status; therefore finding and keeping jobs has been crucial and essential to all Asian Americans. As the cultural, economic, and educational backgrounds of Asian immigrants differ, there have been various patterns of employment among Asian immigrants and their American-born offspring. Figures from the 1980, 1990, and 2000 censuses indicate that, in general, the older and more established Asian Americans—Chinese, Japanese, and Asian Indians—are distributed in more prestigious and better-paying occupations than the more recently arrived Pacific Islanders and Vietnamese. Specific employment patterns also exist among certain groups of Asian Americans. For example, Japanese, Filipinos, Koreans, Hawaiians, and Guamanians are usually employed in the technical sector, Chinese and Indians in the professional sector, and Vietnamese and Laotians/Hmong in the laborer sector. The overrepresentation of Asian Americans in the small-business sector continues as a pattern. In the 1980s and 1990s, 76 percent of Asian American businesses did not hire paid employees, but were operated solely by family members. Of those Asian American businesses, 87 percent were in retail, food-service, health service, and construction.[53]

In addition, some Asian American groups have a monopoly in certain occupations. For instance, there are so many Asian Indians in the motel business that the saying of "motel, hotel, Patel" has circulated among

---

[52]Che, interview. See also Ling, *Chinese St. Louis*; and Freeman, *Hearts of Sorrow*, 369–73.
[53]U.S. Census 1980 and 1990.

the general public, noting the large number of motel and hotel operators who bear the common Hindu surname Patel. Korean entrepreneurs predominate in the grocery business; about 1,000 of the 1,200 independent grocery stores in New York City were run by Koreans in the 1980s.[54] Pyong Gap Min's recent study indicates that more than 60 percent of Korean business owners are concentrated into two categories—dry cleaning and nail services (31 percent) and retail services (30 percent).

Kinship networks are a critical factor contributing to Asian American entrepreneurship. Studies of Korean American entrepreneurship recognize the importance of personal and family savings, usually ranging from 60 to 80 percent of the initial investment in the business.[55] Studies on Chinese Americans have agreed on the vital role ethnic networks play in starting and operating Chinese American businesses.[56] A similar pattern is also present among Asian businesses in Canada and Southeast Asia. Peter S. Li found that in Canada, kinship networks have been crucial to starting traditional Chinese businesses such as food services and retail.[57] Similarly, Linda Y. C. Lim noted that in Southeast Asia, new immigrants rely heavily on ethnic networks to find housing and jobs.[58]

Interracial Marriage

Along with the improvement of Asian Americans' socioeconomic conditions in recent decades, interracial marriage has become more visible. In New York City, interracial marriage among Chinese Americans remained at 27 percent of total marriages in the 1970s and 1980s.[59] In California, a substantial minority of Chinese Americans, 35.6 percent, were intermarried in 1980.[60] In the San Francisco Bay area, American-born Asians were more likely to marry outside their own ethnic group; in some ethnic groups, the rate of interracial marriage was as high as 80 percent.[61] Among interracially married couples, more Asian women than Asian men had

---

[54]John Greenwald, "Finding Niches in a New Land," *Time*, July 8, 1985, 32–33.

[55]See Bang, "The Self-Help/Mutual Aid Component in Small Business within the Korean-American Community," 86; Min, "Korean Immigrant Entrepreneurship, 160; and Min, "Patterns of Korean Immigrant Business in New York."

[56]Ling, *Chinese St. Louis*, 155; and Wong, *Patronage, Brokerage, Entrepreneurship and the Chinese Community of New York*.

[57]Li, "Chinese Investment and Business in Canada," 219–43.

[58]Lim, "Chinese Economic Activity in Southeast Asia."

[59]Sung, *Chinese American Intermarriage*, 10–11.

[60]Shinagawa and Pang, "Intraethnic, Interethnic, and Interracial Marriages," 95–114.

[61]Walsh, "Asian Women, Caucasian Men," 11–16.

married non-Asians, most often white Americans. A 1990 sampling of marriage records for San Francisco County showed that four times as many Asian American women as Asian American men married whites.[62] Some high-profile Asian American women's marriages helped to make the phenomenon more noticeable: politicians Elaine Chao and Julia Chang Bloch; writers Bette Bao Lord, Maxine Hong Kingston, and Amy Tan; and newscasters Connie Chung, Wendy Tokuda, and Jan Yanehiro. Interracial dating has been so ubiquitous at West Coast university campuses that such jargon as "Asian-American syndrome" and "Asian-women-alcoholics" depicting the wide-spread interracial dating between Euro-American males and Asian American females has begun to spread.[63] These terms certainly infuriate Asian American women, but reflect the growing numbers of interracial marriages.

Scholars have analyzed the interracial marriages among Asian Americans since World War II, with Milton Gordon's classic work, *Assimilation in American Life*, spearheading the assimilation theory. This theory sees interracial marriage as a sign of the growing acceptance of a minority group by the majority group.[64] Most studies of assimilation theory suggest that interracial marriage serves as an indicator of the assimilation of Asian Americans into American majority society.

Meanwhile, an alternative theory of intermarriage has emerged. Challenging the assimilation theory, the hypergamy theory has seen intermarriage as a function of the inequality within a society stratified by race and class. This theory was originally applied to marriage patterns in India, where a high-caste male could use his social status to obtain a wife with beauty, intelligence, youth, and wealth of a lower caste. Similarly, interracial marriage in the United States allowed both partners of the marriage to benefit, as a minority male with higher socioeconomic status but lower racial status might upgrade his racial position by marrying a female with the opposite characteristics.[65] After a decade or two of unpopularity, hypergamy theory has reemerged in recent scholarship. Drawing upon this theory, Larry Hajime Shinagawa and Gin Yong Pang have argued that intermarriage was more likely determined by the marital partners' birth-

[62]Walsh, "Asian Women, Caucasian Men," 12.
[63]Walsh, "Asian Women, Caucasian Men," 11.
[64]Gordon, *Assimilation in American Life*, 80. See also Tinker, "Intermarriage and Assimilation in A Plural Society," 61–74; Kitano et al., "Asian American Interracial Marriage," 179–90; and Sung, *Chinese American Intermarriage*.
[65]Davis, "Intermarriage in Caste Societies," 376–95.

place, gender, age, education, and socioeconomic characteristics.[66] Paul R. Spickard has analyzed intermarriage from various dimensions of social structure, demography, class status, and intermarriage behavior, and contended that class, generation, and ethnic concentration in the surrounding population have shaped patterns of intermarriage. He has further claimed that there was a distinct hierarchy of intermarriage preferences.[67]

Both theories provide meaningful interpretations of intermarriage, yet neither can explain intermarriage completely. Assimilation theory has hailed intermarriage as an indicator of a minority's acceptance by the majority, and asserted that love and attraction were primary motives of such marriage. However, it has failed to explain why minority members (both male and female) with higher socioeconomic status or native-born minority members were more likely to intermarry. The hypergamy model has viewed intermarriage as a deal in which the white marital partner traded his or her higher racial status for advantages of physical attraction, youth, or higher socioeconomic status brought to the marriage by the partner of a racial minority. It has excluded the factors of love and romance in an intermarriage.

In reality, most marital partners of intermarriages (with the exception of picture brides) have claimed that love or attraction was the major reason that drew them together. Clearly, the role of love and mutual attraction in intermarriage should not be overlooked. However, few individuals claim love at first sight—love grew gradually during the interaction between the two partners. The interaction often occurred among individuals with similar educational, occupational, and socioeconomic experiences; therefore, intermarriage should be understood in these terms. When a minority member moved to a new socioeconomic setting (often an institution of higher education or a professional occupation) in which he or she had the opportunity to meet a prospective marital partner of the majority group, his or her status was already upgraded, since the majority group tended to enjoy better socioeconomic conditions. Therefore, one may infer that a minority member's assimilation into the majority society was determined more by his or her education, occupation, and class status than by an intermarriage.[68] This pattern is seen among the women interviewed for this volume.

---

[66]Shinagawa and Pang, "Intraethnic, Interethnic, and Interracial Marriages," 98.
[67]Spickard, *Mixed Blood*, 6–9.
[68]Ling, *Surviving on the Gold Mountain*, 174–77.

Part 1
Chinese

Beth Low and Lisa Wang, who were born in the 1910s and 1920s in San Francisco and Boston respectively, are among the first American-born, or the second-generation of, Chinese American women.[1] These second-generation Chinese American girls received high school or college educations, entered the work force, and began choosing their own mates. The stories of Beth and Lisa show the family structure of the Chinese immigrants, in which the husband was the family's primary provider while the wife was in charge of the household's daily maintenance and supplemented the family income by working in sewing shops. Early Chinese immigrant families tended to have large families as a strategy to cope with the uprootedness of the immigrant life. The Chinese Six Companies, the self-governing immigrant community structure established in 1862, dominated the immigrant society through Chinese language schools, as seen here.[2]

The life histories of the women who braved the Pacific Ocean and landed on the new shore reveal the multifaceted dimensions of their immigrant experiences. Ling Ng, Erin Zeng, Gena Chen, and Liz Sing came from Chinese populations, both in China and in the Philippines, Hong Kong, and Taiwan, during the post–World War II era. Ling, Erin, and Gena all came from families of Chinese intellectuals—educators and musicians—giving them a head start in their academic and professional training in the

---

[1]Ling, *Surviving on the Gold Mountain*, 95; and Chan, *Asian Americans*, 109.
[2]On the Chinese Six Companies, see, for example, Ling, *Surviving on the Gold Mountain*, 47–48; Ling, "Governing 'Hop Alley'"; and Lai, "Historical Development of the Chinese Consolidated Benevolent Association/Huiguan System," 13–51.

United States. Yet they all encountered the universal difficulties for most new immigrants—language barriers, emotional loneliness, and academic stresses. With advanced academic degrees, these women were able to find employment and enjoy a life of "model minority,"[3] even while enduring subtle forms of racial prejudice and discrimination. Liz Sing and her parents came to the United States from Taiwan in the 1980s. To escape the stiff competition in the Chinese restaurant business in the major cities, the Sing family settled in a small midwestern town to open a restaurant. Liz's experience of running a Chinese restaurant typifies the hard work, long working hours, and consequent isolation from community activities.

As Chinese Americans' socioeconomic conditions improved in the last decades of the twentieth century, interracial marriage in America became more visible and acceptable.[4] At the same time, the normalization of Sino-U.S. relations and the increasingly globalized world economy has brought men and women of different cultural and racial backgrounds together. As a result, interracial marriages occurred not only between native-born Chinese Americans and other groups of Americans, but also between white Americans and Chinese when Americans studied or worked in China and fell in love with the local Chinese. Martha Reeves's marriage reflects the interracial romance sprouting out of the transnational cultural and economic soils. For Martha, the interracial marriage enabled her to come to America, an opportunity desired by many Chinese youth, but she found herself stigmatized by her countrymen who thought she only married an American to emigrate to America.

In the field of higher education, the young Chinese American women (foreign-born or native-born) shared similar characteristics of ambition, strict self-discipline, and familial values of Asian traditions, yet encountered somewhat different college experiences. Rita Chang came from Taiwan to pursue a higher education in the United States in the 1990s. Unlike their predecessors who came to America decades ago and

---

[3]On model minority, see, for example, Osajima, "Asian Americans as the Model Minority," 165–74; Peterson, "Success Story, Japanese-American Style," 20–43; and Suzuki, "Education and the Socialization of Asian Americans," 23–51.

[4]On interracial marriage, see, for example, Labov and Jacobs, "Intermarriage in Hawaii, 1950-1983," 79–88; Lee and Yamanaka, "Patterns of Asian American Intermarriages and Marital Assimilation," 287–305; Ling, "Family and Marriage of Late-Nineteenth and Early-Twentieth Century Chinese Immigrant Women," 43–63; Root, *Racially Mixed People in America*; Spickard, *Mixed Blood*; Stephen and Stephan, "After Intermarriage," 507–19; Sung, *Chinese American Intermarriage*; Waters, *Ethnic Options*; Wong, "A Look at Intermarriage Among the Chinese in the United States," 87–107.

had to struggle both academically and financially,[5] the Chinese students in the 1990s were from more affluent families in Asian countries and could therefore concentrate on their academic works without worrying about making ends meet. Yet the newer generations still had to battle language barriers, unfamiliarity with American culture, and unfriendliness from American peers. This was not the case for all. Sandy Lee, the native-born Chinese American college student, enjoyed a complete social integration with her white peers. Her experience indicates that cultural differences, rather than racial prejudice, more often prevent different racial groups from merging into one.

[5]On Chinese students in America, see, for example, Ling, "Changing Patterns of Taiwanese Students in America and the Modernization in Taiwan," 179–207; Ling, "Chinese Female Students and the Sino-US Relations," 103–37; and Ling, "History of Chinese Female Students in the United States," 81–109.

1

The First American-born Women

Beth Low was born in 1917 into an immigrant family in San Francisco's Chinatown, where she grew up and had a high school education. Married to a Chinese professor of economics, she has been a housewife and mother of three sons, all of whom have advanced degrees. She lived in Kirksville, Missouri, at the time of the interview in 1992.

I was born in 1917 in San Francisco and grew up there. Being in a city like San Francisco, we went to public school in the morning and early afternoon, and Chinese language school in the evening. In the Chinese language school, they taught Cantonese, so we learned Chinese in Cantonese. The Chinese language school ran from five to eight PM Monday through Friday, and from ten AM to one PM on Saturday. We paid one dollar a month for tuition. I went to Nanqiao Xuexiao (the South Bridge School). The school was built by the Chinese Consolidated Benevolent Association in that district. Since the association owned the property, income from the property was used to build a school. The association also did other charitable things. Now the school is free. The all-male Board of Directors was selected by the Benevolent Association and met several times a year. The schoolteachers, however, were both men and women. Some were students who went to school during the day, then came back to teach after their classes. Some of the Chinese language schools were connected with the Methodist Church. The Catholic Church also had a Chinese language school. While the Chinese schools usually went up to the high school level, the classes got smaller and smaller, and so I quit in junior high. You do whatever the others do.

My father was a merchant when he came to America in the early

1900s. Then he worked for the First National Bank. He was selling drafts to Chinese merchants who bought and sent them to China to buy merchandise. The bank closed in the 1930s during the Depression. So my father, then in his fifties, took an early retirement and received a pension.

My mother was born in China. She came here a year after the San Francisco earthquake of 1906. There were seven children in my family: four boys and three girls. My mother and about a dozen other women worked at a sewing shop with machines set up on a rented floor. My mother worked there during the day, then came home to cook lunch for us. Hours in the shop were very flexible and there were no time cards. They were paid by the piece. The pay was very low, but the work kept them busy.

There were two opera houses in San Francisco then. Before the age of movies, they held performances in the evenings, especially on Saturday nights, which women and older people often attended. Cantonese opera troupes from China performed there. The shows usually started at seven o'clock, and admission was a dollar. If there were seats left, they would sell tickets for a quarter until nine o'clock.

Early immigrant women often went visiting friends. My mother went anywhere she wished at any time; she and the majority of women her age had natural feet. My mother was very independent. She didn't know English, but she would walk or take the train downtown to do shopping or to Oakland. Streetcars and cable cars were the public transportation in those days. She had relatives, including my uncle and cousins, in San Francisco. My mother was illiterate, but she was outgoing. My father could write and read in both Chinese and English; he was better off at that time compared to most Chinese. In the 1930s, people earned one dollar a day. If you could support your family, you were fortunate. The Chinese in San Francisco all had big families; five, six or nine children in each family were common. People of my generation, on the other hand, have smaller families.

My parents treated boys and girls the same. We didn't conflict with our parents; we just followed the tradition. Usually parents had the say. Although we had our own opinions, we considered our parents' ideas more important. My father and mother were from a village near Canton. Back in China, people usually lived in villages. Because all their relatives were in the United States, my parents never returned to China. Additionally, it was not easy to go back once they had children. We spoke Cantonese at home. I learned sewing from mother and also took sewing classes in junior high. Sewing is like a hobby to me.

I didn't start dating until I met Dr. Low (my late husband). Most of us married other Chinese. Interracial marriage was not popular then, though there were some interracial marriages during the war. In San Francisco, there was a big Chinese population, so there were plenty of Chinese boys to choose from. We preserved Chinese traditional holidays, which were more traditional than those in China.

The first time I went out of the town was when I went to California State to visit. I felt different and depressed. However, I soon found a job that took the pressure off. Chinese students would come to our place on Saturdays to play bridge. After playing, we would go to a Chinese restaurant together. There was a Chinese student association and there were always a lot of things going on.

Like many women of my time, I didn't go to college. In 1935, I graduated from high school at eighteen. After my graduation, I went to work during the Depression. You were lucky if you could finish high school. But being with my husband and his colleagues helped me. After the war, many people went to college assisted by the G.I. Bill. With soldiers returning after the war, college and university enrollment exploded.

My husband and I met in San Francisco. His uncle was operating a jewelry shop. My husband first arrived in San Francisco and studied at the University of California for one semester, then transferred to Stanford and stayed there for one year. After that, he went to Oregon State University for his MA in agriculture. He worked in the Office of War Information in San Francisco during World War II because at that time China and the United States were allies. For several years until he finished his MA, he worked as a language technician. He was in translating and broadcasting (he went to the University of Beijing and could speak Mandarin). We dated, went to movies, walked around downtown, window-shopped in the evening, and enjoyed the walking. He was very versatile, having an interest in many subjects.

We married in 1946. My husband was then studying at the University of Wisconsin for his doctorate in agricultural economics. Our wedding, a civil ceremony in front of a judge, was in San Francisco's City Hall. Afterward we went to Santa Cruz for a few days. From there we took the train to Boulder, Colorado, stayed there for a few days, and then went to [live in] Wisconsin.

In Wisconsin, I worked for a wholesale company, running a bookkeeping machine. Before I was married, I used to work for an insurance company in the accounting department, so this was something I had done

Wedding of Beth Low, a second-generation Chinese American woman in San Francisco, 1946. Huping Ling Collection (Courtesy of Beth Low).

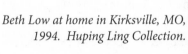

Beth Low at home in Kirksville, MO, 1994. Huping Ling Collection.

before. I worked full time, as I hated to stay in the apartment alone.

After my husband got his PhD in 1950, we went back to San Francisco because it was hard to find a job. A year later, his advisor in Wisconsin called and told him that they had received a grant from the state. So we went back to Madison in 1951 and stayed there until 1954. That year, his advisor told him of an opening at the Northeast Missouri State Teachers College. A professor had retired suddenly and they needed someone right away. Dr. Ryle, president of the college, called him, and my husband was hired.

We came to Kirksville in January 1954. Kirksville was different then from now. Campus was different and smaller. We didn't have the Student Union, Pershing Building, and Centennial Hall. Dr. No-Yong Park, a Korean American lecturer, was there before we came. In the 1940s he taught one or two years at the college. Then he lectured. He was outgoing and funny. After we came, Mrs. Dun (the wife of a professor at the local medical school) also came. We lived in an apartment on Elson Street. We later rented a small house near First Street and Mrs. Dun rented our apartment. Our friendship started in 1954.

I didn't work in Kirksville because there were few job opportunities in a small town. In 1956, our first son was born. After four years, we had two more boys.

We were active participants in college activities every year. Before school started in the fall, the college had a banquet in the hallway of Kirk Building, where all the activities occurred during Dr. Ryle's presidency. Besides the annual banquet, there were the Lyceum programs (a program that brings art performances to campus), basketball, football, etc.

We didn't have a car until we moved to Grim Court in 1967. Before 1967, we lived in three different rental houses. Rent was very reasonable, $65 for our first house, $75 for the next, and $85 for the third. We didn't have the College Park, Bell area then. We didn't have town and country. We didn't have any fast food on Baltimore Street. For $1.50, you could get a good meal at a restaurant called The Old Trading Post. The Traveler's Hotel had a dance hall where you could have banquets.

Now I prefer to stay in Kirksville, where I am used to living. Usually we cooked Chinese food. Lunch was usually noodles. For dinner, I had rice dishes. We also had American dishes—roast beef, for instance, once or twice a week. Because my children didn't like rice all the time, I cooked Cantonese food. Dr. Low didn't do the cooking. In Oregon, he lived with some students who did the shopping and cooking. But after marriage, he didn't cook unless we had company, then he would help me. We speak Cantonese at home. Dr. Low was gifted academically; after being born and raised in Canton, he went to Beijing University after he passed the entrance examination in the 1930s.

My oldest son's wife is a Korean American [while the other two daughters-in-law are white Americans]. They both went to University of Missouri and met there. They married in 1980. He has a MBA. My daughter-in-law has a MA in textile and clothing. My second son went to University of Missouri and received a MS in electrical engineering in May 1992. He is going to a PhD program. He met his wife in St. Louis. She came from Kansas City and went to Washington University for a master's degree in physical therapy. They married in October 1989. My third son went to Michigan for undergraduate, where he met his wife, a software engineer for Hewlett-Packard. They married on 13 June 1987, in the St. Rose of Lima Catholic Church in Hastings, Michigan.

Lisa Wang was born into a Chinese tea merchant family in Boston in 1925. She has a master's degree in Oriental studies at Yale University and was married to a prominent Chinese American scientist. She has three children who are all professionals. She was a retired librarian from Shrewsbury, Massachusetts, at the time of the interviews in 1992 and 1995.

I was born in 1925 in Boston. My father was a tea merchant from Guangdong. He first arrived in San Francisco at the turn of the century. Later he moved to Oakland, California. He then went to Boston, where he was one of the earliest Chinese in the town. My father started as a bookkeeper, but he did well and later he owned his own tea shop. He made enough money to get married, and soon became the first Chinese to buy a house in Boston.

My father spent many years saving enough money for his marriage. By the time he had enough money to support a family, he was already a middle-aged man. He went to Guangdong, China, to marry my mother when she was sixteen, twenty-seven years his junior. My father spoke *Toishan* (Taishan, a variation of Cantonese) dialect, while my mother spoke *Sam Yap* (Sanyi, a variation of Cantonese) dialect. It seems that she came from a middle class family. Therefore, my mother's family had a slightly higher social status than my father's. My mother was eager to come to America. Influenced by her parents and other people, she believed America was a great place. My father treated my mother very traditionally and my mother listened to him all the time.

There were nine children in my family, six of them girls. My father knew he was alone in this country, as he did not have any relatives here, so he wanted to have many children as security for his old age. My mother sacrificed her whole life for us. She stayed at home to raise children and she cooked for the family. Every morning, everybody had to have an egg, because she thought eggs were important for growing children. When we grew older, my mother worked at a sewing factory for ten years. Before she died, she learned to read and write simple English.

My father didn't want us to speak English at home, so I spoke Cantonese with my parents. To preserve our Chinese language, we went to a Chinese language school after public school, from 5:30 to 8:30 PM, five days a week, and 10:00 AM to 2:00 PM on Saturday. We went to Chinese school until we were tired of it. I graduated from the sixth grade. I remember I had a very entertaining Chinese teacher. He told us Chinese fairy tales. I compiled these tales and had three books published later. In addition to the fairy tales I also published two Chinese cookbooks.

The girls were older than the boys in my family which might explain why we girls all had an education. My father sent us to schools in Boston. We all got scholarships to go to school. I went to an all-girl's high school in Boston and got my bachelor's degree from Simmons College in library science. I also earned a master's degree in English from Clark University in Worcester, Massachusetts, in 1967. I got another master's degree in psychology counseling from Anna Maria College, in Paxton, Massachusetts in 1982.

I met M. C. Wang when I was working for my master's degree in Oriental Studies at Yale University. He was sixteen years older than me. He got his bachelor's degree from Qinghua University in China. Then he went to University of Edinburg in Scotland for his master's degree. He got his PhD from Cambridge University the following year. When he met me, he was working in experimental biology at the Worcester Foundation in Shrewsbury, Massachusetts.

At that time, I was dating two Chinese boys of my age. They warned me against trusting this man and that in time he would not be nice to me. But M. C. Wang was older than they were and, therefore, more sophisticated. He phoned me every day and came to visit me every weekend. He told me,"You are so expensive." I asked him why. He said, "I spend so much money on telephone and trains." He also told me, "If you marry me, I will take you to Europe." So he finally won.

From the beginning of our relationship, he took charge of everything. Wherever we went, he arranged plane tickets. I just followed him. He was a male chauvinist. He treated me like how my father treated my mother. Because of my upbringing, it was easy for me to accept this. My mother used to say, "Never fight with men."

Now, because my husband has died, I am more assertive. He died in 1991 at the age eighty-two without leaving a penny for me; he donated all his money to China. A part went to Qinghua University where he went to school, a part to an elementary school, and another part to a museum in his name.

In 1950, Premier Zhou Enlai called for Chinese overseas scholars to return to China to participate in constructing a new China. M. C. Wang considered going back. But when he looked at me, he changed his mind. He said, "Living in China with three small children will be too hard for you; you cannot take it." Therefore, he always felt he owed China. He continuously sent money to China. He donated money to build a primary school in his hometown, in suburban Taiyuan, Shanxi.

My husband was very liberal. He was for Chairman Mao. He believed Mao did a great thing in unifying China and kicking out foreigners. He never liked Chiang Kai-shek. He thought Chiang was too selfish and did not care for the common people.

We went to China in 1972. Premier Zhou received us. I thought Premier Zhou was very charming. He asked me what kind of work I did. I said I was a librarian. Then Zhou replied, "Chairman Mao was a librarian at Beijing University." He made me feel like he was my old friend. He asked me what I liked about China. I told him my favorable impressions of China. Then he asked me what I disliked about China. I told him that I didn't like people spitting on the ground. Premier said, "We can try to take care of that." Therefore, people around us did not spit any more; however, spitting remained a disgusting habit of some people. My husband went back to China several times. As for the Tiananmen Incident, my husband did not agree with the students. He thought students should be more tolerant. He said, "Only foreigners welcome a China with political turmoil."

I have three children. They are all professionals. My eldest daughter, forty years old, is a chairperson in the department of anthropology at Sweet Briar College in Virginia. She and her husband are both anthropologists and they have a five-year-old daughter. She leads a busy life and works hard. Every summer she goes to Greece to do field work. In 1997, she received a $136,000 grant to do research in Kazakhstan and another $20,000 grant to write a book.

My son was trained as a lawyer. He is now at a foundation that gives grants for worthy causes. My younger daughter was my husband's favorite child. Now thirty-six, she has been engaged twice, but never married. She has two master's degrees from Berkeley—one in civil engineering, another in architecture. She works for the government, and is in charge of twenty men at her work. She has no desire for me or anyone else to arrange a marriage for her.

I was head librarian at the Shrewsbury Public Library in Shrewsbury, Massachusetts, for five and a half years. Then I worked at the Shrewsbury School as a librarian. I am writing a biography of a famous person from Shrewsbury.

2

Foreign-born Women
in Professional Fields

Ling Ng was born into a family of educators in Beijing, China, in 1931 and immigrated to the Philippines with her parents in 1941. She came to the United States for her higher education in the 1950s and then returned to the Philippines to marry a wealthy Chinese Filipino factory owner. She came to America again in the 1980s to accompany her children who were attending colleges in America. While her children returned to the Philippines after graduation, she stayed and became a guidance counselor of the public school in LaPlata, Missouri, where she worked at the time of the interview in 1995.

I was born in Beijing, at that time it was called Beiping, on April 1, 1931. When I was born we did not have a Western calendar; we only had a lunar calendar, so I do not know what month it was in solar calendar, but I know it was 1931.

I don't know the school my parents went to, but they were trained as teachers. My mother had been a teacher since she was sixteen. Her father was one of the founders of the Peking College of Chinese Studies. The other founder was a Presbyterian, Dr. Petit. The school actually started in Shanghai, but it moved to Beijing. It's a Chinese culture, language, geography, and history school for foreigners. My father and mother both taught there, and that's where they met. They married, and I am their only child.

At the school where they were teaching, they were not allowed to speak English. There was a method that after three months of learning you can speak straight Chinese. My father was a teacher first, then he became assistant dean and dean of that college. Their students were adults: Japanese,

French, Germans, Americans, and Russians. They were missionaries, employees of oil companies, government officials, and military men. They came to China and wanted to learn about the Chinese and their language. My parents were very good at their jobs.

We have always had maids. In our home it was my parents, the maid, and me. We did not flaunt it, it was just comfortable. My parents were very strict with me. I still remember my mother saying things like, "Oh my, don't speak unless you're spoken to," or, "you're never allowed to sit when you have *zhang-bei* (senior) in the room." To be proper, proper, and proper…it was just very strict in the old-fashioned way.

I attended an all-girls private school in Beijing then. We wore uniforms, we were clean, and we walked or bicycled to school. I really liked it because my school was near a park. We went there every afternoon to have fun. I was very happy as a little girl in China. I loved the seasons. I loved my cousins; we had fun every weekend. It was a happy time.

The curriculum at school was terrible! I went to school from morning till evening, and then I had lots of homework. I was not a good student. My parents were so strict that I remember very clearly that I was punished. Everyone would go outside and play, but I would stay in and practice calligraphy. I remember my desk. I had my own room, and under the desk I had all the ink and other stationary. I remember that, as my punishment, I had to write six or eight pages of calligraphy. Oh it was terrible, I cried all the time. Well there was *guo-wen* (Chinese language), there was *maobizi* (Chinese calligraphy), and there was history, geography, and physical education. Oh it was hard, and we had to memorize many things; but I learned a lot. It was good, old-fashioned teaching. I studied the Chinese language from the time I was in elementary school. My father also taught me with flashcards. I had to learn thirty words in a week; if I learned then I was rewarded, and got spanked when I couldn't remember.

I lived in Beijing from 1931 to 1941. Because of the Japanese occupation of China, my parents were called to start another school, a branch in the Philippines. They were not the only ones invited. There were Min, Chou—about six or seven teachers. My father was the principal. He was the leader, and because they were not allowed to bring family, he took only those people who were willing to leave their loved ones. My father was the only one who was allowed to bring family along.

Four church groups sponsored and invited him: the Presbyterians, Methodists, Congregationalists, and Baptists. Their boards supplied transportation and all other expenses. My parents and other teachers taught the missionaries from these churches in the Philippines. They became exclusively teachers for missionaries. This was their chance to flee from the Japanese, but they thought they could still go back to China someday.

Life in the Philippines was not good. It was there that I began to learn English. I had a private tutor, an American with a Chinese name. My father gave all the students who came to his school Chinese names. Her name was Fern Harrington, so my father said "Han" for Harrington and "Feng" for Fern. Therefore, her Chinese name was Han Feng. It is a very meaningful name. When I first went there I was a big girl already, eight or nine years old, but I was put in grade one with all the Filipinos. Since my private tutor taught me English, I knew how to say "good morning" and some other phrases. She used a catalog, Sears or Montgomery Ward, as a textbook. She taught me by using the pictures in the catalog.

She was my father's student and a Southern Baptist missionary. All these people that have taught me or helped me grow up were missionaries. I am a product of missionaries. One taught me to type, one taught me English, another taught me to play piano, to sing, and to sew. I had almost a completely Western education. I was passed mainly from auntie to auntie. I was like theirs too because I was the only child at the school and they all loved me. However, my father said, "you must teach her, don't spoil her." He was very strict, so strict that when I started to speak English, he told me that I speak Chinese at home so that I would not forget the language. When I was little and started learning English, I disliked it at first, but soon grew to truly enjoy it.

As I was so young, I just played and went to church and followed the missionaries. They were my role models. In the war and in the concentration camp, all the women and children were put together. I didn't learn much because I was with my mother, and she was put to work. So I played with all these other Fujianese and Cantonese, then I began to speak Cantonese and Fujianese because they could not speak Mandarin. We were together for a year, so we became friends. We were freed in 1942, and my parents then taught the Chinese the Chinese language. The missionaries were still in the camps. The churches could no longer support them, so that was their livelihood. My father had a lot to do with teaching the Chinese teachers how to teach their children in the Philippines.

In 1946 we went back to China after the second World War was over. My father was asked to go and teach when everyone returned. They had about two hundred teachers, and maybe two or three thousand students. The students were not just missionaries; they were U.S. Standard Oil, military, and embassy people. My father taught at a Chinese language school for foreigners in an old hotel building at Beijing. My parents had a bedroom, I had a bedroom, and we had a kitchen. It was enough for us; it was very nice. But we couldn't have any company!

In 1949 we went to Qingdao, Shandong Province, and took a plane to Shanghai. We stayed there for several months and were guests of some Southern Baptists. We were there through Christmas. On January 1, we left for Baguio, Philippines. At this time they were employed by the foreign mission board of the Southern Baptist convention until they retired, so they were teaching and helping missionaries. My mother and some missionaries started the Chinese Baptist Church in Manila. My father and the Chinese started the Baguio Baptist Church.

I did not decide to come to the United States; my father decided for me. Miss Harrington was determined that I would come to the United States for college; I guess she thought I had the potential. She told my father she could help me get a scholarship. I was not deserving of a scholarship. My father asked me if that was what I wanted, because I could go to the Philippines Women's University in Manila. But he felt that since the Philippines wasn't "Chinese" Chinese, that "American" America would be better for me. And since my parents weren't rich, they weren't sure they could pay for my college. They asked me if I would like to teach, which I did. Fern Harrington had graduated in the 1930s from NMSU (Northeast Missouri State University) at the top of her class. She wrote to Dr. Ryle and he said he would give me a full scholarship for as long as I wanted to study. I only had to pay my room and board, and at that time it was less than $50 a month. My mother did not want me to go, but my father said that four years would go by very fast.

I lived in the dorm. My parents sent me money, but I worked in the dorm switchboard and in the library. That gave me money to buy toothpaste, shoes, etc. My father wouldn't allow me to work in a Chinese restaurant. He said I may work in the library, the dorm, or work as a teacher, but there were certain things he wouldn't let me do. So in the summer I worked in camps, all religious camps.

My first year was so hard. I flunked every English test. I didn't have the background. I was so embarrassed, but I knew I had to hang in there. The last test was on punctuation and I not only passed it, I passed with flying colors. The teacher said "Good for you, Miss Ng" and he passed me for the quarter. At that time we had the quarter system. I had classes with Dr. Park, Dr. Ruth Towne, Dr. Kohlenberg; all these teachers were wonderful and so kind to me. I worked very hard, and did the best I could. I have the education I do today because of my parents, NMSU, and the missionaries. They were all so good to me. I never experienced any prejudice.

There were two Oriental students, myself and Suzy Wong from Hong Kong. But she was only here for two years and then went to New York, so I was the only Chinese left. If you look in the 1955 yearbook at that time we had the largest number of students in the international club ever; there were about thirty members, and I was the only Chinese.

Dr. Park was an older gentleman who taught in the social science division. He was very smart and was a good teacher. He had a really good sense of humor. He was very funny and both he and his wife were very kind to me. She wrote to me not long ago. She is in Oceanside, California, but she really misses Kirksville. I also had Dr. Zhou as a professor. Dr. Zhou, Dr. Towne, Dr. Wade, and Dr. Nobb all taught me. Dr. Nobb, who has since passed away, was my advisor. I had many other professors. I really learned when I was there. All the teachers helped me learn, even now. Dr. Carol Jones, Dr. McNeil, they are all wonderful. This is what I really appreciate about this school.

I did not really have any bad experiences. I made some beautiful friendships and dated. I went out with two American men, but my father's teachings were always in the back of my mind. I had a good time, but I never thought about marriage. It was fine just to be friends, because I knew I eventually wanted to go back home. When I was young my father had so much influence over me. However, as I got older, it was my mother who had more influence.

We were a very traditional family, but my parents were very democratic for Chinese. They quarreled on bad days, but they considered each other equal and had a lot of faith. They prayed. They did not go to church, but they were very religious.

I returned to the Philippines after I graduated from NMSU. Dr. Ryle offered to let me stay and get my master's. That is one of my regrets because I could have finished it in one year. But my father wanted me to come home, and I was homesick. I went back and taught at the Chinese school, Grace Christian, for two years. Then I taught at an American school in Baguio. It was called Brandt School, an Episcopalian school, kindergarten through grade twelve. And then I got married.

My husband and I knew each other for ten years. We met each other in 1949 and married in 1959. I think he had the idea of marriage before I did. We had a difficult time because he is from a Fujianese family, a huge family with fifteen brothers and sisters, and two mothers (his first mother died and he had a stepmother). However, my father respected my husband's father very much because he knew he was fair. His father was a business-man; he owns something from the north of Luzon to the south of Mindoro now. He was a *Shouling* (leader). Ng is a huge family; he is well known, very

rich and very famous. But he him-self is a very upright person, so my father considered it a good match. His only condition was that we didn't live with anybody; he didn't think I could deal with all those in-laws. And so there was a very big ceremony. The engagement was something; there were a lot of banquets.

My husband graduated as an architectural engineer and civil engineer from Magoa University in Manila. Magoa is like the MIT (Massachusetts Institute of Tech-nology) of the Philippines. He's brilliant. He studied very hard and learned business from his father. His father came from Fujian as an assistant cook when he was sixteen. He was penniless when he came to the Philippines. He saved and taught himself; by the time I mar-ried my husband, he owned lumber companies and grocery bins with rice and sugar cane. His first wife gave him thirteen children. The thirteenth (Victor) is an ear, nose, and throat specialist; he works in

Ling Ng came to the United States from the Philippines in 1951 to study at the North East Missouri State University (currently Truman State University). Ling Ng at the Moore Farm in 1953. Huping Ling Collection (Courtesy of Ling Ng)..

New York. When my mother-in-law was pregnant with Victor, she had cancer with a tumor the size of a coconut. The Philippines is a predominantly Catholic country because it was occupied by Spain for 350 years and by Americans for 50. She had to make a choice, and because they were Catholics, they would sacrifice the mother to save the child. And that's what they did. And today, at the University of Santo Thomas, her tumor is in a jar; I saw it. After his first wife died, my father-in-law chose a second wife, and he picked the one who could cook. It's because he knew the kids had to eat—never mind if they're dirty. She was the daughter of a man who gambled and lost, and she was sold to my father-in-law. It's very sad but true. She gave birth to seven children, but five of them died in various ways, mostly from illness. So there are only fifteen children in the family, and my husband is number six.

When we married, my husband was the purchasing agent for his father. He would buy goods for the store, do accounting, etc. Although he graduated as an engineer, he never practiced. After we got married my father-in-law gave him some money and he built seven factories. He started with State Steel and built two of those. Then he built Philippine Rope (two of those factories) and Cable & Wire factories. Because of his family support, he could go to Japan, Italy, and Germany to buy machines. At first it was a process of trial and error, but gradually he became very good at it and became a successful businessman. He's semi-retired now; he had two strokes, but he's doing well, thanks to the support provided by his large family.

I have two children. Our daughter helps her father in the factories. Our son has his own business. They all live in Manila, but they came to the United States for college. My daughter went to school in Tennessee at Carson-Newman, a Southern Baptist college, and then transferred to Furman, another Baptist university. My son also studied there. He then came to NMSU, but he didn't graduate.

My daughter went into elementary education when she was in college. My son declared this, that, and the other major, but he didn't finish school. He left with one year remaining. My children liked their lifestyle better in the Philippines because they lived like a prince and a princess. Here you have to do your own laundry; you're not the boss. Back home my daughter opens her mouth and everybody jumps.

I came back to the United States when my children were here during college. Actually I came back in 1981 because I was checking on them. I only came in the summer and went back when school started. I did that from 1981 to 1984. Then I said to myself, "I'm coming here every year, I might as well be going to school." I talked to Dr. Towne and she wanted me to do a master's degree in social science. I ultimately decided to do counseling because at home, I felt like I needed to find my place. So I started and kept at it. Meanwhile, my son and daughter went back to the Philippines and I stayed. My second time here was wonderful. I learned and thoroughly enjoyed it. I can now say I'm more self-assured, useful, and independent.

That was my major reason to stay, but I also wanted to take care of my parents. My parents, after living overseas for so long, did not want to go back China. They were not willing to live under that system and there was no home for them there. They had retired and had been living in the Philippines for all these years. After their retirement, they went to Taiwan and lived there for more than ten years because it was the next best thing to China. They had their retirement fund, and that took care of them very well. They didn't think they could survive in China. They didn't think it was the same China they left, but Taiwan was more or less the same. They were happy there and made a lot of friends, mostly Christians. Every year they would come visit me or I would visit them. They were very able. However, I wanted them here because, as I was applying for permanent residency at the time, I could not process my papers going back and forth. At that time, I could not fly anywhere. I wanted them to come here so I could take care of them.

I think it was in 1985 or 1986 when they got here. I was going to school and took care of them. It was then that my mother's health started to fail; she had been diagnosed with Alzheimer's. She died five years later and my father died seven years after that. He was bedridden for the last year and a half.

I graduated in 1987. It took two years for me to finish my master's program. I didn't start on my degree until January of 1985 and graduated in May of 1987. I worked in town for Living & Aging Concerns Inc., a counseling office. Many summers, I also worked on campus for Upward Bound. I did these while I was in school, and I also taught Chinese cooking at the vo-tech, a vocational school in town. I did various things to make money. I didn't want to depend on my husband, although he will still give me money, all he asks is how much. He's like that—very kind, very gentle. There's really not much difference between my husband and I. It's just that my parents could not go to the Philippines to live because the Chinese could not live there. I needed to take care of them, and so this was the logical place. I couldn't work on my master's in Taiwan. I think there is some conflict between my husband and I as far as raising the kids; just ordinary husband and wife things. I do not want them to live like a prince and princess; I want them to know the dignity of work. He calls and we still talk, but circumstances require that I stay here.

I never really applied for a job, and I didn't have to have one. But once you get a job you can process your papers faster. One summer after I came back, there was a message on my answering machine from Mr. Burns, the principal at the local school. He said, "Mrs. Ng, we need a counselor in La Plata schools." I had known that they needed a counselor, but I never thought they would ask me. He said, "The university placement rated you very highly. Would you consider coming in for an interview?" So I called and got an interview with the principal of the high school and principal of the elementary school. There was no application, no resume, and I was hired on the spot. Normally they advertise nationally when hiring someone, and they also go to different colleges for interviews, but the board voted and I was picked unanimously.

I am the guidance counselor for kindergarten through grade twelve. In the elementary school, it is a lot of teaching, curriculum, getting to know the kids, and helping coordinate career days. In the high school, it is more complicated. It is a lot of career days and exploration, and they have to know what they're going to do after high school. I help with financial aid, scholarships, and college visits. I coordinate the recruiter meetings. I also go in the classrooms. I do a career planning profile for the lower grades. I like to bring in some character when I teach, practicing responsibility, honesty, and respect. I do a lot of correspondence work and public relations. I also visit with the parents and help the principal. I feel that I just listen. I've made friends with everybody, especially the teachers. I talk to them, listen to them, and serve as a resource. Every day of my job is varied. I try to get fee waivers. I give tests to special education students. I do all the intelligence tests and gifted tests. We have a testing schedule to follow, we have things on the calendar, but day to day, it's up to me. This is a wonderful system here; they just give it to me. I do as little or as much work as I want. My office is usually always open, but during the summer the door is closed because this room has air conditioning. They treat me very well. I like them all and I think they like me.

There are cultural barriers, but I always give them the benefit of the doubt and do what's right for here and now. One of the lessons I received at university was never to impose my beliefs and my values. However, for the little ones I do tell them. I think they know through human nature the difference between right and wrong. To cheat is wrong, for example. As human beings we are by nature sensitive; we have a sixth sense. This is what I do; I carry myself and let them see it. You cannot say one thing and be something else, it just doesn't work. I am me and this is me, that doesn't mean I'm perfect. However, I think by my actions and the way I respond, they know what I am made of. So they know the things I approve and the things I don't. I never have to say, "This is wrong, you shouldn't smoke, you shouldn't drink." They know that. I feel you don't have to say anything; we just behave the way we should behave. If people are smart, they will see. I have never encountered a situation where parents or students think that I don't know where they're coming from because I am Chinese. Truly, I've never been treated so kind and been so accepted. I share, but I don't give advice because I'm not in their shoes. But if they ask me, I'll make suggestions because there are always alternatives to a problem.

I have many friends here. All my friends are my age or younger and we get together often. Most of them are female unless they are husbands. I am married and I have a husband so I do not have male friends unless they are professional friendships such as my superintendent. I belong to the First Baptist Church, but I don't go every Sunday. I have church friends, school friends, professional friends, neighbors, Jen and her family.

Jen runs a farm with her sister and co-owns three Subway sandwich stores. I have known Jen since college and we are best friends. I invited her to live with me because I cannot live by myself. We cook together. I want to try to be on my own, but I'm not used to being alone. We each have our own jobs; she runs Subway and farms. She graduated from the university with an agricultural degree. She can do anything: build a house, weld, and plant. She is a very capable person. She can do crafts and paint, and she can fix cars. That's why I live with her, because I don't have to do much. It is not easy to keep a strong friendship all these years. She's been to the Philippines and to Taiwan; she helped with my parents, with my children. She is seven years younger than me.

We used to own a grocery store, More-of-Ling, in this town. It was on Jefferson Street, by the post office. She and I tried to run it; we tried to keep busy. It sold just canned Chinese food, Chinese crafts, and Chinese cookware. It was a very nice store. We had it for two or three years. A lot of our stuff was sold to Gatsby's, a reputable local food store. We sold it when I got the counseling job because we did not have time to go to Chicago or San Francisco to buy supplies. We went to buy our products in person because we wanted to make sure what we got was fresh and right. A lot of Chinese are not very nice. The store was not profitable; we broke even. It was more of a service. However, because we were teaching Chinese cooking, we could buy wholesale with a tax number. We could not do it again—we do not have time to shop. We wanted it clean, neat, classy, and inexpensive. It's hard. We went as far as California, as near as Chicago and St. Louis. We had fun, but would not do it again.

That's not the only way you can be rich. My husband is a multimillionaire. My father's teachings are very strong, and I believe that whatever your calling is, is what you'll do. I believe in integrity. Jen and I are thinking about what we'll do when we retire and we think we'll do crafts. She's started already. We want to make things that are useful, that will not just hang and collect dust. So we're thinking and exploring. We'll ask for a fair price—we don't want to make a killing.

I will get my citizenship soon. I have a green card now but I don't have an American passport and I cannot vote. But I want my citizenship for two reasons. One is that I want my children to have a chance to come here, if they want to. Right now they don't want to. But what if in their forties or fifties they want to come here? My husband can leave them zillions; I don't have that. So I will give them another option in life. That's why I'm here, to serve my children and give them something if they want it. They can't come to stay. They can come as tourists. But if they want to come permanently, they have to wait for a quota. With a quota, such a wait can be endless. From the Philippines, it's just too long. Because I was born in China, it was easier for me to get a quota. My husband does not want to come here; he has no desire. He has already traveled the world, so have my son and my daughter. They have been to Africa and the Middle East.

I miss my kids more than anything. I miss my daughter; she's in my blood. She is thirty. I call her and she calls me. I think they want to get married someday. I miss them, but it is worth it. They said to me, "Mom, after you get your citizenship, you negotiate with us, because we do not want to go."

I like this area. For instance, this morning I went to renew my driver's license and people called me by my name. I went to the restaurant and they knew me. It's so easy to do things; they trust you. Sure I've thought about moving; I like the Southwest, Arizona. I've been to Mesa and I love it. I like California too, but it's too crowded. The thing I like best about this town is that it is a college town. It is more invigorating and you have things to do—go to bookstores or eat out. I eat at Thousand Hills, Country Kitchen, and Best Western, and then Manhattan sometimes. We go to the Wooden Nickel as well.

I also like the small town where I am living now, because it is very quiet, very peaceful, and because I am getting older. I think I'm the only Chinese here. There are two Filipino ladies; there might be a Mexican gentleman. I've lived here now for four years. I used to live in the university town but I decided to move here. The residents here are mostly involved in agriculture, but many of them also work in other nearby towns. They work in the hospitals, in the school system, in the factories, and in the nursing home.

There's not really anything I don't like about this area. Well, I don't like the winters. I don't like the extreme heat or the extreme cold. That's why I like Arizona. While Arizona in the summertime is 105 or 110 degrees, it's different because it's a dry heat. Other than that, there's really nothing that I don't like. I'm a person that is easily content, easily satisfied.

I also have my depressions, my moods. Well, one person I give credit to is my roommate Jen; she analyzes me and we talk about it. I'm a very talkative person—I'm very honest. So I will tell her, "I resent you. I do not like it because I feel it should be this way, this way, this way." I can communicate, so we work it out. I do have very sad times, when I miss my daughter. But then I just pick up the phone and call her, and tell her, "Right now I miss you so much." I never feel stressed about my job; I just love it. I get tired; however, it is a good feeling. I am so content and satisfied.

Erin Zeng was born into a family of educators in Hong Kong in 1938. She came to America for higher education in 1955 and later became a successful chemistry professor at a state university in Ohio. She was married to a European American, a colleague in her deparment, at the time of the interview in 1990.

My father was a Hakka (subgroup of Han Chinese), growing up in the backward countryside of Mei Xian, in Guangdong Province. It was so mountainous that it was hard for people there to get to any nearby town. My father was very bright. When he was a teenager, he met a missionary who found out his talent and encouraged him to go to university. He later attended Fu Jiang University in Shanghai and got his degree in Chinese literature. In 1930, he went to the United States and worked on his PhD in education at Stanford University. He got his degree in two years.

Then he returned to China. He held positions in several leading Chinese universities. He was the dean of the College of Art at Qinghua University. Later, he started South China College in Hong Kong in 1936. During the Japanese occupation of Hong Kong, he moved his college to mainland China. Before the Communist Party took over in 1949, he moved his college to Hong Kong once again. He became a professor at Chung Chi College (the current Chinese University of Hong Kong). He wrote many books on elementary, high school, and university education. He wrote the university textbook *Da Xue Zhong Wen* (Chinese language for university students), which was used in many universities in Hong Kong and many other southeastern Asian countries.

My mother was born in Shanghai. She received her college degree in sociology from Denison University in Ohio in 1930. Then she returned to China and met my father on the ship. They got married in 1931 or 1932. She taught college English for all of her life.

My parents worked very hard. They were so busy that they did not have too much time to spend with us. My father was busy traveling to raise funds for his college and my mother was busy making a living and raising children. Those years were full of turmoil. We moved a lot.

My mother later became the dean of the Women's College at Chung Chi College after my father died. In 1960, my mother came to the United States to live with me. She worked in the library at the University of Chicago for four years when I was a graduate student there. She followed me to UC Davis, where I was a research associate and lecturer in chemistry for two years; however, she was too old to find a job there. My mother got her U.S. citizenship in 1965. She died in Oxford, Ohio, in 1986.

My brother was born in 1934. He is four years older than me. In 1950 he graduated from high school in Hong Kong, then he went to Zhongshan University in Guangzhou. During his university years, he went to Hong Kong to visit my family and my mother went to China to visit him. After graduation, he was sent to Changchun, Jilin Province. As soon as my mother got her citizenship, she began to work for my brother's visa. The visa was ready five or six years before my brother came to America, because he had trouble getting his passport from the Chinese government. In 1978, my mother was very ill, which allowed my brother to get a passport. He came to the United States alone in 1981. His family (his wife, a son and a daughter) came later in 1983. He had a hard time at first, but he received his master's degree in geology at this university. Later he found jobs—first in Toledo, Ohio, then at Stanford University. Now'he works for an optical company. His wife learned English and driving after she came here. She is working in the same company as he does as a technician, making about $25,000 a year ($7 hourly pay), which would be equivalent to a bachelor degree holder's pay. If the company needs her, she works ten hours a day and some hours on the weekend.

My niece attended the university here for a year; she had a hard time adjusting. Then she went back to China to enroll at Fudan University in Shanghai and earned her BA there. Later she got a master's degree at a university in New York.

I was born in Kowloon, Hong Kong, on February 8, 1938. Because of the turmoil during the World War II years, I didn't have a formal education until 1949 when I started high school at Pei Ching High School, a well-known Chinese high school in Hong Kong. Before my high school years, I had never learned English.

I came to the United States for my undergraduate work in 1955 when I was seventeen years old. My father paid my traveling expenses with the royalties from his books. My benefactress, Alice, who was the mother of my mother's close friend, gave $18,000 to Berea College in Kentucky, which was enough for four years schooling. Berea College has very good reputation and it is very hard to get into it, but the tuition is very cheap.

In the first year at Berea, I was very shy because I could not speak English and I looked different. Berea had an international reputation and there was a large racial element. But I was the only Oriental there. There was also an Indian fellow. When we ate in the dining hall, sitting at the round table, I was speechless, just smiling. But I could get along with my classmates and roommates and did not feel lonely, for I was so interested in what I saw and so busy studying that I did not have time to think I was lonely. My childhood experience also helped me. We traveled from place to place when I was little. I can speak five Chinese dialects. To me, coming to America was the same as coming to a new town. I passed the entrance exams. I was behind in English, but I got high scores in math and other science courses. I had to take a 100 level English course. The difficulty in English kept me very busy.

I stayed in Berea from 1955 to 1957. Then I transferred to the University of Chicago, which was close to where my benefactress lived. Using the money from my benefactress and the money I earned over the summer, I was able to support myself. Entering the graduate program at the University of Chicago, I got a scholarship. I never felt that anyone discriminated against me. I was always the only female in my class. I was treated like a queen. I felt I was special.

I was well treated until I earned my PhD. I had a hard time finding a real job. I was a post-doctoral research associate and instructor in chemistry at Illinois Institute of Technology for two years from 1963 to 1964, and research associate and lecturer in chemistry at the University of California at Davis from 1964 to 1966. After that, I was a research associate and visiting scientist at Argonne National Laboratory in Argonne, Illinois, from 1966 to 1969. I felt Argonne was an ideal place for my research, for the equipment there is advanced. Unfortunately, the government cut off the funds and I had to look for a job somewhere else.

I found my first real job at this university in 1969. I met a professor from the university when I was at Davis. He was interested in my research. Later he invited me to give several seminars at the university. The search committee then decided to hire me as an assistant professor. Four years later, I was promoted to associate professor.

I feel that in scientific fields, the scientists are very fair in value judgment and recommendation, whereas in the humanities and social sciences, there is a greater human factor there. If you are a woman, if you are a Chinese, you have to work harder. It seems that there is no prejudice there, but every little element can add to the difficulty.

When I teach graduate level science, no students complain about my accent. But when I teach freshmen level, these freshmen would say: I don't understand her, she has an accent. They could have understood me with a little effort, but they don't want to make any effort! If I am in a good mood, I would just laugh at these evaluations. But this could be a source of depression. Language is the major source of hardship for me. I have to work harder than my peers. I am upset that I am still criticized after I made a great effort, whereas some of my colleagues don't even prepare before their lectures. You are fighting a battle that you can't ever win. Like my niece and nephew, when they speak out in the class, everyone looks at them carefully, questioning in their mind if they can speak English. Even if you could speak perfect English, they still feel it different, for they look at you differently. You are socially handicapped.

I met my husband Mark in the chemistry department here. We are both physical chemists. At that time, I was thirty-one years old and thought I could never get married. When my mother found out about our relationship (she lived with me), she could not be happier. She did not mind the racial difference, as long as this man is nice. Mark is a very nice person. He came from a farmer's family. Unlike my mother, his parents didn't have any knowledge of foreign cultures, but they were all very nice. Mark introduced me to his family and relatives. We got married in 1971 when I was thirty-three, and he was thirty-one. We didn't have a ceremony. We thought we were old, so we didn't want to tell friends and relatives about our marriage.

I am very happy about my marriage. I became a U.S. citizen in 1973, two years after we got married. I never judge people based on racial background. If you work with somebody, then you might develop a relationship with him, which is what happened to us. My husband appreciates Oriental culture. He has a great knowledge of Chinese history and geography. He made the whole transition a smooth one. I have no problems adjusting to a white American man, for I am totally Americanized, but I feel that I understand him better than he understands me. I have been a foreigner among natives—he has never been in the same situation. The first five years of my marriage were very difficult. There were all kinds of adjustments with work and family. Then both of us felt we should not have children.

I like American men. They would make better husbands and fathers than Oriental men. They are capable and hard workers. My husband can almost do everything, physically and mentally. He can fix everything. He knows almost everything. Sometimes I feel sorry for my husband; he is working all the time, doing all kinds of thing for other people. He never refuses other people's requests.

I am very Americanized. When my brother came, I had to learn to adjust to him. But my judgment and sense of value are still Chinese. I have a Chinese attitude. I am proud of my Chinese culture. I would be upset if somebody thinks I am Japanese. I think I am very fortunate to be Chinese. I think Chinese culture is still at the top of world civilization, except for classical music and science, which are pretty Western-oriented. I like Chinese culture, but I also appreciate Western classical music and science.

I appreciate some American characteristics: generosity and encouragement to speak out. On the other hand, I consider superficial values to be a bad feature of American life. For example, in political campaigns, people's judgments are sometimes very superficial. I am very interested in American mainstream politics. I have voted every year. I sympathize with the two cultures.

Even though I am Americanized, I don't feel I fit into American society. I don't think I fit into the professional situation in a deep sense. Superficially, I fit. I don't fit into China either. I can talk to my husband about my feelings, but he is not my entire world. I have to face students, my job, and other problems. When I faced age problems, I was also unhappy about my teaching. Students demanded that exams be easier and easier. The national education level is dropping. At this time, I sometimes feel as if I have no spiritual and moral support system.

Gena Chen was born into a family of professional musicians in Hangzhou, China, in 1946, and later moved to Taiwan with her parents. She came to America in 1963 to study piano and taught at Peabody Conservatory in Baltimore, Maryland. Married to a prominent Chinese American scientist, she has two sons and has lived in St. Louis since 1998. She was teaching piano at her own studio at the time of the interview in 1998.

I was born in Hongzhou, China, on January 3, 1946. When I was six months old, my parents, who both went to music school (my father was a violinist and my mother a soprano), went to Taiwan to look for jobs and never had a chance to go back. That was how we stayed in Taiwan, even though that was in 1946, three years before the Communist takeover in 1949. My father got a job in Taipei Symphony Orchestra and my mother taught music at a high school. They liked their jobs and settled down. Why did they choose Taiwan over other places? I think one of their professors went to Taiwan and recommended they go there.

My paternal grandfather, Chen Shizhe, was born in 1891 in Nanan County, Fujian. He was a revolutionary and joined Sun Yat-sen's 1911 Revolution. He was very well-liked by the local people. In 1925, he was arrested and executed by a Chinese warlord. My father, who was then five, and his sister, who was eight, were raised by their mother alone. After my grandfather died, people in his county erected a big monument commemorating him for what he did for the area. During the Communist regime, the whole monument was knocked down. In 1989, my aunt, my father, and some relatives made the government donate some money to rebuilt the monument. When the new monument was erected, it was a big event, a big celebration, and a book was written about my grandfather.

My maternal grandfather, Xie Touba, was an artist. He was born in 1902 in Xiamen, Fujian. He was fond of drawing at an early age. In 1919, he went to Philippines, studying fine arts at Philippine University. He graduated in 1925 but continued to study painting at Philippine University. During the afternoons and evenings, he taught at a local Chinese school. In 1928, he was sponsored by his cousin who resided in Vietnam to go to France to study western painting. He enrolled in a fine arts college and graduated in 1934. It was very unusual that he went to Paris for ten years when he had family in China. Then he returned to China, taught at Fine Arts Academy of Xiamen, Fujian Normal School, National Academy of Fine Arts at Hongzhou, and Fujian Normal University. He served as dean of Hongzhou Yizhuan [National Academy of Fine Arts of Hongzhou]. He passed away just two years ago. I have a large scroll that was presented to him by one of his students at his ninetieth birthday celebration. People say "Bei Xu Nan Xie." Xu is Xu Beihong (a famous painter of Chinese style); Xie is Xie Touba. He had many students who guided the art world in China. I also have a painting, which I have had for over ten years, created and sent to me by one of his students who went to Taiwan. When we moved to St. Louis, we hung it up in our home.

My father, Chen Dunchu, was born on November 20, 1920, in Fujian. He graduated from National Fujian Music Academy in 1940, specializing in violin. My mother, Xie Xueru, was born on May 22, 1926, in Hongzhou. She also studied at Fujian Yizhuan [Fujian Academy of Arts].

In the 1950s, even though Taiwan was not very prosperous, we did not feel poor. We had all we needed. We had two servants who were from the countryside, one taking care of the kids, the other doing household chores. It was quite common for people to have servants. My father worked at the Taipei Symphony Orchestra as a violinist. He later became concert-master and conductor. Later, he did not want to conduct, and so he became manager for the Taipei Symphony Orchestra for many years. He did many things for the orchestra, one example being the Taipei Music Festival. It was very successful. President Li Denghui was Taipei's mayor at the time. President Li was a very serious classical music lover. One of the things they did during the Taipei Music Festival, rather than traditional concerts, was that they promoted a lot of traditional Chinese music, and folk Taipei music and opera. At the festival, President Li translated for Faust (the German Chancellor) a huge work from Chinese to German. His German must have been excellent in that he could translate the whole opera into German. President Li had his early education in Japan, and it was probably there that he learned German.

I have four siblings, and I am the oldest. Next comes my brother, Chen Langu, born in 1950. He is four years younger than me. I have two sisters: Chen Hongqi born in 1954, and Chen Baiqi born in 1956. We all work in the music world. My brother is a violinist, educated at Yale and Columbia University. Both of my sisters are cellists. One also graduated from Yale, the other from the Music School of New York. In the last generation, children did not have a choice to do what they wanted to. They all listened to their parents. That was what happened to us; our parents made the career choice for us. At least I know my parents made the choice for me and I like it very much—I do not know about my siblings. Between my siblings we have a large age gap. When I came to the United States, my brother and my two sisters were very small. My brother and I are five years apart, and my brother and other sisters are another five years apart. I came here when I was seventeen. Therefore, I do not know if they fell into music willingly or not. However, they are all doing very well.

My brother just came back from Beijing. The first time he was there, he could only stay for two days to give a lecture. Some of my mother's teachers had retired from Beijing Yinyue Xueyuan [Beijing Music Academy], but he met some of my parents' teachers. They were very moved seeing their students' child now lecturing at Beijing Yinyue Xueyuan. I am really happy that people of both sides (mainland and Taiwan) could come and go very easily. My mother did not see my grandfather for about thirty years. When they met [again], it was very emotional for both of them. My mother went to China every year and every time she went, she just stayed at home to give my grandfather company. My grandfather was living in Fuzhou and passed away three years ago. My grandmother had died several years earlier. This is a historic tragedy for all the families. However, it is getting better, so I am very encouraged. I know I have a lot of aunts and uncles in mainland China, scattered all over the country. They [the government] send you to work in a certain place. I am not very familiar with my family history because my parents did not want to talk about it before. I think now they are more open to say things. However, one of my aunts did go to Taiwan to visit with my mother five years ago.

When I started playing piano at six, I had a lot of practice, about two hours everyday, very regimented. Practicing was part of my daily schedule. Because we lived in the staff housing area for the symphony people, all the children there were practicing music. Therefore, you do not question when you hear your next-door neighbor practicing. It was, in a way, a very good environment. You do not feel you are left out because everybody was outside playing [some musical instruments]. Every day, I was at home practicing. I had a very nice childhood. My practicing did not affect my academic work; I did very well at school. I went to Taipei First Girls High School. It was very hard to get in. After junior high, my parents already realized that my life would be going in a musical direction and that the high school work would hamper my practice time. However, I did take the Liankao, the high school entrance examination, and I did get into high school. I then went to Taipei Yizhuan (The Taiwan National Academy of Arts) to concentrate more on music. There I had fewer academic demands and more time to practice. Taipei Yizhuan was like a high school. Most people went there after junior high, at fifteen, like me, but others went after high school. It is a five-year academic program, focusing on music in my case. They also have arts-related subjects, such as painting, fine arts, and movie making. It is not equivalent to a BA; instead, you get an art diploma. I stayed there for two years and then I came to the United States.

I first came to New England Conservatory of Music in Boston in 1963 when I was seventeen. At that time in Taiwan it was true and it is probably still true that you can not come to the United States as an undergraduate. I was the second one from Taiwan, after the government enacted a new law, called Tiancai Ertong Chuguo Banfa [The Measure for Talented Youth Studying Overseas], to encourage talented musicians to go abroad after rigorous exams. They say you should go to develop your skill rather than wait until graduate school. I received permission from the government by taking a lot of tests to prove that I was worthy. I got four scholarships. At that time, the Taiwanese government only encouraged graduate students to study overseas. If you were a male, you could go overseas only after you served in the military.

I was quite prepared when I came to America. Other than English, where we had to study Shakespeare, no courses gave me a hard time. I had no problem at all with musically-related subjects. Because my foundation

Gena Chen, a pianist and former piano faculty at Peabody Preparatory in Baltimore, Maryland, studying at the New England Conservatory of Music in Boston, Massachusetts, 1965. Huping Ling Collection (Courtesy of Grace Chen).

Gena Chen at home in St. Louis, Missouri, 1998. Huping Ling Collection.

in Taiwan gave me a jumpstart, I was much more prepared than a lot of my classmates. Before I came to America, I had learned two or three years of English in my regular high school English class. However, the Boston accent gave me trouble. I did tape a lot of lectures. I also had a lot of helpful classmates. I would listen to lectures several times. I would study my friends' notes and my notes and usually I ended up having better grades.

How was life besides academic work? I had no life. It was academic work and practice, period. I was probably very naïve, unlike many American girls or boys at seventeen. I had never spent a night away from home before then. I had led a very sheltered life and did whatever I knew how to do, which was study and practice. I basically did the same thing in America, except everything was in English. I was not very different from what I was in Taiwan, but I did miss my family. I really realized I was away from home when I went back to my dorm and saw that my bed was still not made, because the servants made my bed at home. That was first time it hit me hard. I was sad for a while. However, after a while, I was okay. I just accepted it and did the best I could.

I stayed in Boston for five years. After I graduated from the New England Conservatory of Music, I went to Mills College in Oakland, California, which had excellent teachers there. It was a good time. It was during the Berkeley turmoil, and so I experienced things like sit-ins. I did not participate; however, it was an exciting time for a young person.

Did I have any social activity? In Boston, I participated in Chinese student choirs that are found at several colleges in Boston. I did the same thing at Berkeley. There was a choir company for the Chinese students there. My life was still mostly work, study, and practice, however. I do not think I was a very social person. As I get older, you may see me gradually becoming more outgoing.

I met Frank in Boston. He was at MIT; there was a student activity and we met there. We met again when we were at the UC San Diego during our separate careers. I did not know he was there, but when we met again, it was good. We started dating. I was in a PhD program and had my committee proposal prepared, but I did not finish my PhD. I was probably one year away from finishing it, but my focus was not on a career then. Because Frank had to do his postdoctoral studies at Johns Hopkins University, we moved to Baltimore. We wanted to have children and I had some health problems. Otherwise, I might have finished my program. I do not regret what I did. I know I can still go back to finish it, but it is not that important to do it, because I like what I do now. I knew I always wanted a family. I think my generation is a cross between the old traditional values and the new options. Some people are very torn because they could see both sides. However, in my case that was not a problem, because I know I am not idealistic enough to pursue a performing life. I always wanted to have a family. I knew that kind of life could not accommodate a nice family life. It just worked out well in my personal case, even though I did have a choice, because I chose not to go the other route. I still have a professional life and I enjoy it very much. [By teaching], I can make a direct influence on a one-to-one basis. People I am fortunate to have worked with over long periods of time say that I have made a huge difference in their lives. I find it very rewarding for me personally, and this way I do not have to be torn between family and career. Hopefully I do both well. You can only try your very best and deal with whatever is given to you.

When my children were younger, their demands on my time were not as great, so I continued to give recitals. When they got older, they became involved into all kinds of activities. With these factors, in addition to my teaching, it became unrealistic to keep a set schedule. I have two boys, Gregory is twenty-one and Jeffery is twenty. It has been a long time since I have seen them; when they do come, it is only for short periods of time. They are both in California. They are involved in the liberal arts; they are not going into science or music. One is interested in business, the other is interested in law, but they may change.

Gregory has a girlfriend, Michelle, a very nice girl. Michelle is white. He was, like me, a late bloomer. He never dated in high school. I think this is his second girlfriend. His first relationship did not last very long. Gregory and Michelle have been dating for over a year. I do not care what race his girlfriend or future wife is, as long as they have the same values, they are good people, and good for each other. I am sure I have preferences, but it is not up to me. I do not let them know what my preference would be. I always tell them they have to find a nice person that is good for them, that is more important. But my second son told me, without me asking him, that he definitely wants to marry someone Chinese. He is not dating seriously but somehow got this idea. My sons are so close to each other in age and come from the same family, yet they have different preferences.

They both speak Chinese fluently, though they cannot read and write Chinese as well. But they both went to Chinese school and they took Chinese in college. They grew up in Baltimore, where we lived for twenty-two years before we came to St. Louis. There were Chinese language schools there. My husband was very active in all these affairs. He was the chairman of the board for the Chinese language school for eight years. The Chinese language school was just taught one day of the weekend for two hours, just like the Chinese language schools here in St. Louis. I think in Washington DC there might have been more intensive Chinese language schools, but not in Baltimore. My husband insisted that we speak Chinese at home. He is very good in this way. He came here to America at the age of five, so that is even more incredible. I have a very nice, very admirable mother-in-law. When they [my in-laws] came, they were the only Chinese family in Denver. They came to the United States in February 1948 with their two boys— one five, one three. They both had student visas, which I thought was highly unusual. Usually one spouse would come and the other would stay behind. I guess my mother-in-law is a very capable person. She was born at the wrong time—thirty years too early. They stayed in Denver until my husband went to college. My father-in-law had another job, so they moved to Buffalo, New York, then retired to Fremont, California. They are involved in math or chemistry, more traditional Chinese subjects. They are very interesting to historians. My mother-in-law would give daily Chinese lessons in history and geography. She was very persistent. Before her sons were allowed to go out to play with their friends and do their regular homework, they had to learn Chinese. They had to go through each book made available to them. I found my husband's drawing of what provinces the Changjiang (Yangtze River) flows through. My mother-in-law did not work when her children were young. When they were older, she taught at a high school for sixteen years. All three children—although the youngest one, Jerry, was born in United States—speak perfect Chinese, which was unusual for that time. My husband speaks Chinese with a Peking accent, while I speak with a Taiwanese accent. His family was from Jiangsu Province. But his parents went to Nankai Middle School, a boarding school in Tianjin. Then they went to Xinan lianda (the Southwest Associated University) during the Sino-Japanese war.

Am I a strict mother or a lenient one? I would say half and half. I am not very strict in a traditional Chinese fashion. We usually talk about reasonable discipline when we need to. I even do not remember if they had to sit in time-out or were not allowed to watch TV, though my children probably remember. Even if it did happen, it was very rare. They did not go through a teenage rebellion. They were okay, not as bad as people predicted.

I think my boys and I are as close as possible. Being boys, they tell me things that they think I need to know; no more, no less. They write e-mails, they know to call every Sunday. They do not discuss problems they had with me. At their age, they make a decision and then they tell us. Sometimes they ask our opinion, but we do not tell them what to do at this point. My husband is very westernized in this way. Sometimes, between him and me, we have different ways of looking at things, and he is very democratic. I think it's too much—just let them decide—it's definitely not the Chinese way. He has high standards such as honesty, integrity, and a sense of civil pride, which he wants to instill in them. Choice of lifestyle is a personal choice. It's up to them.

I didn't participate in any social organizations. I was very busy with Peabody where I taught and I had a lot of responsibilities. I taught part-time at first, and gradually I became full-time as my children's demands lessened. I also participate in a lot of statewide or local music clubs and organizations.

I taught one-on-one at Peabody; I also taught enrichment classes. That's a repertoire class, teaching students from various stages. Once a week different students would come. I taught a couple of classes for students, a combination of music theory, music history, and ensemble. We played for each other; that's why we call it enrichment class. There were usually six students in each class and the parents also would come. These students came to Peabody after their regular school. They call it prep school. Prep schools have many missions; they can prepare people who want to go into music, but they can also accommodate people who just play an instrument for enjoyment, not necessarily to go into music as a career. We had a full range of students, and also a full range of ages, from child to adult.

When taking students, I select parents. When children are young, everybody can be educated. It depends on the parents' dedication, whether they have the right expectations and the right kind of attitude to guide their children. I feel that if I can get along with the parents, if we have the same kind of values, the children would definitely come easy. There were cases in which parents needed to guide the child. I enjoyed being very close friends with the parents because we all have similar outlooks. Students and parents became long-term friends. Basically I teach children between ages four and seventeen. I had fifty students when I was in Baltimore. Now I teach no more than fifteen students, because I want to practice more for my personal growth and accommodate my husband's job.

My husband moved here because he wanted to do biomedical engineering. There is good support here at Washington University from chancellor to dean. It was also a good time, because our children were old enough to go to college. We didn't have to worry about uprooting them.

I think Johns Hopkins is a very conservative place, and my husband's career was at its pinnacle over there. There was certainly a glass ceiling. He was named the medical school's full professor ten years ago. He was the only Chinese American to be named to this position in over one hundred years of Hopkins history; after him, no other Chinese American has been named, which I think is not logical at all. I am sure there are many deserving Asian Americans, but people still have very tight-knit outlook of others. There he reached the highest he could go, but he feels that he can make a big difference. He is also very concerned with making sure there are role models of Asian American professionals in his position. He wants his children to know that you can be a leader and that you should be assertive. He also mentors a lot of other friends' children, and they seek his advice, so he feels it is important for him to be a chair in a very good program. Maybe indirectly, it allows other people to have some role models. I am very proud of his determination. A lot of time we say that you have to be twice as good in order to compete with the mainstream, which shouldn't be. Unfortunately, sometimes even twice as good is still not enough.

His work now is wonderful. He has wonderful support. They are determined to make biomedical engineering the top priority at Washington University. He is very happy. Washington University is the third-ranked medical school in the country, and all the top biomedical engineering programs are associated with very top medical schools. Right now the program is just in its first year, and it's already ranked number twenty-two. He got his degree in the late 1970s in biomedical engineering; he was among the first wave of scientists involved in biomedical engineering development. In a way, the field has been in existence for almost twenty years, and it has become extremely important. They have wonderful students, all graduate-level, which is exceptional.

His job is demanding. He stays at work very late, but this is no different from before. He always works hard. It's definitely not a nine-to-five job. He has to recruit faculty, which takes a lot of time. He has to write a lot of grants and find the right kind of people for students to work for, so all of this takes time. He is involved in the lab as well. He enjoys it. His office is at the engineering school and his lab is at the medical school. He spends more time doing administrative work than writing grants and doing research. It is no longer a research job in which he tells his research fellows what to do. They correspond with him from Baltimore on how to use and maintain their grants. This is different from what he did before; it is more administrative; he manages the department. He wants to make a big difference at all levels, from undergraduate education to graduate students. He does this not just for himself but for every area where he feels he should be. He is a pioneer in this place. He enjoys the administrative work more than he thought he would. Before when people approached him for that type of position, he wasn't ready and he thought he wasn't interested in it. He is very good with figures, very determined and methodical, the scientific type. Some people cannot do administrative tasks. He is very good, because he has been doing a lot of that anyway. In a big way, doing grants is similar to administration.

In the family affairs, I influence him a lot. We are very good at compromising if we have differences. If I feel strongly, I still do it my way. If he feels strongly, certainly he will do it his way. If it concerns our children, we definitely have the same idea. We talk about it away from the children. We come to one decision. We don't tell them different things.

Do I have any religion? No. But this is also funny. This has probably been very Chinese. My parents decided I would live away from home, since I never spent a night away from home in Taiwan, and it was decided that I should go to Boston rather than New York, because in my mother's mind (and it's probably true), Boston is a safer place than New York, even though she has never been outside of Taiwan. She somehow found out that Boston is a Catholic town. I was converted, I went through the training of how to become a Catholic, and became one in name. My mother felt that it was a way she could protect me—send me to a safe place and have me join the majority religion. It's very moving actually when you think about it because that's all she could do for me being physically away so far. In name, I am supposed to be Catholic, but I never practiced it. My religion is very much a Chinese kind of thing, which is just being a very nice person, trying to be helpful, and living the way your conscience leads you. That's my religion. My husband doesn't have any religion either. I have to come to peace with my own conscience.

What is my typical day? In the morning, we get up very early. After my husband has breakfast, we will talk about our day. He sometimes gets up at five-thirty. I will get up at seven. After he leaves, I practice, then do yard work. By that time, it is almost noon. Then I run errands. I will start teaching in the afternoon. Usually the class goes from early afternoon to late afternoon. The day goes by very fast. I might spend two or three hours at piano, two hours in the yard, do a couple of errands, start teaching, and cook dinner when my husband comes back. Sometimes, I cook dinner before I start teaching. I cook every day. Very seldom do I take orders out. I enjoy cooking, so it's not a problem. Before the children came, I did a few cooking classes. I enjoy food. After dinner, we spend some time together. During the school year, we are out a lot of time on weekdays, either recruiting or going to school related functions. So we have a lot of social events. This is another reason why I can't teach a lot, because I have to go out on a couple of nights when I have class. I noticed that, last year, I had to go out often on Wednesday nights. They do keep us very busy. For instance, last week, we were out four nights. We often invite people, senior members, trustees, or potential donors, into our home. I cook for those occasions. I coordinate department functions, such as dinners with graduate students and faculty; I deal with schedules and catering.

———————◆———————

Liz Sing was born in Taipei, Taiwan, in the late 1960s and came to America with her family as a teenager. Her parents first owned a Chinese restaurant in Columbia, Missouri, and then moved to Kirksville, Missouri, for better business opportunity. She became manager of her family restaurant after graduating from the University of Missouri-Columbia with a degree in business management in the early 1990s.

I was born in Taiwan. I lived in the capital, which is about the same as New York. Not in population, but in terms of the people and the traffic, it's the same. What you could see in New York, you could probably see over there. It's a pretty westernized place; I think sometimes it's too westernized.

I came to America with my family when I was a sophomore in high school. I don't know why we came to the United States. It probably started with my dad. He decided to move to the United States where he had many relatives. They gave him a lot of business, and then he decided to move his family to America.

We didn't live in Kirksville to start. We lived in Columbia, Missouri, for about ten years, then we moved up here. When we first moved into the town of Columbia, I guess I didn't really like it, because in the capital of Taiwan, when you go out, you always see people around, and there is a nightlife. In Columbia back then, one of the things that really surprised me was that when I went to the downtown, I didn't see anybody walking on the street. It was pretty much just businesses there, just one or two people walking around. I was shocked because I knew that downtown would be the place that attracts a lot of people. Actually, it turned out the other way. On Sunday, people in Columbia would do outdoor activities, like playing football, or do things with family, whereas on Sunday in Taiwan, everybody goes shopping; nobody plays football. Columbia took me a couple of years to get used to; but once I did, I really liked it. It's getting bigger, but it's not too big. If you want to go to the license bureau in Taiwan, it takes you forever to get finished. Columbia is a really good-sized town.

Kirksville is a very quiet town. It's really good to do business because you don't get many mean, tricky, and crabby customers. You get it occasionally, but not in large numbers. But it doesn't make very much difference to me, working in a restaurant. When I go home, I go to sleep.

Our restaurant business actually started out with my uncle, who has a restaurant in Taiwan. My mom and dad helped him out. When they came to the United States, they decided to open their own restaurant. If you look at the Columbia area, it's pretty much saturated with restaurants like ours, so we decided to come to Kirksville. It only has two or three [Chinese] restaurants, so we thought this would be a good area to start the business. We're serving Chinese food, but we want customers to be able to carry out the way they do with fast food. Normally if you go to a dining room restaurant, you might have to wait a little while to get served. But here in our restaurant, I think you will bring people food and service a little bit sooner, and people will come back for that.

I would say that the way Chinese food is served to Americans and the way it is served in a traditional environment in Taiwan is probably about the same. You have to chop the vegetables, prepare the meats, and it's cooked about the same. But when you serve it, it's a little different. In Taiwan, if you serve a family, you have the entrees in the middle of the table, enough to serve four or five people. In America, you pass around the entrees. But the Chinese people don't do that; you take the chopsticks and pick out whatever you want to eat. You usually have the soup after the meal, but in America you have the soup before the meal.

I like to meet people through our restaurant. You talk with them, you

The kitchen of a Chinese restaurant in Kirksville, Missouri, 1997. Huping Ling Collection.

serve them, and later on you become friends with them. It's just another way of making friends. Another thing I like about the business is it gives me some experience on how to deal with people—not only customers, but also employees. For example, when they are late or when they have a problem and cannot make it to work, how do I deal with them and how do I manage the whole thing? I would say the worst part in the business is the long hours. I like working here, but I don't like such long hours all the time. If you are involved in the restaurant business, you can't have any time off. It's really hard. If you take the day off, you spend the whole day thinking, "Okay, there is something wrong at the restaurant." You also think, "Something is going to pop up—something is going to happen." You think about it all day. That's what I really don't like. You won't be able to take a day off unless it's Sunday.

If the community—like the police department, or the Red Cross, or the Chamber of Commerce—asks for a donation to help with certain activities, we try to help since we don't have time to participate.

I finished a college degree at University of Missouri–Columbia. I graduated in 1992 with a bachelor's degree in business management. Nothing really in particular stands out about my college experiences. It just started out as college life.

I can only compare the educational systems of Taiwan and America at the high school level. I wouldn't know the difference in college education between the two countries. In America you get so much freedom on what classes you want to take. In Taiwan you need to go to more classes than you do here. Everything is fixed. Everybody has to be taking the same class and doing the same thing. All the way through high school and college, you get tremendous pressure in Taiwan.

I would say that the family upbringing in the two countries is about the same. Family is the same everywhere. There are arguments. Mom and Dad care about you very much. And sometimes you might care too much, and always are worrying. But I would say it's about the same. I would say the kids really have to respect their parents in Taiwan. But I'm not saying that Americans don't have to respect their parents. I just think that if Americans were more caring about each other, they wouldn't have such a big gap between parents and children. That's a pretty significant difference between the two cultures. I would say that Americans are much more individual-oriented. But we Taiwanese are much more family-oriented; everything you do, you think about family first, you think about other people as well. You don't pursue your own goals and say, "This is something I want to do." So that is quite a big difference.

I have gone through the formal citizenship procedure in the United States. I think citizenship is more of a formality; it doesn't matter. As long as you are not Caucasian, people will still think you are Asian and a foreigner. In a way it bothers me, but I'm getting used to it. I think it has to do with the whole country. You get all different kinds of people, but people don't recognize the differences. You might get all different races, but they're still Americans. I guess some people don't recognize that.

As a female, there's no doubt about discrimination. There is a double standard in this society. I can't think of a specific example; it's just kind of a feeling you get. But I don't think it has so much to do with race. As long as you want to get a good job, you want to make a living out of it, and you work hard, it doesn't matter what race you are. It's not as though if you are a Caucasian American, you don't have to work hard.

Economically, I think there is a big difference right now between the United States and Taiwan. Since I immigrated, I can only see that there is a certain price increase. A package of Little Debbies used to be sixty or seventy cents, now it's up to ninety-nine cents. The price of food, produce, and everything else is pretty much steady. In Taiwan, I would say there is a huge price increase in all the basic needs that you need to have.

3

Interracial Marriage

Martha Reeves was born in Chongqing, China, in 1976 and grew up in Xian, China. She met her husband in Xian, where he was a foreign student, and came to the United States with her husband after they got married in 1995. She lived in Columbia, Missouri, with her husband, who was a student at the University of Missouri-Columbia, at the time of the interview in 1996.

My English name is Martha. Ed [my husband] gave me this name. I didn't know why he chose it. He just said that's good for me. I was born in Chongqing, Sichuan Province, in China. I never knew that until very recently. Before I left China I had to fill out papers for my visa, and at that time my mom said I was born in Chongqing, Sichuan. I don't know when we moved to Xian, Shaanxi Province. I always lived in Xian as long as I can remember. I thought I was born in Xian but my paper says I was born in Chongqing, Sichuan, and I must use that paper for my visa.

My parents are both retired. They stay at home and take care of house and everything, including my nephew and my brother. My father was a manager of a traveling company. His job was very easy. He did not have to spend a lot of time at work and he did not work too hard because he was old. He is sixty-three now. My mother is fifty-eight. She was an inventory clerk and she took care of everything in her factory. She did a very good job. She was very busy. Both my parents were very busy when I was young.

Before they had jobs, they were peasants in a village in Hunan Province. My father had a very limited education; he didn't graduate from elementary school. But he went into the army at sixteen. After my mother graduated from middle school, my grandfather said to her, "You don't need more education because you are a girl. After you are married just stay home and take care of your husband and baby." So they didn't let my mom go to high school. I think in the village that is very common. The girls just need to know how to count so they can pay the bills.

I graduated from high school and I came to America. School is twelve years in the Chinese school system—six years for elementary school, three years for middle school, and three years for high school. Ed told me that here it has just two years for middle school and four years for high school.

Many people go to university in China, but it depends on what university. Qinghua University in Beijing, for instance, is a very good university. If you go there you must have good grades and money. In the United States, you can borrow money from the bank, but in China most people depend on their parents. Some parents have good jobs and can save a lot of money. But some parents are very poor. You can probably get a scholarship if your grades are very good and if your high school tells the university that you're very good. If you are excellent, the university is free for you. There are only a few cases like that, and most people go to an average college. They are not good but they can provide you with a diploma to prove that you graduated from university. I have never been to a university in China, but I went to Ed's university in Xian. I thought that for foreigners it is good, but for Chinese, it is just a library. They give you one big room to study at night. It is very crowded. I don't know anything else about it because I did not attend university. My parents made me study when I was younger. I really regret the time I didn't read a lot of books.

In the late 1970s the Chinese government issued a law permitting only one baby per family. That time my mom was seven months pregnant with me, they wanted my mom to abort me. My mom said, "No! If you want to kill my baby, you first kill me!" They didn't do that, and I was born in 1975. My family is considered big in China. I have three brothers. My first brother got married some years ago and they have a baby, my nephew. He is three years old. All of my brothers are older than me. I think my first brother is now thirty, my second brother is twenty-four, and my third brother is twenty-three. They all have jobs. My first brother is a driver, my second brother is a hotel worker, and my third brother does his own work as a salesman. It's not a really good job; it's just something you do when you have free time. For instance, right now I work at Hardee's. Study is important. I just need a little money from Hardee's, so I work there. In China, I worked at Xian Hotel as a shop assistant. My section of the shop sold polished jade and wooded statues. The other section sold clothes.

When I was very young, my father loved me a lot. When we grew up, I tried to think we were all the same. My parents wanted me to go to school and study. They want me to study a lot and study hard. All the Chinese parents hope their children do very well. In China a boy can always go out, but a girl can't, especially at night. In my life, before I married Ed, only two boys came to my house. One was my classmate, the other was my work-mate. The first boy came to my house just to give me a book that I left at school. The second one stayed at my house with all my workmates. After an half-hour he left because my father didn't like me to meet boys.

Ed is a brave and special boy. He is not my first boyfriend. I had two boyfriends before I met Ed. One was my first love. I was dating the second one when Ed was in China. After we broke up, I met Ed. At that time I didn't think I would marry him because he was a foreigner. We were just friends. But the next year, he came back to China again just for me. Oh, he just came back for me, how exciting! Then I thought we understood each other. I knew he was really good to me. After we decided, we were married. I didn't tell my parents about it. One night, I just told my parents I was married. They said, "What? You married a foreigner?" But they didn't go against it because they knew I'm a donkey [very stubborn].

So I introduced Ed to them. For people their age, my parents are open-minded. After they met him, we often ate out together. During the Chinese New Year, Ed was at my home with us. Everyone in my family thought that he was a normal person, a part of the family. After that I often brought him to my home to spend time with us. They often talked with Ed and that made them understand him. At first they did not like or dislike him because they didn't know him. They just thought, "Ha, he is a for-eigner." When they knew Ed better, they liked him, especially my mom. They just hoped he was nice to me. They didn't want anything from him, they didn't care if he was rich or poor. They even didn't care that he was a foreigner, that he looked different, and that he had blonde hair and blue eyes. I think if Ed were Chinese, he would be in much trouble. But because he is foreigner, he doesn't understand some parts of our culture, such as the boy going to the girl's house. He is very lucky in that way. My parents and my brothers would like to play with him, but they didn't want to make it too difficult for Ed. So they tried to be so nice to him, especially my mom. She always asked, "Is he cold, is he hungry?" I really miss that time when we spent time together.

It's not good to be a foreigner in China. I met some Chinese here in

Columbia. When I told them my husband was an American, they didn't say anything. But I could see that their eyes just looked mean, as if they were saying that I just wanted to marry a foreigner to come to America. I stopped talking with them; they're not my type. In China, when I walked with Ed on the street, some people would say, "Oh! That girl is dirty!" At that time I was not used to it, so I was very mad at Ed. After a while I got used to it; I just thought: I'm marrying him, your bad words mean nothing to me. When people said some bad words when they saw me with a foreigner, I just looked at them. Only a few times, some teenagers saw me and said, "Oh, she is a translator." I was very happy because they didn't think bad things about me, like you make love with him, you live with him, you want to spend his money. That always made me angry.

Chinese boys treated me differently than Ed did. When I am with Ed, he tells me everything. He always lets me choose what I want to do. But in China, all the boys already made their plans and you just go with them. They cared about your dress and they cared about your appearance. When I was with my Chinese boyfriend, I always felt nervous. While with Ed, I'm very relaxed. I want to do everything that I want. I can do anything with Ed. I don't worry about him being angry because he likes everything I do. Going out with my Chinese boyfriend, I must bring money with me. Sometimes I paid and sometime he paid. When I am with Ed, he always pays, but that's not what matters. I feel Chinese boys are not strong. They are not like men, but like young boys. With Ed, I feel very good and very relaxed. He is just my friend. I feel very happy and very free with him, and I want to do everything and to make noise. That's what I like most about Ed, his temperament. Even if I'm very angry and very crazy, he is always very nice, always makes me feel better, quiet, and calm. He makes my heart feel good all the time. Sometimes I fought with my family, then I would go to his dorm and be very angry at him. He would calm me down and I would go home to my parents and we were all together again. I like that. If I did that with my Chinese boyfriends, they would say, "What's wrong with you? Are you crazy?" They always did that to me.

When I was with Chinese boys, we couldn't hold hands. But I could hold Ed's arm to go down the street or go shopping; I felt it was very natural and not strange at all. When I was with Ed in China, I never touched his hand. I never let him touch me. We just walked on the street and I went to his dorm just to study and to listen to music. I never let him touch me. The first time he kissed me, I thought, "Oh, this is a foreigner. This is foreigner's kiss." It felt very different and I just thought, "Oh, this is for-eigner's kiss taste."

This is how I first met Ed. I remember that in the disco my friend Bobby said my friend wants to be your friend. At that time I thought, "Oh, he could be my friend." So I walked to Ed and spoke to him. I said hi, he said hi and then I went back. At that time I was thinking, "Oh, he has a beard, he is very old." You know Chinese boys doesn't have beards. Then one day he shaved his beard. Standing in front of my workplace, he showed his face to me. I thought, "Oh my God, it's so strange. When I saw him first time, he looked like he was thirty. Today he stands in front of me and looks like he's fifteen or seventeen." That time I thought he was very different, but I felt very strange. I had never seen a boy before and after he shaved his beard. I had never seen Chinese boys like that. So I just thought, "Oh, he is a foreigner and he is very interesting." I never felt he was different from us. I liked studying language. I wanted to know different cultures and different countries. I could study English from him, and he could teach me English. That was what I thought about Ed then.

I want to have two children. I want to teach them about my Chinese heritage. We will bring them to China, because I want to show them China is a great country and that many cultures came from there. After we have a baby, we will decide if they must speak Chinese at home. When they go to school they can speak English. I don't want them to forget Chinese because they are half-Chinese. I want to teach them like Chinese children. I want them to have knowledge about China when they are young, in kindergar-ten and in elementary school. I want them to speak both Chinese and English. I don't want them to forget either one. I also plan to teach them some Japanese. I studied Japanese in high school for half a year. I want to study Japanese again. If I study Japanese well, I will teach them a little bit of Japanese. I want them to speak a lot of different languages.

If we have enough money, we will send them to a private university because I think the education there is very good. We still want them to have nice personalities. We don't want them to hate poor people because we don't like that. We were not raised poor. We are young; we cannot throw money out. We must study to give our children a good life. I want to do that. Par-ents in China do that. They start saving money for their baby when they are very young. That's why they try so hard to find a good job. That's why Chi-nese teenagers study so hard. They probably don't want it, they don't like it. But their parents want it. So their parents make them study because their parents want them to be very good, hardworking people.

Since 1976, parents in China can only have one baby, and so that baby becomes your king. In China, we call baby the king because he would just sit down there and say, "I want this and I want that." Then his grandparents and parents must get this or that for him. If they don't, he starts crying. When he is crying, the parents and grandparents would say, "It hurts my heart! My poor baby!" So parents and grandparents spoil a child in China.

A lot of girl babies were deserted. Especially now, since you just have one chance to have a baby, most people want a boy, especially in villages. When some peasant women have girls, they would try not to let the government know and her baby girl wouldn't have a birth certificate. After the baby grows to one year or two years old, and if the mother wants the baby to have a birth certificate, she must pay money, about ten thousand or twelve thousand dollars to the government. You must have connection to the government some way. If you don't, your baby would have a very difficult time getting that birth certificate. The birth certificate affects how you go to school and if you could buy your food, because we buy food like rice and flour in government-owned stores. That's important for the Chinese. If you don't have a birth certificate, you can't buy food for the child. That's why those families are very poor and they always run away from government. They don't have a home. Boys are very important in China. That's why they find a lot of girls whose parents don't want them. In middle school, I found that situation all the time. In the back streets, if people look around they could find a crying baby. It must be a girl—it wouldn't be a boy. It's just a girl by itself by the road. Sometimes the parents keep the baby's name and birth date with the baby. In China they still think boys are important. Parents think they can depend on the boy when they are old. That's why they want a boy, but I don't think that way.

If I stayed in China I would be expected to take care of my parents. While in America, old people are very independent. In China, if you don't live with your aging parents, other people would think you are very bad to them. You either live with them or bring them to your house. If you don't do that, people would think you're very bad to your parents. My first brother has a house, but it is not big. China has lot of people; they can't have big houses. My parents are not old now. They can still take care of themselves. My second brother and third brother live with my parents so they can take care of them. Even after they marry, they will probably live with my parents. But they will probably rent a room because too many people living all together is not convenient. If you have only one son, your son will probably live with you. If I were married and lived in China, and if my brothers couldn't take care of my parents, I would bring them to my house. If I married a Chinese boy I would have to live with his family. But some men live with their wives' families because they don't have their own houses or they don't have enough space for the wedding.

Chinese weddings are very different. At Chinese weddings, we must wear a red dress. But in America, people wear a white dress. I don't think it matters. In China, if someone died, we would wear a black or white dress. White dresses are considered bad luck, while red dresses can make ghosts and bad luck go away. The color red is hot. On a Chinese wedding night, we must wear a red bra, red underwear, and red shoes. In America, you must wear a sexy dress. When Ed's mom told me that I was surprised.

In a Chinese wedding, when the groom first goes to the bride's house, he must try hard to get into the house because all the girlfriends of the bride would stop the groom and say, "Give me my money." So the groom must give them money for good luck. After the groom gets in the house, he must rush into the bride's room. The girlfriends of the bride would say that he can't come in, he can't take her away. The groom has to try very hard to please these girlfriends so they would let him come in.

Then the newlyweds go to the reception. Before they start eating, they have to show their marriage certificate. If they don't show it, they would be thought as fake, that they just want to have a reception to make everybody think that they are married. Then they eat, and after that, the groom takes the bride to his home. Then the groom's friends start teasing the bride. If they want to smoke, the bride must light the cigarette. That was just a normal game people play at weddings. The bad game is when the groom has policemen as friends, they would use handcuffs on the bride. Sometimes they beat the bride just for fun. This kind of teasing is really hard to take and sometimes it even makes the groom angry. Before I met Ed, I was thinking that if I had wedding in Xian that it would be very scary. The manager of the hotel where I used to work said at his wedding, he had to eat three candies and then throw them up into his bride's mouth. If you don't do it, your friends will be angry.

In China, we have a lot of American movies. We often see American weddings on TV. But I never thought I would have a wedding in America and that I would wear a white wedding dress. On my wedding day, I thought it was like a dream and I was very sad that day because my parents were not there. That morning when my father called me from China, I was very sad. I cried over the phone, not being able to stop myself. When I went to church I was still crying. "You can't cry! You'll be very ugly if you cry!" I prayed to God. When the clergyman was saying the wedding vows, I was just thinking, "My family is not here." Next month we will send them wedding pictures and videotapes.

My parents were very sad when I left for America and I was a little surprised that they let me go. They didn't stop me, but they just said, "We hope your life is good. If you choose it then you must be there. If you're sad in America you can come back. If Ed is not good to you, you just tell us and we will help you." That was very sad. My mom always cries. Every time when they write a letter to me, I am very happy for a few days. Their letters let me know something about my home and I can think about things there.

I think it's normal for parents to be so supportive of and helpful to their children, especially in China where we always live with parents. My brothers are already twenty-four or twenty-three and they still live with my parents and depend on them. My parents buy food for them and give them money if they need it.

In America when you are eighteen years old, you must go out to work and your parents don't give you money. In China we don't have to. When I was in high school, my parents paid my tuition and fees. But in the last semester of my high school, I paid tuition myself. I paid one hundred dollars; I was very proud of that. There are a lot of people who don't do that; they just depend on the parents. In my family, I am very independent.

Now I understand that my parents are very important to me. But I didn't understand that when I was in China. I thought I could live by myself. I could save money. I could go to work. But I never thought life was not easy. When I came here to Ed's mother's house, I thought we could depend on his parents. We wouldn't have to pay for food, rent, and utility bills. But after we moved to Columbia, I must take care of everything—rent, health insurance, his tuition, and electricity, water, and trash bills. We must plan our spending for every month. At that time I began to feel our life here is not easy. I think it is very difficult not to live with your parents. But when I was in China I wanted to leave my family. It was normal for high school students to want to leave their family.

I really don't have a favorite thing about living in America. I just have one wish. I wish I can speak English like Ed. Eventually, I want to understand everything. I can go to college or university. I want to have a very good education so I can find a good job. I can help Ed because he will go to another school and study for five years. If I can speak English and go to university, I think I can find a good job. It is my wish. In China my favorite thing was riding bicycles everywhere. I didn't have to stop. I would look at everything. But here I am afraid to ride a bicycle. I am worried that I will die in traffic. There are not too many interesting things for me here. I just want to study English all the time.

I will go back to China, but I will not stay there for a long time. I like America because everything is convenient. I think American education is good for our future babies. I want them to study here and grow up here. I will go back to see my parents. I miss them a lot. I have lived here only for four months, but I feel it's been four years. Probably I would just go back and live for half a year, just for a visit. Ed is studying Chinese politics; everything is very good for his study in China.

4

Attaining Education

Rita Chang was born in Taipei, Taiwan, in 1976. She immigrated to the United States with her mother, an accountant, in 1993 as a high school junior for better educational opportunities, because the competition for college entrance exams was stiff in Taiwan. She was a business major at Truman State University at the time of the interview in 1996.

I was born on 24 November 1976 in Taipei. My mom is in St. Louis. My father now works and lives in Taipei, because he just got a promotion there. He goes back to Taiwan every once in a while for conferences. I don't know exactly what he does right now, but before he got the promotion he was an air traffic controller at an airport. He looks at the screen and talks to the pilots. My mom is an accountant and works for a computer company.

I came to the United States with my mom about three years ago, mostly for purpose of education because my parents really don't like the educational system in Taiwan. We thought there was a better system here and we could also learn English. But mostly we came for the education. In Taiwan, you can go to high school or university only if you pass the entrance exam. You can only take the entrance exam once and if you fail it, that's it. So nothing counts but the grade that you receive on the entrance exam. It's like the ACT here, but you can take the ACT over and over. So to get into high school, we have to take a high school entrance exam. It is a two-day exam that covers five subjects, three subjects in the first day and two in the second day.

Three days before the exam, I was in the hospital because I had a high fever. I didn't feel well physically in those two examination days and I was too nervous. I get nervous when I have to take big exams. I threw up after the first period exam on Chinese. I was just like, "Oh my gosh! I have to go to the bathroom." I don't eat breakfast usually, but on those two mornings I ate breakfast because my mom told me, "You're taking this big exam, you should eat something." So I threw up afterwards. Before the exam my teacher would say, "I don't worry about you, you know you should get into at least the top five." In Taiwan there are about a thousand good public high schools that people are trying to get into. My teacher said that I should get into at least the top five high schools. But after the result of the exam came out, I got to the ninth one. That was bad. I felt like I failed it. But there's nothing you can do about it. My parents really disliked the system. My sister was a couple years younger than I am. She likes to play, and doesn't like to study at all. So my parents were worried about her. We have this school system—all the classes are divided into good classes and bad classes. If you belong to one of the bad classes, you don't learn anything. Nobody cares about what you do. It's really bad. So my parents were worried that my sister would learn smoking or other bad things that the bad kids would do. So that's the big reason why we came here.

I have just one sibling; that is my sister. She just turned fifteen. She is in high school in St. Louis, Missouri. My parents have definitely treated us differently since we got here. My mom has changed so much. For example, my mom has gone really easy on my sister for putting on makeup. If you're a student in Taiwan and you put makeup on, everybody will look at you like you're weird or strange. But here it's okay. And my sister has her ears pierced, which is inappropriate for students in Taiwan. When I was in middle school, if I wanted my friends to come over and spend the night at my house, I would have to struggle for that. If I wanted to go out to see a movie with my good friends, I also had to struggle for that. I had to tell my parents two weeks in advance who I was going with, where I was going, what time I was going to be back, and other details like that. My mom just said things like, "Oh well, it's dangerous to go to movie theaters. What if there's a fire? How are you going to escape?" I think they're really concerned about the security. They are still strict, but they have been really easy on a lot of subjects.

I do not necessarily think this is from living in the United States. I guess for my mom, I can't say that coming here doesn't have any influence on her. But I would also think that part of it would be also because she's older and I guess when you become older, you just appear to be easy on things.

I have a green card, so we are residents but not citizens. I do plan to go back to Taiwan after I get my degree here in the United States, maybe after four years because I plan to pursue a master's degree. Right now my major is business. I plan to study either international relations or international studies for my master's degree, but that might also change.

I came here when I was a junior in high school. But only after a semester, I was a senior. It was really different. We have to wear uniforms in Taiwan and our school system is like a military system. Everything is really strict and rigid. We sing. I think you do that in American schools, how you sing the national anthem in the morning and you see your flag rise, just like that. We go to school from seven o'clock in the morning to six o'clock in the evening Monday through Friday, and until twelve thirty in the afternoon on Saturday, so school is a big thing and that is what you do when you're a student. We cannot choose our schedule. Everybody studies the same schedule. And we learn a lot. We have ten subjects in middle school and more in high school. One of them is cooking. We stay in one classroom for three years in middle school. We don't move around the classrooms; we just stay in one. Teachers come and teach us. So I think in that case you really get to know a good friend. We have lunch boxes, not cafeterias. We have heater, like a microwave, and you just put your lunch box in it. The focus is a lot on the academic subjects. We do have physical education (PE), but it's not emphasized. We have an hour of PE and an hour of drawing every week. But, mostly, we study Chinese, along with math, science, geography, history, and stuff like that a lot.

It's such a pain for a year in ninth grade, which is a year before you take the high school entrance exam. Our middle school is from seventh to ninth grade, and then tenth to twelfth grade would be high school. Ninth grade was really terrible because we had to be at school at seven o'clock in the morning and then we went home in the afternoon. Then we stayed at school to study until nine o'clock at night, because if you fail the exam, bye-bye. You have two lunch boxes and you eat at school. You just go home to sleep for four hours and then you get up and go to school again. It was really hard.

I got really tired in the end. That's probably also why I didn't do as well as I should have. I just got so exhausted physically and maybe mentally. For three years in middle school, there were around forty people in my class, which is pretty normal considering how crowded we are in Taipei. I was always in the top fifteen in my class and I graduated from middle school as the thirteenth in my class. My teacher would say, "I wouldn't worry about you. Just relax and take the exam. That's fine. I'll see you in high school." So I was really sad and I really don't like the system because I think we should take into account our performance in school, not only on the exam. That's just too much for a fifteen year old. I felt it was the end of the world when I realized that I didn't do as well as I should. All of these expectations and pressures are just too much.

I think my parents were pretty open on the academic part compared to most of the Chinese parents. But they are strict on the social part, on dating. Maybe they're just too protective. Throughout the three years in middle school, every time I handed my father my grade report, he would go like, "Oh, are you the last one in you class? Oh, you're not. That's fine." And he would go really easy on that. My mom is a little bit stricter. Still, I don't have to be the first one in my class. Myself, I would want to, of course. Every time I do my math, I wanted to be the first one. I caused pressure for myself, but my parents didn't. I guess they were disappointed that I didn't do well, but then they said, "It's fine." I think they were disappointed but they didn't say it. They were just like, "Why don't you just prepare for the exam for the private high school so you can go to private high school." So I ended up going to a private high school close to my home.

I worked at McDonald's during my senior year in high school in St. Louis, Missouri. It was okay to work there. I don't know whether people treated me differently because I was Asian. At the time I still didn't speak very good English and I didn't really talk a lot to anybody that I worked with, so it was just a communication problem. But the managers were really nice to me and the atmosphere was pretty friendly. I worked, and then I went home.

I speak Chinese at home to my mom and my sister. We eat mostly Chinese food. My mom has had a hard time learning and speaking English. But she's getting better and better because she works in an American firm, and she has to talk to her co-workers. It is interesting that she got a job when she didn't really speak any English (now she does). In the firm that she's working for as an accountant, she is directly responsible to her boss who is from China and speaks Chinese. But everybody else in the firm is an American. That she's only directly responsible to her boss works out for her. But then of course she gets contact with her coworkers so she gets to practice her English.

I don't think that I've been treated differently in high school because of my heritage. When I didn't speak good English for the first year or two when I was here, I felt isolated; but I can understand that. Now that I'm here at the university, I've made a lot of friends. I think people here are really friendly. My friends are a mix; half of them are foreign exchange students. Grim Hall is mixed up with one-third international students. I'm really glad I have all those amazing friends. It's cool. Five of my close friends here on campus are Asians; everybody else isn't.

I'm the president of the Chinese Student Association this year, so I try to be as nice as I can. That helps me to get to know everybody. We just get together once a month to have a party. We had the Moon Festival party last month, this month we showed a Chinese movie, and we will have a graduation party for these who are graduating in December coming up next month. We don't have any really big events because everybody is so busy. Once a month we get together and we get to speak Chinese to each other.

In my spare time, I like to sleep a lot. I also listen to music. I like soft music, real soft classical music. I can't stand rock and roll and I don't like country music. I also read, write letters to my friends, or just relax. Recently, I've really liked to play tennis. I think it's a really, really good sport. I just hang out with my friends and do all the things that people would do. I don't go to church. My family doesn't have any religious background.

On the weekends, I study on Sundays, like the day before I have to turn in my work. On Fridays, we definitely hang out and relax. I don't do any homework on Fridays. On Saturdays, sometimes I realize I have big things due on Monday and I'll start work on Saturday night. But sometimes I don't realize that I have to do so much until Sunday and it's really bad. I'm trying to change that habit. During the week, I would say that since I have seventeen credits this semester as I'm trying to graduate earlier, I don't have any choice but to study.

I am interested in our [Taiwanese] politics. But I'm also interested in American politics, maybe 30 percent, I guess. I don't really understand American politics. I haven't ever [taken] any American government course before, so I don't really understand the system. But I'm interested in it a little bit.

Sometimes I ask my friends from Taiwan who are just here for a year or so about what is going on there. They will hear a lot of things from their families. They call their family every day or so. When I call my father, I just talk to him about what's going on in Taiwan. We subscribe to a Chinese newspaper in St. Louis at my house. If I have time to go back, I read it.

Sometimes I just write my friends in Taiwan and they tell me about big things that are happening. We have a Taiwanese newspaper in the library and I also read that.

My friends are what I miss most about Taiwan. Besides that, of course, is the food. We can't just go out and go to a restaurant even in St. Louis and eat a little food. There's just things that my mom cannot really cook. But it's okay. Hopefully I get to go back next year. I'm going to visit my friend in Russia, so I don't know if I have all the money to go to Russia and then Taiwan. Hopefully I'll find a job next semester and try to make some money. I'll try to work four hours more as a tutor so I can get some money. I'm still working on that and I also [plan to] take seventeen hours next semester. It's hard. It keeps me busy so I always eat and study and gain weight. With all this cafeteria food, I can't help it. The first year I was here I would eat until I can't eat any more. I would eat everything they have and it was like, "Oh! Food," every time I wanted any. This year, it was better. I eat until I need to stop. I also get sick of the food. They don't change the menu much. I eat healthy food now; I don't eat hamburgers and pizza.

I call my dad once a week. He comes here every summer and during winter vacation. He has to stay in Taiwan because his job is there and he doesn't want to give up his job and come here and start over again. I am close to my parents. Maybe not as close as American families because that is not the case in Chinese families; you don't get really close to your parents. It's like there's a respect line right there. I don't think, "Okay, my mom is my best friend." But it is not like every time I see my mom I bow to her. I know who are my friends and who are my parents.

I think people here are really friendly and I really enjoy that. You know how you're just walking down the street and people say hi to you. That's really nice. It was a big change from Taipei to St. Louis. But from St. Louis to the university town, it's not as big. Generally speaking I do like the big city atmosphere better. I know I will only be here for five years or so, so I don't mind staying here and studying. But I wouldn't want to live in a community like this for twenty years. Maybe when I become older I will, but I want to still live in a big city and experience all of the excitement while I'm young.

I don't like the feeling of being really homesick. But I can't go back to Taiwan either. I would have nothing to do if I go back. I can't just apply and go to a university like the kids in the United States. I would have to take an exam, which is based on the three years of learning in the high schools in

Taiwan. So I wouldn't be able to pass the exam at all. I want to graduate with a master's degree here and then go back and try to get a job in Taiwan.

---·—————

Sandy Lee was born into a Chinese-Indonesian American family in Holland, Michigan, in 1977. Her parents came to America in 1973 for better educational and occupational opportunities. She was a jounalism/communication major at Truman State University at the time of the interview in 1996.

I was born on 15 June 1977 in Holland, Michigan. My parents were both born in Jakarta, Indonesia. My dad was born on 28 September 1942 and my mom on 21 September 1944. Both of them went to high school and college in Indonesia. I am not totally Indonesian. I am Chinese-Indonesian and I guess they are stigmatized in Indonesia. If you are not Indonesian, you are oppressed. That is kind of the sense I got from my mom.

In Indonesia, she really wanted to be a psychologist. She applied twice to the school and she didn't get in. She ended up dropping out because she was so discouraged. My dad went to undergraduate in Indonesia for a few years, then he went to Germany to finish his undergraduate. When my parents moved to the United States they went to Texas, where my dad got his master's.

They came to the United States twenty-three years ago. I know we have relatives in the States. I don't know if that is why they went to Texas specifically. I'm not exactly sure why they wanted to move. It could have been that my dad wanted to continue his education here.

Both of my grandfathers are dead so I never met them. My grandmas live in Texas and California. I really don't know when they came to the United States. I think it was probably after my parents. Both my grandmothers speak Indonesian. My grandma Testus, that is my dad's mom, doesn't know English very well, but she knows more than my other grandma. We call my grandma in California Omar and my dad's mom grandma. When I was maybe nine my grandma came to Holland [Michigan] for a year or so to spend time with my mom. She is a pretty old lady and she didn't know any English really. So we sent her to the community education center just to teach her English. She would get these workbooks with pictures of shoes and books, and she would have to write the English word. She was just so slick. I was just a little sucker. She had me doing all her homework. "Grandma, that's a book. That's a shoe, grandma," and she was just writing it down. I don't think she realized that she was that sneaky. It was funny. I don't see them very often though since they live across country.

My father is a product engineer. I live in a town that has two really big office furniture places. He works for Herman Miller, Inc., a big company. They design and manufacture office furniture, like tables. He works there as a designer. I have always known he was an engineer and then I found out engineers can do several duties, so it is kind of hard to nail down his specific position. I know that he does something with product design.

We used to own a store and we had it for twelve years; we finally sold it about a year and a half ago. My mom used to be the one running the store while my dad worked from eight to five. But now that we don't have the store, she stays home gardening, busy as ever. She always is. She likes being at home.

The store we used to own was a little grocery store. It started off as an Asian food store, because we were in Holland, Michigan, and there is a pretty big Asian population. It's not huge, but it is nice to have someone who knows about Asian culture, so there was a market for it. Holland also has an incredible Hispanic population. Within a year, it ended up being at least about 80 percent Hispanic and 20 percent Asian. We sold the store to a friend from Chicago. He is Hispanic himself and he owns stores. It is kind of sad because he doesn't know about the Asian products so he has kind of rounded that out. It's because he doesn't know what to get. A lot of people I know in Holland are really disappointed with that, just because our store is where they would come. My mom would always give advice on how to cook things. That is a complaint that I hear a lot. He has done a lot with the store, so it is growing. We owned it for about twelve years. For a long time, my parents were running it and we kids would help out once in a while. But towards the end, it was just my parents and that was a lot of work for them.

I have three siblings, two brothers and one sister. My oldest brother is twenty-four. My older sister is twenty-two. My little brother is thirteen. I'm not the smartest kid in my family. My siblings are all really, really smart— better than I am in school. My sister is working as an architect in an firm in Detroit. My little brother is in high school and he is just brilliant. He is a little genius. I am pretty normal. I get Bs and everything. I try, but I'm definitely different from my brothers and sister. My parents have always known that, as much as they say it really doesn't matter. I've got the worst grades out of all of my siblings. But they really stress that it really doesn't matter. It is pretty much me that is putting all the pressure on myself.

I've never been to Indonesia. I don't know if I'd like to go there. I know Indonesia is a really tourist-oriented place. My sister went a couple years ago because she really wanted to. She stayed with relatives. It was good for her to go there but she came back and said that there were a lot of things about Indonesia that she didn't like. Environmental issues are just terrible. They are just so corrupt there. She was sick for the first week and she didn't know why. She went out of the tourist area and went into the real Indonesia, and it was like garbage. It smelled really strongly, and she couldn't tell at first, but then after a while she figured that something wasn't right. She was there for two months; the first month she stayed with relatives, which was like a big family vacation and so it was kind of a drag. The next month, she pretty much toured around Indonesia herself and she sketched. She visited people that she met at school. I think it was a better experience for her; she was kind of independent. I think overall she got a lot out of it.

I would love to travel anywhere. I don't know that Indonesia would be the first place that I would want to go. Eventually I would like to go there, but right now I am looking towards Hawaii and Europe. One day I hope to go to Indonesia.

The language of Indonesia is Indonesian. My parents still speak it. They have been here for a long time, but as the years go on I notice that they don't speak it as much anymore. I can expect that if they just came here. But they have been here for ten years and all of a sudden they have started winding down. My parents are pretty multilingual anyway. They have a lot of other languages up in their heads. They learned Spanish from the store and just from meeting people. So they know Spanish. From living in Germany, they know a little German. My dad is pretty fluent. And they know just a little bit of a lot of languages. I don't know how they did it. My mom has a gift for language.

They badly wanted us to understand Indonesian. But this is not so much anymore, because there is not much they can't tell us, or that we don't understand. I know a few words like, "get over here." When my parents speak, sometimes we can pick a few things out, or you can tell what they are talking about just from their body language. I couldn't rattle off, though. It is just dialogue.

My parents instill everything about their cultural values in us. I guess I am pretty hardworking. They are hardworking. My sister is hardworking too, but hardworking in a different way. At the same time, while they are really hardworking at school, I'm not. It is kind of hard to say what they did to instill their culture in us because it wasn't uniform at all. I'm sure there are ways they did, but there are things I don't recognize as cultural values. I just see them as things that have been there from the beginning.

There are some Indonesian foods that my mom does cook. She will go in kicks. She will go on rice kicks and we will have all rice, and then she will go on soup kicks and she will make soup all the time. She makes things and she makes us eat them every once in a while. We have rice every day with pretty much everything. I hated rice when I was growing up. It was such a treat when I did not have to eat something with rice. We have a rice cooker and we only use gasin rice, a certain type of rice.

I even have gasin rice, but Minute Rice scares me because it is not supposed to be that quick. It should take at least twenty minutes to cook, so that rice is like fake rice. My roommates get it and I am like, "What's that? That's not rice." I never really had Minute Rice until last year in the dorms and you know for the first time rice sounds real good, and I got it and I was like, "What does this look like? What does this taste like? What is this? Is this Styrofoam?" It tasted very different.

If you go to an Asian restaurant you know you would get gasin rice and that is the kind of rice that I will eat. It might be jasmine rice, or it might be different. But it has some kind of fragrance to it, something like that. I don't think you can get it at a local grocery store. I think it is specialty stuff and you may have to order it at a certain place. I've got a twenty-pound bag of rice. My parents gave me this big bag when I left for college. I have made it twice now and I have nineteen and a half pounds to go. It is like feeding people in third world countries.

I have never really been a fan of soy sauce so I don't put it on my rice, just salt and things. If I am just eating rice I have to put something on it. I usually eat it with something. Salsa is a huge favorite. I love salsa. At Wal-Mart there is a salsa that has black beans and corn in it. All of a sudden, I am just a salsa fiend. I just inhale bottles. It's good. I know my roommates make fun of me. I should just buy a case or something like that because I go through big bottles. They go through spaghetti sauce bottles.

I have some of those Indonesian recipes from my mom actually. I like my mom's food a lot. I can't make it as well as she does, but I try. I want to cook her recipes. Most of the time I just don't succeed because they are not easy. I am so impatient. I hate making pasta. I just think that I can't cook.

My mom and I get along pretty well. I think I have always been the tough child of the family because I was pretty much a hellion. I'm not like my sister; I am the social one. I do things differently and I am very stubborn. My parents both know that and I guess we have a love/hate relationship. I know that we get on each other's nerves and I know that we get along at times. I think I am the only one in my family that really talks to my parents. Not that my brothers and sister don't do that, but I actually tell my mom things that happen. It's different and I think my mom really appreciates that. We kind of get along when we are both in the mood. My relationship with my father is pretty much a typical dad/daughter relationship. My dad is cool, but I see a lot of things in him that I don't want to find in someone. But that is typical for everybody. We get along fine. My dad is kind of a sucker; if I want something it's mine. But I try not to take advantage of that and I'm not really greedy. My older brother and sister and I are close. My little brother is in high school. I can't really be close to him.

I can't go home all that often and everyone is spread around. I have been home once and that was over midterm break. I probably go home about six times a year, which isn't bad. It is only eight or nine hours away. My brother is in Wisconsin. My sister is in Detroit. My family is in Holland. We're pretty far apart. But we'll all see each other on Thanksgiving and Christmas. There are things we will still come home for. I don't e-mail anybody as much anymore. I am just sick of e-mailing. But I call them and sometimes they call me.

My parents think education is essential. It wasn't even a question of whether or not I would go to college. It was just what I was going to do. It was understood. But I didn't even think about not going to college. That's how education is ingrained. I don't know many people that don't go to college. Where I grew up is a pretty conservative town; everyone was geared towards higher education. Even if that wasn't the case, I would end up going to college anyway. My parents said it doesn't matter what you do as long as you move out of here.

I have a friend that is going to school here. I am living with her right now actually. We wanted to go to school together. I guess that is kind of a bad thing. She is one of my closest friends, and we went through a lot together. This is a cheaper school. It would be like the University of Michigan for me in state, because it is about $10,000 for Michigan and Michigan State. It's cheaper here and they have a good biology program too, so that is why I came here. It fits. I'm breaking apart from Michigan too. I definitely wanted to leave, but where I went wasn't a huge factor. I would have even gone to Michigan [State] University. It was weird coming this far away but I don't know. It will probably end up being better in the long run.

I am a journalism/communication major. I was thinking about going into public relations, something in that field, maybe mixed in a little with advertising and designs. I would like to work with art in public relations somehow. I like working with other people. I have always been able to get along with people; it is my forte. I just like when company comes over. When I was at home, my parents always wanted me around because I was entertainment. I can be as cocky as anything and adults just eat that up, and I knew it. That is where I come in. I'm the social one.

I was a biology major, and it is really interesting to me and I would have probably gone into botany if I would have done that because I love plants and gardens. But that is more along the lines of the scientific, analytical sibling group. So I really needed to break apart from that, but that is what I had to do, kind of like coming to this school. I didn't have to go to the University of Michigan like both of them did, and I didn't have to get the same grades as both of them did. And this isn't intentionally one way to break apart of that whole technical career mode. It suits me better than anything else I think.

I've had some difficulty in school like in Spanish. I didn't drop the class. Spanish isn't easy. I guess I have a hard time focusing because I like my friends so much and I just love my room and I love the people next door, and it is always fun hanging out with them. It's hard to say, "I need to work now." It's always, "I want to play." So that is probably the hardest thing for me, just buckling down. I don't know if I really study efficiently or not. I don't think I do, but that's me. I probably spend about two hours a day studying, which is not a lot at all. I wish I could say more. Weekends I will try to study hard and I think the weekends are keeping me where I am. I have class pretty much throughout the day; I have a few hours between them when I have to work; additionally, I have another job that I work at. It just feels like I have no time, and the time that I do have I want to see my friends.

As far as relations with my classmates, in particular in my Spanish class, our class is divided. We have a few really vocal people and we have a few that just sit there, that just try to stay afloat. I only know a few people and I am trying to meet more people. But it is hard because everyone in that class is scared to death. It depends on how the teacher treats it. If the teacher fosters the community then it's really easy to meet people. But if that doesn't happen, obviously we are just one of many faces in the crowd. I won't really make an effort to try to get to know a lot of people if it is not part of the class. I am probably one of those people who just listen. It really depends on what class it is. Like in Spanish, I think I will say something, just because you have to say something. But in classes like my mass communications class, I am pretty much quiet even though I know it is part of my grade. I've been more and more outspoken though. I'm just kind of being more vocal. It's my major. I'd better be.

Probably the thing I like most about the university is the friends that I have here. The whole registration thing made me really leery of the school. Small class sizes, small school systems really bug me. I just wish they could be bigger, just one space bigger. I do like big cities. I like having options. That is probably why I got a job. So I would have a little something to do on weekends making a little extra money. There is nothing else to do.

I have really close friends here. The people who are my closest friends have been here since freshman week. I met them last year while living on the first floor of Dobson Hall. Living in the dorm was a good experience. I liked my hall. I live with my friend from home, and the other roommate is her old roommate. The people next door are all AKLs [Alpha Kappa Lambda fraternity]. We just love them to death. We get along pretty well. There are some little minor things, but we get along pretty well for the most part. They are people that I have really clicked with. I know that I should find the time to visit a lot of people more often. But it is really hard, especially living off campus now. But the people that I have are my friends; I don't ever think I have had closer friends than that. Of course, I haven't had to be around people twenty-four hours a day and seven days a week. I'm sure that leaves room for either hate or disaster. We do get along pretty well. Those are my closest friends and they keep me here.

I'm not dating anybody. I just had a big talk with a male friend of mine yesterday. It was actually kind of neat. We laid everything on the table from last year. It was a big deal. It's been about a year and a half and we never talked about it. Yesterday we kind of defined everything and decided, "Well, it's going to happen." It was good because I have never had a talk like that with anybody. It was totally open and honest. I know that he hates that kind of thing so much. So it was so cool to make him start that because it was all on his shoulders. He had to initiate it. That relationship right now is the biggest thing. We're just kind of going to figure things out.

Things are good; we felt the same way. We are leaving the door open to anything in the future. I can't say anything else. I wish I could but I can't think. It is kind of hard to say what is going to happen because it is complicated. But we know how everybody feels now. We'll see what happens in the future.

In my spare time, that oh-so-abundant-time, I usually hang out with my friends and listen to music. Music is huge in my roommates' and my life. We always have music playing. We listen to nothing really hard at all. I like a lot of different things as long as it is pretty mellow. I like R.E.M. a lot. I like 10,000 Maniacs.

I read a lot actually. I usually like feminist books. I was reading a book called *Earth Vibes*. It is about environmentalism and feminist theories. It is very interesting. I don't know if I would agree with a lot of things, but it is an interesting perspective. I would like to read more about that. I haven't had much time to read on my own for enjoyment since this summer because there is so much to do and I am so far behind.

We don't have a TV at all. I love not having a TV. I don't have any time for it in my day. I don't know how a TV would work out. We have a TV that we keep in the closet because I wouldn't want to pay. But if we didn't have to pay, we would definitely have it plugged in. But now I have gone through it and I know what it is like to not have a TV. I just love it so much that I don't know what I would do if we had one. It seems like I never do anything productive anyway. If I am just sitting there watching TV, I feel bad about myself.

A lot of times my friends and I just sit around, cook, and talk. We hang out and do homework. We go to Pershing [the gym] to work out. My friends are pretty athletic. They like to go to work out. I go swimming there. I do that quite a bit actually, but none of them really swim or none of them want to go swimming. That is as far as I go and I like it a lot. It is a good challenge for me. I tried swimming in health and wellness class. I just got hooked. I love it so much. In high school, I ran cross-country in my freshman year, but realized that I hated to run. I stayed on it because I enjoyed the team. Then I played soccer for three years. I would love to play soccer here, but the players here are pretty good, better than I am. I would love to play if I had a chance, but I don't think I have that chance.

At the university, I take pictures for the *Index* [a student newspaper]. I work at the Career Center. I do not really get involved in other school activities here. I wish I did. I used to be in the astronomy club. I was the treasurer. I was a terrible treasurer because I am so unmotivated and I didn't want to do it because it was a pain. It was a lot of responsibility and I didn't want it in the first place. I don't know anything about astronomy. I think they just organize nights to go out. They got telescopes and we got to go to the observatory one night and look up the sky, pretty dumb stuff. It was cool for a while, but then you get into all the technical club stuff, and that's what's not fun.

My parents do finance my education. See, that is the thing. I told you that my dad was a sucker. If I want something then I get it. Well, I am really aware of that and I have always been so independent. Even now I am paying for independence. This summer I worked two jobs because I wanted to earn enough money so I could help out a little bit with my education. But this summer I found out that my brother and sister didn't get a job after their freshman year. My parents definitely paid for their education. They just sat around and did yard work for my dad. They both wonder why I have so many jobs (I have three jobs here). I work at the coffee shop that is on the downtown square on Washington Street. I work at the Career Center and I also take pictures for the *Index*. I don't even know if I'm getting paid for it. Actually I am not even on a time card now. I just got this job. This is the second time I am going out. I haven't worked anything out with anybody yet. But it is not a big deal. I don't mind volunteering. My siblings just wonder why I have jobs. That is always the way I have been; I always work. I like making my own money and I have always been a hard worker. So I do end up paying for a little bit, I think. But my education is mostly paid by my parents.

I took pictures of the swim meet. I am in beginning photography so I don't have a lot of experience. It is kind of intimidating because they gave me this big set of cameras and they say, "Okay, take some good pictures." You've got to be critical on what you pick. It has to have all the right compositional elements. I end up getting nervous and I take terrible pictures. It's hard, but I have only taken pictures once and today I'll take pictures of the blood drive. I am taking the class on photography and I learned how to develop film. I love developing, or working in the dark room. I saw the ad in the paper and thought it would be good.

I want an internship too. This summer I am planning on going to Washington DC because I have a few friends that are going to DC too. That is a good place for us to go. I want to try to get an internship in Hawaii next semester; I would like to work somewhere like the National

Tropical Botanical Garden. I want to go so badly, although I am not a biology or botany major, but a journalism major. To go there to pull some weeds—I would love it. I was thinking about being a biology minor actually because I have the course work behind me already. I found out about the Hawaii internship by working here [at the Career Center] and playing on the Internet. They have cabins on the beach and your door opens out to this huge deck. It is right there on the beach.

Let me tell you, I would like to go out right now, get a job, and get a life. I'm pretty sick of school. I would really like to be on my way so I can have something to say, "That's my own." On prom night it's like, "Oh, that's my parents and I am really glad because I am really lucky to have my parents." They worked hard to pay for it. But I don't know; I would like to get up in the morning and have people waiting for me to come because I've got to do something. I like the feeling that I am making it on my own. I like independence. So I just want a house to renovate. I want an old house to fix up and just live there. Seriously, my biggest dream right now is to have the money to buy a house and fix it up, but that is pretty narrow-minded.

I have basic expectations. When I get married I want someone who appreciates me for me, someone who loves me and wants me to be an independent person; at the same time, I want someone who is always there, being helpful. I would want him to have a job. I haven't really given it much thought.

I don't think my parents have any expectations of who I should marry. I haven't brought anybody home for them to consider. Well, actually I brought one person home. We were home for midterm and he and my mom hit it off. It wasn't like meet the parents kind of thing, but to see our town, to see where I came from. I felt weird at first. But he loves my family a lot, so that was good. I like that person, with whom I defined everything yesterday. I'd probably want someone like him, but not now.

My parents have never placed any emphasis on my dating or marrying an Indonesian. We never really talked about the whole dating thing. And they know where their lives end and my life begins. They see that I see really clearly, but they have never said anything like that.

I don't know if I want a life with children. I could mess them up. I've thought about that for a long time. I just probably wouldn't want that, at least not right now. Now, thinking about the future, I don't want that. To be perfectly honest, I don't think I would be better than anyone. I would be scared to have children, but if I did, I definitely want them to be hard working. I've never done anything bad. When I was a little kid, I never stole anything or broke anything. I never threw things—random acts of violence—that was not me at all. I was a good kid. I would just want them to be the same way, which is tough. I just want them to be good. I don't know Indonesian. But I wouldn't say it was a really important thing to teach any kids I might have, just because I don't know it myself. I don't know how that affects or doesn't affect my life. I definitely want them to have interests, to go out there and see for themselves, just like any other culture. It doesn't matter. I just want them to be pretty multicultural and multilingual. That's cool.

Part 2
Filipinas

Many Filipinas came to the United States after the 1960s to fulfill the demand for personnel in the health industry. Among them was Amihan Perez, a first generation immigrant woman. As a young girl, she helped her parents with the family farming when school was not in session; she also helped with household chores. Although she had demanding daily responsibilities, she did well at school and earned her teaching certificate. Like most of her compatriots, Amihan immigrated to the United States to seek a better life, aided by her daughter who worked in America as a nurse.

The Filipinas working in the health industry experienced various degrees of job satisfaction and acculturation. Bituin Perez, also a first generation immigrant, had a similar childhood to Perez. As a patient-unit clerk at a university hospital in the United States, her daily responsibilities included filing, typing, and answering the phone. She was satisfied with her job, finding it "not stressful," and was happy with her work environment, where five of her co-workers were Filipinas. Diwata Lopez, another first generation Filipina, came to Chicago as a nurse in 1964 under the exchange program. As a registered nurse, she worked in the operating room where the staff often dealt with extreme emergencies. Although her job was stressful, she enjoyed the fast pace at work and the "great salary and good benefits" from the job. Similarly, Marie Bornales came to the United States to respond to the need for nurses in the health industry. She took great pride in her profession, and especially enjoyed working with newborn babies and helping doctors. However, she was frustrated with the subtle discrimination she faced at work resulting from her racial and cultural background. While well assimilated into the American health industry at work, all these women were consciously preserving the Filipino culture and traditions at home.

They continued their ties with the motherland through correspondence, remittance, and irregular visits.

The younger generation of Filipino Americans were struggling to define who they were and what their identity was. Leonora Juliano was born in St. Louis, Missouri, but was largely influenced by the Filipino American culture when growing up, as her parents were actively involved in the Filipino community affairs. Although she appreciated her Filipino heritage and felt that she had benefited from it, she still had to cope with her dual identities of Asian and American. At school, she was expected to be a "smart" Asian student excelling in math and sciences, while she was actually more interested in subjects in social sciences. Dalisay Lopez, a second generation Filipina from Chicago studying nursing at St. Louis University, had more tumultuous relations with her parents. Growing up, she often defied her parents' restrictions, especially those regarding dating. The classic cultural and generational conflict was evident in her life. While her parents wanted to raise her the "Filipino way," she felt they should mix American and Filipino values, and remember that "we're in America and not in the Philippines." Dalisay Lopez felt she wouldn't be able to raise her children—if she had any—the traditional way. Sarah Perez lived in the Philippines until her sophomore year of high school and then immigrated to the United States with her parents. With Filipino upbringing in her most formative years, Sarah Perez did not experience much cultural conflict with her parents. However, her comparisons of life in the Philippines and in America provide interesting references on differences of the two cultures.

While a first generation Filipina involved in an interracial marriage with a white American has often been stereotyped as a military wife or a mail-order wife, Maria Herman's marriage clearly challenges the stereotype. A professor of nursing at a Midwestern university, Maria Herman was married to a European American, and was often mistaken as a military wife. Her strategy to deal with the stereotype was to be continuously devoted to her profession. Her husband (a nurse when they met and later a fellow professor in nursing) works with Maria and they mutually respect and support each other. They also shared household responsibilities and made family decisions jointly. Enjoying a successful interracial marriage, Maria Herman also wanted her children to be immersed in Filipino language and culture at home while assimilating into American society.

5

Immigrant Women at Work

Amihan Perez was born into a farmer's family in Batac, Ilocos Norte, the Philippines, in 1917. She grew up under harsh conditions and later became a teacher. She immigrated to the United States in the 1970s to join her daughter, a hospital clerk, and worked as an assembler. She was retired and lived in Chicago, Illinois, at the time of the interview in 1994.

I was born on October 12, 1917, in the town of Batac, in the province of Ilocos Norte, in the Philippines. My parents did not have any kind of formal education and were farmers. I had ten brothers and sisters, but two of them died while they were still very young. Of the eight surviving siblings, I had three brothers and five sisters. Together, my family raised agricultural products such as rice, corn, and vegetables.

When I was a young girl in elementary school, I helped my parents with the farming when school was not in session. While my parents did the actual farming, I aided with the housework. Sometimes I cooked for them while they went to the fields to work. I brought food to the field for them because they did not come home for lunch. During the summertime, while they were eating, I used to try planting tobacco seedlings. During the rainy season, I did not plant the rice seedlings.

For the most part, we earned little money and had just enough food for the family. However, if the harvest was poor, we had to buy rice from the market for the family to eat. We did not hire any workers; it was completely a family venture. In the region where we lived, every family had their own piece of land to cultivate. They mainly produced food for themselves, but if they had extra, they sold it to others.

When I was in elementary school, I used to help my parents with household chores. Every day, after cooking and washing dishes, I had to do my school assignments. However, when I was in high school, I did not have time to help my parents because I studied in another town. This school was not exactly a boarding school; there was no boarding school in that area. I stayed in a boarding house. On Saturdays, I brought my parents food in the fields, which I found to be enjoyable work.

All of my siblings and I were expected to work for the family. Jobs were different for boys than for girls. The girls usually helped with washing in the house while the boys helped with the farm work. During the rainy season, the boys helped with the rice planting. During the dry season, they had to help plant tobacco. They also had to help with the harvesting of the rice, tobacco leaves, and corn. The boys also tended to the animals.

After high school, I went to a government school. It was called Philippine Normal School, but was changed to Philippine Normal College after my graduation. I graduated with an elementary teacher's certificate and became an elementary school teacher. I had a little difficulty at school. I stayed with my uncle, and everything was just the same as when I was in elementary school with my parents. I did the chores at my uncle's home. In the afternoon when I went home, I did the cooking and washed the dishes. Afterwards, I put the kitchen in order. I would stay up for a long time cleaning the kitchen. It would often be nine PM when I began studying my lessons. Sometimes I could not finish all of my lessons because of all my household chores, so I had to cram during my bus ride to school. I used to ride in an electric car when I was in college. I usually read during the ride. My main difficulty was balancing my chores with my schoolwork. On Saturdays, I used to go to the library at the school just to catch up and to be able to study. If I stayed at home, I usually did the housework instead of my schoolwork.

I was not very sociable during my school years. I did not go out with my friends socially except when it was a school activity, like a dance. If it were compulsory, I would go, but if not, I did not go out. I stayed home to study my lessons or to help with the household chores. To me, the most important things in my life were my family and my studies.

My relationship with my teachers was good. They were friendly and understanding. My teachers did not really realize that it was hard for me to find time for my studies because I was doing well. I had a few small troubles; even between class periods I would try to read so that I could take part in the discussion. Even then, I did not often take part as much as the others.

I decided to come to the United States because my daughter was here. She was very much interested in coming to the United States because of the job opportunities; also, the wages were higher here than in the Philippines. My daughter's supervisor wanted her to stay in the Philippines so that if she retired, my daughter could take over her place. When my daughter came to America, her supervisor was greatly disappointed. The earnings in the United States lured my daughter enough that she ignored the advice of her supervisor. Because she was in America already, I was also very interested in coming here so I could work and earn money too. Then I could bring my other children, so they too could discover a better living.

Life in the Philippines was hard. The pay in the Philippines is low compared to here. Even though one works and is paid well, the salary is still not enough to buy all of the things one might need to survive. In the United States, as long as one works, one receives enough pay to buy everything one likes. That is why we came to the United States—to improve our life.

When I first arrived in the United States, I had an immigrant visa. I was naturalized and became a U.S. citizen in April of 1983. I was an assembler at an electronic company, Shore Brothers in Evanston, Illinois (in the northern suburbs near Chicago). When I worked there, I had a good relationship with my coworkers. When I first got the job, my coworkers had to help me so that I could finish the daily quota. There is a certain amount to be finished, and they taught me how to do it. They were pleasant and I did not experience any kind of racial prejudice or sex discrimination. They were friendly and cooperative. My relationship with my boss was friendly too. Normally, I was not stressed when I was working. Sometimes it was a relaxing atmosphere, but other times it was not, especially if the job was new. Some jobs were easy, others were hard. It was hard to finish the required quota. I had to work fast in order to finish. However, if I was given a job that was easy, I was relaxed. I never had any conflicts with my co-workers or with my boss. The salary and benefits were fair and substantial. The thing I liked most about my job was that it was usually easy.

A typical product while I was an assembler would be the microphone. I had a hard time putting the small pieces together. For the big ones, I had to use a machine; that was easy. I managed. When the work exports were slow, they had to lay off workers. I was laid off four times, and then I was called back again. The last time I was laid off, though, I was not called back.

I got more money here as an assembler than I did as a teacher in the

Philippines. Teaching was harder because one had to prepare. One had to make the lesson plans every night in order to be ready for the next day. If one did not have lesson plans and the supervisor happened to come around and see that, then one would be reprimanded. My relationship with my coworkers when I was a teacher back in the Philippines was also good. I had no conflicts with anyone, even the boss. That job was more stressful than my job as an assembler, as assembling required no thinking at the end of the day. But when I was a teacher in the Philippines, I went home, attended to chores like cooking, then I attended to the children, and after everything was finished, I had to do the lesson planning and writing. In the morning, I woke up early to get ready for school. I did not have any free time to relax when I was a teacher. This was the main difference between my work here and my work in the Philippines. When I was here in the United States, we used to go out of town on the weekends. In the Philippines, nobody went on vacation for pleasure. We just had to stay in our homes and do work. Occasionally, if there were parties, we did not work.

I met my husband in the Bicol region when I was a teacher. My brother was in that region in a gold mining town, working as a miner. After graduation, my best friend and I decided to go there because my brother was there. We taught together in the same school. We talked together and stayed together. On weekends, we went to visit our brothers, and that is how we met.

My husband was a history teacher. After World War II, he went to school. He was unable to finish his college education before because his father died early and his brothers, who came here to the United States, did not remember him anymore. His mother provided for their needs. He only finished his education after the war because of her aid. After graduation, he could not find a job as a high school teacher in our town, so he went elsewhere to work for about ten years. When his friend became principal at a local high school, he hired my husband as one of the instructors there. At first, my husband was a high school teacher. Then he became an administrative officer and retired as one.

With my husband in Mindanao, another region, I had quite a hard time raising my children. Although I had two helpers, it was difficult as Monina was still a small baby. I could not attend to my children because I was teaching in a barrio school (a rural school). I made many of the family decisions, which made it almost like being a single parent. My husband's money was sent to one of my daughters. My income was for all of us: Winston, Junie, Erwin, Edlar, and Monina. I had a hard time. Whenever I needed money, I had to get a loan. My husband was supportive of my work.

After we came to the States, we spoke Ilocano at home, which is a dialect that we spoke to our children. We also ate Filipino food, Chinese food, and Pansit noodles. There were many Chinese in that region, so we had to follow some of those recipes too. One of the things I like most about the United States is that it is easy to get what you want because money is easy to make. I have more money here than I did in the Philippines because my children give me money; I have Social Security too, so that I can buy what I want. The thing I like least about the United States is the cold weather in the wintertime. Other times, it is nice. I can go anywhere, even if I do not drive; I can take the bus and go any place I like as long as there is a bus going there. I prefer living here because all of my children are here. All of my children, except for Monina, have married a Filipino. I prefer that she marry one, as well as my grandchildren, because you can trust Filipinos about money and relationships. I spend my spare time watching TV. I read the newspaper and magazines. Right now, Monina is buying *Time* and *People*. I follow life in the Philippines by watching Filipino news. I also go to church every Sunday at St. Genevieve. Kids are easier to manage during church in the Philippines. They are more obedient because they ask no questions. Here, they talk back and they think their teachers are better than their parents are. They mingle with other American children.

6

Filipinas in the Health Industry

Bituin Perez was born into a farmer's family in Batac, Ilocos Norte, the Philippines, in 1947. She was a teacher in the Philippines but decided to immigrate to America in the 1970s for a better life. She worked for the University of Illinois Medical Center at Chicago as a patient-unit clerk at the time of the interview in 1994.

I was born on 10 September 1947 in the town of Batac in the province of Ilocos Norte in the Philippines. My mom and dad were only educated through the sixth grade. They both worked on the farm, which they owned. They produced a lot and the products depended on the season. There is a tobacco season during the summer. During the rainy season, they plant rice and corn. They grew vegetables and sold them to the market. Sometimes buyers would come to our house to buy our products because we had a surplus. We had to hire some laborers to gather the fruits and vegetables. It was a family business involving everyone. Even though I was still in elementary school, when we got home we had to go help with the family business. During the weekend, Sunday was market day, so we picked fruits and vegetables and sold them. When we were in high school, we had many more products, which forced us to hire laborers.

I have two sisters and four brothers and not all of us had a college education. My second brother and I finished college. Another brother only went to college for two years because he got sick and then decided to help my parents on the farm. One thing that I appreciated about my parents was that they treated all of us equally. There is only a one-year gap among the first three of us, while with the fourth one, there is a seven-year gap. As a result, my parents had to make more sacrifices for the first three of us.

Sometimes they would borrow money from our relatives just to help give us something to continue our studies. When my other brothers and sisters were in school, they had better lives because we, the oldest three, were helping them. They did not ask or tell us to help. It was just in our minds.

I finished college with a bachelor of science in elementary education. Our parents tried their best to let us study since they did not finish school themselves. They tried their best to help us finish our studies because education was very important to them. They said that education was the greatest inheritance they could give us, as they were below average in education.

I do not exactly remember what elementary school was like in the Philippines, but it was not hard for me. When I was in high school, it was more difficult than elementary because it was demanding, the same as college. You have to study all the time and you will not pass without helping yourself.

I never thought of coming to America before. I did not have any ambition to come, but then, when I got married, I learned that, from time to time, coming to the United States results in a better life. That is why we were encouraged to come, to try life here in the United States. I have an immigrant visa. I think that I can apply now if I want to have full citizenship. We did not have a comfortable life in the Philippines. When I got married, a lot of my husband's friends and relatives helped us. We had a more comfortable life than other people did. However, if we were on our own, I do not think we would have been so comfortable, because life is hard in the Philippines. You can stay wherever you want. You can stay at home, but if you do not work, how will you earn money to buy food and eat? How can you survive? The chance for a better life drew us to the United States. I was working a lot. I worked hard there but still it was not enough. We still needed help. I worked as a teacher full time and I had a business during the weekend. I went to the remote barrios just to sell some fruits, like mangoes. I also had a store where I really worked hard. My husband was working the same way. He was working in a bank in the Philippines and he helped me to run the store.

I met my husband in the Philippines in 1970 or 1971. He was my coworker. Although I finished college, I had to pass the teacher's board, but there were many teachers there. I had to wait. I looked for another job besides teaching and was employed in Manila in a senator's office with my sister. I volunteered to help with the senator's campaign. When he won the election, I got a job as a telephone receptionist. My sister was a stenographer.

But after working there for one year, I decided to return to Ilocos Norte. I found another office job there where I met my future husband. Five years later, I got a teaching job.

I do not think that we have more leisure time here in the United States. There is more leisure time in the Philippines. We could relax more there, but then again, it is not like here. You must be a workaholic here in order to live comfortably. In the Philippines, you had to work hard to make ends meet. I think my work in the U.S. is easier. I am paid what I deserve. But in the Philippines, I was working hard from 7:00 AM to 5:00 PM and the salary was not worth it. It was very little, not enough for us. Here, it is okay. We have a nice apartment and a couple of cars, but we have many bills. We are just trying our best.

I do not remember what my relationship with my classmates was during college. I think it was great, but it has been twenty-eight years. During the first year, it was okay because whoever your classmates were, you had the same classmates for all of your subjects. But when we were in our second year, another subject meant another set of classmates. We only saw each other when we met for class. Then it was not like high school when you do everything together—eat, go to the library, and go out. In the United States, sometimes you do not trust anybody. You have to always be careful. You have to watch what you say.

I am a patient-unit clerk. I do office work: filing, typing, answering the phone, and using the computer. I do not have stress from my job compared to my work in the Philippines. If I compare, I really like my work here. I do not think that I have been discriminated against in my work. Sometimes the assistant head nurse, who is white, notices that there are five Filipinos working. He says, "Now I'm the minority." That is fine because he is not discriminating against us; he is just joking. He did my evaluation and rated me nicely. Sometimes when I go to other places, I know that some people are looking at me because I'm a Filipina, but I do not mind.

I have not had any confrontations with my boss yet. I hear that sometimes other workers are experiencing something, which is not good, which I do not want to be exposed to. For example, a few months ago, our unit director was changed because the previous one was promoted. The new one is making new policy changes in which the staff really is not interested. These changes make some of us hate each other. Particularly, we do not like that unit director and now he is really watching us because of that. He blows even a small mistake out of proportion. That is why we need to be careful.

Right now, we are just trying to keep calm with the unit director. If we hear something that we do not like, we just have to shut our mouths to have less trouble. Everybody is like that. I am not satisfied with my salary although it is good compared to what I made before in the Philippines. I would like more. For benefits, we have fifteen days of paid vacation and fifteen paid sick leave days. We have free medical insurance and a discount for our families. There are dental benefits. It is all good.

I like the fact that my job is not stressful. It is relaxing but sometimes it is boring if there is nothing to do. Sometimes I like it if it is busy so I am not bored. I do not like it to be busy all the time, but I also do not want it to be slow. I do not like the extremes. I just want a fair amount of work.

My husband and I have a good relationship. We both work now, we share household responsibilities. We talk together first before making decisions on family matters. He always gives me the final decision. I do not feel like doing that all the time. I ask him to decide also. He is not pushy. Now, the only issue is that our son wants a new car. He has to save first, to have at least the down payment for the car ready to go.

From what I see, I have a wonderful relationship with my mother-in-law compared to others, especially in the Philippines. They fight with each other. I do not fight with my mother-in law. She is nice. I will never know another person like her. She is always ready to help me and I am ready to help her.

We speak Filipino at home. We speak it to our children too. We sometimes mix dialects between Ilocano and Tagalog. Both of my children know Filipino and Tagalog. That is what they learned at school. Filipino is our national language. But there are many dialects there. We all have to learn Tagalog so that when we meet with others from different regions, at least we can speak with each other. If we do not, we cannot understand each other because they have their own language. That is why we have to master English and Filipino from the start of elementary school.

English is one of our school subjects even in kindergarten. In fact, we have more English subjects than Filipino ones. In the Philippines, we do not speak English at home. Sometimes they would fine us when we spoke Ilocano at school when we were in the English-subject classes. They just wanted us to practice using the English language. The only problem is that we have an accent. Sometimes Americans do not understand us even if we are speaking the correct grammar. This was true, especially when we were new here. But eventually, we understand each other.

I cook Filipino food most of the time. I cook *pinakbit* (mixed vegetables), *abobo* (chicken and/or pork), and what you know as chocolate meat. Part of the reason that I do this is because I like to give my children the Filipino culture. I think that my children already have a large amount of Filipino culture in them. They were already grown when they came over here. They still understand and observe Filipino culture. My son works in Dominick's [a grocery store] instead of Burger King. He transferred because his coworkers were using drugs while he was there. He did that to get away from that situation. I appreciated his good sense.

I prefer to raise my children in the Filipino way. I differentiate both ways. In the American way, the children have to be independent when they are eighteen years old. If possible, they do not want us to tell them what to do. I do not want that. If they still want our guidance, I think it will be better for them. If they are ready to support themselves, that is fine. That is why I am telling them to finish their studies so that they will have a better future. I think that it would be better for my children to marry someone that is Filipino. If they find someone they like, though, it is up to them.

What I like most about living in the United States is having a job and making lots of money so that when we return to the Philippines, we will be fine. If I worked in the Philippines, the retirement pay would not be enough for the duration of my retirement years. If I retire here and decide to go back, I think we will have enough money. The worth of the U.S. dollar there is very high.

Sometimes during my free time from work, we go to Lake Michigan. When we have money, we go on vacation. Sometimes it is hard on our budget to have a vacation. I try to keep up with current events in the Philippines. I watch the news rather than read the paper. I also go to church at St. John's and at St. Genevieve's. I do not participate in anything other than the service and family activities. But when I was in the Philippines, we participated in church activities.

There are some differences between the Catholic Church here in the United States and those in the Philippines. Some people help with fundraising in the Philippines. There are also more prayers and rituals involved there, but that is true with many religions. When someone dies, it does not end with the funeral. For example, we have to keep the dead person in the house for nine days so that everyone can pay his or her respects. There are no funeral homes in the Philippines. Every day that the body is in the house, the priest will come and say a prayer. A year later, we pray in honor of that dead person. It is only Catholics. It is the culture.

If I could have the same work and benefits there as I do here, I would like to be in the Philippines. We are here because of the economic factors and for the future of our children.

———————◆━●━●━◆———————

Diwata Lopez was born into a family of educators in Manila, the Philippines, in 1943. She immigrated to the United States in 1964 under a visitor's exchange program for a nurse's visa. She was working as a registered nurse in the operating room at Cook County Hospital and living in Chicago, Illinois, at the time of the interview in 1994.

I was born on 20 March 1943 in Manila in the Philippines. My parents were high school teachers. They each had a bachelor of science in education degree. My father was a history major and English minor. My mom was a home economics teacher. My parents had high expectations for me, but it was not until I was in high school that I really felt they expected a lot of me. In grammar school, I did not feel this pressure. I did not work while I was in high school or even in college. In the Philippines, we do not work while we're in school. My mother did housework in addition to her teaching job. I have four brothers and one sister. I think that in Filipino families, the parents are stricter with the girls than the boys. The boys and girls could be out late, but girls had to have a chaperone. The girls were more sheltered.

I decided to come to the United States to see another country. At that time, people were going to see other places. If I did not come to the United States, I would have gone to another country. I came to the United States in 1964. I first came to Chicago, Illinois. I was part of the visitors' exchange program for a nurse's visa. I had a choice between Chicago and Philadelphia. Chicago was more popular, so I chose it. We read a lot about Chicago in the Philippines. We knew that Sears & Roebuck was in Chicago and that it was a big city. I thought that the Americans were nice. I got the same impression when I got here. I was living on the south side of Chicago in 1964 and everyone was so kind. I got my permanent residence or green card in 1971. I became a citizen of the United States in 1976. I just filled out the forms and filed them with immigration to get my citizenship.

I did not work much in the Philippines. I worked, before I took the board exam, as a private nurse. I worked in a nursery for babies for three months. It was just like taking care of healthy babies. When I was done with my nursing degree, it was nice to work. I enjoyed getting the money and being paid for working. I got my degree at the University of the Philippines in 1963 and it was believed to be the best degree in the Philippines. I majored in public health. During our senior year, we had to choose between teaching and supervision, ward management, or public health, which is working in health centers. We had to study hard because where I studied, if you did not pass, you were out. The standards were lower at other places.

A typical day at school involved many things. We had to study hard. It was a lot of reading and lots of reporting. We had to study journals and submit our findings. Especially at the University of the Philippines, we had a big campus; one had to run from one building to another to get to class. In the morning, we would have our clinical work in Manila. Then we had to run to our school. We used to have to run to catch the public transportation to campus. My children's college experience is the same as mine as far as being away from home, but they have cars. I did not have one. As far as reading and researching, it is similar.

I was in a sorority in the Philippines. We had initiation and hazing. I used to live in the dorms, so I (as a pledge member) used to hide from the active sisters. I used to go to my other friends' rooms and stay there. If I was caught, they would boss me around and make me clean their rooms. In the Philippines, we use mosquito nets and they would make me hang them up. They would command me to act like a certain person. They would also ask me to interview someone for them, especially if they had a boyfriend or a crush on someone. They could ask me to give that person a rose.

The name of my sorority was Delta Lambda Sigma. The reputation of my sorority was one of the best on campus. At one time, our grand archon was a member and president of the UP Women's Club. The office of the club was a popular position and there was some campaigning involved. It was an honor.

When I was a freshman, the UP Women's Club encouraged sororities to have parties. There was one every week, but there was no drinking involved. We had dances and balls with a brother fraternity. I was more active during my first two years because the second part of nursing was harder and we had to leave campus to be closer to the hospital. In my senior year, I was not very active, but when I lived on campus, I was very involved.

We also had cultural events such as musicals and presentations about the culture of the Philippines. We did fundraising and we are currently trying to organize our alumni in the United States. We have one chapter in New York and another in California. Many of my sorority sisters are now working and living in America.

I went to work right away after graduation. However, when I was here in the United States, I wanted to continue my schooling. The hospital that I worked at was on the south side, far from downtown where all the schools were. I wanted to obtain a master's degree in nursing. Many graduates from my school were doing the same thing, which was expected of me too—go as high as you could. I kept on writing the schools and getting information, but most of them were too far away. Most graduates of the University of the Philippines who were working at Cook County Hospital (my current employer) were able to finish their master's degrees at DePaul or Loyola because they were right there, close to the hospital.

I had a bad relationship with my nursing instructor at the University of the Philippines. I was negative. I always asked questions, and it appeared to the instructor that I was not agreeable. I always had a question with whatever they were doing; I guess it was mostly with the student teachers because I was critical of their work. I was not very friendly with them.

The educational training in the Philippines is based on the U.S. system. Most of our professors have master's degrees from the United States. There is a big American influence there. Our books were all American. We used what they were using here in the United States. Now I am done with trying to advance. I will probably go on with the job I have now until I retire. I am happy, content, and also well-paid. It is what I know. Why should I change?

A typical workday at my current job can be very hectic because I work in the operating room. I work the night shift and we are dealing mostly with emergencies. Sometimes it is a busy day because we are dealing with extreme emergencies like stab wounds or gun wounds. There are also times when it is quiet, like on a very cold day when not too many people go out. It is boring if there is nothing to do. Yet, if it is too busy, that is not nice either. I like working. I enjoy what I do. I have a good relationship with my colleagues because I have worked with most of them for a long time. We have office parties for birthdays, etc. I also have a good relationship with my boss. Right now, my job is not very stressful because I am used to it.

When I was working in a private hospital, it was more stressful because we were working with doctors who were already finished with their residencies. They were more particular and demanding. When I first started this job in the County Hospital, where we worked with doctors in training; it was nice. The doctors we have now are less demanding because they are learning themselves. We, the nurses, have been there longer and we in fact help the doctors. I really like working at the County Hospital.

I do not feel like I have ever been discriminated against at work because of my nationality or gender. I do not think that I have been discriminated against outside of work or in other countries either. Maybe I went to places without discrimination. Maybe in these other countries, I did not experience discrimination because I was a visitor. All the people at my work are minorities. But even when I worked in a private hospital, it was mostly Caucasians and they were okay. When I just started in 1964, it was fine even though there were only a few Asians on staff.

I have had some conflicts before, though. At one time, I wanted to be off on Christmas, and my boss would not give it to me. I was mad because I had been there for a long, long time. I had to tell the other supervisor, who was in a higher position than my supervisor, about the problem, and I got the time off. I was not happy still, so I changed my shift to the day shift. I was hurt because I should have had priority since I had worked the night shift for a long time. I did not understand why she should not give the priority to me.

However, I have a great salary and good benefits from my job. That is why I stayed for twenty years. We get twenty-five vacation days a year, or two days a month. Sick days are cumulative up to one hundred fifty. I get more holidays than any other institution gives. Health insurance for me and my family is also provided.

The thing I like most about my job is working with people, especially with patients. I like doing what I know and I am happy with what I do. In the beginning, however, I did not like working nights, but now I am used to it. I had to work nights when my children were still babies. It was harder to stay up then. Now I am used to it and prefer it. I get more errands and chores accomplished during the day.

I met my husband in Chicago. His niece used to stay with me in the nurses' dorm apartments and she introduced us. That was the beginning. He was very patient and persistent. Even if I tried to discourage him, he was still patient. Our relationship now is very good.

We share household responsibilities. I do the cooking and most of the housework—cooking, cleaning, and washing. He does most of the carpentry, and fixes the car and the house. We usually cook Filipino food at home, but we also cook other kinds of foods. We still have rice every day. We talk about our family decisions and we have to agree on them. Sometimes if it is about cars or things like that, I let him decide. He asks my opinion on other matters. My husband is supportive of my work, although in the beginning he would not let me work overtime. When there was no need or when my children were younger, he did not want me to work overtime while others could.

I also had a good relationship with my in-laws. They used to live with us and took care of the children while my husband and I worked. They also helped cook. We lived in an extended family atmosphere. We all got along okay.

I speak Filipino at home to my husband, but not to my children. We did not teach the children Filipino, because at that time we thought it would be better if they spoke English. We did not want them to have an accent and we really wanted them to master English, especially when they talked with their friends.

However, I prefer the Filipino way for raising children. The American way is more permissive; there is too much freedom. With the Filipino way, I think, there are more limitations. We have more parental control. We still want to teach our children, even though they are now young adults, that they cannot do anything they like. We want them to be guided by us. At a certain point, we will be less strict, but we will always be concerned. We will not kick our kids out when they are eighteen years old. They can stay here until they are married, and even then they are still welcome here.

I prefer my children to marry an Asian, but I would also respect their choice because it is their life. When I say Asian, I mean Chinese, Japanese, Koreans, etc. This is because I think our cultures are more or less the same. They all have an Oriental orientation.

I am fond of many things about America, but most especially I like the economic comfort and freedom. In the Philippines, you have to brown-nose those politicians in order to get a good job. Here, you are on your own and you are chosen by merit. The things I like least about America and Chicago are the drug problem and the crime. There is a problem with these two things in the Philippines now as well, but I think it is because of the times we live in and the influence of the United States. In the Philippines during my time, we did not have those problems, but now I am hearing about those problems surfacing. This is true in Manila, especially now.

Manila is like Chicago; the countryside in the Philippines is like Missouri, safer.

In my spare time, I like to do many things. I like to go to plays, go to the casino, dine out, or go on vacation. My husband does not like to go on vacation. He just wants me to go with my children and send him a post-card. I also read the *Chicago Tribune* and nursing magazines. I follow the daily news all the time. We watch the news on TV. I am interested in American political issues too. I think that Clinton is doing okay, but I am a Democrat and I will always say that they are doing fine. I also go to church. I do not participate in church activities anymore, but when my children were attending grammar school there, we always participated in the carnival and other events. Now, we just go to church. Most of my friends are Filipino. I think that we will go back to the Philippines to retire with our American money because it is safer and cheaper there.

Marie Bornales was born into a family of educators in Ilocos Norte, the Philippines, in 1931. She came to the United States in 1954 as a nurse under an exchange visitor's program and then returned to the Philippines. She immigrated to America in 1961 and had since lived in St. Louis, Missouri. She was a retired nurse at the time of the interview in 1999.

My name is Marie Bornales. I was born in Ilocos Norte, in the northern part of the Philippines, in 1931. My parents completed only a grade school education, which was basically the only thing that existed in the Philippines at the time, but both became English teachers later in life. Most people in the Philippines were like my mother and father in terms of education. I have eight siblings: five sisters and three brothers. Two of my brothers didn't finish college, and the other died early, when he was forty. Two of my sisters finished their college education (one is a nurse, one is a teacher), but my older brother and sisters got married early. Since we had so many children, I was sent to live with my grandparents at a young age, which is common in the Philippines.

I came to the United States for the first time in April 1954, when I was twenty-three. I had read in the paper that registered nurses were being recruited for an exchange program with the United States. I entered on a visa especially for this exchange visitor program. Under this program, we could only stay in the United States for two years and then we had to return to the Philippines to teach what we had learned in the United States. I ended up coming back to the United States a few years later because it is a beautiful country and I really liked it here. Everything is available and the quality of education is much higher these days than when we lived in the Philippines and it is more progressive. The number of opportunities and the ability to advance is what I like most about living in America. It is still the best country I have ever known.

Most of the time, speaking the language in America was not especially difficult; when I was in the Philippines, we learned to speak English. Sometimes, though, I had difficulty understanding my teachers, especially their pronunciation. My classmates were very nice to me; they helped me a lot, taking me out to dinner or the movies or opera house because we lived around St. John's Hospital near Kingshighway Blvd. They were mostly American; I was the only Filipino at St. John's and I became homesick. After a year, I moved to a city hospital and took a post-graduate course in operating room techniques, and then I moved to St. Anthony's Hospital, where there were more Filipinos.

I started my university education during my first trip to the United States, attending St. Louis University. Then I moved to Chicago. By that time, the two years of my visa was over, and so I returned to the Philippines. During my time there, I worked in a hospital for about a year. Before I came the United States, I had graduated from the nursing school of that hospital, so they made me a head nurse in one division. While in the Philippines, I also married and had my daughter. The three of us came back in 1961 with a green card. After eight years, in 1969, we became American citizens, along with my daughter, who was still young at the time, and gained her citizenship through me.

When I came back to the States the second time, I planned to be a registered nurse and then continue my education at the same time. I was a nurse for thirty-two years. My coworkers were always friendly and helpful. Some of my bosses were very nice and understand me. But some of them constantly tried to find fault with me and that was why I was upset once in a while when I was working. However that did not matter to me as I always worked hard and I was devoted to my job and my patients. I especially loved working in labor/delivery with the newborn babies. Working with the newborn babies and helping the doctors was my favorite part of the job. Sometimes, if we had a difficult baby, it was hard. I felt bad for both the parents and the child.

I felt job-related stress sometimes. If the problem was with my coworkers, I confronted them, but you can't confront your boss. It was also not good to just say "yes, yes" to everything. I tried to give my own opinions, but my boss never listened. Sometimes I felt that people discriminated against me since I was not only female, but also Asian. Nurses in the United States work hard. In the Philippines, if you are a head nurse, you only supervise your staff and the students; you don't work at all. When I retired twelve years ago, the pay was not good. The Nurses Association complained and demanded that nurses should be paid more.

I met my husband in the Philippines when I was in nursing school. We had a mutual friend. I came to the United States before him (I arrived in April, he came in November or December). Coincidentally, it turned out that he came to St. Louis to work at St. Anthony's Hospital. I was still at St. John's at the time, so he came to visit me until I started to work at St. Anthony's. We fell in love there working together.

We have only one child, a daughter. My daughter is about forty now. She has three children, ages sixteen, thirteen, and eleven. I have a sister living in Hawaii; her children are in Chicago and St. Louis. I also have a brother in Los Angeles. Some of his children are there as well, and some of them are in St. Louis. My third sister and her children are here, too.

My husband helped me a lot around the house, because we both worked. We don't have maids here, unlike in the Philippines, but we have appliances and electronic equipment, which do help a lot. I worked full time. During that time, my daughter stayed with a woman who babysat several Filipino children. We thought about adopting a second child for three years. But because we both worked, we couldn't afford to stay home for two years to adopt, so we ultimately decided against it.

I didn't have any problems with my in-laws, since we only made short visits to the Philippines after we were married. We had a good relationship, though. They were very nice people. I was close with my parents. As a child, I visited them every day since they lived within walking distance. They also stayed in the Philippines because of their age. My father died in 1961, and my mother is also dead.

As a child, I didn't do any housework; I only played. I only learned to cook when I came to the United States. I cook Chinese food—chop suey, egg rolls, bouillabaisse—which is similar to Filipino food. In the Philippines, the wife stays at home, raises the children, takes care of her husband, and does the housework. Wives are more submissive there, but in America, my husband and I talk with each other, express our opinions, and then agree on whatever we decide. In America, women have options. Life is much easier in the United States, because here we have appliances. In the Philippines, it's necessary to get a maid or stay at home full time.

I would like to think I was strict in raising my daughter, but you do have to be more relaxed in the United States. In the Philippines, you have to ask your parents' permission where you are, where you go, and what you do. If we didn't want my daughter to go somewhere, she just insisted and left. I wanted her to be home at a certain time and I stayed up waiting for her—she was my only child, and I didn't know what happened out there when she was away. We also disagreed on the way she dressed. She didn't clean much in the house, either—she would just pull out her clothes and throw them on the floor. I tried to help her with homework, but she insisted that what she was learning was different from what I learned in the Philippines. At home, we speak Tagalog or Ilocano. When she was young, we always went out to eat, we spent time outdoors, and we loved to travel. We went to Europe, Hawaii, and California when she was growing up.

Nowadays, my husband and I go out to dinner and drive to Florida. We also spend a lot of time with our grandchildren. We don't get any news from the Philippines unless my sister calls me. We're quite interested in American politics and news though, but my husband is a Democrat and I'm a Republican, so we argue sometimes. We participate in some Filipino community activities, such as the Filipino American Nurses Association. They have fundraisers, barbeques, and dances. There is also the Filipino American Association, which had picnics and entertainment such as folk dancing. We go to Assumption Catholic Church at least every Sunday. Sometimes I will go multiple days, and my husband attends every day.

We have some friends from church and the neighborhood. We go out for dinner or lunch once a month with my neighbors, just three couples. We meet both Americans and Filipinos when we attend parties and dinner dances. It doesn't matter if a couple is Filipino or American, though Americans are more friendly and approachable.

I tried to raise my daughter to be Catholic. She went to Catholic school, and was the only Filipino or foreigner there. She grew up here, since she was only a year old when we returned to the United States from the Philippines. She went to dance class when she was three. In grade school, she played softball, volleyball, and joined Girl Scouts. She was very active socially. Since I was working at the time, I didn't have the time to drive the distance to many Filipino cultural activities, so she was not active in the Filipino community. In that way, she was raised as an American. She had a few Filipino friends from her babysitter when she was younger, but she grew up with more American kids. She's very Americanized. I tried my best to raise my daughter in the right way. Now she's raising her own children; it's different, but she doesn't like it when I interfere or criticize her children's behavior.

In the Philippines, I was taught to be respectful and helpful, especially to older people. Attentiveness and kindness were also important. I tried to instill this in my daughter and grandchildren. My grandchildren are very respectable, sweet, and lovable, and they listen to you ... sometimes. I think many American parents try to instill similar values in their children. I knew the parents of my daughter's friends well, and they were all very nice. All in all, I am very happy I came to the United States. If I had stayed in the Philippines, there would have been no advancement or opportunities. I would not have gone to college. America is a very nice country. We have traveled to several countries and there is no place like the United States. It is still the best place to live. We have everything—advancement and education, culture and opportunities—what else do you want?

7

The Younger Generation:
Defining Identity

Leonora Juliano was born in St. Louis, Missouri, in 1979 to Filipino parents who immigrated to America in the late 1970s to escape the political persecution in the Philippines. She was a sociology major at Truman State University at the time of the interview in 1999.

My name is Leonora Juliano. I was born in 1979 in St. Louis, Missouri. My parents are originally from the Philippines. They came over a little while before I was born, in the late 1970s. My grandfather and my family were heavily into politics. They were kind of an opposing entity, against Marcos and his martial law. It was probably safer for my family to move to the United State when they did. It was a good thing.

I have three brothers and four sisters, and I am the youngest. My mom was more active than my dad with raising the kids. I think my mom was more lax with me because I was the youngest. I know she was a lot stricter with my older sisters than she was with me. I'm the only child who was born in the United States and went through the entire educational system here. I think that had a lot to do with my upbringing. I also think that the Filipino society is more about respecting your parents and obeying everything they say and in the United States, it's not like that. My mom tried to adjust and be more relaxed when it came to dealing with me. I think I am the most assimilated out of all of my siblings. They spent more time growing up in the Philippines, while my formative years were spent in America.

When I was growing up, my parents really socialized a lot with other

Filipinos and were really involved in the community. There were always other Filipinos around. But when I went to school there would be maybe only a few other people who were Asian American. In high school I knew three other Filipino kids and we all stuck together. It was hard because people would call us "the Asian crowd" and thought we were separatists. We didn't look down on Americans, but we could really relate to each other and we had similar issues at home. Our parents were all friends, too. I miss having them around to relate to them. It's hard to talk to other people about it that wouldn't understand because they've never been the objects of racism. But I do think I was more sensitive to Asian American issues when I was around other Filipino Americans. I think it was because we were targeted more as a group.

My parents went to college when they were in the Philippines, but that's all I know about their education. As far as I know, their educations were pretty similar. I went to school in the United States for a few years, until second grade, and then my family moved back to the Philippines. I went to school there for about three years before coming back. Those transitions were really difficult, going between the societies. In the Philippines, school is very strict. They expect a lot out of the students. If you don't do what they ask you get punished. It's very regimented. I think the American system tries to be more lax, a little more understanding. On my first day of school in the Philippines, I was yelled at for not standing up when answering a question. There were little things like that which I wasn't accustomed to doing, and had to unlearn once I got back to the United States.

One thing that made the transition easier was the fact that my parents spoke their native language at home. Initially they would speak Filipino and I would answer in English, but eventually it grew on me. It wasn't as hard of a transition because I had the background at home before we went to the Philippines. Sometimes I worry that my Asian part is lost. My mom sometimes complains that I'm becoming too American. But what can I do? I'm not around Filipino Americans all the time. People take from what's around them, and I'm generally around Americans.

My transition to junior high was bad. It was awkward because I wasn't used to the American school system. I felt like I had missed out on a lot of American history and culture and geography. I remember the first day we did an activity where we wrote down as many of the states as we could. I could only name about two because I had never learned them. That wasn't part of the curriculum in the Philippines. I only knew Florida and Missouri so those were the only ones I wrote down. My parents had talked to my teachers and told them I had been gone, so they kind of understood. But they still were surprised by what I didn't know. I didn't have as much trouble in math and science.

My teachers never brought up my background in class, but it never bothered me. It's not a major part of an American history class. The Philippines was once a possession of the United States, and that was mentioned a few times. But other than that there was little talk about it. It was never really an issue growing up. We didn't learn a lot about Asian American issues or the history of the Philippines. But we were such a small percentage of the school and I learned a lot at home and especially when I was in school in the Philippines. I would have missed out on a lot of my heritage and culture if I hadn't moved there, so I'm glad that I did.

I do think that a lot was expected of me from my teachers because I'm Asian American. I've actually written a paper about it. I noticed it especially in math courses. I think I was expected to be the smart, hardworking Asian math student, but I wasn't. I was the exact opposite. They put me in higher-level math classes because I tested high on something a long time ago. They expected me to do well in those classes but I didn't at all. I remember teachers signing me up for math contests; I don't know why they did. I was a disappointment to all of my math teachers. I did better in English and creative writing. I don't think it's like that here at college.

I think in general, though, that my teachers were open-minded. In English, my teachers tended not to stereotype me as an Asian American. Whereas in math, I thought they did. I could have just been overly sensitive, but that's what I thought. I remember once when I was in high school there were announcements for yearbook photos. They called for everyone in the math club to go and a girl turned around and asked me if I was in it. I told her I wasn't. I had never talked to this girl before. I guess she equated Asian Americans with the math club. I don't think there is any basis for that stereotype; I think it's just been perpetuated. I think that the hard work ethic is there, especially from parents, but my friends and I tend to be the opposite. I grew up in American culture and have similar interests to most students. One of my sisters doesn't look as Filipino as the rest of the family, and she didn't feel the pressure as much at school. Her outward appearance was different, but she did have that culture at home.

Most of the pressure for me to succeed came from home. I was jealous of some of my American friends because they could get Cs and it wouldn't be a big deal to their parents. Whereas if I got a C, it would be a big deal. My parents would ask what was wrong. They drove me to be perfect and to get perfect grades. It's still like that. Of course my parents also always wanted us to be happy. They would try to create a balance, but I could tell my performance wasn't always up to their standards.

My mom definitely expected more from the girls than from the boys. A couple of my brothers went to college but didn't graduate. One of my brothers is a doctor. I tend to think my brothers had it easy; they were underachievers. They were good in sports, so that's what they focused on. My mom focused on academics for us girls. For the most part, my sisters went to college and were on the straight and narrow goals because there was pressure from my mom. I've thought about it a lot and I really don't know why. I went to an all-girls school in the Philippines, so I didn't associate much with boys. I don't know if the difference in treatment between boys and girls is a cultural thing, or just my mom.

I think that gender roles are more emphasized in the Philippines. Women are expected to stay home and fit some sort of mold. I think women in the United States have more opportunities. But I'm still surprised by some of the ideas that boys grow up with. They can have false ideas and be ignorant of feminist issues. Sometimes they make crude jokes about women. It surprises me sometimes. I think in general the university community is pretty understanding of women. But, then again, sometimes I think I'm fooling myself. There are some people who are sexist and upset me.

I wasn't worried about my background affecting my chances in college. I thought if anything it would help me more than hurt me. Colleges probably try to recruit more minorities. But I do think I'm expected to have a more active role. The Multicultural Affairs Office always tries to contact me to get me involved, but I don't feel a pull to be part of the Asian-American community here at college. Maybe I'm just too apathetic and lazy. I would like to get more involved in Asian American issues; it does interest me, but I just don't take an active role here. I do know a few other Asian Americans here, but only through work. There aren't many of us around or a lot of opportunities for me to get to know them. I think there is an Asian American student alliance set up by Multicultural Affairs. I think they're doing as much as they can with such a small population. I think it would be different if I went to a bigger school. I would probably take on a more active role. But that wasn't a consideration when I was applying to schools.

I've heard members of other minority groups complaining that Multicultural Affairs focuses too much on blacks. But I've never experienced that. Sometimes when I'm looking for books about Asian Americans, I can only find a section from a book about minorities. I think there is more of an emphasis on African American issues in general, but just because there is a larger number of them in America and they take an active role in their situation.

Since I work in the International Student Office I think people assume I am one. It's just people's perceptions here because there isn't much diversity. So when people see someone from a different background they'll assume they're an international student. I don't take offense to it. But sometimes I wish I could just be an American student. Over the years I've accepted that I can't because people make assumptions based on appearance, and my appearance is Asian American. It's something that I have grown up with and understand that it's how people see me and make assumptions based on that. Sometimes I can tell people are apprehensive because they aren't sure if I can speak English well and are surprised when I do.

Sometimes I forget that I look different. I'm reminded by little things here and there. I think I have been the object of racism, but not a lot. I think it's generally out of frustration. If people are mad at me, the first thing they can attack me with is my appearance. They call me Jap or Chink or something like that. That reminds me that I'm not really an American. It's hard to create an identity that's both Asian and American; it's two totally different cultures. Sometimes I feel more American and sometimes I feel more Asian. I try to create a balance. The duality is frustrating sometimes. But I do feel like I have assimilated into American culture, as much as I can. I have lived here for the majority of my life.

I am a sociology major. I'm not exactly sure why I chose that field; it's just one that interests me. I took an anthropology class and was interested in it, in studying and understanding different cultures and their practices. It's something that has always interested me. I think being a minority is a large part of that. I am an Asian American, but I'm also an American student. I try to understand both cultures and who I am and create an identity for myself. I perceive it as a personal struggle.

I haven't taken an Asian studies class but I really want to. When I write papers for my anthropology courses I find myself focusing on Asian American issues. I'm interested in the topic and it's something I can relate to. I wrote a paper on the model minority theory to help me understand myself more and to learn more about the topic. I also tend to focus on gender issues as well. I try to figure out who I am and my place in society. It's difficult because I have two blows against me, being a woman as well as being Asian American. Next semester I'm taking an Anthropology of Gender course. I talk to people who work at the Women's Resource Center and go to some of their programs. I think it's an important part of the university community. I try to understand feminist issues. I think part of it comes from the fact that my mother was such a strong woman. Her success influenced me to be a stronger person. My mom is one of the strongest people I know. For her to grow up in Filipino society, I know she had to work even harder than she would have here. She has overcome a lot of obstacles.

I have had one Asian American professor at college. I had her for French. I went to her office once and she asked me where I was from. I told her I was from the Philippines and she told me she was from Laos. Maybe she perceived a connection, but I didn't see it. I think she wanted to find out more about my background, but I wasn't really interested in sharing it. I think it's harder to bind Asian Americans together because each group has a different experience. My home life had a big impact on my life. My parents put a lot of emphasis on being Filipino, whereas some other parents don't. I'm glad they did because it helped me to understand my background more.

I think being Asian American has an influence on what I do and my interests. At school I'm active with *The Monitor*, the student newspaper on campus. I think that stems from being the object of somebody's racism. I try to preach being more tolerant of other races. I think *The Monitor* is all about tolerance and trying to be open. That's what I'm interested in. Being an Asian American, I wish society would be more tolerant and open, and *The Monitor* perpetuates that. Working at the International Student Office also helps me understand what it means to be in a minority group. It gives me a sort of satisfaction helping other students who aren't part of the majority.

My freshman year, I had an Italian roommate and we both felt like we didn't fit in. We weren't average students here. I saw how she struggled and thought it was similar to being part of a minority group even though she was white. People still treated her as a minority because of her accent. She wasn't treated like a normal person. I saw her struggle to fit into the community and I wanted to help out in my own little way. So I started working at the International Student Office. I think it's hard for international students to adjust. I do see them bonding, because they all have similar struggles that bind them together.

I do plan to continue with my education. I don't know if I'll be ready after my graduation here, but I really want to go into Asian American studies in grad school. I think it's probably more selfish than anything. I want to understand where I come from and what other Asian Americans go through. I do want to take my interests a step further and have a more active role.

I don't know what I want to do in the future. I've been toying around with the idea of working with the Asian American community in St. Louis. I would like to do something along those lines. I would like to give back to the community. With my experiences growing up, hopefully I can lend an open ear to those that are struggling with the same issues that I did. I think my parents expect me to. They are very active with the Filipino American community in St. Louis. They socialize and have meetings and they want me to be more involved. They push me towards that, but they understand if I don't want to; they don't try to force me.

If I have a daughter someday, I hope to instill in her pride for her heritage. I hope I can teach her about her background and Filipino culture and traditions. I want to create a balance, like my parents did for me. I want her to understand her culture while still being part of American culture. I would help her create an identity and provide her with information. Hopefully she'll take something away from that.

———————

Sarah Perez was born into a middle-class family in Batac, Ilocos Norte, Philippines, in the 1970s. She came to the United States with her parents in 1990. She was a sophomore nursing major at the University of Illinois at Chicago at the time of the interview in 1994.

I was born in the Philippines in a town called Batac in the province of Ilocos Norte. My parents were both educated. My mom graduated with a degree in education and became a teacher. Although I forgot what degree my dad had, I think it was something to do with business. My father worked at a bank in the Philippines. Here in the United States, he works at a company sorting mail and stuff. My mother works in the United States as a hospital clerk.

I think my parents have high expectations for me about school. I do not feel that this is linked to my gender. I think it is more value-based. I have one brother. He is a junior in high school right now. I do not feel that my brother and I are ever treated differently because of our gender. I feel that my parents are fair.

We came to the United States in May of 1990. I do not really know when they decided that we were moving to the United States. They told me a month before we were going to move to the States. I was surprised because although we knew we were going to come here someday, my brother and I did not expect it so soon.

I think that my parents decided to come to the United States for a better life. Things were getting hard in the Philippines. Money was hard to come by and everything was expensive. The first airport when we arrived was the O'Hare Airport in Chicago, Illinois. We came to Chicago because our family lives here; my dad's parents, sisters, and brothers all live in Chicago.

However, at first I did not want to move here. I told my parents, "I'm not going with you and I'm staying here!" I wanted to finish school in the Philippines, not in the United States. My friends were in the Philippines and I did not want to adjust to a completely new environment. Now I have an immigrant visa and I like it here. It is okay because I have adjusted and have new friends. I finished my sophomore year of high school in the Philippines. I graduated from high school in the United States, from Von Stueben High School. Now I am a sophomore majoring in nursing at the University of Illinois at Chicago.

There are a few major differences between my schooling in the United States and my education in the Philippines. I would say that the teachers in the Philippines are stricter, and there were more subjects in a semester. We studied biology, chemistry, and physics; all of the sciences and math in one year. We had twelve courses every year. I think there was a bad part to that system; we could not really concentrate on one subject. There were more subjects at once, but you did not learn as much about each subject. Here in the United States, we took biology and algebra in one year. I would say that this is better. It allowed me to concentrate and explore each subject more extensively.

For high school in the Philippines, I was in a special science class; one had to have a certain average grade to stay in it. If that requirement were ignored, they would expel one without any question. They did not use corporal punishment in high school, but they did use it in elementary school. The teachers would hit you with a stick or pinch you. We spent more time in school in the Philippines. We would start school at 7:00 AM, get out at 11:00 AM, go back at 1:00 PM and leave at 5:00 PM because we had more subjects.

There are also differences in my relationships with friends there and in the United States. I was closer to my classmates in the Philippines because I knew them better. We went to school together since kindergarten, and we knew each other well. Here, I had just met my classmates; they were like total strangers.

Teenagers here are more open, though. They kiss in public. When I first got here, I would see people hugging and kissing in the streets. You did not do that kind of thing in public in the Philippines. We are shyer because if someone saw you doing something like that in the Philippines, they would talk about you. Now I am used to it.

Another difference is that I have more free time here in the United States, especially now that I am in college. I usually go out in my free time. Sometimes I study, but most of the time I go out. Right now I am taking biology, chemistry, and math—all 100-level classes. My classes are very big with two hundred people in lecture. That is very different from high school where we had much smaller classes. It is okay, I guess. For the big classes, it is only for lecture. Once a week they divide the class into groups of twenty-five to discuss whatever we learned in the big group. The average class size in the Philippines was thirty people.

I work now too. I work at the Jewel Food Stores as a cashier and I like it. It is easy, I get along with my coworkers, and we hang out too. Almost none of my coworkers like my boss, but he is okay with me. I have never had any conflict with my coworkers or with my boss. I did not work while I went to school in the Philippines. We spent more time in school, so most students did not have time to work. Here, working and going to school is like a normal thing. There, school is the only thing.

I have experienced discrimination once. At school, I was waiting for the bus and there are always African Americans there. I got pushed while I was trying to go up into the bus. I heard someone say, "Hey, that Chinese girl is going up!" or something like that and then he or she started laughing at me. I did not really say anything and blew it off. I was going to correct them—I am Filipina—but I thought, "Forget it." I was mad because I was waiting for the bus for a long time and they just pushed me and laughed at me for no reason. I was madder at the fact that they pushed me than I was at the racial slur. I have never experienced any discrimination at school or at work. I have been to Wisconsin, Indiana, and Canada, all of which are predominantly Caucasian and I never experienced discrimination in those places either.

My plans for the future include finishing nursing school and getting a job. I am not going for a master's degree in nursing; I will think about that later on. I was first attracted to nursing when I was a kid. I wanted to be a doctor, but that takes too long. Nursing is hard enough right now, but I enjoy science. I want some money; I am not interested in business or in anything else, so I decided on nursing. I hope to stay in Chicago because I like it here. Some day I would like to go back to the Philippines just to visit. I would not want to live there again. Life is easier here. Things are more expensive in the Philippines; I cannot work and go to school there. It is hard to get a job, and the weather is hotter too.

I like everything in the United States. Despite this, I have been raised in the Filipino way. Most children are let go at the age of eighteen. I am nineteen and still living at home, and I like it. This is normal for Filipinos. We still eat Filipino foods, but we eat other kinds of food now too. I am not sure if I will marry a Filipino or not; I am pretty open-minded about it. I hope that being a woman and an Asian will not affect my chances of getting a job here in the future.

Dalisay Lopez was born in Chicago in 1976 to Filipino parents who immigrated to the United States in the 1970s as a mechanical engineer and a registered nurse. She was a nursing major at St. Louis University at the time of the interview in 1994.

I was born on 23 January 1976 in Chicago, Illinois. Both of my parents finished college. My mom has a BSN (bachelor of science in nursing), and my dad is a mechanical engineer. They are both professionals. There are no expectations of me just because I am a female. My parents have high expectations because of the way they raised me and because of the education I have been given. I finished high school at probably the number one high school in academics in our state and I am in a good college. So far, I am doing pretty well.

I think that my parents were stricter with me because I am a girl and because I am the youngest—it makes it worse. I guess I did get a lot of freedom when I was younger, but I abused it and I am not going to go into details with that. Since I abused that freedom, it seemed like the older I got the stricter they became. For instance, I had to be home at a certain time. There was a double standard for the boys and me. But they are not too bad.

However, as far as guys and dating, that is where the boy-girl differences surfaced. I had to wait. Many things happened. I just was not allowed to date as freely as my brothers did until now, actually. Even now, I still have this fear of dating freely because my parents would say, "You're not going to have a boyfriend until you finish college." That was not the way it would happen, but that is the way they wanted it. Whenever I would argue with them when I was younger, everything would come down to "because you're a girl."

That shouldn't have been a reason for them restricting me as far as being able to go out and come home as late as I wanted. The reason should not have been "that you're a girl." It should have been because I was too young. In addition, young would have been a more convincing reason than "you shouldn't drink because you're a girl." They do not mind my brothers drinking. My parents' reasoning is that "girls shouldn't drink because that looks bad." They just say stuff like that.

They wanted to bring us up in the Filipino way. But with us being raised in America, they had to learn the American way and how to mix the old-fashioned traditional Filipino values as well as the American ones and keep in mind that we are in America and not in the Philippines. Dating at a young age is American. Dating and going through several guys (for women) and girls (for men) is American. Going out with one girl or one boy that you are going to marry, and kissing only that one is Filipino. Dating other races is American and dating only a Filipino is Filipino.

I think about how I am going to raise my kids when I have them. It is hard to say the way I am going to do it. Someday I do want to have a family, but I am confused right now on how I will raise my children. I am not so concerned about raising the guys. I rather understand that double standard. I would not tell my daughter "because you're a girl." I would find some other reason to give even if it's "just because I said so." It is hard to be fair. As far as American and Filipino traditions, it is hard to say which way I am going to choose to raise my children, because I do like the Filipino way but I guess it is too rigid. You need that for children though, but I am not saying that the American way is all freedom. I am going to have to somehow do what my parents did. I do not know. It is too hard to put it into words.

I have two older brothers. I guess that they both receive the same kind of education except that they both go to public universities, which does not make a difference; it is just cheaper. My tuition is expensive.

I go to St. Louis University (SLU). I am a nursing major. So far, I am not set on nursing but it is the direction I am headed. I am sure I want to be in the medical profession. I do not want to be in business. It just seems like you must have that kind of personality or a certain kind of drive to become a businessman or woman.

I did not choose a university in Chicago because I rather wanted to get away from home. I wanted to be on my own. That is a reason I did not pick a school in Chicago like Loyola or University of Illinois at Chicago. I did not pick Northeast University because I have never lived in a small town and I do not think I would want to. In addition, I wanted cultural diversity. At SLU, it is pretty mixed. It makes me feel a little more comfortable.

I have never experienced any kind of racial prejudice at SLU. Throughout my life, I might have bumped into somebody that would say something. It is not so much that I remember an incident. It was not really a problem. I just thought I would be more comfortable at SLU because that is where all my friends are. I have many friends that are from different cultural and racial backgrounds.

Academically, I was prepared for college. I have the same kind of study habits. I have to discipline myself a little more because I do not have to be in class straight through. I have more time to just do nothing. Socially, since my school is not big on fraternities and sororities, I did not join one. That was not a big deal in getting to know people. Even though it probably would have helped me, I really did not have a problem with meeting new people. I do not think that I am going to join a sorority. Some of my friends actually did join sororities. I wish I had gone through rush, but I did not.

It is weird because it seems like the kind of people I am hanging out with or starting to hang out with at SLU are similar to my friends in high school as far as being from different backgrounds and listening to the same music. I guess those are the kind of friends I get along with really well and connect with the most. I like to go out and dance, so we go out to clubs. We have been to the raves [underground dance parties], to a club called Felix's. It was a bar, but they have dancing there. We like hip-hop, techno, rave, and dance music. I usually hang out with mellow people, those who are not too hyperactive and somewhat laid back.

In high school, I was comfortable so academics did not really stress me. I was stressed in high school, but because I was comfortable with my friends and with being at home as a security, I was able to have a lot of stress relieved. As far as it being that way at SLU, it is stressful because I was uncomfortable. I was adjusting. I was stressed out. I feel like I am still adjusting, but I am more comfortable than I was earlier this school year.

I expected the city of St. Louis to be like the city of Chicago, which was somewhat disappointing. It is not culturally diverse; it is mainly a black and white mixture, which disappointed me. There is not that much to do, not a lot of places to go either, unless I have not found these places. I am getting the impression from people that live here that they think St. Louis sucks. I am not saying that it does, but no one is making me think otherwise. The University is fine. I have only been here for a few months.

I see myself finishing nursing at SLU, but as far as graduate school, I see myself going somewhere else. Right now I am just thinking about going to graduate school for nursing. I am thinking about going to graduate school in Chicago. I would really like that a lot. Medical school is also in my mind; it is an option. But unless I have this burning desire to become a doctor, it is not going to happen. I want to be in the medical profession because I like just helping people, being around people, and making things better. It's not only about that—making people better or helping them. Being in the medical profession, especially in nursing, it is easy to find a job. You pick your own hours, and the pay is good.

I am not antisocial at school but I am not a social butterfly. I can talk to people but I do not usually approach people. My own group is kind of building now. I did start hanging around with a group, but we all rather faded. I guess that in the two months that we knew each other, we all went our own ways. We found out that we did not have a lot in common or something. There are many people around to meet, and still I do not know everybody yet. The friends I did meet are in sororities, and they are separating because of that. They have other things to do and they have their own groups.

I have not really talked to any of my professors so I don't have a relationship with them. I have two lecture classes, about two hundred students in each. I do not talk to my professor a lot, but I do talk to my TA (teacher's assistant). I always ask him questions during our chemistry lab. Other than that, I talk to my English teacher because it is a class of twenty students. It is somewhat easier to talk to the teacher. However, as far as large classes, they probably do not know who I am.

There is not that much to do for fun at SLU. It is not a party school. They do have parties, but I have not been to any fraternity or sorority parties yet. There are raves in St. Louis. I have been to a couple. At raves/underground parties, many bad things happen as far as drugs. I am not into that. I like to dance. It is a very free environment. You feel so free there. It is a free party. It is like a party for you. You can do anything you want. You can meet people, but there are a bunch of weirdoes; you have to be careful. There was a rave right behind my dorm because at my school there are warehouses. So many people from my school went. We went back and forth from the dorm to the rave because they stamped our hands. If we wanted to rest, we could just leave. We could have gone back and danced if we want to.

I also have some family and friends in St. Louis. I have my god-mother who lives twenty minutes away from St. Louis. I have family friends down here who live fifteen minutes from St. Louis, but I have not called them or talked to them since my parents dropped me off at SLU. It is just nice to know I have somebody to call and who will be there for me.

I have not volunteered or joined any social clubs or any kind of club at SLU, besides going dancing and raving. In high school, I was in Club Asia, an organization for those interested in Asian culture. We just met every other week and went on outings to Asian restaurants. We put together traditional Asian dances. Actually, we only did a Filipino dance—*tinikling*—using two bamboo sticks. I did a show for Open House. We did not have a Festival of Nations [a cultural exhibition within St. Ignatius] because we have it every other year. Therefore, we had a Mini-Festival of Nations.

There are different cultural clubs in my high school and each club puts together a dance from their own ethnic group for the Festival of Nations. Club Asia usually does *tinikling*. It also has other dances, like the two dragons' dance from China; I do not know what it is called. We also have Japanese dances. The Middle Passage, an African American Club, does African dances.

I was also a tutor in high school. I tutored at an elementary school in the Pilsen neighborhood on the south side, a predominantly Mexican neighborhood. I did not feel any kind of discrimination there. They welcomed us. We felt very comfortable there. I thought of it as a great experience to work with kids. I want to get involved with tutoring in college because I know they have that as far as volunteering. I have not done that yet because I was too busy adjusting. I know that's probably a poor excuse, but I would like to do that again. I really miss tutoring and working with young kids because it gives me a feeling of accomplishment. I also did a lot of volunteering in soup kitchens.

I have tried to get up for church on Sunday at SLU, but it is hard to get up. That also is a poor excuse because they even have a mass at 10 PM at night for college students. I have tried to go when I could.

I have been outside the city because St. Louis is not really all that big. It is not hard to get out of the city. I have been to Washington University. Washington University, to me, is a party school. They are probably stressed out and need to party because I think more than 50 percent of the students are pre-med. They are crazy. I like going there. It is fun. I have not been to any parties there, but I have a couple of friends that go to Washington University and we hung around there.

I have a boyfriend. He goes to a community college in Chicago. We have been together for a long time, so we thought it was time to see other people. We had no reason to break up so we kept the relationship and can see other people. I do not have a boyfriend in St. Louis because none of them have really worked out yet. I met a guy. I still talk to him but nothing has been said about liking each other. I know he likes me but he also likes many other girls. However, I am not looking for any kind of commitment. I am just looking around, dating, and having fun.

I would not do it any differently than going to school at SLU. I would not be at home. Being away or not having other people that I knew around was quite an experience because I am not used to not having anybody there for me. It is teaching me to be independent because I did not realize how dependent I was on my parents. Of course, I am financially dependent and will be for a while. I just relied on coming home from high school every day. Unless something bad happens in St. Louis, I think I will be here for a while. However, I do not think I will get a job here. I could not live in St. Louis. It just would not be a good place for me to live. It does not seem like there is much to offer me. There is just so much to offer in Chicago. I have not traveled outside of the Midwest recently. I traveled to New York and California, but it was a really long time ago. There is no place I can say I'd want to live because it's been such a long time. I am sure that other places have things to offer.

I like Filipino food. I guess it is because I do not have it anymore. I miss it. I do not know all the names of the foods. I like *pansit* (noodles), *palabuk*, egg rolls, all the popular stuff. In fact, one of my Filipino friends and I went to church together and went to an all-you-can-eat Filipino food buffet after church at a restaurant near SLU.

I went to the Philippines once. I don't remember any feelings or sensations. I see pictures, and the only reason I say pictures is that I look at pictures from the Philippines. All I can say is that it was hot; there were many beaches, a lot of dusty roads, and street markets. I would definitely want to go back there to visit because I am older now. I will remember everything better. I will have the whole experience of being there and just going there instead of being dragged there when I was a kid.

As far as my relationship with my relatives of the same age group that have come over from the Philippines, we were raised by the same kind of Filipino parents. I did not really get close to them until they adjusted to America. They think American education is behind Filipino education. They think it is better over there. I do not know why they would think that because they come here to get educated and work. I personally get along well with my cousins, but many of their friends are first generation. They all speak Filipino and I feel alienated sometimes. The fact that we do not know Filipino is another bad thing. I feel like an outsider. I have experienced more prejudice among them and I do not feel comfortable. It is a reverse racism. Being American is not so bad, to remedy it, there has to be a realization of this on their part.

8

Interracial Marriage

Maria Herman was born in the Philippines in 1954 and came to the United States as a nursing student in 1978. She is married to a European American professor of nursing and has three children. She was a professor of nursing at Truman State University at the time of the interviews in 1995 and 2003.

I was born on 13 April 1954 in the Philippines. My mother had a sixth-grade level education. At that time, they said that in the Philippines if you finished the sixth grade, you could teach. My dad graduated from high school. While my dad worked as a driver, my mother had a small business. It was not really a grocery store, but a mixed store, kind of like a dime store. In the Philippines we call it a *sari-sari,* a small type store, where kids could go and buy some candy, snacks, and small toys.

My parents had high expectations of all of their children, not just the boys. I don't think my parents treated the daughters any differently than sons. They wanted us to have more education and better lives than they did. They expected that everyone get at least a college education. I have three brothers and three sisters. My oldest brother made it through most of college, but didn't finish his last year. My other brothers finished college. My oldest sister did vocational training and the rest of my siblings finished college.

I'm the second from the youngest, so I grew up with older brothers and sisters. I probably was treated differently because I was an unexpected child. My older sister was five years old when I came. Then there's another one! I was treated differently at that time after I had a little sister. We were different by age, not by gender.

I came to the United States in 1978. The reason I chose to come to the

United States was really different from most people. My boyfriend at the time wanted us to get married, and I wasn't ready for a marriage. Therefore, I thought that if I could go somewhere for a year, I could put off the marriage.

I initially had a diploma degree in nursing, a graduate nurse certificate from the Philippines. I graduated top of my nursing class and was the valedictorian in my school in the Philippines. While working as a nurse in the Philippines, I went back to school and completed a baccalaureate degree in nursing.

I thought I was very good in English when I first came to the United States. However, to my surprise, I wasn't that good. I learned English from Filipino teachers, so the accent was really different. I was really scared the first time I was in an American hospital listening to reports, because I realized that I didn't know English that much. I couldn't understand what they were talking about, or the way they talked, because it was very fast. That was my initial shock with language differences. It was hard.

While working as a nurse here in the United States, I thought about going back to school. I had to take the Test of English as a Foreign Language (TOEFL) before I left my country. I didn't think I would have problems in graduate school. Since I was always an honor student in high school and college, I was very confident. I think that sometimes self-esteem and confidence really help you. At that time, I felt I was not really excelling the way I was used to. However, I didn't really have any problems. I completed my comprehensive exam and passed.

When I was working on my thesis, I did the whole project and realized I probably was not the good writer I expected myself to be. It took me a year to get my thesis done so I could pass my committee—whew! I realized then that, at the university, there were a lot of foreign students. I also realized that we all had problems doing our thesis or dissertation. The problem was with our writing style, and it sometimes really didn't meet the expectations of the professors. It was hard and it took me longer than I expected to finish my thesis.

I met my husband in one of the small towns in the Midwest where I was teaching in a nursing program. He was a nurse too. We knew each other about a year before we got married. We really have a very good relationship; I can't complain. We communicate well and we respect each other. I think the main thing is that we are very sensitive to each other. He is a very sensitive and very caring person. He is also religious. He has good, strong morals. He is really very straightforward.

One thing that I really like about our relationship is that I can cook and he can cook. I can do laundry or he can do laundry. I can clean the bathroom or he can clean the bathroom. There's really no separation of duties in our house. He changes the oil on the car and that's the thing I don't do. He mows the lawn too. But there is really nothing else. He is wonderful with raising the children. He bathed the kids when they were little. He puts in his share of taking care of the kids. There's no separation of labor between genders. That's the big difference between my household here and the way I was raised in the Philippines. I've never seen my dad cook dinner. He never did work that my mom would do. Therefore, my present family is different from the family I grew up with.

At first I didn't plan to change my citizenship. I had my permanent residency already, and I wasn't bothered by not having citizenship. Permanent residency meant that if you were a professional and had an employer here, then you could apply for a permanent residence, saying that you were a valuable employee, a taxpayer, and then immigration authorities would allow you to stay. I came to the United States on an H-1 work visa. The hospital recruited some other nurses and me from the Philippines, and sponsored us to come over. Then, later on, if you wanted to stay, they asked you if you would like to apply for permanent residence. That is what people call a green card. When we [my husband and I] decided to adopt two kids from the Philippines, we thought if I was an American citizen it would help with the adoption process. We had problems bringing the children back here because of immigration. We thought that if I became a citizen, it would be easier to bring them back here. Therefore, I went ahead with the citizenship for family reasons. However, in fact it really didn't make a difference.

I have three children now. My daughter and my older son are the two that we adopted. After we adopted them I got pregnant. Then I had three kids! Before we had children, I was diagnosed with Crohn's disease. I got pregnant once and then had a miscarriage. My gastroenterologist said it would be better if I didn't get pregnant. So we decided that since we were both professionals, we were both working, and we were loving people, we could give love to children! We wanted children, so we decided to adopt. Actually, the daughter I adopted is my sister's daughter.

So then we went home to the Philippines and asked if she [my sister's daughter]—she was seven years old at the time—wanted to be with us. We told her that we would like to adopt her. She said yes. So we checked on legalities on how to go through the adoption and came back here to the United States. Then we received a call from home in the Philippines saying that my oldest sister was pregnant and that it was an unwanted pregnancy. We were asked if we wanted to adopt this child as well. We had prayed about it a lot at first because we were already committed to this little girl. We had already talked to her. She had already said yes. So we prayed about it, and we said, "Okay, we will adopt the unborn child too when you give birth." We took care of the expenses of my sister while she was pregnant until she delivered the baby. So we knew the little boy was going to be ours even before he was born.

The reasoning behind adopting Filipino children was that when we went to an adoption workshop, they told us that if we wanted to adopt a baby it would be a long wait. It would have been almost impossible because we were a mixed marriage. When they go through the process, they have to look at the placement of the children. They would rather have a white kid in with white parents. And where will you find a mixed Filipino American kid? So you would probably wait ten years or even twenty years. But when we spent our vacation in the Philippines, the topic came up and we were asked if we would adopt this little girl. So we talked about it and discussed it.

Our child raising is mixed. I initially told them [my daughter and son that came from the Philippines] that they were supposed to talk to me in the Filipino language. This was because I really wanted them to be bilingual. My son, after starting school, almost completely lost the Filipino language. My daughter is still bilingual or trilingual. She talks to me in the Filipino dialect, and now she's learning Spanish. She is also mastering English. I want to take them back to the Philippines five years from the time they left and I want them both to be able to communicate with everyone.

So that's why I'm glad for my daughter. She started school in the Philippines and then came over here last year to be a freshman in high school. I told her it was okay and that she would catch up with the others. She's a sophomore now and a straight A student. Last year she had a B. She was very upset about that, because I guess in high school it's cumulative GPA that counts. You see, up to sixth grade, she was in a different school system. I told my daughter, "You should be proud of yourself for catching up with these kids now, because when you finish high school or college you will not have the same problem as I had in graduate school."

The differences between the educational systems in the United States and in the Philippines are the technology. When I was doing undergraduate research, I had to do a lot of manual work, like using the Dewey Decimal System in the library. Here, you can just do a computer search. It's fun going to school in the United States. It's the technology available to us over here that makes learning very easy. I remember going to school over there in the Philippines. We could not afford to copy materials in the library, so we had to stay in the library, read the materials, and take notes. Here when I was in graduate school, every reading that I had to read, I could run it through the copier and bring it with me. Then I could read it and mark in it as much as I wanted.

Going back to school for a doctoral degree is probably the thing I'll have to put off for a while. Before having kids, I was taking courses and planning to go back to school. Then children came along. Maybe I can go back sometime in the future. Robert, my husband, is going back to school in the summers. I have to be the mom and the dad every time he goes back to school. So work-wise, I'll probably be working, either in education or at the hospital. I quit working for about a year, when we had the first two kids. It was really hard, as I had been used to working. I enjoyed staying with my kids, but I stayed as a PRN, as needed, just to be with professionals. I liked being at home, but at least once a week I could be with professionals.

I am a nurse. My specialty and most of my working background is as a critical care nurse. It's the area in which I really work a lot. My typical working day usually starts at six o'clock in the morning, five thirty when we're in the hospital. Otherwise, I usually do office work, preparation, and departmental meetings. Being a new faculty member means a lot more work. I never thought it would be this hard. I worked eight years at my last job, and I had folders for everything I wanted to teach. Here, teaching new stuff, I never remembered how hard it was to start planning lectures again. It's really a lot of preparation that usually doesn't end until four o'clock on clinical days, or five thirty, six o'clock on non-clinical days.

However, I have changed one thing lately. I would like to get out of here earlier—at about four in the afternoon. I stay at home, bring my work home, and I do it in the middle of the night. Usually I do it from midnight to four in the morning. I generally spend my whole evening with my kids. My kids go to bed very early. They're usually in bed by seven thirty or eight. After they go to bed I take a nap too. Then I get up at midnight when every-body is quiet, and do my work. This year and the next will be the hardest years for me since we have a new curriculum. Hopefully, it won't be as hard after that. You can spend less time in preparation. After this semester, there's going to be new assignments. We have extra work to do, so it's pretty hard. But usually, in my experience, the first years are the hardest until I learn the curriculum and know how things are done. For course preparation you have to start from scratch. That's why it's the hardest.

In my house, instead of having potatoes and bread for meals, we have rice. We eat a lot of rice. I do a lot of stir-fry and some Filipino cooking as well. However, my kids are very open to eating. My two little ones like peanut butter and jelly, and macaroni and cheese. What they are fed in school really affects their eating habits. However, the only person that really likes Filipino food is my daughter. I hardly ever cook now because I'm too busy. When I cook something that's Filipino, my oldest son would say, "Oh Mommy, that's yuck! I don't like it." But I would say, "When you were a baby in the Philippines, this was your favorite!" And he would say, "Really Mommy?" Then he would try to eat it. That is important to me.

When we were in Prince Rupert, British Columbia, there was a big Filipino community. My kids really liked it there. It was really nice because there were a lot of cultural events such as the Filipino Christmas celebration. They were celebrating the holidays there in a group, a communal celebration. It was really good for the kids. It was a good transition for my kids to be from the Philippines over there in Canada. We moved to Canada because we couldn't bring the kids here to the United States. So from the Philippines, my kids came to Canada for a year, then we moved back to the United States.

One of the things that I really want my children to keep from the Filipino culture is being respectful. Filipino culture respects the elders and the parents. I think that's why I really don't want my kids to forget about Filipino culture. My daughter has strong Filipino background. It's nice to see her being very respectful.

Another thing about my family is that when we make family decisions, it's usually a dual decision. We do a lot of discussion, especially on major purchases. Usually any major decision is a husband and wife decision. Even buying furniture, we always go together and shop for the things we want instead of just him or just me going. It's close to the family I grew up. My parents made a lot of joint decisions too. My husband is also very supportive of my work.

My husband is an American. His parents are wonderful and I have a wonderful relationship with them. When I first met my husband, I probably would not have really dated him or would not have had a serious relationship with him, had I not met his parents. His parents are both professionals. His father is a professor at a university, and they're just wonderful people. The reason that I felt it was important for me to meet the family when I first dated my husband was that I had all this at the back of my mind. If you married somebody not of the same culture as yours, usually you get discriminated against. I was very aware of that. Therefore, meeting his parents and brother, as well as his grandmother, and seeing how they reacted to me affected my decision. They were all really nice. If they weren't really nice, I probably wouldn't have seriously dated him. My husband knows about that.

A good relationship was very important to me, because I came from a very close family. In fact, when I announced to my family that I was dating this American guy and I was serious with him, they all said "No," except my dad. All of them were scared—even my younger sister told me—that I would regret it. "Americans will just marry you, divorce you, and leave you, and that's it." They said these things because of the stereotypes. One situation that happened to someone else in our neighborhood was generalized. So it was very important for me to know his family. They are nice people. We all have an excellent relationship. I can't complain.

The things I like most about living in America are the freedom and convenience. It was so wonderful to me, when I first had the experience of being able to vote. I never voted in the Philippines. We pay taxes here, but then we have so much the government gives us in return, like good facilities, good schools, and good roads. I also like the peace. You all probably don't realize, living here, that you take a lot of peace for granted—that a lot of other countries have never even known it exists. That's what I like.

I do not like the impersonal things about living in America. Sometimes we become so busy with our lives that we forget about people around us. People in the Philippines are so hospitable and friendly. People have time for each other. Here we're all working, and we're all so busy that we're blind. We forget to say "hi" to our neighbors. That's the thing that I don't like.

There is another aspect of being in America that I don't like. I never realized it until I married my husband. A lot of Filipino women have married Americans who have been in the Philippines in the military. I learned it from experiencing it and also through a friend of mine in San Antonio, Texas. Down there a lot of Filipinas are married to military guys. It isn't a surprise when people think down there that you met your husband in the

Philippines through the military. I remember when we lived in Alva, Oklahoma. Everywhere we went, everyone asked my husband if he had been in the military. Everyone assumed when he or she saw a mixed Filipino American couple that he was a military guy and that we met in the Philippines. My husband always said that he'd been in the military, because he was in the army before he met me. Then they would always say, "I didn't know there was an army post in the Philippines." He would say, "No, I was in Germany." Then everyone asked how he met me. He would tell them that we met in Alva, Oklahoma. I guess there is a stereotype that when an American marries a Filipino woman, he was a military guy and that the woman was not a professional.

I remember that when we moved here, whenever my husband said we met in Alva, Oklahoma, everyone asked what I was doing there. He said that I was a nursing faculty. Everyone was surprised by this. That was really the stereotype that we [Filipino women] were not educated. Moving here to Kirksville, I didn't have a job initially. Robert was the only one with a job. And I said that I would look for a job when we got here. Once we were unpacked and the kids were settled in school, I could always find a job. I usually took our little one for a walk while the other two were in school. One time when we were walking, I told a neighbor, who was a babysitter, that soon I would be going to work and that I was going to need a babysitter for my son. She asked what kind of work I liked to do. I told her that I had this clinical educator job offered to me at the hospital, and her eyes just went so big! She asked what degree I had and I told her that I was a nurse. Then she asked if I was a one-year nurse or a two-year nurse. I told her that I used to teach nursing. Then her eyes went really big to realize that I had a degree to teach! I told my husband that I thought the lady was surprised to know I had a degree. But I guess that I was not surprised by her reaction.

Sometimes people think that if you are not white, then you are not educated. We encountered that when we were moving here. The counselor in the high school placed my daughter in a terminal math class without even asking her if she planned to go to college. We were very angry. I'm explaining that to my kids. Sometimes it's really hard. My daughter is coping with it. The first semester of the first year was very hard for her. Robert and I had to go to the high school several times just to see that the kids don't pick on her. She came home and told us that the kids say things like "We will shoot you." It was very traumatic, the first year. I had to keep telling her to just work very hard and that if she was very smart, then people would be okay. I had never even witnessed racist things like that before in my experience.

Amy Bragg was born in 1971 to an interracial couple. Her lawyer mother was a Caucasian and her psychiatrist father was from the Philippines. She grew up in St. Louis, Missouri, and was a college student majoring in theater at the time of the interview in 1994.

My father is from the Philippines, a little town outside of Manila. I do not know how big the town was because I was raised in the United States. My mom is Caucasian and is from Kentucky. My parents got married in 1968. When my parents were still married, we traveled to the Philippines before I was one year old, so I do not remember the trip. I have many relatives there; I have an aunt and about four cousins who have families of their own. However, I do not know them at all, so it is a bit strange.

My father went to the University of the Philippines. The schooling is a little bit different there because one attends college at a younger age. He came over to the United States as a medical resident in 1963 or 1964. My father came to the United States because many Filipinos wanted to flee the Philippines because of the poverty, and he came for medical school. He went to Baltimore first and then proceeded to St. Louis where he became a resident at Malcomb Bliss Mental Hospital, where he met my mother. She was a social worker. That is how they met and came to be married.

There was no problem with race when they got married, and I thought that was very odd. That was in the late 1960s and apparently there were many problems back then, but neither family had a problem with them getting married. I guess that was rare. I never felt any prejudice or strangeness simply because one of my parents is from the Philippines and one of my parents is white. I never was made fun of as a child. I think I am very lucky. After I got older, I saw all of the prejudice and racist behavior that still exists and I feel very fortunate that I did not have to go through that.

I have one full blood sister, a stepbrother, a stepsister, and a half brother. My parents got divorced when I was five years old, and both of them got remarried about ten or eleven years ago. My stepfather had two children from his first marriage. My father, after he remarried, had a son.

I still have a very good relationship with both of my parents. I am very close to my family, and when they got divorced, my dad actually wanted custody of both of us. In the decree he did not get custody, my mom did, so we were really traveling back and forth the whole time through my childhood. I know them very well. However, I identify more with Caucasian culture; I feel the easiest around white people. Most of my friends are Caucasian, probably because I was raised with my mom. I really was not that immersed in the Filipino culture. My dad, however, really tried to give me Filipino culture. We were always around his friends who speak Filipino in the community in St. Louis. I never picked up the language that he speaks, which is Tagalog. He never really tried to teach it to me. I think if I had been around it consistently day in and day out, I probably would have learned it. I just know a few words. So I guess I am illiterate about the Filipino culture in many ways.

In the Filipino community in St. Louis, where my dad lives, there are several different associations. There is a Filipino Medical Association, a cultural society where they do the traditional dances and have many get-togethers, and other social organizations. Filipinos enjoy having parties and socializing within their community. Being half-Caucasian, I think this is the only difference. I felt like I was particularly different because my mom was white.

I thought that they treated me differently, but I think that was just because my parents had a bad marriage. They really should not have gotten married. But I am glad they did because my sister and I would not be here if they hadn't. My dad has had many bad feelings towards my mom. I thought from the way I was treated by the other Filipinos, although I do not know if it is true, that he was bad-mouthing my mother. I talked to him about it later, and he said that he did not. But I never really knew because I never understood Tagalog. That further alienated me from the Filipino community and I still have some resentment. I am trying to get over that resentment and to embrace the Filipino culture and learn more about it.

I feel guilty because I did not do this earlier. At first, I never considered myself a racist, but I had a lot of resentment toward the Filipino community because I felt like an outsider and I thought that they thought badly of my mother. I did not feel accepted by them. Because I had a lot of resentment, I was probably racist in my thinking. I think that was brought about by my parents' relationship, and my not feeling accepted. Now I try

Tinikling Dance, a native folk dance in the Philippines, 1999. Huping Ling Collection (Courtesy of Kit Hadwiger).

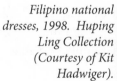

Filipino national dresses, 1998. Huping Ling Collection (Courtesy of Kit Hadwiger).

to be more open. I realized that it is impossible to say that you do not have any racist tendencies because even I realize that it is not so.

I still have family in the Philippines. My father had an older brother who was killed in World War II, and another brother and two sisters. My father's brother was not in the war. He was just a kid running around in the streets—a bomb was dropped and he was killed. There is a lot of pain; my dad never spoke about things from the past. His family was not wealthy, but they had more money than anyone else did because it was very poverty stricken over there. My sister saw this firsthand a couple of summers ago. I found an excuse not to go because of summer school.

I did not want to go. I did not know these people at all, even though they were close relatives—my aunt, uncle, and my cousins. But I did not want to go for some reason, which was somewhat strange. It is a very different way of life over there. I'm very glad that my dad came here and that I grew up in the United States because I would not have nearly as many advantages there as I do here in the United States. That was one of my father's objectives when he came here. It was not only that he married for love, but also it was a better life for him. He could send, like many of the doctors, money back to the Philippines to their relatives because they make so much money here. My father never forgot his relatives there. He is always sending money back. That kind of thing is so important there, and family is important to him. There are many things he can get here that he could not get in the Philippines.

He does not go back to the Philippines very often. The last time he went back was about six years ago. He, my stepmother, my sister, and my half brother went back. Before that, the only other time he had gone back was when my grandfather died. He went because they were burying him in the Philippines. It's very expensive to go back over there unless there is a death in the family.

None of them [relatives living in the Phillipines] has ever come over here. I do not think my dad's sister has ever come here. But my grandfather and grandmother came over and were living with my father and his brother when I was very young. My grandmother died before I was born, and the grandfather who lived here is the one whose funeral my dad went back to the Philippines for.

I think that I would like to go to the Philippines, but I would like to wait three to five more years until I am older and more mature. I still feel very young, still a child. I'm still overcoming many resentments so I think it would be better if I matured a little bit more before I went to the Philippines. By resentments, I mean that I do not have a very good relationship with my father. Filipinos are a very patriarchal society and it is hard growing up with something like that because they are not very liberated. Actually, they really would like to have boys born first. I know that my sister and I were supposed to be boys, because boys carry on the tradition, the family name, etc., etc.

I feel resentment towards my father because of this. Just being a female was very hard, and Filipinos have a difficult time letting their daughters grow up. In respects of education, they want it to be equal for their sons and daughters. The Filipinos wish their children to become doctors and successful businesspeople. Education is extremely important, but dating is different. It has not been that long since there were arranged Filipino marriages. When I was fifteen or so, it really annoyed me when I attended these Filipino functions. I had no way out and I was merely trying to appease my dad by going because I knew he wanted me to be there. But specifically, one time after a wedding, my dad was standing there talking to this other man about his son and how they should get the two of us together, implying that I might marry this guy one day. I was like, "No way. Sorry." This is not the Philippines and I am not going to marry someone that my father arranged for me to marry.

I will not marry a Filipino and that probably goes along with my racist thinking. I would just be too afraid that I would get someone like my dad. There are many things in that culture that I disagree with. As if how you must kowtow to the man; if you are married to a Filipino, what the man says is always right. He takes care of everything and you do not question it. That is not a stereotype because I have been around several Filipino families and their kids. All the time their parents had the same attitudes; dating is a big deal.

Even with the Filipino dances I went to, I have always dated white men. That is just how it was because I totally identified with white culture. The dances were big Filipino functions. The Filipinos like to dress up, spend a lot of money, and have fancy balls. That is another huge part of the culture, wearing those big fancy gowns. There is actually a big Filipino debutante ball and I know my dad would have loved my sister and I to be a part of it. But I think in actuality the Filipinos were racist towards us. There have been other interracial marriages between Filipinos and white women, and the mixed daughters were rather excluded. They always wanted full-blooded Filipinos to be in these pageants. I just merely said, the hell with it, because there was just too much non-acceptance. Even as a female, I felt it.

I have never been good friends with any Filipinos because I was always wary of them. Many of the kids grew up with the advantages their parents did not have. In coming to America, Filipino parents, if they had money, tended to spoil their kids rotten. These kids would have designer clothes, and for a while, I tried to fit into that culture. I was into it as much as they were, and when my true self came out, I realized I was not like that. So I never really developed a close relationship with those Filipinos. It makes me a little sad and regretful, but that is just the way things turned out.

I went to school with many Filipinos too. I think the biggest religion in the Philippines, besides Buddhism, is Catholicism. I grew up as a Catholic, but I do not practice it any more; I do not really consider myself Catholic, even though I have had all of the sacraments. Nevertheless, I went to St. Clemons School and to mass every day except for Saturday. Religion was crammed down my throat. In St. Louis, where I lived out in the country, there are scores of Filipinos. I went on to Visitation, there were numerous girls from privileged families, and it was just an extension of that type of isolation. It was not for me. There were many Filipinos there too. There was this one family, the daughters all had Mercedes or BMWs and thought that everyone on earth was there just to please them. It was really somewhat sad because a lot of those doctors and their wives were very materialistic.

My parents got divorced around 1975, I was about four or five and my sister was less than one. I lived with my mom, and she kept the house in the county. My dad moved down to South St. Louis. He was living with my two aunts, my uncle, and my cousin. My mom was terrific about my dad taking me to all of those dances. Even though my father was very belligerent and hot tempered and hard to deal with, she never said one bad thing about him. She realized that he was our father and that he deserved respect. She never said anything about him taking us to dances; it was fine. Whenever we needed to be somewhere, she took us.

I resented having to go to all of those functions because I felt like an outsider, so did my sister. This is interesting—I look more Filipino, I have dark hair and dark skin, but my sister, who is my full blood sister, looked whiter and more Caucasian. She is about 5 feet 7 inches, has pale skin, and looks like a white person. She said that she felt much excluded from these events because when we were at these functions in the Filipino community, she just felt as if she did not belong. She suspected that people treated her differently because of her appearance.

I do not think, like other minority women including Asian American women, that the feminist movement has excluded me. This is because I have always felt that I was white. Since I was lucky not to be a victim of racial prejudice, I never really had to deal with that issue. Therefore, I never thought that it was a big impassioned deal of mine worth fighting. I identify more with the white culture; I cannot label myself and say I am Filipino American or Asian American. I was born in America. I consider myself a feminist. I guess the biggest cause I have is for women's rights, unity with all women, no matter what color they are. I think that the women's movement is striving for the same causes that I am, and I do not feel alienated at all.

I do not consider myself a minority, or believe that I have been mistreated. I think a lot of it has to do with economics because I was born into a privileged family. My father is a psychiatrist and my mother is a lawyer. Although money has not been so great lately, I do not want it to seem like I have had an easy time with being a doctor's kid, because I really have not, except maybe when I was younger. I think that if I grew up with the same parents but without money, I would have been a victim of racial discrimination. Money has a large effect on discrimination. When you have more money, people are going to treat you better than if you are without money.

I think that this happens in the Filipino community as well. Filipinos stick to levels of money. Many Filipinos perform menial labor and they just do not mix because of the levels of money. Numerous Filipinos that I knew and grew up with are really into status, power, and things like that. They would not mix with people that they considered lower than themselves. I think that they were overcompensating. No matter how much money they have, they are still a different color. They are the minority here; they would not want to associate with poorer people. That would make them less accepted by the white community. Just like the white community with money does not want to associate with poorer people. I think that it is similar with blacks and Cubans too.

I am a theater major but not enrolled right now; I am taking a break. Since I have been out of school, I really appreciate the schooling I have. Recently I found a job at the Country Kitchen where I am a waitress.

While I was in school, I felt no prejudice from teachers. Maybe I would have if I were a dumb student. I really think that if you do not have money, if you are not as intelligent as others, and if you are a different color, these things make a big difference in regards to prejudice. I was lucky to be smart, and hell, I was in a county where people had a lot of money, so people just did not act prejudiced, and the racist behavior was frowned upon.

I do not eat a lot of Filipino food. I used to be on a big health kick; I was a vegetarian but that went downhill. I have been eating a lot of junk food lately; standard American fare, hamburgers, French fries, that is what I like most of the time. I never really liked Filipino food that much. When you go to a Filipino function, they are like, "Eat this, eat that." When you go to a Filipino's house, they always say, "Have some more," and they are offended if you do not eat it.

My dad never cooked. Most Filipino men do not cook; it is not in Filipino culture for men to cook. The women cook and take care of the kids. My aunt, when my dad was living with her, did all of the cooking. Filipino food is really similar to Chinese food. There are a lot of noodles and vegetables. They also like seafood a lot. I have never cooked Filipino food. I would go to these functions, but I just stuck with the rice and noodles. It is funny that the Filipinos like fast food, because there would be Kentucky Fried Chicken at the functions too.

I think that when I have children, I would like to teach them the Filipino culture. I think that I would be learning along with them. I think one day that will be important to me. Even now I've been talking to my dad more about what he knows about our past. I would like to do an extended family tree, and go far back from both sides on my family. I am much more appreciative of the Filipino culture. When I do have children, I probably will be learning with them because I will want them to know where they came from and where their grandfather came from.

I feel that I am at the point where I would like to go to the Philippines now. I am leaving those childhood resentments against the Filipino culture behind. Actually, it is terrible that I have denied my heritage. I had this fantasy, but everybody makes mistakes. I have done a lot of studying about Native American culture, and I always wished that it were my other culture. I have moved past that dream now though. I would like to teach my kids about their Filipino heritage. I would like them to be proud of their heritage, which I unfortunately took for granted.

If I had had a better relationship with my dad, I would have been more willing to accept the Filipino culture. He had a bad temper. He never physically abused us, but he did emotionally. I never talked back to him. I think that also relates to the difference of cultures. It was so different growing up as an American girl as opposed to a Filipino girl. I saw my friends yelling at their dads. I would never think of doing that. I did not question anything my dad did, even if he was wrong. When I saw the other Filipino kids growing up, they were as much into their culture as their parents were. They embraced both the American culture and the Filipino culture and thought it was cool to be different. They had pride about it, but my sister and I did not. Now that I am older, I can understand those feelings. My dad has heart problems, and recently he almost died. That has made me forgive, not necessarily forget, and I was much more understanding. I wanted closure on everything with him. Now he talks to me about the past and treats me as more of an equal, which is good.

I am actually proud that I have this heritage in my life. People thought it was neat, having two parents from different cultures. I am not as closed up as I used to be. I hope that as I grow older, I can be as proud of it as other people I have known.

Part 3
Japanese

The U.S. concentration camps for Japanese Americans have been one of the most controversial topics in Asian American history, and there is a rich body of scholarship, biographies, and media productions on the topic.[1] Shigeru Yamaguchi's reminiscence of the concentration camp experience calmly but eloquently depicts a dark page in our nation's history. From her seemingly simple and emotion-free recollection, one can easily sense the depth of emotional scars left on the surviving internees, and be outraged by the injustice done to Japanese Americans and the violation of their civil rights during World War II. Her family history also adds to the existing literature on the socioeconomic conditions of Japan and the causes for Japanese migration to the United States in the early twentieth century.

Interracial marriages between Japanese women and American servicemen was one of the inevitable and particular consequences of the U.S. Occupation of Japan and the close economic and military ties between the two countries in the post-war era. Anna Crosslin's interview focused on her mother, who has been married to two white Americans, one serving in the military and the other a former servicemen. These marriages typify those of Japanese women who married American servicemen. Her Japanese grandfather's reaction to his daughter's interracial marriage reflects Japanese ambivalence during the U.S. Occupation when the country lost its sovereignty to a thirteen-nation coalition dominated by the United States. Her mother's unpreparedness for a new life in a new land was characteristic

---

[1]On the internment camps, see for example, Austin, *From Concentration Camp to Campus*; Daniels, *Concentration Camps USA*; Daniels, "Incarceration of the Japanese Americans"; and Daniels, *Prisoners Without Trial*. For memoirs, see for example, Houston and Houston, *Farewell to Manzanar*.

of the experiences of many military wives who had limited English-speaking abilities and lacked basic survival skills such as driving a car. The mysterious death of Crosslin's father compounded her difficulties. The interview, however, shows her mother as a survivor with strong characteristics of intelligence, pragmatism, diligence, and determination to be Americanized.

Kazuko Miller's marriage resembles that of Crosslin's mother's in many ways. Similarly, she felt the consequences of World War II in her life. Her father died in 1945, leaving her family in poverty. The hardship of life and the shortage of food in her family during her childhood made her especially appreciative of food. She married an American Navy enlistee because of his "tender kindness" despite her family's rejection. Her patience and open-mindedness earned the trust and affection of her American father-in-law and members of the community. Although still speaking fragmented English, she felt herself an American and enjoyed her marriage, one not filled with money but love.

Masako Smith's recollections provide vivid and useful information on how the marriage ceremony between an American serviceman and his foreign bride was conducted. Because of the opposition from the bride's family, typical in interracial marriages of this nature, and American immigration requirements for the entry of an alien bride, couples often passed up a formal and elaborate wedding in favor of a simple and brief civil ceremony. Masako's husband-to-be wore a jacket borrowed from one friend and a pair of pants borrowed from another. After the staff member at the American Embassy stamped the marriage license and pronounced them as "man and wife," the ceremony was complete.

Mina Yoshida's life history differs from the other Japanese women in several ways. She came to America as a student and met her European-American husband at work in a pharmaceutical company. Compared to Japanese women who married American servicemen in Japan, she was more prepared for her interracial marriage, as well as for her profession as a research biologist. However, she was disappointed at the cultural and gender biases she experienced at work despite the good salary and benefits from her job.

Japanese students provide unique insights on the Asian American life. Although some intended to return to Japan after completing their education in the United States, their American experience enriches the general Asian American history and therefore is worth examining. Maiko

Yamamoto, Yuko Saito, Mayumi Honda, Yukiko Tatsumoto, and Ayaka Tanaka were international students at various midwestern universities. Although their personal situations differed, they shared some common experiences during their stay in America, especially the frustrations of language difficulties and the consequent social isolation. However, they enjoyed the choices and flexibility of the American higher educational system and hoped their educational experience in America would benefit their future careers in Japan.

Christie Smith, a second-generation Japanese American girl, represented a break from the "model" Asian American youth; she was not always interested in academic work. She was, however, interested in learning more about her Japanese heritage so she could better communicate with her mother who spoke fragmented English. Ethnic sensitivity is clearly shown in her life history.

9

The Concentration Camp Experience

Shigeru Yamaguchi was born on Terminal Island (in Los Angeles County), California, in 1925. Her father immigrated to the United States in 1917 and her mother joined him in 1924. Her family was interned in the concentration camp in Grenada, Colorado, during World War II. She was a retired clerk living in Denver, Colorado, at the time of the interview in 1994.

I was born on 10 June 1925 on Terminal Island, California, which no longer exists, but it was in Los Angeles County. My name, Shigeru, is really a boy's name. When I was born, my father already had four girls and really wanted a boy, so he named me Shigeru. Eventually, my parents did have a son. My dad was a gardener for a while and then owned a wholesale nursery business. I really do not know what my dad did in Japan; I think he managed a business, but I do not know what type of business it was. My mother was a pearl diver when she was in Japan.

My dad had an older sister who was blind, so my grandparents adopted a girl to take care of the older sister. When the adopted girl got married, she decided that she did not want to take care of the older sister. In Japan, the oldest son gets everything and because her husband took the Okuno name, which is my maiden name, he got everything from my grandparents. This left my dad with nothing, so he came to seek his fortune in the United States in 1917 or 1919. He left my mother and my four sisters behind in Japan. In 1924, my mother came to the United States to join my father. She brought the two oldest daughters with her and left the two younger ones, who were seven and nine, in Japan. Later in 1924, the immigration law passed stating that if you were from Asia, you could not come to America. Because of this, they could not bring the other two daughters here and both my parents died without ever seeing their two younger daughters again. It is a sad story. I saw the younger one of the two for the first time two years ago, in 1992, and again this past April. I saw the older one of them in April for the very first time. It is kind of like the story *The Joy Luck Club*.

I do not think that I have ever felt prejudiced against. However, one incident bothered me. When we bought our house here in Denver, a representative from Moore Realty showed us our house and that was it. He never came back, so we had to buy our house through the builder. That is the most prejudice we ever encountered. The area where the house was located was one that was predominantly Caucasian. My friends moved into their house only a few blocks away. Maybe the neighbors did not want us in the area because we were Japanese. They felt that when Japanese came in, the blacks would come in and, "Uh-oh, there goes the neighborhood." However, that did not happen; it is still predominantly Caucasian. The newspapers used to refer to us as Japs, but I do not think that I have ever been called a Jap to my face.

There was no Japanese language school back then in Denver. I went to Japanese language schools in California, and I used to write a lot of *kanji* (Chinese characters used in Japanese language), but when you get away from it, you just lose it, unless you are with people who speak it all the time. I think that most *sansei* (third generations) regret that they did not learn the language, but our *nisei* (second generation) Japanese was so poor that we could not teach them. I went to school in Los Angeles—elementary school, junior high school, and high school—but I did not finish above the twelfth grade in Los Angeles. I finished in Amache High School, which was in the concentration camp we were sent to before I graduated during my junior year. I remember that, afterwards, we never spoke about being in the camp. I do not think we held it back on purpose; it was just something to forget. The camp was located just south of Grenada, Colorado. A reunion was held in Las Vegas last month for those still living and they are planning to make the place a park or a monument for the people who were in the camps.

In order to leave the camp, you had to have a job. Someone came to recruit for maids in Chicago, and my friend and I went. My mother gave us permission to leave. Because we were young, they had a place similar to a dormitory for us to stay in. My friend and I worked in a hotel before finding another job in the transformer factory. That is where my future husband was working because he had left a camp in Arkansas and went to Chicago also.

Life in the camp was like living in an army camp, I guess. We had blocks of twelve barracks, a mess hall, a laundry, and a latrine. There were six units on each side of the barracks. Our room was about fifteen feet by fifteen feet. All we had was cots for beds and everything else had to be made. We got five dollars a month, a clothing allowance, and a Sears catalog. Sears made a lot of money off the camps. We do not shop at Sears anymore, and that is why Japanese people do not shop at Sears today. You never knew what you were going to get from the catalogs. You would order one thing and they always sent a substitute. Our camp was quite lenient. We did not have harsh guards. There were two guard towers, but there were no guards watching over us.

10

Interracial Marriage and Immigrant Women in Professional Fields

Anna Crosslin was born in Tokyo, Japan, in 1950 to an interracial couple. Her father worked for the American Air Force in Japan when he met her mother, a Japanese woman. Her mother immigrated to America in 1952 and became a U.S. citizen in 1957. After her father's death in the line of duty, her mother married another white American, a former serviceman; the marriage later ended in divorce. Her mother ran a family restaurant for thirty years. Anna Crosslin was a professional woman living in St. Louis at the time of the interview in 1999.

I was born in Tokyo, Japan, on 24 August 1950. My mother grew up in Himi, a small town nine miles from Toyama on the island of Honshu. My grandparents on my mom's side had a very interesting history. They had always been relatively independent themselves and my mother followed that spirit. My grandparents met when they both played instruments in the imperial marching band. My grandfather was a well-respected Go-master, and at one time, he was rated number three in Japan for his mastery of the game. Throughout his life he made his living by teaching the game of Go to the children of wealthy families. My grandmother died shortly after my mom's birth. My mom was the youngest of eight children—one sister, who was twenty years older than her and essentially raised her and six brothers. Her father remarried and she had a half-sister, but she was never close with her stepmother. They were not wealthy, but they were comfortable. By the end, some children had died in childhood but she lost most of her brothers in World War II. After the war, only

133

her stepmother, her sister, and one brother survived. Her brother and his family live near Mt. Fuji and her sister, who is in her nineties, still lives with her family in Himi.

As another result of the war, opportunities for work were few, so her family moved to Tokyo where she found a job in an office and met my father. He worked as an interpreter for the American Air Force, as he spoke Japanese and Russian, and was stationed overseas during the Korean War. There are a couple of different stories I have heard from my mother as far as the reactions my mother's family had to her interracial marriage. She always told the story that her father was not happy about it and rejected her because of the marriage. In later years, he came to accept that it was perhaps her way of creating separation because she knew she had to leave her family. I understand, from my American grandmother, that my father told her that my Japanese grandfather had come to visit my father before they left Japan and had begged him to take care of my mother and to treat her well and to say that he wanted to maintain contact with the family. I know that throughout my childhood my Japanese grandfather would send me presents on my birthday, and so he maintained contact through letters and through acknowledgment of his grandchildren. I am inclined to believe my American grandmother's interpretation of the situation rather than my mother's. I think they [my Japanese grandparents] accepted the marriage, although I also think they would have preferred that she not marry an American and leave the country.

My father's history, I think, is as equally interesting as my mother's. He was the last of a long line of pioneers on his side. His was one of the earliest founding families in America, as some of our ancestors were on the Mayflower when it came. Some of our ancestors fought in the American Revolution and were also among the pioneers, who moved across the country, resettling various portions of it.

My grandmother was born in Colorado and although her parents farmed, she went to a teacher's college; she was a teacher and later became a social worker. She outlived three husbands and in fact outlived all four of her children, including my father. My father was her last child alive, she accepted it wholeheartedly, and after his death, she became the backbone of the family. She had a pioneer spirit and was very much a survivor. I think my father saw the military as his way to go further west, go to other countries, and continue the pioneer spirit.

My father had a high school education. After high school he attended the Monterey Language School in California. Monterey is the language school the military uses when people show proclivity for languages. While he was there he learned to read and speak Japanese and Russian. He apparently had a strong language ability. He used to say he spent the Korean War sitting on a hill listening to the Russians. But he never talked much more about his work because he was in the intelligence area—it was one of those subjects that isn't discussed. I do not know how many years he had been working, but he was over there for a couple years before I was born, in 1950, and came back in September of 1952. In December of 1952, my sister Linda was born. I have a brother who is deceased. I also have a half-sister and a half-brother who were born in the sixties to my mother and her second husband.

I know a fair amount about my mother's life when she first moved to the United States. She had been home-schooled during high school because she had tuberculosis. My American grandmother, her third husband, and my mother then spent nine months in the hospital. In those days, the only way they had to deal with tuberculosis was isolation. They didn't have modern medicines. Penicillin had been invented but Dimineech had not. We now see all these stories about how they sent people to sanitariums, and that is essentially what they did for her. My sister Linda was born at Fitzsimmons Hospital that December while my mother was a patient there and she was immediately removed from my mother. My mother tells stories that she wasn't allowed to even touch or hold her because they were afraid she was contagious. My American grandmother came, picked up Linda, and took her back to Utah. And so my grandmother took care of my sister and me for the first year after our arrival in the United States. My mother was released when my sister was nine months old, so she would have been in the hospital for twelve or thirteen months altogether; she has had no reoccurrence of the disease after that time.

After that, I lived with my mother and father. We lived in Utah and then we moved to the state of Washington to Larson Air Force Base because my American grandmother and her husband had moved there. My step-grandfather was a carpenter and he built houses. My father was really seeking more of a support structure to help my mother and us adjust, and so he wanted to be near his family. I began kindergarten at Larson Air Force Base and attended part of first grade there. In 1957 my mother received her American citizenship; she had to wait five years to get it. I have a letter from my father telling some friends she had gotten her citizenship.

In March of 1958, my father went ahead of us to fly back to Japan on a military transport for another tour of duty. He was going ahead to find housing and do all those things for the family and we were to follow him four months later. He never reached Japan because the plane crashed. It was at the time, according to newspapers, the largest air search of the Pacific that had been conducted. To this day they have never found any of the wreckage or any indications of what happened to the plane. It was reported that the crash occurred between the Waif Island and Japan. We don't know if the plane was off course. There could have been problems with its mechanical devices putting it off course and therefore the search crew would have been searching the wrong part of the ocean. This happened . during the Cold War; it could have strayed into Soviet airspace. There are a lot of things that could have happened and we will never know. I think that security information relating to it may have possibly been declassified. If I were to do some searches I might be able to get some more details, but quite frankly, it has been so long ago that I have not really felt like opening up the issue again.

In 1958, there was a long period of three months before they declared him dead. It was a very difficult situation. I still remember the funeral because all there was up at the altar was a photograph of him. There was no body. Because he died in duty, there were a variety of ways in which the military helped us along the way. I think it was always very difficult for my mother because she didn't have proper closure. After that, my American grandmother really took over in terms of guiding the family and providing the stability because it simply was not possible for my mother to survive with us on her own. She still spoke limited English, but she lacked basic survival skills; for instance, she didn't know how to drive a car.

A year later, in April 1959, my brother ran out in the street and was hit by a car in front of our house and killed, and there was another funeral. A year and a half later, my mother remarried. She married a man who had been a childhood friend of my father's and who had visited us while we were in Seattle. He had been in the military also. When he came out of the military, he came over to visit my mother to pay his condolences. I think he reminded her a little of my father. He had blonde hair and blue eyes and was about the same height. My mother began to develop a level of independence during this second marriage. My grandmother had taught her to drive and we moved to Seattle where my stepfather had a job. She began to meet neighbors and interact with them. We were not in a neighborhood where there were very many other Asians, but we made through it all right. Then, when I was in the seventh grade, my stepfather, who worked for United Airlines, lost his job and so they decided to buy a restaurant. My mother became actively involved in the restaurant. They had a decent marriage for the first five years but then it deteriorated for a variety of reasons and eventually ended in divorce.

She continued to run the restaurant for thirty years until her retirement ten years ago. The restaurant served American food—sandwiches and soft ice cream. In fact, she was best known for her hash brown potatoes, not her Japanese food—not that they would not say she made great Japanese food. She made wonderful soups, split pea and others, and people would come from miles around for her American cooking.

My mother raised my sister and myself in an American way. She was convinced that we would have to survive in America and she was deathly afraid we would grow up speaking with accents. Over the years, she herself became so Americanized that the few Japanese remnants and mementos around the house slowly disappeared to the point where, now, I cannot point to any specific Japanese mementos. Because she was so conscious about raising an American girl, the opposite took effect. Children can really be curious about their heritage and who they are when they do not really know or are not taught about it. My sister and I both have, in fact, tried to learn about our Japanese heritage and eat Japanese food. When we go to Seattle, we always go out to a Japanese restaurant. She enjoys the food. My nine-year-old daughter, whom I had when I was forty, is also learning Japanese traditions and isn't embarrassed when she uses chopsticks. My husband's parents have both died and were from German decent. He is very supportive of me. He has worked as a photographer for the *St. Louis Post-Dispatch* since 1970.

My mother is very much a survivor and very pragmatic. She's a little hard to take sometimes—by phone once a week is tolerable. My sister who lives in Seattle sees her more frequently and is subjected more to her ups and downs. There is no question that her persona influences my personality. One of the things that she is probably most known for is her expedience—doing something the quickest way rather than stopping to study it from many different perspectives. It is something that, at many times, dismays my husband. For example, I might pay a bit more for something because it is here rather than looking at three other stores. I am not much of a comparison shopper. If I decide I want something I go and buy it, I will not fool around.

My mother is a very creative, intelligent, and emotional person. She had hoped to be able to pursue higher education with her ability in math, but that was not really an option for women in Japan during the period she lived there. I think she could have done several things in terms of a career in her life. To this day, she can work an abacus as fast as many people can work a calculator and she can add up long columns of numbers in her head, she has that kind of memory. She also paints. She likes watercolors, oil paintings, and she likes to do crafty things. She has worked on pottery and can sew and make quilts. She makes incredibly intricate quilts for Barbie dolls and sews zippers, sets in sleeves, and makes buttonholes in sweaters for these dolls and sells them.

Despite her characteristics of being a hard-nosed, practical woman, our relationship is strong but separate. When I went away to college, it was very hard because I was the oldest daughter. Years later, at family parties, she would mention how she had tears on her floor six months after I left. College was a place where my biological father, in an interesting way, was able to help me, even though he was long gone. Due to his death in active service, I qualified for benefits for college under the Veterans/War Orphans Bill. This bill provided me with a little more than two thousand dollars a year to attend college. In 1968, two thousand dollars a year would get me in just about any college in this country in terms of tuition. In addition, the government had started to pay my mother Social Security benefits for my sister and me as surviving children. All through those years after she had remarried, she had simply put that money into the bank for college rather than spend it on our upkeep. So, when I was ready to go to school, I could pick just about anywhere. My mother actually had very little control over where that school would be. I was able to attend Washington University in St. Louis, because of the War Orphans Bill and Social Security.

I graduated from Washington University in 1972 with a bachelor's degree in political science. In the spring of 1973, I returned to Washington University to work in the Office of International Studies where I stayed until August 1978 when I began working at the International Institute. I worked as an assistant for Stanley Spector who was a Sinologist, and who has died recently. The office develops study abroad programs. It also coordinates with the office in dealing with visitors and dignitaries. I did learn to write grants, and that skill helped me more in my present job.

Anna Crosslin (right), President of the International Institute of Metro Saint Louis, interviewed by Huping Ling, 28 May 1999. Huping Ling Collection.

Now, I am the president of the International Institute. We were established in 1919—this is our eightieth anniversary. It was a small non-profit organization with nine paid staff collectively working on $110,000 a year. In 1998 we had a staff of seventy and a 3.4 million dollar budget. About 70 percent of the budget comes from the federal government through contracts and grants mainly for refugees, and mini-grants. The rest of the money comes from fees for services, donated services, and charity. English teachers, tutors, doctors, and nurses volunteer to help further our cause and computer experts help us with our software needs. We have about five hundred volunteers for our festivals and about two hundred volunteers annually. The institute has various programs in charge of education, job placement, human services, and cross cultural services.

My responsibilities include overseeing agency operations. I write grants and I am in charge of fundraising, although we have a fundraising director. I serve on various communitywide committees involving issues of hate crime and diversity. It is very difficult to find representatives from each of the ethnic communities so we have to be the voice for every ethnic community and share their concerns.

A typical working day includes working from 8:15 until 5:20, which correlates with my nine-year old's school schedule. Half of my time is spent talking with people, either meeting them or talking over the phone. Other times I try to get caught up with work. The months of June and July are particularly bad because they are the deadlines for federal grants. By late August it slows down enough that I am able to go to Seattle to visit my family. In September and October, I organize the International Festival. This year will be crazier, because once the festival is over, we will have to do some packing for the move to our new facilities and raise funds to complete the construction there. We still have half a million dollars left to raise.

The refugees we work with should be settled no more than a bus ride from the institute. Most of the refugees are located in South County. Within 120 days after their arrival, 85 percent of adult refugees work in light manufacturing or the tourist industry, such as hotels, motels, gambling boats, and restaurants. There were 1200 job placements done a year by International Institute.

After a period of time, some of them buy houses and stay in the south city area. Some move into other professions and they have to move to the area of their new job. There is upward mobility in their jobs. We keep in contact with some of them, many come back and participate in the International Folk Festival in a dance troop, and sometimes they come back and work as volunteers.

⸺ ⸺ ⸻ ◆ ⸻ ⸺ ⸺

Kazuko Miller was born in Japan in 1942 and grew up in hardship as a result of her father's death in World War II. She married an American serviceman stationed in Japan in 1974 and came to America with her husband the following year. She was a housewife living in a midwestern rural community at the time of the interview in 1999.

I was born in 1942 in Japan. I have been married for twenty years and we do not have any children. In Japan, I went through a junior high education in a public school. My father died during World War II so I am not sure of the education he got, but my mother had something equivalent to a college education. She wanted to get more education so she could make more money since we were poor. My father was a cook for a Japanese company and my mother did not work. She took care of the children and made kimonos. I have two older brothers and one older sister.

After my father died when I was three years old, my mother had a hard time raising my siblings and me. She also wanted the best for us; she wanted us to get more of an education. But my siblings and I had to work hard rather than furthering our education. In Japan, if you go to high school, you have to pay the tuition. We did not have the money, so I was not able to continue my education. After junior high, I quit schooling and worked at the same company where my father used to work. I worked the night shift, making thread.

My sister wanted to continue her education too, but could not since we did not have money, so she became a geisha. She did this after my father died and when my mother became really sick. My oldest brother went to work for a farmer. Japanese farmers are not poor—they have a lot. They have vegetables and raise cattle. If they need money, they can sell their land because the land in Japan is expensive and you can make money from it. Now my brother has his own restaurant. Because we grew up poor, money is very important to everyone in my family except me. Now I spend every cent I have; I cannot save money. When I was young, I did not have much to eat, except for what we could get with the little money we had. My mother sent my brothers and sisters to work for a farmer, who was our babysitter, so we could have more food. Because my father died when I was so young, my mother was concerned that I did not know of my father's love. She felt sorry for me and kept me with her while my older siblings had to work for the farmer. My mother taught us that, even though we were poor, we should not touch someone else's belongings—do not steal, do not touch. Now that I am older, I appreciate good food.

I came to the United States in 1975 when I was in my early thirties. This was a year after I got married. I decided to come to the United States because my husband was an American serviceman. I met my husband in Japan. I was on my way to work and he stopped me in the road. He was going someplace and asked me about the direction. At that time, I could not understand English, but that's where and how I met him. I was working at the navy commissary store, and after a little while a friend of mine introduced us. We got along well. But my family did not like it. They wanted to know why I was going to marry an American, that Japan had men too. I told them that I didn't know. He was really nice, I guess that was why. He retired from the navy and the United States government said I had to come with him, so I did. Now we grow vegetables, which we enjoy, and sell them at the farmer's market on every Saturday. My husband worked at K-Mart but he lost his job when it closed down. We also do odd jobs— mowing lawns and cleaning houses for people.

I like my husband's tender kindness the most. He never hit me. We are poor though, that is our problem. We talk over everything that comes up, such as money and other matters. If we are going to make some decision, we talk it over. I don't make decisions by myself. My husband takes care of everything. When I am working outside of the home he helps with house-work and when I am not working outside, I take care of the house. I used to work at the university, but I quit last October. I am a housewife now.

My father-in-law had a hard time understanding me at first. I talked to him, he couldn't understand me. I thought I spoke English, but he couldn't understand me. So I had to explain to him three times. I told my husband that I was speaking English and I wanted to know why he couldn't understand me. My husband said that he is not used to me, that's why he couldn't understand me. After I stayed here for a long time, though, my father-in-law could understand whatever I said. He was a real nice guy. We visited him once a week. He is gone now, so I don't have any living in-laws.

My husband speaks a little Japanese. If there is someone around that he does not want him/her to understand us, he speaks Japanese. Mostly I cook Japanese food at home. I have my own food and he has his because my husband likes the typical American food—meat, beans, and potatoes. I like Oriental food because American food tastes too heavy for me. I do eat American food sometimes too, but I like Oriental food better.

I like the open space that America has in abundance. Japan is so small, and too many people live there. In Japan, everything is too close together. Houses are so close that in the summertime, you can open your windows and tell what the people next door are having for supper and hear every-thing they are talking about. But in the United States, there is lots of space, lots of air. I like that. We live out in the country. I have a backyard here; no one in Japan does. Myself, my husband, two dogs, and one cat live here. The dogs' names are Cocoa and Toby, and the cat's name is Kitty-ko. I talk Japa-nese to them sometimes when I get mad. It comes out automatically. I

Kazuko Miller (third from left) learning English, Oxnard, California, 1977. Huping Ling Collection (Courtesy of Kazuko Miller).

Kazuko Miller (bottom left), her husband and friends outside a Japanese temple, San Diego, California, 1978. Huping Ling Collection (Courtesy of Kazuko Miller).

learned most of my English from talking to my husband. I really like living here. The air is clean and people are nice; there is not too much to dislike. I do not like how some older people are not very open-minded and are so stubborn; it is difficult to explain to them.

I do not have American citizenship, but I do have a green card. I am kind of old to take the citizenship test; I am fifty-two! I would have to study harder, I do not know if I can remember things very well. Maybe I should have taken it when I first came here. We do not have kids, and if something happened to my husband, I could stay in the United States or I could go back to Japan, whatever I wanted. I could go back to Japan, but it is a matter of pride. Oriental people have pride, like the samurai a long time ago. For example, even if the samurai were very hungry, they would put a toothpick in their mouth and walk around like that. They would do this because after you eat, you usually use a toothpick, and this would make them appear as if they had just eaten.

That is how it still is for people of my age. Young people, I am not sure of now. There are a lot of differences. The young people do not have manners; the older people are more proud and the younger people do not have respect for the older. They are not friendly in the way they talk; it is similar in the United States. We were polite as kids; we were raised to use polite language around older people. Younger people today refer to older people on the same level, like they are friends. I cannot say one way is worse over the other; that is just how things are today.

One of the things that bothered me when I came to the United States was that Americans keep their shoes on around the house. In Japan, we open the door, come into the house, and take off our shoes. We take our shoes off because they get dirty, then the floors get dirty, and then they lay on the floor to watch television. Sure, people vacuum, sweep, and pick up, but I still think it is dirty. When I first came to this country, I would ask visitors to take off their shoes, but I don't say it any more. It does not bother me now; I have gotten used to it. But you think about it anyway. When you take off shoes, the carpet will keep clean and last longer.

Japanese eat with chopsticks. But you can't eat a hamburger with chopsticks no matter what. That is common sense; different food requires different ways to eat. I can't understand people eating rice by grabbing with fingers. It does not bother me when people eat chicken or hamburger with fingers though; I can't think of a better way to eat those foods than with fingers.

I have been married for twenty years and I am used to living here. I am used to American ways. I can't tell any differences. I think of myself as an American.

———————◆—◆—◆——◆———————

Masako Smith was born in Tokyo, Japan, in 1941. She married an American serviceman working in the American military base in Tokyo and came to America with her husband in 1968. She worked at a Japanese restaurant as a cook. She was a housewife living in Denver, Colorado, at the time of the interview in 1994.

I was born in Hachioji, Tokyo, Japan on 18 June 1941. My maiden name is Uchida. My father worked for the train system in Tokyo. My mother was a homemaker. She did not have an outside job; she stayed at home and took care of the kids. I have three brothers and three sisters. I was the middle child, but I was also the second oldest daughter in my family.

I did secretary work on the American air base in Tokyo after I got out of high school. I did not go to college because my brother was the oldest son. This meant he had to help take care of the family—this is a Japanese tradition, taking care of the family is the eldest son's responsibility. I became the first one in my family to come to America when I got married. My husband is from America and in the military; I had to come back here with him. My husband was part of a communications group for the Air Force. He stopped by an officer's club one night. He and his friend came to the club while I was working at the base in Tokyo. I was dancing at the officer's club when my husband first met me. We got married later, but we did not have a wedding ceremony. We stopped by the American Embassy and signed a marriage license. A man stamped the license and said, "Now you're man and wife." My husband did not even have his own suit. He borrowed a jacket from a friend, the jacket was too big, and he borrowed a different pair of pants from another friend. He looked funny. The ring was too big for me because he had to order it from a catalog. When my parents found out I was marrying an American, they opposed it. They did not want me to go too far away from home. Family is very important in Japanese culture. They were unhappy about me going to another country. Plus, I think my mother wanted me to marry a Japanese man. She does not hate my husband; she just wanted me to be closer to home.

We came to the United States in 1968. We lived in Delaware, Little Rock, Arkansas, and a couple of other Air Force bases. A few years before my son was born, we came to Colorado Springs. I did not work until we got to Colorado Springs. That was 1972, right before my oldest son was born. I worked at a Japanese restaurant as a cook; but it was not real Japanese food, it was similar, but not the same.

I wanted my children to learn English first because they live in America, but I regret not teaching them to speak Japanese when they were little. I am very excited that my husband is finally learning to speak Japanese. Sometimes he will try to speak in a conversation with me, and I look forward to that.

I was raised to believe in the Buddha; but I believe in all religions and that if you live a good life and are a good person, you will go to heaven. I used to go to the First Baptist Church. I think I get along well with my husband's family. I think his mother is really nice and I really do not have many problems. We get along fine.

I do not find it easier to become friends with other Japanese or Asians than Caucasians. I am not around many Japanese people here. I make friends with all kinds of people. If they are honest people, good people, they will make a good friend. Nice people respect other people and have lots of friends. People, white or not, always have friends, they do not have any problems. I like to talk with my friend Mitsue because we're from the same place. Both of us have a similar life. Mitsue knows other Japanese women, but I do not really know any others. I do not think there is any difference in making friends with Japanese people or other kinds of people.

I want to go back to Japan to visit my family and relatives next summer, but the trip would be very expensive to make. I want to take my children with me since they have only been there once, but they need to save money.

––––––◆◆◆◆––––––

Mina Yoshida was born in Yamagata, Japan, in 1954 and came to the United States as a student in 1981. She was working at a pharmaceutical company in St. Louis as a research biologist at the time of the interview in 1999. She was married to a European American, a fellow researcher at her company.

I was born in Yamagata prefecture, Japan, in 1954. Both of my parents had high school educations. I have one big brother. My father died early, and my mother was running a liquor store to support the family. My mother had high expectations for both of us. She had the idea that I should go to a girls' school, but I did not, because my teacher did not recommend me to go to the girls' school. I like to mingle with both males and females, so I went to the co-educational school. After my mother learned my decision from my teacher, she was more accepting of it.

I graduated from Kanagawa Kenritsu Gaiko Daigaku, which is specialized in English study. I came to the United States in 1981 with a student visa. I first arrived in Kansas City, studying at Kansas City College and majoring in microbiology. Then I earned a master's degree in biology from the University of Illinois. When comparing the educational systems in the United States and Japan, I thought that a college student in Japan is much more immature than the students in the United States. The American students are more independent, especially financially. At my school, a lot of students did not go to school with their parents' money and they work their way through college. In this sense, I think they are much more mature than the students that I met in Japan.

I am a researcher in my company. I have worked there for sixteen years. People say that in the United States, everybody has the same opportunities, but the reality is not so. My company is one of the biggest of its type in the world. However, only 5 percent of management personnel are women. It is hard for women to climb up to the upper level management. If you are Asian, forget it. If you are Japanese or Chinese, you are not going to get there. Maybe Indians can as they are more aggressive. I have seen a couple of Indians getting up there, but again, they are men, not women. So there is a cultural and gender differentiation. Asians and women cannot get up there. But I would not think it is racial prejudice, it has more to do with one's cultural background. I think if we try hard, the managerial job is not hard to handle. Actually, I don't want to be one of them, to be politically involved. My field is pretty narrow and we are all professionals. Everybody at work has a master's degree or a PhD. I don't feel I am discriminated against. But I do think there is racial problem in the United States and this is what they are trying to cover up.

I went into medical technology because the pay is good there. I have a good salary and benefits from my job. But what I like most about my job is the freedom. I can do whatever I want. I can work whenever I want. It is not because I have worked here for a long time, but because I don't work for anybody else. I have a big boss but I don't see her at all. I can plan the work from my own experience. I can figure out what I have to do. Before I came to the United States, I worked in a city hospital for a year and I hated it. The job was boring and the people around were nasty, and I did not get along with the nurses and doctors there. We could not go home before the boss went home. We had to respect older people even though they were pretty incompetent. Here in America it is really serious. If you are incompetent you are laid off, because you are evaluated twice a year. So one's ability is more important than one's seniority in the United States.

I met my husband in 1984. We work at the same company on the same floor. He is very sensitive for an American, while many Americans are not so sensitive. Most people are only superficially sensitive. But my husband is sincere from bottom of his heart. He knows a lot of things. If I choose someone as my husband, he has to be more intelligent than me. He is very intelligent and he knows every field. He knows astrology and botany besides his own field. We dated for a year and then got married. My mother did not oppose it and she only worried about if he was a black. I think if he was a black, my mother would have observation.

I do most of the household chores and my husband only cleans dishes. It is not because I love household chores, as a matter of fact, I hate them, I do most of them because my husband is very slow and he does a perfect job. If he does some chores, he takes all day to do it. But I am quick. We make decisions together on family matters. But on the important things, he makes decisions as he is more thoughtful and thinks more carefully, while I decide things quickly.

My husband is supportive of my work. We work in the same company and we have to be supportive of each other, as our company lays off employees all the time. Who knows, one of us may lose our job someday! Just thinking out that when I started working there, I was one of 160 employees. Now only 30 of these people survive in the company. Those who were laid off come on and off. My husband's good friend was just laid off. If we had more stable jobs, I could quit my work if I want. But now I cannot quit.

I have a very good relationship with my parents-in-law. I feel lucky to have relatives here in this country. Otherwise, I would have felt very lonely. I think the biggest problem of an international marriage is not the cultural difference, but the parents—how receptive of each partner's parents would affect the marriage.

I cook Japanese food most of the time. I have two children. I speak

Japanese to them at home, but they reply in English. In terms of child-raising, I think a combination of American way and Japanese way is good. I want my kids to have respect for everybody and I want them to learn the Japanese culture so I try to instill the Japanese values into them. We try to go back to Japan every two years. It is up to my children to choose their nationality and cultural identity, and my daughter said she would like to be an American.

My first ten years living in America was wonderful. But after ten years, I started feeling annoyed by Americans. Many of my friends were going back to Japan after living here for ten years. America is not that wonderful a country. But the first ten years, you are going to love it! Why was the first ten years wonderful? Because you don't know much about the country, so everything is interesting and exciting. What I don't like about America is the superficiality of people, the homeless problem, and the education, although there are also homeless in Japan and I don't know much about Japanese education. I don't expect much from the schools here. I think all parents should have confidence and knowledge to teach their kids. I think more Japanese have that kind of knowledge and cultural background than Americans. Only 25 percent of the population in America has college degree and that is not good enough.

I feel it is easier to make friends with Japanese than with Americans because we have the same language and culture. I spend my spare time writing essays in Japanese and it is my dream to write my own book someday. Both my husband and I are atheists so we don't go to any church on Sundays. I don't like the weather here and I would love to live in Hawaii! I don't want to spend the rest of my life here. If we can, I want to live in Japan after we both retire from our work.

11

Attaining Education

*Maiko Yamamoto was born in Tokyo, Japan, in 1973 and came to the
United States as a student in 1995. She was attending the University of Missouri-Columbia, seeking a graduate degree in journalism, at the time of the
interview in 1996.*

I was born in Tokyo, Japan, in 1973. In Japan I studied American and
British literature and received a BA (bachelor of arts). Here, I am a fifth
year student at Mizzou working on a graduate degree. My mom had a
bachelor's degree and my dad had a master's degree. My mom is a housewife. My dad has just recently retired but he still works part time as an
engineer. I have one older brother, who is a college student, and one
younger sister, who is a freshman. My brother is studying Japanese law, in
Japan. He doesn't want to be a lawyer, he's just a law student for now. I
think my parents expect more from him—to get a good job and obtain a
higher status.

I came to study in the United States because I wanted to study journalism and English. I could not get a journalism degree in Japan so I
decided to come here, but I am planning on going back to Japan. I have
had a lot of difficulty in some of my classes. All of the teachers interrupt
me, especially in discussions. All of the students have their own opinions,
which, I think, are kind of irrelevant and incoherent. It is also very hard for
me to pick up expressions.

It is very hard to start relationships with classmates. I think they see
me as kind of embarrassing because I am always asking people if I can look
at their notes. They are very tough. I cannot feel discriminated against just
because I cannot speak English that well though. Language is a very big

150

gap between other students and me. Some people care for me very much and pay a lot of attention to me, but I cannot respond to them. I can't understand them, and so I think that is one of the reasons that they think I am a very uninteresting person.

I feel pressure in America to get a very good GPA and to go back to Japan and get a good job. I do not think that getting a degree is as important for women in Japan. Marriage changes a lot of things though. A lot of companies like Zenith allow women to keep their jobs if they want to get married; they want women to get married. Some companies are presenting themselves like that. It is really bad. It's against the law, but there are still invisible laws among companies. I also think that Japanese men are changing a lot, but a lot of men have jobs with one company and work for that company for their whole lives. They are with the same company and it is getting much more political. For me, I think, it is still harmful to be an international student with American students. I think it is a good idea for me to marry a Japanese guy.

I usually spend my free time in college doing something for class— usually I am reading six books. It's so boring. Or shopping, I go shopping and hang around downtown; I will get some coffee or just walk around. In Japan I would shop too, but the shopping styles are very different there. We have a lot of different restaurants in Japan, and the department stores are very specific. There are a lot of brand name shops in Japan, but I cannot find any such shops in Columbia. In Japan, I dated a lot. Friends and I would go drinking in places where they have very good Japanese food. These are not only restaurants for eating, but also for enjoying Japanese alcohol with Japanese food.

People are very kind to strangers here. They say hello to strangers— this is very unusual in Japan. It's kind of strange for me to say "hello" to someone I do not know; in Japan I would run away. I like that in America; if a guy likes me, he will date me.

When I was younger I went to school from eight o'clock to three o'clock. After that, I could do anything I wanted. It is not so strict in Japan; when I was a high school student, I dated boys. I was very old-fashioned in my thinking. Younger kids have a lot of freedom about dating others; I think it is kind of a social problem in Japan. A lot of companies and enterprises use high school kids as targets for their products. I do not know why students have so much money that they can buy things like Chanel bags or lots of expensive brand-name clothing. Many girls work at bars; maybe that is how they supplement their income.

Girls and the expectations placed upon them are different in the United States and Japan. My brother does not have to help my mother wash. He does not have to clean his room or do his laundry, but I have to. I do not know what the difference is between Japanese life and American life. I do not know what American girls are expected to do by their parents.

There are also differences between what is expected from men and women in Japan and in the United States. In Japan, they measure your involvement by how efficiently you care for your children and parents. That is why, I think, a lot of companies don't want to make their working situations more equal. I think we [women] are struggling to achieve equality. Even if the same education is given to boys and girls, I think that when they are compared three years later, the male workers would be much higher up in status than the female workers. I think that it is very difficult for a woman to move up because of societal restrictions and that this is very wrong. There should be a lot of support for women within the home so that they can work outside of it. They could significantly change the institution. It is my hope to change attitudes in Japan, which is why I want to be a writer.

I think there is a difference in the emphasis on beauty in the United States and Asia. I usually wear high heels in Japan, but noticed when I was in Spain that Americans had shorts on and tennis shoes while everyone else had a skirt and high heels. I think Japanese girls are always thinking about current fashion. They chase the latest styles, which change quickly. I think that girls here use really good stuff for many years. I am always thinking about what others think of me. In Japan, if I went outside my house for five or six minutes, walking to meet my friends, I would not wear strange clothes and I would wear makeup very neatly; it was terrible. I am much more comfortable when I do not have to worry about what other people think.

The notion of a women's job being in the house is a very big problem and we need a lot of time to change it. I think a lot of housewives and other housekeeping jobs should be for care for other children, so that some women can work. The number of children women have is getting fewer and fewer. Having one child is safe, but having six children to have to care for is a very big problem. The role of women in society needs to change, but it is going to take a lot of time. I think there has been a kind of women's movement in Japan. There is a very radical group that a lot of men belong to in support of women's rights. I think women should get along with men more and we should also get support from them, but women will eventually need a political movement.

———◆━━◆━◆━━◆———

Yuko Saito was born in Yokohama, Japan, in 1966 and came to United States as a student in 1994. She was a business major at Northeast Missouri State University at the time of the interview in 1995.

I was born on 18 February 1966 in Yokohama, Japan. My father is a plumber and owns his own business. He is the only one who works there and therefore his schedule varies, sometimes he can take days off, other days he works twenty hours. My mother is in insurance sales. She also works very hard; she leaves home at six in the morning and gets home at nine or ten at night when she has to come home and cook for the family. They are both high school graduates. I have two younger sisters, one is twenty-four years old and the other is twenty-one. I also have a younger brother who is twenty-two. One of my sisters just graduated from high school and my other sister and brother have both graduated from a two-year college. They are all single.

On an educational level, I do not think that my parents treated me any differently from my brother. I think that maybe I am kind of lucky, because my family had many financial problems. When my brother was young, we had financial problems, he did not go to kindergarten and it affected his writing skills and overall education. I think my parents expected too much from me because I am the first daughter in the family. The educational system in Japan, compared to that in the United States, is very strict. The students in Japan go to school from eight until three. Then they go home for a couple hours and then to a private tutor at six or seven o'clock until ten or eleven. Most of the parents are very strict with their children; I actually talked about this topic in Chinese class. Our parents just push the kids in their studying—no housework and no part-time job. Students should study for as long as they can. Some students only sleep for three hours.

My dad does not like to work around the house. He does not like to do housekeeping work, so my mom does everything; even if my mom gets home late, he does not do the cooking. She has to do everything by herself. Since I am a girl, my father thought that I did not need a higher education and that is the reason that I worked hard and brought myself here. My dad made most of the decisions, but after we had grown up, we made most of the decisions for ourselves.

Some of my friends got married when they were twenty-one years old, but I think that the age to get married is different for everyone. Since we live in the city, the average age for marriage is higher, maybe twenty-five or twenty-six for girls and twenty-eight or thirty for men.

There are a lot of things that are different between Japanese and American relationships. Japanese men like to have love affairs. They have what they call love hotels. It costs a certain amount of money for a certain amount of time spent there. Many people have these love affairs—that may be because we have such small houses. Overall, people are still really conservative but they like to hide it.

Right now I am here on a student visa. I first arrived in January of 1994. I came to this university because I like working here. English is my main purpose and I like to study, and I found out from Peterson's student's guide that this university is cheap and offers a good education, so I choose this one.

When I first came here, my score on the foreigners' grading scale in English was 500, which meant my English score was low. Whenever I went to class I could not understand what the teacher was saying; I had a really hard time. Then I stayed with Japanese friends because I could not speak any English. I still have difficulty while studying for school. I do not have any difficulty listening. Sometimes professors use different terms so I have some difficulty, but overall it is all right. At home everyone has to study six years of English, but even after that six years we cannot speak it, we do not like it. The hardest thing is speaking to the professors, we just had to get used to it. If there were other things, cultural things, such as the food, that we were not accustomed to, we have gotten used to them.

I do not care much about my relationships with my classmates, since it is my opinion. I do not like to borrow notes from other people in the class, even if I do not go to the class because my English is not very good now. I have borrowed American friends' notes before, but they have a hard time with me borrowing notes. I do not like to do it. My professors understand that I am a foreign exchange student and that it is harder for me than it is for most students.

My major is business. I would like to be a businesswoman some day. I hope that I can get a job. I have considered going to China to do business as well. I think I am going to work when I graduate, and I may go to graduate school later if my GPA is good enough. I would like to permanently immigrate to the United States. For that I would have to work in a company for six or seven years. We still have problems between the equality of men and women in Japanese society. There is a big difference in promotions in America; there is more freedom for women here.

In Japan I did mostly secretarial work. My relationship with my colleagues in Japan was different from how I would act here because I am a student. Here I do not have any partiality towards people. I have to pretend or act very kind, even if I do not like a person. In Japan, I had a lot of job-related stress, mostly because my job was so boring. There was a lot of gossip between the girls; the type of job and its environment condones it. I am kind of old, compared to the other workers—I am twenty-six. When I came here, I found that there were differences in my ideas from the other Japanese girls. My friends asked me why I came to the States and wondered why I did not get married and have children, even though I work for a living.

In Japan, I usually get up at six thirty in the morning, prepare for thirty minutes and leave at seven. I catch the train for work and I arrive at the company at nine—it takes me almost two hours to get there. We have a break from noon to one. After five most of the girls are released from the company. After work I take the train for another two hours to get home. Usually, once we leave the city, the girls go to some kind of a culture school; there we learn traditional things like floral arrangements and tea ceremonies or something of the sort. We go to school once or twice a week. Sometimes the girls get home at ten o'clock or later.

When I have free time here in America, I write letters to my friends. I also cook dinner, go out with my friends, sometimes we go to the bar—the Japanese love to drink. I also listen to music, pretty much the same things Americans like to do. I do not read a lot of newspapers, but I do follow the news; for instance, before I came here, I heard that the Missouri River had flooded—it was on CNN. I try and stay away from the political issues. I do not participate in any community or outside activities or in any religion.

I think it is easier to make friends with people from my own country; you can share the same topics. Most of my friends are Japanese. You cannot make friends with Americans very well. One of the things that make it difficult is the language barrier, but there are other things too. We are totally different. We cannot talk about TV programs. There are a lot of things you cannot talk about when your backgrounds are so different. Right now, I am living with two people that are from Taiwan, we all speak English.

I like the people of the United States and the freedoms they have. I feel that I can do anything I want here, unlike in Japan. Some think that I am not cooperative with people; sometimes it is good for the people, and sometimes it is not.

The way of living in the United States is different from that in Japan. My house in Japan is very small. There are two rooms. If you like to live in the city, you have to spend a thousand dollars a month. That includes a kitchen and one bathroom. Our house is very small. The apartments in New York are much bigger. The people that I live with here care more about each other. Some people in the city are not very kind, but overall, they are very kind compared to Japanese people.

Besides New York, I have also visited lots of other places when I traveled by myself five or six years ago. I took Amtrak from Los Angeles to New Orleans and then to Miami. It is from Miami that I went to New York and stopped many places along the way. The United States is an immigrant country. It has many cultures, but they can all communicate with each other. In Japan, it would be hard for a foreigner to become accepted among the Japanese; they would have a hard time fitting in. The Japanese are not as accepting of foreigners. We do not like to have many immigrants in the country. We have Chinese people, but their appearance is not very different from Japanese; the Chinese people are very interesting. A foreigner would experience hard times in Japan. The Japanese people want to make friends with the blue-eyed, blonde, English-speaking tourists. A Southeast Asian or the Middle Eastern person would have a harder time unless he or she could speak English.

I have one bad memory of a trip. It was morning in Houston, Texas, and I was hungry, so I went to a restaurant. An American man was studying next to me. I did not do a thing. He moved and hit my hand. He said, "Oh my God, I touched a Nazi-Chinese." I was not angry but I was sad, and that was the first time I was discriminated against. Also, in my mind I thought I am not Chinese, I am not a Nazi-Chinese, I am a clean Japanese. At first I had a very nice time, and thought, wow, America is a very nice country. My feelings have changed now, since I have been here longer. The Japanese do not discriminate against Americans and Europeans; they just admire you and want to make friends with you. Houston changed my mind because being discriminated against by someone is so sad, so disgusting. It is really hard to explain.

I like America, I love New York; it is my favorite city. It opened my eyes to the wide variety of nations that are represented here. Many Japanese want to be more like Americans. Other Asian countries look up to Japan; but we see the American culture and like American things. Ballpoint pens, which here are very cheap, would make a lot of money in Japan. We feel that our economy has improved; we can complain that we make lots of money, but then the American people complain to us, so it works both ways. I think that they have opposing viewpoints on the Japanese economy. Some people look down on the economy, maybe to a point where we look down on ourselves.

The prices here are a lot lower than the prices at home. The food is cheap. If you go shopping in Japan, a small bag of groceries would be quite expensive—a small sack will cost maybe fifty dollars. We can buy a big bag of potatoes for one or two dollars here. In Japan they are expensive; beef is very expensive, too. I like how everything is inexpensive here.

I also love spaghetti very much. I cook spaghetti when I eat American food. I had to get used to American food, but there is not a big difference. Eating American food was very interesting at first, but now it is normal. My friend from Taiwan used to microwave her salad because the Taiwanese cannot eat anything raw. Now they have gotten used to it. It is a natural thing for Japanese to eat salad. In Japan, we have several Western foods besides the Asian food, Chinese food; we have Red Lobsters in my hometown, and we have McDonald's everywhere.

Mayumi Honda was born on the island of Shikoku, Japan, in 1972 and came to the United States as a student in 1991. She was a political science major at Northeast Missouri State University at the time of interview in 1994.

I was born on the small southern island of Shikoku in Japan in 1972 in the prefecture called Koji; it is an area developed by fishermen. I lived there until my fifth grade year, when we moved to Tokyo because of my father's business. My father's company deals with the transportation of vegetables within Japan. They are transported by truck and boat. They also transport furniture and moving equipment. My mother is an English teacher at the university. I have a brother who is two years older than me and a sister who is three years younger than me.

My brother is studying business at a university in Boston and my sister, who is a junior in high school, is studying for a year in Australia. She might not want to come to the States and study; maybe she will go to some other English-speaking country. I visit my brother about twice a year, on holidays and during summer vacation. I keep in touch with my parents while I am here. I usually call them once a month and I write them when I have time. I think it is hard on my parents, having us away studying. My mother could not go abroad to study. She is an English professor and it was her wish to go abroad since I can remember—I got my idea from her.

I had never been to the United States before I came here in an exchange program. I did the program my senior year in high school, it was called Youth for Understanding and I stayed with a family in Iowa for a year. At first I could not understand any English. Within six months I had gradually improved. My history classes were particularly hard. It was really interesting to see what America's perspective is on what happened in World War II and how it was they decided to drop a nuclear bomb on Hiroshima. I had never thought about it before; there are so many things that we do not learn about in Japan, there are still so many facts the government hides about what Japanese people did. These classes at the high school told us about how Japanese troops invaded Asian countries and about imperialism; these things helped me decide whether or not I wanted to come to the United States to study.

I think American education is more flexible and open to anyone. It does not keep the opportunities limited only to young people, but rather anyone who is willing and able to study. At a Japanese university, there are not many students ten years older than me, but here you find people of all ages.

I transferred the credits of the classes I took in Iowa to my Japanese school, so when I went back home I was able to graduate. I got a diploma from my Japanese high school. I did not know that when I left the high school in Japan that I wanted to study at a college in America. I began to study at a Japanese college, but towards the end of the first year, I realized that American education was better. I took an international relations class, a typing class, and a class on the business industry. These classes were something that I had never taken in Japan before and I felt, at that time, that if I studied in the States more, I would be able to learn about certain fields that I am interested in. In Japan we do not get to choose what we want to study—it all depends on the grade you get on the entrance exam, usually business, finance, or literature. If you fail the examination, you have to wait until the next year to try again. I did not want to waste my year preparing for the examination. I knew that I had to study at these schools for a year and I may not get a chance to go to the university the next year either. I did not want to take the risk, and I decided to come here and start studying what I was interested in.

I waited until January to come to the United States for school. I went back home about July (after high school), received my acceptance letter, and was told to come back here at the end of August. However, I wanted to be with my family longer than one month, so I decided to start in January. That is an advantage about this university—you can start each semester. I am a junior this year—I will be a senior next semester. This is also an advantage because in Japan you have to follow year by year. The first year you are a freshman, then sophomore, etc. You have to be there at least four years. But here if you want to go ahead and graduate in three years, you can do it. I will be graduating next December because I took a semester off last year.

I am studying political science. My field includes the study of Asian countries. As I mentioned before, while I was studying in Japan I realized that there are a lot of things that our government keeps from us, that it does not want us to know. Japan is a democratic country, everything is free, open to the public, but still you have to find it by yourself. I realized that if I study in the United States or some other country for my master's degree, I can study Asian countries from a third person perspective that would be more objective. I would like to build a bridge between Asian countries, because Japan is kind of isolated in Asia. We feel left out among the Asian countries. I plan to get my master's in America, or somewhere else, but not in Japan.

I took a study abroad program last fall to Austria to study German. It was also a different experience because while I was studying in Kirksville I met a lot of new friends, American friends as well as international friends. When I got to Austria, I met many more new foreign students from Eastern Europe since Germany is kind of the border between Western and Eastern Europe. It was an interesting experience. I traveled a lot, more new languages were introduced to me, and I got to learn about different cultural aspects of the country.

I studied German for two semesters, but before I came to the United States I had studied English for six years. When I got here, I could not speak it; I could not understand people. I realized that the best way to learn a foreign language is to go to that particular country and learn. I confused some English and German while I was there though. I learned German much faster, I think. I took one semester off because I wanted to improve my German a little bit more and so I lived there until May.

Asian parents are more supportive of children until they graduate from a university. My parents wanted me to concentrate on studying rather than work, but now, for example, I am working institutional hours on campus. That does help me, of course. I work for a professor and I also tutor in Japanese. This is really an interesting experience for me. I am also interested in teaching languages, if I can. Even if I did not work at all, I do not think I would use those eight hours to study. I would rather use those hours to relax; teaching Japanese makes me relax.

Right now I share an apartment with my close Japanese friend, I lived with her last year as well. While I was in Japan looking for an apartment in Kirksville, I got rid of everything before I left, so I did not have anything and I did not know many people. My friend told me that her friend was looking for an apartment and roommate too, and that is how we came to live together. When I first came to Northeast, I lived in Ryle (an all-girl dorm at the time). I am glad that my friend told me to choose Ryle. She graduated from the same high school in Iowa and came one semester earlier than me. She is my closest friend here and she told me to sign up for Ryle. I did not believe that I would benefit from coed housing, but I think at the beginning, not knowing anybody here, it would have been much harder to get to make friends if I lived off campus. I participated in some events in Ryle Hall, and since I lived on campus I knew what was going on. I think I adapted to college more naturally than others because I was close in age to all the other students living in Ryle. I liked that. Some people really do not care about international students, and this does not only happen in the States. People are busy with their own stuff. On the other hand, I realized that people were more tolerant of their friends.

Sometimes I felt sorry for some other international students who never had the experience of living with an American family. They think that American food is the food they get in the cafeteria in the dorms. The American people do not like this food either, though; they do not even consider it American food. In that sense I really appreciate being able to cook my own meals, now that I live off campus.

Here, we use really effective equipment; in Japan you usually do not have an oven. Now we are modernizing, but a lot of houses still do not have ovens and it still takes a lot more time to cook food. Since I use an oven, it is a lot easier; I can put everything in and it is finished in an hour. I cook American, European, and Japanese food. I like cooking in my free time. I make bread from scratch. I also like to play tennis—I have been playing since junior high school.

I decided to come to this university because of a teacher I had in Iowa. The teacher who taught us international relations took us to a Model United Nations. He graduated from here and that is how I got to know this university. I visited this campus with my friend before I began classes. I really liked the International Student Office and Mrs. McKinney and how they work for us. She is great. We did not really know anything about the area; we needed someone to take care of us and I feel the International Student Office does this very well compared to other universities. In other words, I did not look at any other universities. I am pretty lucky; it turned out really well. I like this university, even though it is really competitive and hard. I think it makes me study.

I still keep in touch with the family in Iowa that I stayed with. I am planning on visiting them in January, after New Year's. While I was staying with them I realized how important my real family is. Even though I have such good times with my American host family, a real family cannot be replaced with any other. Even though I do not go back home much, I appreciate my real family much more than before. I am worried about my parents. Asian families take care of their elders; for instance, my mother has to take care of my grandparents. It is really hard for her to do that and maintain the household as well. I talked to my mother this summer before I came back and asked if I should stay and help but she wanted me to stay in America and follow my own path. This past summer was the last time I was home; I had not been home in a year so I was really excited to go.

If I could see myself doing anything ten years from now, I would like to work to create a bridge connecting the Asian nations. I see myself having a family in the future. My parents do not mind different nationalities; they said it is my decision whether I marry a Japanese man or someone else; it should be someone who is right for me.

———————◆━◆━◆———————

Christie Smith was born in Denver, Colorado, in 1976 to interracial parents. Her father, a European American, worked in the Air Force, and her mother, born in Japan, worked in a Japanese restaurant. She was a business major at Colorado State University at the time of the interview in 1994.

I was born on 13 January 1976 at the Swedish Medical Center. My father was in the Air Force for a while and then he retired and started working for Hewlett Packard. I think he stayed with them for eighteen or nineteen years before starting his own company, a consulting firm, where he still works. My mother is a housewife. The stories I get from both my parents as to how they met are different. Mom says that they got married because she was supposed to marry someone else but she felt sorry for dad. Dad says that mom lied about her age, so dad thought that he was marrying someone younger than he was. I do not think either of their stories is true, but who knows.

I am currently in my first year at Colorado State University majoring in business with a concentration in advertising. I am not so sure I really like college that much. I really miss my friends and miss seeing my family and home. I am tired of school and I'm not confident that I can talk to anyone here about anything. It is not that I do not want to get a good education; I just miss everything. School is not extremely bad; I still have fun, but I do not like my teachers, and I really don't feel like I can talk to the girls that I hang out with.

Plus, I am tired of all the organizations calling me up all the time. I have never considered myself Asian, but someone from the multicultural group keeps calling me. It does not bother me that it is a multicultural group; I was in the one at my high school, but I hate when people are always hounding and calling. It gets kind of annoying.

I would really like to learn more; someday I might actually try to learn how to speak Japanese. When I finish school, I think I would really like to do something with advertising, especially since I like art so much. I would love to do what my dad does and start my own company, but I want at least a good paying job.

Most Asian girls I knew in high school were brainy and nerdy so I never talked to them. Since I do not look Asian, and since there really are not that many Asians living around here, I do not really think it matters; it should not matter. I have never been treated differently because of my background. I was able to apply for special scholarships based on the fact that my mom is Japanese, but I did not receive any of those.

I think that it would have been really neat to be able to speak to my mom in her language. I guess I regret the fact that I was not taught how to speak Japanese at an early age. I cannot talk to my grandma unless I learn how, which is quite disappointing. Right now I am just confused about what I want to do with my life; maybe when I get things straightened out, I will take Japanese.

I think that for the most part my mom and I understand each other well. Mom has finally started to understand my taste in clothing and other things, and we always do stuff, like shopping, together. I sometimes wish that I knew why she says or does the things that she does. Sometimes she will give advice, but I am not quite sure what she really means. It also does not help that her English is fragmented. That is another reason I think that I want to learn Japanese. I also want to know what she says about me when she talks to her friend in Japanese.

I'd like to learn more about both sides of my background; not just the Japanese stuff, but my dad's side too.

***

Yukiko Tatsumoto was born in Tokyo, Japan in 1965 and came to the United States as a student in 1994. She was studying art at Coe College in Cedar Rapids, Iowa, at the time of the interview in 1995.

I was born about thirty or forty minutes from Tokyo's main downtown on 20 March 1965. Both of my parents were thirty-eight when I was born. At that time, they were poor. Now Japan's economy is good but when I was small we were very poor. My father is handicapped, but he worked as a graphic designer. When I was ten, we struggled to get a house. Before that, we lived in an apartment. It was like a dorm room, a single dorm room without a bathroom, so we used public baths.

I have one older sister, who is seven years older than me. My mom is a housewife. My parents married late, when they were thirty or thirty-one. My mom worked before they got married. She was a dressmaker; she also taught dressmaking at schools. She was tired, she said she just wanted to get married and rest. She planned an arranged marriage and got married.

My father's father died when he was three and my father's mother remarried, so older uncles and younger uncles and an aunt of mine have different fathers. They do not have a good relationship and so each family is very nuclear. Because my mom lost her parents very early I do not have a relationship with my grandparents on my mom's side.

Growing up in Japan, I went to a public school for elementary and middle school. I went to a private, all girls' high school, then I attended a two-year college. Because I went to college ten years ago, people told me that if I go to a four-year college, I would not be able to find a job. At the time, the company just gave me a job as a secretary because I had a higher education. Most women got a job after high school or a two-year college. Women went to a four-year college to become specialists. There were not a lot of jobs. After I finished at the two-year college, I got a job at a computer software company and I worked as a programmer for eight years. I changed companies only once during that time.

I came to the United States on January 25, 1994, because the economy in Japan was bad and because my job was really stressful. I had a kind of mental depression because I could not sleep for a long time. There were maybe three to four months when it was hard for me to sleep when I went to bed. I could not sleep, I just dozed continually for a long time. I wanted to change my life. I was busy, working continually, fifteen to sixteen hours a day. I would go in at nine and finally leave at eleven or midnight. I think that after the war, Japan was brainwashed by American thought so that money became the important thing.

I like to read books. I found a book about the English as a Second Language program at colleges in the United States, and Coe College was listed as having a good program. I had liked English since I was in high school, but I could not speak it well. I wrote a letter to the director of the department of some of the colleges listed and was pleased when Coe College wrote a letter back. It was so personal. Other big universities sent me letters addressed "To applicant" but Coe said "Yukiko." The signature was original. I felt so familiar and warm and I chose Coe. I tried to get information about another university in Washington state or Oregon on the West Coast. I though it would be easy. But I got a scholarship from Coe College and another college said they would not give me a scholarship, so I decided to stay here.

Before I came to the United States to study, I had made short trips to Boston, New York, and Los Angeles to visit my friends, but still my English was not very good. The fact that I could not speak English created difficulties for me. The first three months I felt so frustrated. English as a second language was taught very well. The teachers tried not to treat us like children, but because our speaking ability was like a child's, because we could not speak in complete sentences, people sometimes treated us like children.

But I am an adult and they did not understand that, so I felt frustrated. I told some of the teachers, and they said they would try to help me and they did. It is hard to make friends here. Of course, if I were in Japan and a foreigner came and talked to me in a very slow childish language, I would understand, but sometimes I feel so lonely.

Depending on the region of the United States that I am in, sometimes I feel like a minority. Here, in the Midwest, there are not so many Asians. It is interesting when I go to Sears or the mall. Sometimes I do not know Asian women working in the mall but they just start talking to me. They will ask, "Where did you come from?" Maybe they feel familiar talking to me. They are very kind to me. That would never happen if I were back home because everyone is the same.

It is convenient to live here. Because it is college, I do not have to wear good clothes or makeup. In Japan, when I was a college student, I had to wear good clothes, high heels. Some of the Japanese female students who come here look like prostitutes. People just expect women to be pretty and feminine and to obey. For the Japanese, hairstyle and color and how smooth the skin is and shiny and healthy hair are how we view beauty. Because of the way we grew up, some girls adjusted quickly. When we were kids we did not wear makeup—we were just children. But in middle school and high school, I think we separated. I could not obey because I had a feeling that it was not equal or fair. I always complained. I could not fit into my society. For example, when I got a job, I was expected to clean up all of the other workers' desks. Maybe forty or fifty other people's desk every morning and there was only one woman in the office. I was not hired as a secretary or a cleaning lady. I was hired as the other workers, as an engineer. I told my boss that I had a problem. I had a right to complain. But in Japanese society, you can't.

When I came here, I had conflict because I could not finish my education in my country. I graduated from a two-year college, but the social expectation changed and women now needed a higher education. I did not have a degree and I really wanted to get one. The companies needed better-educated people. But the university education system had not adjusted to the need yet so it was really hard to get into a college. At universities here, you can transfer or go back to school. It is very systematic. If I wanted to get a four-year college degree over there, I would have to take an exam. I would have to start as a freshman. The exam is only once a year, not like it is in America. That is why many people come to the United

States from all over the world.

I am studying art at Coe College; I am a sophomore. I have not decided what I will specifically study, probably painting; I am just taking basic courses now. I am not sure what I want to do when I get out of college. I might go back to Japan. I really enjoy studying here. The small classes and faculty are very helpful. Because my English ability is very limited, I have to work harder than others, otherwise I will fail. So far I am doing all right; I have good grades. It is not so different relating to my family now that I have gone away to college. I had already been independent of them because we lived in different places. It might be different to go back home, though.

My hobbies overlap with my major. I enjoy doing my art homework, making ceramics and doing photography. I never had the chance to do these things in Japan because I was so busy. I do not plan on getting married either, because I do not have time to meet people. My life is like a monastery. I like it that way; I do not feel stress. Life becomes very simple. I just study by myself, go to class, study, eat, study, and go to class. I like writing. I think it helps me.

Other people may have fun. But for me, I cannot tell them my age. Of course, they know, but I do not say it. They are so young and I do not want to be separated by generation, because I am already separated because of my race. Age is really important for us because it determines our way of talking. There is an altogether different way of talking here. Here, students talk to their professors like friends and sometimes call them by their first names. This would never happen in Japan. That is why if I tell them my age, they would change their way of talking and maybe think, "She is different from us." So, I do not want to tell them. I pretend. Even to Americans, ten years difference can be big.

I do not have many Asian American friends. There is this one person I met at Sears, a girl who just talked to me. She touched my hair and she said, "You have really shiny, straight hair." She was born here; she is a Korean American.

When we watch movies, about Japan, China, or Korea, they just do not know what the difference is between the three. We laugh at some karate movie because the Japanese were not using beds; they were just sleeping on the floor as in a traditional movie. Sleeping on beds is a Chinese custom, but the setting was in Japan. Speaking is so strange in Japanese movies. For example, Madame Butterfly was funny. People expect Oriental women to be obedient creatures. I think most generations of Japanese came from a different society, we do not talk loudly. Since we don't say our opinion loudly, people say that Orientals are shy. But we are not shy, some of us are extroverted. People just want to think that way, but it is not true. Sometimes, because we are stubborn, we do not want to show ourselves to outsiders. Americans think because we are shy that we are hiding ourselves. I just do not want to show myself.

Last year a Chinese girl, Mary (a black girl), and I lived off campus. It was hard to get an apartment because we were rejected. Mary said it was because she was black and the apartment was owned by a retired person. Most of the landlords were old ladies and men. Mary has a white friend and her grandmother rented the room for us. Actually, those old people were nice, some of them just do not know how to behave. They wanted to be friendly but one person came and said "hi" and slanted his eyes. It was terrible for me but it was not meant to be that way. They wanted to be friendly. I couldn't tell them not to do that again. It was a terrible experience.

Another person I met at Sears (I always meet Asian Americans at Sears) said she came from Hong Kong. She just came to me and started talking to me. And she said, "I'm Linda." But her pronunciation was very different from Americans'— she had a very strong Chinese accent. I asked her if Linda was her original name. She said, "No, I changed it." Her name was Li Wang, but she said it was really convenient to get a job that way, and suggested I change my name. At the time I thought, "I'm not going to do that," because if somebody called me Linda, it would seem so funny. Now, I live with a Japanese girl in the dorms and she says it is really hard to make friends at Coe. One reason is that people cannot memorize her name. She is thinking of picking an American nickname, but she always says she will change her name later. I think there is a very clear difference between Japanese and Chinese; if it has benefits, Chinese will change their names. They say they do not care, though maybe some do.

I like a lot of things about America. If I want to research something, I just go to the library and it is easy to find papers or periodicals. But in my country, it is not so convenient. If I wanted to do it by myself, there would be a lot of difficulty, but in a group it is easier. Individuals have very little power. It is not convenient to look for something by myself in Japan. I just know college life here in the Midwest. Here, people just do what they want. They just do individual work. It is different in Japan because over there everybody works together for one purpose and it works really well. It is easier to create friendships and enables people to become closer. Here, you do not know who is doing what.

There are also differences between the Chinese and Japanese. I think that Chinese are more united. They have Chinatowns everywhere. They hire each other when they need a job and therefore they have more power. When we got to Chinatown in San Francisco, I found that most people could not speak English. They came to Chinatown, stayed there, and did not have to know how to speak English. There is also a difference in our religions. Almost no modern Japanese have strong religious aspects, but many Koreans are Christians. They go to church. Cedar Rapids, Iowa, also has a Korean Church. Church gives them a good opportunity to unite. The Japanese are not so united. I have heard that the Japanese dissolve more quickly. Sometimes we are weak, but sometimes we are more liberal and that has an impact.

Sometimes people in America are aware of our Asian distinctions and it makes some of us feel good when they notice it. I have a female Cambodian friend who has become American now. Her last name is Chhen. The double "h" describes she is from Cambodia. Here, when she wrote her last name, a student said, "Chhen, that's cool." That was it. But when she went to graduate school, one person came up to her and asked, "Did you come from Cambodia?" She knew that some people knew of her background and she felt safe.

There are some people who, when they find out about our differences, are shocked at what they discover. I, personally, do not have a religious belief. That amazes a lot of people. Anna, my other international friend, says, "Why don't you have a religion? You should have a religion." I think of before World War II, and how Japan used to have a religion—Buddhist or Shinto. We still have some, but it is not so strong now. We pray sometimes if it is convenient. Not too many people have a strict religion, which can be both good and bad.

I plan on graduating from Coe before going back to Japan. I want to graduate next year, but I have already borrowed $10,000 from my parents. If I can borrow more money, I will be able to graduate next year. My parents are not actually supporting me in school because they are both retired. I asked them to loan it to me, but the $10,000 was not enough. I worked in the summer at a company where I worked on computers and answered the phone to earn money.

My parents and my sister have never come to the United States to visit me, they are too old and do not understand English. It is hard because it is up to me to go and visit them. My sister is thirty-seven. I am not really close to her; her life is so different from mine. She got married when she was twenty and has two kids. She has a happy family life and is always railing on me about my marital status. She tried to arrange for me to marry someone. When I was working before college, she blamed me. Now that I have quit my job and I have come to the United States to become a student, she is really angry with me. This summer, my sister and I argued a lot and we did not contact each other. That is sad, but it is too late to change.

———————◆◆◆◆◆———————

Ayaka Tanaka was born in Nagano, Japan, in 1971 and came to the United States as a student in 1989. She was an exercise science major at Northeast Missouri State University at the time of the interview in 1994.

I was born in Japan, in the middle of the main island, in Nagano in 1971. Because of my father's job I moved around a lot when I was younger—seven times in sixteen years. My father works for one of the big cosmetic companies in Japan—Shiseido. There are many branches to the company and my father is now working in Canada, which is where I lived for a while after living in Singapore. My mother is a housekeeper. She used to have a part-time job in Japan. I have two sisters. My little sister is very young, she is only fourteen and still lives with my parents. The other one is twenty-two and is also studying in the United States, at Indiana University in Bloomington, Indiana. She has played piano since she was three years old and may go to a music school here in the United States or in Germany.

I, personally, do not have a religion; my mother did not force me to become Buddhist. My mother is from a small, religious town and there are big temples near her house. If I had a religion, I would really have to limit myself and attend one place, but I would want to try everything. I felt this way when I was in Singapore; there were Muslims, Hindus, and Christians. If I were to have a specific religion, I would not be able to enjoy all the different religions. I have not visited a church here. It is nice to know about a religion, but I think that if I were not, for example, Christian, it would be rude to the people who are. In that way, I am kind of scared. I do not want to be impolite.

I attended preschool, kindergarten, and junior high in Japan; public schools were everywhere. We took entrance exams to get into high school. It was very hard. I entered high school in 1986 when my father was asked to move to Toronto, Canada. I had to quit my high school there and we moved to Singapore. There, I enrolled in the International School, a school specifically for international students. Not many American students were there because there is also a school called America's School and most Americans went there. I stayed there for five and a half years. When I graduated, I went to the community college called the American College, which is actually connected to the International School. They have American programs that proved to be beneficial to me later. They have a British program at the International School, so I had to adjust a little bit.

When I graduated from there with an associate's degree, I decided it was not enough to get a job and I wanted to continue my education at a university. I thought I would have a better chance to get a job in Japan if I came to the United States to study. If I had gone to an American school I would have had to graduate by the time I was twenty-one years old. If I had attended ESL (English as a Second Language) I would have had to start at the beginning level and I would not have graduated in time. Now I am a senior, this is my third semester at the university. I am majoring in exercise science. After I graduate from here, I think I want to take the general test for aerobics instructors and personal trainers to get my license so that if I want to go back to my country, it will be easier for me to get a job.

Citizens of Singapore are multilingual. Sometimes they speak English, sometimes they choose Mandarin, which is Chinese, sometimes an Arabic language, and sometimes an Indonesian language called Bahasa. I spoke English in school. The first time I had contact with the language was when I was thirteen. Usually in Japan you started studying English when you were in junior high, but I never studied much. When I moved to Singapore I had to study the language; I did not even think of studying it earlier.

I think I have a fairly good understanding of English. If the teachers talk about a subject and relate it to life, I can understand it very easily. But if they talk about the human body, the digestive system, it is very difficult and complicated. I have to look some things up to see what they are talking about. There are two things that bring my grades down. One is a lack of a general understanding; the other is lack of knowledge in general—subjects I would not understand even in Japanese. The teachers are very helpful and understand my situation.

I have been in college a little bit longer than other people because I did not learn written English at the International School, I just learned to speak and read. I did not know that many American people used writing often; it is very tricky to me. Before I was accepted here I had to study everything again. It took three and a half years to graduate from the community college in Singapore. Then I thought about going back to Japan and getting a job, but when I thought about it, I realized I had gone to an institution that provided me with information about United States, so I might as well use it.

Because my parents were in Canada, I chose this university by myself; I was still in Singapore at the time. I came here from Toronto, Canada, by way of a plane to Kansas City, then I took a Redwing airplane to the Kirksville airport, and an international student picked me up. I had to visit this institution to see what kinds of majors were offered and I chose exercise science. There are not too many international students in my major classes, but I still feel accepted. I feel a little bit alone, but at the same time, it is challenging for me. The majors offered by colleges in the United States are completely different from those in my country. In this country, I had to decide what I wanted to do, and then I had to look at tuition fees and living fees. Because I spent a long time in school, I had experience and knew my best study habits, and so I knew I had to choose somewhere in the countryside. If I were in a big city, I would screw up because I would party. Singapore is kind of an exciting place. This place is okay.

I hated changing schools so often. But now I cannot stay in one place for more than three or four years. I like moving around now. I plan on finishing school and getting my degree here. Then I plan on going back to Japan. I have been planning this for quite a long time. I have not been to Japan for five years; I went back once for a week, and that was it.

When I went back, I stayed in Tokyo for three days and I traveled around the countryside. Then I went back to Singapore. Basically, I have not been back for seven years. I am sure there will be a culture shock. But I want to go to my country one more time to get a different point of view. I do not think I would like to live there the rest of my life, but I want to go back to Japan. If I go back I want to live in Tokyo, it is just like living in New York. It is very busy and very stressful. I could stay there while I am young because I have more energy, but as I get older, I would probably have to go somewhere else.

Besides living around the world, I have also done some traveling around the United States and Southeast Asia. I went to Florida. I have a friend who used to study at the same school in Singapore. He is at a small university near St. Augustine. I went there and had some other friends come too; we had a big party. I went to Washington DC and I have been to

New Jersey and Atlantic City while visiting my sister. I have also traveled to Indonesia and Malaysia. I love the island of Malaysia. When I got there, I noticed how quiet and beautiful it was! I had never seen the sea like it is there. I would like to go back there some day. It is fun to visit Southeast Asia.

Most of my friends here are international students because they were the ones I approached when I first got here. I have some American friends, but compared to my international friends, I cannot say that we are very close. We know each other, but not very well. I came to Kirksville before I started classes so that I could see the school. At that time, the International Student Office introduced me to a Japanese girl and through her I met another of my current friends, so I met two Japanese girls right away. If anything happens, I call them. We are still friends. I hang out mostly with international students—from Japan, China, and European countries too—because we are in the same situation, being in a different country. I want to know about other cultures, so that is why I came here. Sometimes I want to know about other countries too. By talking to other international students I can get a better idea, otherwise, all I can do is look at a map.

I am not dating anyone here. I am kind of old. I am going to be twenty-four soon and most of the students here look young. There is no reason to tell somebody "I like you" because I am going to be leaving soon. Most of my friends, international students, are leaving too. We try not to be too involved with each other—that way I will not have to worry about leaving when I do go. It does not matter if I date a Japanese or not. Maybe my parents want me to have a Japanese boyfriend, and maybe I will meet my husband in the future, but I keep telling them that they cannot force me to love someone. Ever since I left Japan, I have never had a good experience with a Japanese guy. My parents said, "Well, it's only certain people, maybe you will find one." I hope so!

When I have kids I do not know if I will move them around like I moved around with my family. It depends on my future husband. Anywhere I live, I will not put my child in a public school though; if they were, I would have to tutor for them on the side.

On the weekends, we like to have parties at someone's house. We play music and eat and drink liquor, because most of international students are above twenty, which is the drinking age in Japan. Most of our countries are not that strict about the drinking age. Society is not strict, we would have a problem if we drink too much. The driving age is different here too, for a motorcycle is sixteen, and for a car, it is eighteen.

Where I grew up, we had a good transportation system. We had the metro and the buses. The last place that I lived was Chiba, next to Tokyo, and it is very busy. People rode bicycles to the metro station, which was not far, but we are a very busy people and wanted to get there quick. From there my father usually spent one and a half hours trying to get to his job in Tokyo. We are actually close to Tokyo; other people spend up to two hours on the metro. To do that you have to ride bicycle to get to the station, if you are late and miss a train, then you will be late to work.

I have had jobs before. I worked part time in Canada in a warehouse. I basically counted the products in the boxes and sent them. This warehouse was a part of my father's company. He did not let me begin at office level, he said, "Start from there, you are not supposed to be here." I experienced the basic job, and I think it was a good idea. I have also worked as a waitress in a Japanese restaurant in Singapore. Now it is very hard to get a job, any kind of job. Some people say there are no jobs for girls.

Those jobs had a specific Japanese style. I had to wear a traditional Japanese costume and was unable to have a manicure. It is very important to the people who come to the restaurant—they want the Japanese experience. No matter what, I had to be nice to customers. I was scared before I started, but once I did it was kind of fun; it is nice to meet people and learn about their culture. It does not mean I have to be serious about my job.

Just three years ago, there were a lot of job opportunities in Japan, but suddenly, one and a half years ago there were no jobs. They were gone, the bubble burst. The economy is very tight right now and it is very hard for girls to get jobs—even an office job. If I were to go back to Japan and could not find a job right away, I would settle for any kind of job. At the same time, I would like to work as an aerobics instructor at a community center, even if I did not get paid for it. I would continue looking for a job in the area I would like to work in, and when I found one, I would leave my old position.

Women's roles are different in America, not just with jobs but with other things too. Here, women tend to state their opinions more, though men often do not like to hear a lot of this. My father has been outside of the country for a long time like all of us, so he is very liberal. He is very different from other Japanese fathers. My sisters and I are very westernized and we voice our opinions all the time and we try to argue about what we think does not make sense. My father does not like it sometimes. He has to escape from our house, but we just grew up that way. Getting American-ized was difficult.

Here on campus, I live in Campbell Apartments and can cook for myself. My roommate is Taiwanese and she also is a good cook. I like the privacy of living in Campbell and I am able to keep the place clean, I like cleaning up. I think I will stay here next year too; everything pretty much fits in the room right now. At the same time, though, I think I will look for a close friend who wants to move in. I will probably choose an Asian girl rather than a Caucasian because the food we eat is similar—I like Japanese food.

I eat rice, bread, and all kinds of other foods. So far I have not found any food I cannot eat. I eat American food a lot; sometimes I go to Main Street Market (in the Student Union Building). When I lived in Ryle Hall during my first semester, I had a twenty-meal plan and around midterm break, I realized that I could not handle the food. The food is not so bad, but I just take it day by day. Sometimes I think, "Oh my God, I need some-thing simple." During my second semester, I just had a fifteen-meal plan. It was at that time that I moved to Campbell, so we had a kitchen. I basically ate in the cafeteria during the week and at home on the weekends. I cook noodles a lot and eat some seafood. We only have salmon and catfish. It is okay; I can deal with it. Some people cannot though, and have to go some-where else to eat.

While I am here I try to keep up with news about Japan. Sometimes there are reports on CNN, and the Kansas City news has been running sto-ries about Japan recently. Otherwise, I have not read a Japanese newspaper since I have gotten here. Maybe that is a mistake, but I am busy. Outside of class, I like to catch up on my sleep, talk to my friends, watch television, read magazines, exercise, and just jump around. I also like to go to parties at my friend's place.

If I could see myself ten years from now, I would hope I would be an aerobics instructor, but not only that. I want to work in a health company and do a little bit of desk work. In ten years, I will be thirty-three and will, maybe, have two children then. I think I want to travel across the United States by bicycle. Actually, I have wanted to do that since I have been here, but I am so small that no bike will fit me! I want to go to other countries to see my friends who were in my class here or in Singapore. I keep in touch with them still. I learned my best friend died a few months ago though, so that was quite a shock.

Part 4
Koreans

Korean American adoptees Liz Hwang-Mi Brown and Lisa Burton were both born in South Korea and adopted by European American couples at an early age. As adoptees, they were puzzled about the meaning of their Korean names, who their biological parents were, and why they had been abandoned. However, the most troubling difficulty was their dual identity. They were raised by European Americans and grew up among whites, with the values of white Americans. Yet, they encountered racial discrimination or prejudice because of their non-white physical appearance. They were teased in high school and their treatment by the larger society resembles that of children of Asian immigrants. At the same time, they were alienated by other Korean American youth as a result of their lack of the Korean language and culture. Therefore, the search for roots and dealing with their dual identity have become the major anxieties for many Korean adoptees.

Jin-Hee Cho's story reveals the life of Korean immigrant women. Cho and her older brother took care of themselves since she was in the second grade as her parents were rarely at home before seven or nine o'clock in the evening. The common phenomenon of immigrant parents working long hours and leaving their children home alone is typified by Cho's personal account. Katherine Larson's story about her mother reflects an immigrant woman's struggle in overcoming the language barrier. After living in the United States for twenty-five years, Larson's mother still had a thick accent no matter how hard she tried to lose it. The story rightly points out the connection between her associating mostly with Korean immigrants and speaking Korean, and her language handicap in English. While the ethnic solidarity certainly provides comfort in a foreign land, at the same time it hampers an immigrant's cultural assimilation. While placed under the section of interracial marriage, Yong-Mi Jones's interview also largely reveals the struggle and success of the Korean immigrants.

Su-Hee Sparks's story about her mother's interracial marriage and her own provides rich materials to compare two different patterns of interracial marriage among Korean American women. Her mother's marriage typifies the unions between American servicemen and Korean women who worked at or near American military bases and were longing for a better life in America through marriage. Su Hee Sparks's mother married her father, a white American serviceman, because he told her "I am a rich American." Mismatching expectations of both parties, the Korean bride's inability to speak English, and her lack of knowledge about American culture brought tremendous difficulties to the marriage.

Spark's own interracial marriage represents those among the second-generation Korean American women. Similar interracial marriages are also found in Su-Yi Edwards's and Yong-Mi Jones's interviews. Daughters of Korean immigrant women, compared to their mother's generation, are more compatible with their marital partners. They met their partners in educational or occupational settings that indicate the similar socioeconomic and cultural conditions between the two partners. Consequently, these interracial marriages would have better chance of succeeding.

The relationship between Christie Kim, a high school student at the time of the interview, and her parents explicitly exhibits the conflict between individual aspirations and parental expectations among the Asian American youth. Kim's parents placed education and academic performance as high priorities, which Kim both appreciated and resented at the same time. Her story also explains the causes behind the stereotypical Asian American academic success.

12

Adoptees

Liz Hwang-Mi Brown was born in Pusan, South Korea, in 1974 and was adopted by European American parents. She was attending Northeast Missouri State University and majoring in English and minoring in German and biology at the time of the interview in 1995.

I was born in Pusan, South Korea, on 12 December 1974. I'm almost twenty-one. I was adopted. I know absolutely nothing about my birth parents. My mom's Swedish, a third generation Swede. My dad is French. My parents are both white, WASPs. My dad's a mutt and so is my mom even though she likes to say she's mostly Swedish.

My name was Kim Hwang-Mi when I came to the United States, that's where my middle name came from. Koreans always give their surnames first. It would be like Kim, Hwang-Mi. I don't know if Mi was my middle name but they always just say Kim Hwang-Mi. I don't know what you would say first if you were friends with someone, whether it's "I'm Hwang-Mi" or not. I don't know what it means, which is another big disagreement in my family. My mother told me it meant "grand beauty" when I was young, but now she tells me she never said that, so I don't really know what it means.

As I said, I was born in Pusan, Korea, on the very southern tip of the peninsula. I lived there for two years until I was adopted. My parents were thirty-eight at that time. My mom tried to find out about my birth parents, but she couldn't find anything. I think it was because of the culture, because they were Americans and the Koreans are really racist. Also I know a lot of other people my age from Korea. It always says the same thing on the adoption papers of anyone I've ever talked to—she was found abandoned. I do not believe that at all. It also says that they don't have any record at all of our pasts. Again, I don't believe that. So I guess I don't know anything about my birth parents. It's really very weird to think that I could have brothers and sisters out running around.

My parents decided to adopt because they had two boys. It seems that if your second child is not a girl, you might as well stop, but they wanted a little girl…and my mom decided that she didn't want to keep trying, since she had a hard time with her pregnancies. Plus, my brothers were running her so ragged. That's why they decided to adopt. They went to Korea because they were thinking about Vietnam or some other war-torn country. Not that Korea was really war-torn, but they also thought that they would get an older child, like a toddler or even older. Because my parents were getting older (they are fifty-seven), I think they just wanted someone from Asia. I think they would have even taken a child from India. My dad always thought Asian features were beautiful. It's kind of frightening to think that was the reason they wanted to adopt from Korea.

My fiancé studied in Korea this past term and he spent some time in Pusan. I asked him if he saw any old ladies running around that looked like me. I'm the one who got him interested in Korea because he loves me. He was never that interested until we broke up, then he was all gung ho with Korea and Koreans. He loved Korea, except the Korean men. He says they are all chauvinistic. He's so tall that he could step on them.

My father went to the journalism school at University of Missouri and got his degree there along with my other uncles and my aunt. He works for the 3M corporation, the Minnesota Mining and Manufacturing Corporation. 3M is divided into groups and sectors and he's below the group vice-president. He's a marketing manager of a group and does a lot of foreign stuff with marketing. I don't know a lot about what he does. I've never wanted to know enough to spend a day at work with him. He's pretty much a suit except he gets to wear sport jackets on Friday or a nice sweater. After he retires, he's planning on doing consulting work. He does a lot of graphics and related work.

My mother is a domestic engineer. That's the p.c. (politically correct) term for a housewife. She takes tennis lessons and walks around our pond. She's always ironing clothes and watching the O. J. Simpson trial; it's so sad. My mom says she needs to get a job to pay for my wedding. I tell her, "Mom, you don't have to do that! We have plenty of money for a wedding, it's not like I'm asking for a wedding of two thousand people with crab cakes and lobster and a honeymoon across the universe." She's taking computer classes so she can learn to use our personal computer. We're a very computer-oriented family. I have a laptop, my dad has a laptop and a desktop, plus two more desktops in our basement. Additionally, he has his own computer at work and he's getting a new power PC as soon as it comes out.

I have two older brothers. One is thirty-two and the other is thirty. Both are my parents' biological children. I don't think my parents put too much pressure on me to succeed. Of course, they wanted me to succeed in whatever I tried to do, but I always had high expectations of myself. I saw where my brothers had failed and have tried to avoid their mistakes.

For instance, my fiancé's stepdad is a psychologist, so I sat down to talk with him for a day. I just love having relatives like this in the family. I love the free counseling! It's great because he does dream analysis and all sorts of cool stuff. I sat down to talk with him about my parents because I don't get along with them very well. For instance, the day before my fiancé was going to leave last summer, we were going to go over to his house to go rollerblading. I brought with me a bikini top and a T-shirt because it was hot outside and I wanted to get some sun. But when I told my mom that I was going over to my fiancé's she said she didn't like the idea of me going over there in my bikini top without any adults around. I said, "Mom, I don't believe this. I'm twenty-one years old, he is twenty-four, we're both adults! My brother was married when he was twenty-three!" And of course she said angrily, "Well fine then, go ahead." I'm sure she realized how stupid she sounded saying that. They're always telling me, "Don't be late. Get home early." In fact, if I were to come home at two o'clock in the morning they would say the next day, "Boy, you sure were out late last night. I think you should try to be home a little earlier tonight." My dad told me to be home before dark once. They hate the fact that I go out late.

I drive a Nissan Pathfinder when I'm at home, but they just have this idea in their head that people would do anything for this car. They were worried that someone would carjack me or rush up to me at stoplights or something and try to get in. They said, "This car is a really popular thing for teenagers nowadays, and I wouldn't want anything to happen to it or you." I'm staying in Woodbury, which is an upper class white suburb of St. Paul, and if I stay there, nothing is going to happen to me. The worst thing that happens in Woodbury is speeding.

I'm not going to South Minneapolis! They're just so overprotective. This time, it was a lot better. They didn't tell me once to be home by midnight. I've always had extremely early curfews. I still have a curfew even though it's not an official one. My fiancé and I had our anniversary on July third, and we went to see the fireworks and then to his house. I gave my mom a call and told her where I was at about 11:30 PM. She wanted me to come home then. I said we were going to watch a movie, but she said, "Try to be home soon, okay?" I replied, "Mom, it's only 11:30!" She still wanted me to come home right away and said, "It's late and I don't know if I like the idea of you driving home by yourself when it's late."

I think they discriminate. They think it's worse because I'm female and they don't believe that I can take care of myself. They just think all these terrible things are going to happen to me, like I'll get raped or something. I'm just the type of person that if somebody were trying to attack me, I would just go crazy. I would be punching and screaming and kicking as much as I could until I could pry him off me and then beat him some more! I would probably find a garden hose or something and smack him.

My brothers were the same way as me. My older brother would just sneak out. He ended up moving out of our house and into an apartment with his girlfriend at the time, who was three years older. My parents forced them to get married because they were living together. We all hated her, but they've been divorced for six years now.

I'm the "parent pleasing child," which is what my fiancé's father calls it. Maybe this is what sometimes happens with the youngest child. They see what their older siblings do wrong and they try to avoid those mistakes in order to to please their parents. I don't really know though, since I don't know much about psychology. But really, because my brother was bad with credit cards, I know that I will never be bad with credit cards. What really sucks is that I didn't get my own credit card until this year because my parents thought I would misuse it. They're still saying that to me, always telling me to pay it off in full every time. I know that I would pay it off soon, but they don't trust me. All the mistakes my brothers made, they think I will do the same thing. It's really infuriating.

In school, my parents always said that they wanted me to do as well as I could. They never put pressure on me for my grades. I think if I failed a class they would care, like most parents would, but they wanted me to do my best. I never had any problems with any of my teachers. They were all pretty fair, at least on the outside. At my school we had a TCEL program, which was English as a second language. Don't ask me what TCEL stands for because it's a lot more than English as a second language. There were a lot of Cambodian and Vietnamese and Laotian people in there. They couldn't speak English at all, and I could speak English perfectly. My dad told me that I came home once when I was really little and I asked him, "Why don't I have eyes like Mommy?" But I don't really remember any instances of teasing during grade school, and that's when children are the worst. There were some Japanese students that would be in the mainstream classes, because the Japanese start teaching their kids English early. I remember this one kid who came over from Japan when he was about seven, and he picked up English so fast that the next year he was already in our class. I knew a girl who was French. She didn't speak any English whatsoever, but they put her directly into our class, while they didn't do that with the Japanese students. I don't know why.

I was teased more when I was in eighth grade while I was on the bus, by these guys that had nothing better to do with their time. They would sit in the back of the bus, these little Aryan boys with blonde hair and blue eyes, the kind of guys that were caught smoking pot and drinking in the bathroom. They were really low class people and they weren't very nice. They would bow at me and make Chinese sounds. They used to call me Ho Chi Minh. I was only in the eighth grade, and I didn't know who he was, so I looked him up in the dictionary. I saw he was this famous Vietnamese leader. I asked them the next day if they knew who he was and of course they didn't know. I said, "You guys are so stupid, get a life!"

We had lockers that opened in half. Some of the luckier people got the big lockers in the eighth grade. I did because it went alphabetically. Anyway, one time somebody spit on the top of my locker. I don't know if it was intentional or not. And another time my locker was strung open and in it they wrote "gook bitch!" I don't even know how someone would know which locker was mine! But I went home and told my mom and she went to the principal. If you call someone a gook, it means he/she is a Vietnamese. I was called Chink too, that means Chinese. There's no real slur name for Koreans. If you're going to use racial slurs, at least get the right country! I don't remember what happened, I just remember that my Mom started to pick me up after school.

People had grown up a little by high school. During my freshman year, riding home on the bus, these guys who were totally moronic to begin with were now total loners. By this time, I had a bunch of friends and we would make fun of them. But I was reading this book for my Young Adult

Literature class, possibly by a Korean author whose last name was Lee, called *Finding Our Voice*. She wrote about people making fun of her and how others would ignore it or pretend they were really busy. Often, that's what would happen to me. One girl, Anne, who was a really good friend of mine, sat there staring straight ahead while I was bawling. I would stand up for myself and all they did was throw my words back into my face and make fun of what I said. So I learned to just totally ignore them. I remember one time that it got really bad. I was walking down the aisle and they bowed to me and I slugged them in the face! It never deterred them, but I felt better.

I went to a Korean culture camp between fourth and fifth grade. It was a day camp where you learned some of the language. It's where I bought my Korean dress. I don't know what it is called. You can't call it a *kimono* because that's a Japanese robe. It's got these little straps that tie up, and then it is long and straight down to the ground. Around the bottom there are little designs. The Koreans use really bright colors like red and fuschia together, bright lime green and bright blue. And then they have these little jackets. The jackets, depending on the kind of dress it is, have big poufy sleeves. My jacket is way too small for me, while the dress is too long. Actually, it kind of fits me now, since I got it in the fifth grade. At this camp, they taught us some of the language; I think I can still say "good morning teacher" and I also know part of the Korean National Anthem. The camp was for adopted kids and was put on by the Children's Home Society, which was one of the agencies through which I was adopted.

We also learned how to make *bulgoki*, which my roommate has now turned into something completely unlike its original form. But it's really good. You marinate strips of steak with garlic and sesame seeds and soy sauce. It's really good. My roommate puts a lot of black pepper on it so you can't taste anything else, and then we serve it with rice. My roommate still makes it. I made it once during freshman year and then she thought it was really good, so she would cook it and make little changes to it, and now she's the one who cooks it. I make lasagna and she makes *bulgoki*.

My best friend, who I've known since I was three, was talking about how I was her best friend, and her grandmother said, "But Nikki, she's Korean!" And Nikki replied, "So? I don't care!" Nikki was really young back then and already she knew that it didn't matter. Her parents are really nice; they're like a second set of parents to me. They love me, but if Nikki ever dated a black man, she would be in trouble! Anyone that was not a white man was unacceptable. It was fine to be friends, but according to her parents, you just don't marry them. It's interesting because a lot of people don't care if there's an Asian person in the family, but a black person would be totally taboo. Even some people that would have a problem with Asians get over it sooner than with black people. I never quite understood that.

I remember there was a Native American girl in high school during my senior year. When she was a sophomore or junior, she ended up leaving the school because things got too bad. People harrassed her using a derogatory Indian term. They would write this word all over her locker and people would try to hit her in the parking lot. Additionally, when I was a junior, there were less than ten black students in the whole school. There were definitely more Asians in my high school than there were blacks. Typically, the Asians in our town have more money than the blacks, because most of the Asians that came were chemists from China, most of whom work for 3M, so there were naturally more Asians. One day, someone spray painted obscenities about blacks on the track and on someone's locker. It was really bad for a whole week for the black people in our school.

Another interesting thing about my high school was that some of the really popular people were Asian. Emily Barry was an adopted Korean and she was really popular. Sarah Lee, a year behind me, was Chinese. Every year she was Winterfest queen for her grade. And our homecoming queen was a half-Chinese girl. So we had a black homecoming king and a half-Chinese queen, which was really odd given the demographics of my school. I didn't find it easier to make friends with other Korean kids. One close friend that I had was Betty. She's a second generation Taiwanese, but we were friends simply because we were friends, not because of race. Another girl, Amy, was also adopted Korean but she hated talking about that fact; it was a very sore subject with her.

I disagree with the term "Asian American." I think it's good to be proud of who you are and of your background, but by adding Asian, that just sets you apart from everyone else. People say Asian American and African American and Native American, but Caucasian people are just "white." You don't say Euro-American. It just doesn't seem right. They're trying to be sensitive to it, but I have no ties to Asia other than my genes. As far as nationality, I'm American. I guess it should be different if you were born here rather than if you were an immigrant. It's hard to know what to call someone. I guess what you could say is American of Asian Heritage or something. I was in the International Club at my school because I was interested in other countries, and everybody that I was with assumed that I was a foreign student. I think that you can tell the difference between foreign students and American–born Asians even by the way they dress.

I used to have an identity crisis because I wasn't Asian and I wasn't a white American. I always wondered if we got funny looks because there was this white family and then me. I don't think we ever really did. I always felt that when people describe someone, they describe them by the way they look. And it's easy to say "She's black" or "She's Asian" by the facial features. I've never really been offended by that, but nobody ever says "they're white" about a Caucasian person. I guess that's because white people have different features and different eye colors, so it never really bothered me. As for being adopted, people would always refer to me as the "adopted Korean daughter," or "the little girl that they adopted from Korea." When friends of the family first meet me, they would ask if I was adopted. I think that's kind of funny because it's obvious! I still wonder if someone will judge me because of the way I look. It's not something that's easy to hide and there's nothing I can do about it.

I think my experiences are probably typical among other adopted Asians. One kid I know here, Than, talked about it a lot with me because he wanted to go look for his biological parents. His mother actually knows who his birth mother is, so he was kind of thinking about where he fits into things. We had a lot of discussions about that. I think adopted people in general have a lot of the same feelings, wondering about their origins. I guess I don't care and I just want to know for medical reasons. I want to know stupid things like what my birth mother looked like after having kids, if she had easy pregnancies, and if she had breast or cervical cancer so I would know whether I'm at a high risk for cancer or other diseases. I wonder who I look like and from whom I got these dark circles under my eyes.

I've never been treated differently by other Asian nationalities. I think it would be different if I went to that country. People that come here generally want to broaden their horizons and have an open mind. It would probably be different if I went there. I've heard that all the Asian cultures are racist. I think the Japanese and Koreans have the most problems because of the wars. Korea has been bombarded from all around. They've been attacked by both the Chinese and the Japanese. Koreans from Korea would look down on me because I don't speak the language or know anything about it. If I went to Korea I wouldn't fit in. I would scream American even though I look Korean. It doesn't matter if you're of Korean descent; if you're an American citizen, then you're American. They would know that I'm American.

I was never pressured to date within my race. My parents just wanted me to pick a good one, and I picked a winner. He's a great guy. We met at 3M. If you're not a regular employee, you have to sign in. I worked with this guy, Christopher, who had the same job as me. It was my first day of work without having someone lead me in, so I had to sign my name and pick up my badge. I forgot to write something so I grabbed the pen out of this guy's hand, who was getting ready to write something. I said, "Oh I'm sorry. I didn't mean to do that." I was so nervous. And that was Steve. The guy behind him was Christopher. They had known each other for years, practically since grade school. Well I could tell that Steve was giving me the once over. We were introduced and shook hands. Then I bumped into him again where we had to use the computers. He came in and said, "Hi, Chris! Oh, you're not Chris!" and I said, "No, I'm not, he's in there." He went into the next room and when they came out, they invited me to go to lunch with them, so I went. My face was buried in my salad, I didn't say much. He started asking me all these questions like, "Where do you go to school? What year are you? Where do you live?" I gave short answers, and that was our entire conversation. As time passed, we started going to lunch more often and I began to think that he was really cute. Eventually we started talking and flirting more and more. I would ride to work with my dad, because he had a close parking spot in the garage, but he would get off work later than I did so I would start catching rides home with Chris and Steve. Then we were at lunch one day and Steve asked, "What are you guys doing this weekend?" Chris responded, "Well I'm going to a party." Steve said, "Oh I was going to ask if you guys wanted to do something, but since you're busy Chris...." And Steve turned to me and asked if I wanted to do something. I said sure. I found out later that Steve had asked Chris ahead of time if he was doing something so he would be sure it was just the two of us. Isn't that sweet? So that's how we started going out. I was so excited, but I tried to keep my cool. I told him once that I really like Cheddar and Sour Cream Ruffles and he brought me some.

Things progressed and I was a good friend, a girlfriend, and a fiancé all within about six months. He hasn't officially proposed yet, and I haven't gotten my engagement ring, but for all practical purposes we are engaged. I have my gown! But he doesn't consider it official yet until I get my engagement ring. I would have gotten it sooner, but he made this promise to himself that he would not buy a ring until he got a job so that he could buy a beautiful ring. I would love it if it was just on a typical day, out of the blue, and he walked in the door with the ring and said, "Hey, do you want to get married?" It doesn't have to be with dinner and champagne. I want it to be "us."

I think that Steve and I are both equal, because he doesn't let me push him around at all. It's not in his nature to push me around, so we're really on equal ground. To my knowledge his family doesn't have any problems with my being Asian.

My major is English and my minors are German and biology. Everyone looks at me like I'm crazy. I speak German, but I have never really had any desire to learn Korean. I got a scholarship here because I am a minority. I think it's wrong to give scholarships based solely on race, but if it's going to help me, then I don't mind. I just got this dinky little $1,000 scholarship. It would have been more if my ACT score would have been higher.

I was in College Republicans for two years, where I was Adair County liaison last year. We coordinate activities between the Adair County Republicans and College Republicans, but I never went to any of their meetings. I did do a speak-out between Prism and College Republicans. I think you can guess where I stand on the gay rights issues. I'm not Christian; I'm not white or wealthy. I believe we should help the environment, I believe in the woman's right to choose, I believe in equal rights for homosexuals, and I'm a right wing Republican.

I've been in Phi Eta Sigma. I'm currently in LAP (Lifestyle Advocacy Program), the HIV/AIDS education group on campus, and I am Red Cross trained and certified. The office of Multicultural Affairs sent me a letter wanting to know if I would join a group because I was a minority. I said that I'd never seen any groups for Koreans and I thought that exclusive groups only perpetuated racism and never helped anything. Needless to say, they never sent anything else. I did get a letter from the head of multicultural affairs. He nominated me for some award for outstanding minority students. They wanted me to fill out this application to be included in some book. My parents thought it was pretty cool, but I just thought that it was something to put on a resume. I wanted to join the gun and rifle club because I like target shooting, but I never found out anything about it. I also wanted to do Model U. N. because I did it in high school and really liked it. I decided to come to a university in a small town because there are too many diversions in a big city. I would never get anything done.

I worked for a temp company during the summer and for the last two summers I've worked for 3M. I have never had any problems at any of my jobs, except boredom.

I disagree with Affirmative Action. I think that it's good to try to even out the racial lines, and I guess I think the idea behind Affirmative Action is good. It's good to have people with different backgrounds. But as far as getting a job goes, I think you should hire the best person for the job, regardless of race or sex. I think it's wrong to hire a black female when an Asian male would be more qualified for the job.

After I graduate from here, I'm going to get married and then go on to graduate school. I will definitely get my master's degree, then I plan to teach college-level British literature. Steve is going to work in computer science. Then after I'm finished, he'll go into graduate school for philosophy. Hopefully, he'll end up teaching it. Nobody usually puts computer science together with philosophy, but they're both based on logic and step-by-step thinking.

I don't really watch the news. I probably wouldn't pay any more attention to news on Korea than I would to anything else, unless it was something really important, like if Korean-born Americans were awarded $10,000, then I'd really pay attention. I used to wonder, like most adopted children who think they don't belong in their family, if I was an Oriental princess, if I was really the daughter of some nobleman who would come find me and I would be rich.

I'm a Lutheran, but I don't go to church very often. I read *Zen and the Art of Motorcycle Maintenance*, if that counts as studying an Asian religion! I read the *Tao of Pooh*. In addition, I have to read *Siddhartha* by Hermann Hesse for German Culture. It's about Siddhartha Gautama, the Buddha.

Someday I would like to go to Korea. The first place I want to go to, though, is England. There are a few places that I really want to go, like England, Germany, and Italy, especially Florence. Steve wants to go to the Orient. That's fine with me, but I don't want to go there first. Europe is the last place on his list.

At least we agreed on a honeymoon spot. We want to go to the Bahamas or the Virgin Islands. It doesn't mean we're going, but we want to go there—go on a cruise, parasailing, scuba diving, and things like that. I just want to go someplace where the water's blue, the beaches are white, and it's warm but not humid. The beaches here are not exactly white. I can't say the water's that blue either.

I don't think I could teach my kids about Korean culture because I don't really know anything about it myself. I always wonder about the age when kids start to realize that they look different. I think I came home with that question about my eyes when I was in second grade, or maybe first grade. My mom would say [to that question], "Honey, your eyes are beautiful." But that doesn't help me out any, Mom! I don't care what you think; you're not those kids at school! I guess I would say something like, "You know, since I'm Asian, then I know every type of martial art known to man, and I'll just go in tomorrow and kick their asses." But we joke around about martial arts. I really don't know what I would say. It would probably depend on what my kids look like, because some biracial look Asian, some look white, and others look in between.

In movies like *The Joy Luck Club*, Asians have a really positive image. I thought it was a great movie and I cried. Margaret Chou, she's funny, but not because she's Korean. Her show was on for a half a season and it got canned. I didn't see it, though, so I don't know if it was any good. But I think in movies, especially older movies, there was a real negative stereotype about Asians: buck teeth, squinty eyes, hunched over. But I think in recent years, it's been more positive like in the *Bruce Lee Story*. And Brandon Lee was in *The Crow* although he doesn't look real Asian at all. Brandon Lee's sister is also in the *Bruce Lee Story*, and she doesn't look Asian either. It's interesting because Bruce Lee was a complete Chinese and Linda was almost a Swede. It's funny that, genetically, both of their kids turned out the way they did, because I know some kids with one Asian parent and one Caucasian parent that look really Asian. There have been Asians on soap operas; there's one on *ER*. But as far as prominent actors go, I can't really name any.

As far as role models, I used to admire Rick Allen, the drummer from Def Leopard. Even though he lost his arm in an accident, he still went on to be the drummer of a band. He's a good drummer, too. I always admired him because he had the strength to go on and not fall into the depths of despair. Most of the role models I look to now are literary people. I want to be able to write like Anne Rice, how she uses description and draws me into the story. I also admire people like Watson and Crick, who discovered DNA. And I think Penny Hardaway is really cute. I admire people because they could do things I couldn't do. I know how difficult those tasks were for me, so I always thought it was neat that they could do them. I didn't really have any role models when I was growing up. I didn't have any Asian role models. I didn't look up to Connie Chung. I just always thought that she wore too much eye makeup.

———————◆—•—•—◆———————

Lisa Burton was born in Seoul, South Korea, in the 1970s and was adopted by European American parents. She grew up in Crete, Illinois, and was attending Monmouth College in Monmouth, Illinois, with an undeclared major at the time of the interview in 1995.

I was born in Seoul, Korea. I was adopted at six months so I don't know any information about my parents. The files are closed; they don't really have any information about me because I was dropped off on the doorstep of the orphanage. Basically, I don't know anything.

I have never tried to research my ethnic origins. My parents and I are planning a trip to Korea, but I doubt I will ever know anything about my birth parents. We're going to Seoul when we get the money saved up, probably within the next two years, to see what it's like.

Every year a Korean picnic is held in Chicago for adopted children and their parents through my adoption agency. They have a picnic first; they give you their Korean food. It's a nice little picnic, and then they immerse you in the culture. They do some dances, Tai Kwan Do, and then some language practice. They start speaking the Korean language and children start to pick it up. Once my mom tried to cook *kimchi*, the national dish of Korea. It didn't turn out very good; it just didn't taste right.

I've forgotten the Korean I picked up at the picnic. It's kind of hard to remember it when you grow up in America, where Korean is never used, but I want to learn it. There's a Korean church that I'm going to go to this summer. It's basically a Christian church but it offers free classes about the Korean language and culture. There is a school as well. That's part of the reason I'm going to start going to this Korean church, so that when I go over to Korea, I will be able to speak the language a little. As soon as I learn about the Korean culture myself, I'm going to teach my children about it. I want to pass that on to my children so they know where they came from.

I'm from Crete, Illinois, about half an hour south of Chicago. The northern suburbs have a lot of Asians, but the southern doesn't, or at least the town that I was from didn't. There were two Asians in the whole town and I was one of them. The other girl was also adopted and we were pretty close. We talked about being adopted a lot. She was born in Seoul, Korea, too, and her parents adopted her through the same adoption agency. She went through a lot of the same experiences I did.

My adoptive father is a maintenance man at some condominiums and my adoptive mother is a housewife, who does some cleaning and maid work once in a while. My mom is the dominant one in the household. Both my parents are white. I have two brothers that are my parents' biological children. They are both older, one is twenty-eight and the other one is twenty-seven. I'm the youngest, the only girl, and the baby.

My parents don't treat me any differently than my brothers. My parents told me that my brothers didn't like me for a while though, because I was new and I was a girl. My parents paid a lot of attention to me, because I needed a lot of attention when I was a child. They haven't treated me any differently; they look at me as their own. I think my brothers might not have liked me because I was a baby while they were starting to get older.

I had a lot of difficulty at school when I was growing up. I went to a Lutheran school where I was the only minority. It was different! Other children teased me and called me Rice Cakes and other stupid names. They knew my parents and they couldn't understand why I looked different than them. I don't even know when my parents actually told me I was adopted. It was hard growing up, until these kids got to know me, got used to it, and got over it. I remember that everyone was pulling their eyes back into a squint, making fun of me. My teacher helped out by explaining, "Everybody is the same, but we're all different." They also explained the origins of the different races to help me and my situation.

I think there is some conflict in my life because I'm an adopted Asian. On my father's side of the family, I've never known his mom because she's felt bad towards him ever since he adopted outside the family and outside the Caucasian race. It's sad. The main conflict I have right now is with my identity, not knowing who I look like when I look in the mirror. Most people don't think of that because being biologically linked to your parents, you know who you look like. But for me, it's a big mystery. When you're adopted, you don't know anything about your background. For medical reasons, that's scary too. A lot of my doctors said that they can't do much because they don't know my history and why things happen. I've talked with my friend back home who's also an adopted Asian and she went through a lot of the same experiences in her grade school. We talked and she also finds it difficult that she doesn't know who she is and why someone gave her up. I haven't talked to many adopted Asians except my friend, but I think that others' experiences could be similar.

All of the guys I've dated were Caucasian, since that's what I'm used to. I grew up with them and that's why I've only dated Caucasian men. In my high school we had two Asian people and I was one of them. It was a big high school, but it just didn't have many Asians in it. Maybe that's why I haven't dated any Asian men. In my town, there weren't any.

I started dating somebody I met on the first day of school here, but we broke up because things got difficult. I started to date another guy just last week, but we decided last night that we were better as friends, so at the moment I'm single.

I did have a job for three years at a car dealership that sold Pontiacs and BMWs. There I did a little bit of everything. I was a porter for a while, but my main job was as a receptionist, mostly filing and receiving customers. I didn't really have any discrimination problems with my boss or coworkers because of race. I got harassed for being a young female from a lot of the guys. I like the people and most of them were really nice. I also liked it because I got to work with computers a lot, and I was always busy. I don't like being stuck with nothing to do. My boss was great, but that may have been because I dated his son too! He was a good guy.

Right now I'm attending school here at Monmouth College where I'm a freshman. Monmouth is a lot smaller than my hometown. It's quiet here; it's a nice place with a nice campus. But I don't like it when you have to get away and do something on the weekends especially. On the weekends at home, I always went out and did something fun. There was always something to do, but around here there's not much to do on the weekends.

I'm undecided as to my major because I didn't get into the classes I wanted. I was thinking about either psychology or computer science or accounting. I got the accounting course, but I didn't get into either computer science or psychology. I'm good at a lot of things, but I always have reasons for not picking a certain major. I'm going to wait until next semester.

I decided to come to Monmouth because of the money they offered. It wasn't my first choice college, but they awarded me a lot of scholarships. My parents and I didn't have very much money, so I came here. The other schools gave me scholarships, but not as much as Monmouth did. I didn't receive any scholarships because I was Asian. Actually, they made a mistake and thought I was white. They put me down as Caucasian so I still have to change it. I did receive some minority scholarships from Michigan

State and Illinois Wesleyan.

I think affirmative action helps to a point, but I think it is unfair that a Caucasian person might be more qualified, but is not hired since he/she isn't a minority, and that a minority who may be less qualified may get the job. I believe that the job should go to the most qualified person.

I will go on to get my master's degree. Whatever I choose for my major, I plan to get the highest degree I can in that subject. I just have to decide what I'm going to do. I'm still thinking about it. I'm finding a lot of things that I like to do, but nothing in particular that stands out. I think my ambition to succeed has come from the fact that nobody in my family has gone to college. There has been a lot of pressure on me to go to college. They say, "You're the smart one in the family, you've gotta do this!" So I think that's where it comes from. Neither of my brothers have gone to college and my parents are very supportive of me.

In my spare time I have Kappa [Kappa Kappa Gamma social sorority]. I help elementary kids over at Lincoln Elementary School to learn to use computers and I watch them at the library and tutor them if they need help. I'm Lutheran in faith and I taught four-year-olds at Sunday school for my church. It was so great and I loved the kids. I was on the volleyball team, but the practices exhausted me and I was sleeping instead of doing my homework, so I had to quit to keep my studies up. I'm taking an alternative spring break to help cleaning up in the Appalachian Mountains. I'm planning on entering some things into *Coil*, the literary magazine here. I write short stories, fairy tales, and children's stories. I read the *Chicago Tribune* and the newspaper back home. Sometimes I do pay special attention to articles about Korea, like the riots in California between the Korean store keepers and the blacks.

I've never been treated differently by other Asian groups. I have a lot of Asians that come up to me and ask, "Are you Korean?" But those are the ones who lived there and they can tell who is Korean or Chinese or Japanese because of certain physical features. They start talking about how great Korea is and how I have to go and visit. I haven't had any bad experiences with that though. Some Asians give me the stare and I noticed too that a lot of Asians stare at each other. When you see another Asian, you just kind of stare and wonder, "What is she? Is she Chinese, or Japanese, or Korean?" I stare too. I just try to pick them out. "Yup, she's Korean."

There are just not many actors that are Asians in film, unless they are portraying the stereotypical Asian, in the Bruce Lee movies for example, or in the comedies where you'll have a comic relief role, with the crazy Asian man doing some karate moves. Joan Chen, for me, is the only standout Asian actress. *Joy Luck Club* seems to be the exception to Asian stereotypes in film; it's the first serious Asian American film I think I've seen, and it has a lot of strong actors. I always got made fun of and called Connie Chung.

Sometimes the term "model minority" is actually true. The Asians I have talked to are exceptionally smart. I'm smart, but not as smart as they are. I think Asians are very stereotyped, and sometimes it's for the worst. I think that others definitely have a higher expectation of me because I'm Asian. My classmates all come to me for help. They say, "You're supposed to be smart!" The professors might also think I'm supposed to be smart, too.

Resolving my American and Asian identities goes back to the stereo-types. A lot of people stereotype me and say, "You're supposed to be smart." I also always got the "horny" thing. That's another thing I think Asians get a lot of. We're supposed to be sexually knowledgeable. A lot of people in high school would come up to me and say things like "You look like this girl in this porn film," and "Asians are in porn films, haven't you ever seen? They have special movies dedicated to Asian women. They have a whole porn magazine dedicated to Asian women." I also got it in college a couple of times. A couple of my friends were talking about it. Because I grew up in a white-dominated society, in my little town, there have been a lot of ste-reotypes about Asians.

Most of my friends are Caucasian, and all the guys I've dated have been Caucasian, but I have run into a few problems with a few of the guys I've dated; they've been really childish. A few guys haven't gone out with me because their parents wouldn't approve of it. They want Caucasian grandchildren. It wasn't like we were getting married, but it still happened with a couple of guys. Otherwise I've been pretty accepted. I've had some great friends. I've never really been asked out by any Asians. I've had a lot come up to me and talk to me though.

I look to the younger one of my brothers as a role model. It's hard to look to Asians as role models because I haven't known that many. I look to my brother because he has gone through so much in his life. He's in his third marriage and he gives me a lot of good advice. He has a lot of good views on things. He's not college-educated, so a lot of people look down on him, but I respect him a lot because he's very smart; he just decided not to go to college.

13

Life of Immigrant Women

Jin-Hee Cho was born in South Korea in 1977 and immigrated to the United States with her parents in 1984. She and her family lived in St. Louis, Missouri, and her experience growing up reveals the hardship Korean immigrants encountered. She was a college student with an undeclared major at the time of the interview in 1996.

I was born in South Korea. I lived there until 1984 when I was six or seven, then we moved to St. Louis. So I'm the so-called 1.5 generation. It was really a hard adjustment because I was fairly young. I picked up English quickly so people think I was born here. I don't think English was hard, it was just different. I didn't really recognize how different it was. By the time I was older, I had pretty much forgotten Korea so I didn't have a way to contrast it with America. I don't really fully comprehend what I lost, so I am not able to feel any sort of anguish over losing my native culture.

In St. Louis we first lived with my cousins and then after a few years we moved out to an apartment. I think my father's sister is in Chicago and his brother lived in St. Louis, but all my mom's family is in Korea. It's hard for her. She hasn't been able to see them in a while and she's only gone back to Korea once because it's pretty expensive. My grandmother on my mom's side has only been able to come here once because she's fairly old and she can't fly on a plane very well. It's not as hard on me because I don't miss anyone in Korea. I don't remember them very well. I don't know anyone in my family who lives in Korea. My mom's sad about it but she recognizes that she can't do anything about it. It's not something that's under our control.

My mother graduated from a four-year college and she was an elementary school teacher in Korea. My dad went past four years in college

194

and was a physical therapist in Korea. He never worked in the United States as a physical therapist because he was born in Korea. In America you have to take a test to be authorized for it and he did not know enough English to take that test. I have an older brother. He's twenty and he goes to UMSL [University of Missouri–St. Louis]. I think he's a criminal justice major. He wants to go into a law program like the FBI or something like that. First he would have to go through criminal justice and then be a lawyer or some other occupation before they will pick him up.

At first my parents wanted me to be a doctor and I told them I wasn't going to be. Then they wanted me to be a business major, and I said I wasn't going to be a business major, either. And then they told me they wanted me to be a lawyer and I told them I didn't want to be a lawyer. Then they kind of gave up. I'm not really family-oriented, no children from this womb. I would hate to give up the independence. I'll probably work, but I don't know what I'll do.

Because we're Asian, my family thinks very highly of the first-born male. In our picture album first is my mom and my dad when they got married and them on their honeymoon. Then there are a lot of pictures of them and their friends and then suddenly it's only my brother. And you see a lot of pictures of my mom, my brother, and my dad, and then there's me. And then you see a lot of pictures of my mom, my brother, and my dad. There's a lot more emphasis on the son. But it hasn't been extremely detrimental or anything. The curfew was different for me because I was a girl and because I was younger, and I understand that.

I would describe the relationship between my parents as male-dominated but it's changed since my father retired. He can't really take care of himself as well as he once did. He's pretty up there so now my mom takes care of him with my brother. The power balance has completely shifted.

My very first job was not really a job, but I helped my mom out in her store. My mom has a beauty supply store in St. Louis. She owns it and she used to work there with my dad. But he retired and she just hired somebody else. They've owned it for several years. I guess they do all right. Then I worked at two dry cleaners and then at Toys R Us for a long time. I had a job in environmental stuff last summer and that was great. It was really hard work because we'd get in around two in the afternoon and we'd leave around eleven at night, but it was so much fun. Everyone was there for five days a week and was around each other a lot so a bond formed between all of us at the office. We'd go out after work almost every night because all of our other friends had parties in the house. We were out by eleven o'clock and we would go out and have fun by ourselves. We were a really tight-knit group; that was great. It actually was working toward an environmental cause. It made us all feel a lot better, too.

I've always been fairly independent so it wasn't a change for me to be at college. My parents don't really have a huge governing role in my life. They couldn't really help it because when I was younger they worked all day, so my brother and I were by ourselves ever since I was in second grade. We just took care of ourselves. Our parents were rarely there before seven or even nine o'clock at night. Nine o'clock was when my parents were working in the restaurant when we were younger. During my junior high and high school years, they had the shop and they wouldn't get home earlier than seven o'clock at night. We were pretty much by ourselves.

I decided to come to college because I recognized that if I didn't I would be out in the real world four years sooner, taking care of myself. I'm an undeclared major right now, but the only things I'm interested in are English and philosophy. So I'm probably going to major in English and minor in philosophy. I have no ideas about what to do with this degree. I do have a very good relationship with my classmates, peers, and friends. I'm a very social person; my nickname is Social Butterfly.

I chose this university because I really hate the fact that I'm reliant upon my parents. This university is close to home and it is very inexpensive for me to go here, especially with the scholarships. I didn't want my parents to pay a lot for my college so I came here. It makes a lot of sense especially for my undergraduate degree. It doesn't really matter where you go as long as you're going for your master's. I'm happy with my choice so far. I knew it was going to be like this—in the middle of nowhere. It was just what I expected. My cousin goes here and he told me.

I don't really believe in traditional marriage. I'm engaged and my fiancé is one of my best friends in school. We don't believe in the concept of marriage per se, a standardized marriage, because we believe it's an institution we can break out of whenever we want. So if we decide that love doesn't exist then we're going to marry as friends after four years of college. He's Asian, too; he's an American-born Chinese. His parents had a really dysfunctional marriage and so did mine. We both saw that our parents had only married for codependency reasons and they weren't divorcing because it's a real stigma if you're Asian. I guess we just figured it was better to marry as friends than marry for love and have to disintegrate and be alone.

Katherine Larson was born in Baltimore, Maryland, in 1976 to an interracial couple. Her mother immigrated from South Korea and worked various jobs in the United States. Her father, a European American who was stationed in Korea, was the vice president of finance for Western Auto in Kansas City. Her account of her mother reflects Korean immigrant women's experiences in America. She was a nursing major at Truman State University at the time of the interview in 1996.

I was born on 14 October 1976 in Baltimore, Maryland. My mother was born in Seoul, South Korea. My father was born in Pittsburg, Kansas, and graduated from Pittsburg State University. He is the Vice President of Finance for Western Auto.

My mom graduated from high school. All I know is that she had regular school in Korea like we have until three o'clock and then they had an hour off and then they went to a cram school until dinnertime. Then she would go home, do her homework, and go to bed. That is what she did every day. They had the weekends off. My mom didn't learn English in Korea because she never thought she would come to America. She learned English after she came here; she took some classes, but she doesn't anymore. She is fluent in English now, although she has problems with her l's and r's, and she has a really bad accent. A lot of people can't understand her, but she does pretty well.

My mother does odds and ends jobs. We have owned a laundromat in Olathe, Kansas, since I was four. We still own it; we just rent it out now because we moved away from there. It used to be that if I was sick that was where I had to go. I couldn't stay home by myself after school; I had to stay at the laundromat with my mom. Sometimes I had to go there and sit and watch the people working. My dad kept track of all the accounting stuff and my mom worked. Then she worked at Alaskan Fur for a while. She is always wanting to buy new buildings and open up some business. Last year she opened up an alteration and tailoring shop and she still owns it now.

I haven't met all of my mom's family members. She has five sisters and one brother. The reason she has so many sisters is that in Korea when the parents got old the boys would take care of everything. So families would continuously have kids until they had at least one son because girls were never expected to take care of their parents in any way. My grandparents kept having kids until they had a boy, which happened to be the seventh child. My mom hasn't really said anything about her parents. Both of them passed away when I was nine. When my grandfather passed away it was in the middle of the school year. We were in school so we didn't go. My mom went by herself for both funerals. We went over there when I was one year old. I don't remember anything except for pictures.

My mom is pretty close to all her sisters, but not very close to her brother. It doesn't seem like she talks to him as much as her sisters. She is the second youngest girl. The youngest daughter lives in New Jersey. She came over and lived in Olathe, Kansas, with her son-in-law when we moved there. She is married to a Korean man. When we moved to Ohio, they didn't want to stay in Kansas anymore so they moved. Her husband found a job in New Jersey. They ended up moving there and still live there because they really like it. Once we moved back to Kansas City, they didn't follow us anymore. Three other sisters have come to visit at different times. I know my mom still talks to her sisters; the phone bill shows it. Everyone else still lives in Korea except one of my cousins who came to California for school, but he couldn't afford it. My junior year he came and lived with us for a year and went to school in Kansas City because it was cheaper. He didn't have to pay rent, and he stayed in my sister's room.

I would like to visit Korea sometime. My mom has pushed and pushed me to learn how to speak Korean, but I never have because I am terrible with languages. I can't even speak English very well. I know a few words of Korean. I know "thank you," and I know "fart." My mom doesn't say if somebody farts, "Did you fart?" She just says it in Korean, so I know that one. I know "mom" and "dad" and "come here," because she will call us for dinner and she has to say "come here." I know "pretty" but at the moment I can't remember it. I used to hear her friends say, "Oh, your daughter is pretty." It's weird to hear her talk to other Koreans because she'll be talking to her friends and she'll keep on going and going and then she'll get to "Katherine" and I would think, "What are you saying about me?" Then you will hear "volleyball" and you will hear more, and you want to know what they are saying about you, but you just don't know.

My mom and my dad will speak Korean at home every once in a while; they will say something that my dad will remember how to say in Korean. I don't think he remembers a whole lot, either. Every now and then they will say something. Once we got older, my mom would say things in Korean a little bit every day. We didn't want to do it, but we picked up words every once in a while. My mom wanted us to learn Korean and she pushed it on us. She would say, "You never know when you are going to go over there." Maybe someday I'll go there. I always tell her every time she pushed Korean, "You never learned English till you came here, so I'll learn Korean when I go there." She doesn't like that very much.

She belongs to a Korean Presbyterian church. It's all Koreans. All her friends are Asian, some of them are Koreans, but they all speak with themselves. My mom always asks me, "Why can't I get rid of my accent?" I would say "Because you still speak Korean. If you would stop then you wouldn't have an accent anymore." One of her friends who is a lot older has been here for forty years (my mom has been here for twenty-five years now). She stopped speaking Korean for a long time and lost her accent. Then she joined this church and everyone was speaking Korean and she couldn't do it anymore. She had such a harsh American accent when speaking Korean that she couldn't make the right sounds. It's funny sometimes, if my mom doesn't say a word right we try to get her to say it right. She gets frustrated with it because she'll say it over and over again, and we say, "Mom give it up, you can't do it." She tries very hard. This summer my dad, my boyfriend, Mike, and I were eating dinner and my mom had been out. We had ordered pizza or something. She came home and started talking about how we needed our lawn to be cut. I have never cut our lawn in my life. My sister used to do it when we were little and my dad has done it ever since she went to college. We were having this big conversation about cutting the lawn and Mike was just sitting there and had no clue what we were talking about until I said, "I'm not going to cut the lawn." That's the first time he understood what we were talking about. He had a hard time understanding her accent.

My mom pushes food on people, no matter what. If you are not hungry you will have to eat. One time I was at work and Mike was sitting in the living room. She wanted to give him a Coke but he couldn't understand her. I think he finally understood her and he said "No," but she went downstairs and got him one anyway. I told Mike, "Don't take that personally, she has done that to me." If I'm not hungry, she will still fix me something to eat anyway. Almost all the meals that she eats are Korean. She doesn't always make us eat Korean food but she always makes people try things. We don't really have family dinners. Usually not all of us are home at the same time. But if we do, it is usually me and my dad and my sister eating American food, and then my mom will eat at the same time but eat Korean food. My dad doesn't eat Korean food at all. If we all have Korean food, then he will cook a hamburger for himself.

I don't know if that is a custom in Korea or not, but my mom is very superstitious. When she was a kid she was Buddhist and believed in reincarnation. When I was growing up I wasn't allowed to eat while laying down. I always sat in front of the TV and ate. I got in trouble all the time for that. That is probably the biggest thing I got in trouble for when I was a kid. During Saturday morning cartoons, I would lay down, watch TV, and eat. She used to tell us that if we eat laying down we would be reincarnated as a cow, which to her was the most terrible thing because in Korea the cow is the hardest working animal there is.

I guess the biggest value that mom taught me would be respect. I can talk back to her all I want as long as I am alone but the minute anyone else is around I better not say a word or I will get yelled at. She gets pretty mad. But she wouldn't yell at me in front of everyone. I got it in a big way after that and I used to be really bad about it. That is probably her biggest concern. She has taught me respect.

My parents have high expectations for me. I don't know if it is because I'm female but I know they have high expectations of me. My mom pressed school because of the way she was brought up. When I was little I was told that if I got a C I was kicked out of the house. I don't think I really would have gotten kicked out of the house, but I never got a C. They used to tell me stuff like that. In high school if I got a B, then Bs were not good enough; it was always, "Why didn't you get an A?" My dad asks me how tests go and he'll just say, "Well, why couldn't you get an A on it?" It's the same with sports, too. I always have to be the best player. Now I sit on the bench all the time. They understand now, but in high school it was like I always had to be playing or something was wrong and it was my fault. I don't know if it was because I am a female; we don't have any boys in our family. They had the same expectations for my sister. She is my only sister, four years older.

My parents had a lot of influence on my choice of college. When I first started looking at colleges, I was getting recruited for volleyball so that was all I was looking at. There was a school that was my first choice, but I didn't want to go there because it was private and cost $13,000 a year. My dad sat me down and said, "Don't worry about the money if that is where you want to go." He talked to me a lot about my choice. I thought about it for a long time and I decided that if it wasn't for volleyball I wouldn't go to that school. He told me that my sister played softball in college, and it didn't go the way she wanted. She played softball all four years, but I think if she didn't like the school, she would have transferred because softball was not going the way she wanted. But she loved the school and that was really important. In that respect my dad had a lot of influence, but I pretty much made my own decision.

It was expected that I would go to college. I don't think it would have been an option for me to have said, "I'm not going." I don't think they would have made me, but they would have made me feel guilty about it. I just changed my major and now I'm getting a BS in nursing. I was chemistry/pre-med. Since I haven't taken too many hours, right now I could still go into medical school if I wanted to. The only other class I would have to add to my schedule would be organic chemistry, which wouldn't be hard. Since I have so many hours already my biggest semester would be fourteen hours. Other than that I will have eight- and ten-hour semesters. So it wouldn't be hard to add an organic chemistry class. I might still do it; I haven't really decided. For a long time I wanted to be a doctor. My senior year in high school I started going to hospitals three hours a day. That's when I started going back and forth between nursing and pre-med; I couldn't decide. I finally chose pre-med because if I don't make it, I could always go back to nursing. But if I just go for nursing and never try pre-med, I will never know if I could have done it. I went pre-med but changed my mind and went to nursing last year.

My sister graduated in May of 1995. She took her last year off to play professional softball in New Zealand. Now she is back and she is working. She wanted to go to physical therapy school, but her grades weren't good enough. She's going back to community college next year and then she's going to get her medical degree.

I don't really know what my mom thought about my sister taking a year off to play softball. She really didn't say much about it. My dad's life is sports. At first, I didn't think he would go for it, because my dad promoted school a lot, especially good grades. But I talked to him one day after my sister decided for sure that she was going. All of her senior year, she didn't know if she was going, she was just talking about it. Then she decided to go and my dad said, "It is an opportunity she can't give up basically, to go to New Zealand and Australia for a year." Everything was paid for and she got paid to play, so he said, "You can't give that up."

My sister met this guy in New Zealand when she first got there. He is going to graduate from college and then he is going to come over that August. She decided she didn't want to go over there and waste another year. She said "I'm twenty-three and I need to get my life going, having a career. I can't wait another year not really doing much." It was hard; they only talked once a week because it is a dollar a minute on the phone and it takes almost a week and a half to get mail. So she broke it off. She is dating someone else, but not seriously. They are not going to get married anytime soon but my mom always wants her to get married.

My parents and I were not as close as other families are. I wouldn't go to my parents if I had a problem. We talk about once a week, but not for very long. It is more this year because they always come to my games; but last year I never saw them. This year we talk more, but it is not as if I go to them when I have a problem. It's more like, "How's school going? How's volleyball going?" My relationship with my mother is sometimes different than it is with my dad. One thing about that is the way she was brought up in Korea. It's not that it's wrong for her, but it is wrong for us. We're in a different culture and in a different time. Sometimes, in that respect, it kind of drives me and my sister crazy. We tell her, "It's not the same anymore." But it's not really that different. We probably talk to our dad more because he likes sports.

My mom doesn't like the fact that I want to be a doctor. She wanted me to be a lawyer. I have no interest in law so I didn't want to do that. My parents always tell me that I'm a smart-ass; I got it from my dad. My mom wants me to be a lawyer because I can talk back so well. It's not that she didn't want me to be a doctor, but after seeing my sister's grades go down in college, she didn't want me to do that. It was a couple of weeks ago that I told them about my nursing degree. We were in Pittsburg for a volleyball tournament and they came down. We were sitting talking about a lot of stuff.

This has always been my mom's plan: to be a nurse, go work in the hospital, meet a doctor, and marry him. All her life, that's all she wanted. She wants me and my sister to marry someone rich. She thinks all we need to do is shop and be a housewife. That is what she has done for the majority of her life. She has had some jobs here and there, but not a career. She always says, "All you need to do is get your husband's money and go shop with it." I'm not the type of person who could stay home.

I have a boyfriend and we've been dating for almost nine months. My parents like him but they worry sometimes since he is sick. They ask if he is doing okay because one time last year he was with me and he had to go to the emergency room because he was sick. It ended up not being a big deal but ever since then they ask, "How's Mike doing?" Or if I even mention he had to go to the emergency room they start to get worried. My mom just doesn't want to see me get hurt. We have history of cancer in our family, so she is paranoid that something is going to happen. She doesn't want to see me married and have kids and be all alone. Nothing is going to happen to him but I'm not getting married until next year.

I like the university town because I like small towns. I don't know what I like most about it. I have lived in both a city and a small town. I don't have a job now but I'll probably find a job after volleyball season is over. I couldn't have one during the season since I get stressed out so easily. If I get a B I get stressed out because I worry about what my parents are going to say. Then I will talk about it and Mike will say, "It's a B, that's fine." I will say, "No, it's not." For example, yesterday I thought I flunked a test and I got it back and I got a C on it and Mike said, "I know that is not what you wanted and how good you think you should have done." I struggled in organic chemistry; that's why I dropped it. I know some people struggle a lot harder. I don't study as much as some people do. There are two people down the hall, one has a 4.0 GPA and the other has a 3.98. I know that they both study all the time. I study a lot but I don't study all the time. Sometimes I feel like I am having a hard time. Right now I am having a hard time in one class. I just can't get on the same wavelength as the teacher with his questions. I study what I think will be on the test and I'm ready for it, and I get the test and it's like, "What? Did we cover this?" That is not that big of a deal. I'm still doing okay in there. I get stressed out though and I take it out on Mike. I did that the other day and he got mad at me for it. He gets sick of me taking everything out on him. It was about volleyball, too. It was right after practice. It was terrible. Most of the time I go for a walk to get a grip. A lot of times I will just calm down if I have a lot of things to do and get stressed out, and I feel like I am never going to get everything done. I calm down and break things down so I can get things done, make it more rational. When I am not in season, sometimes I work out.

I have no idea how I spend my spare time because I don't have any. What I would like to do right now is catch up on talking to my friends at home that I haven't talked to in forever. I have all these letters that people have written me and I haven't written back. I would probably like to read. I like John Grisham books; I think he is a good author. I usually read what people say is good. Mostly it is whatever my dad gets because he is constantly reading except for corporate books. He always has those. I'm reading the Dennis Rodman book right now. Sometimes we go rent movies if we don't go out, to just relax. But I don't really go out much. I probably spend five to six hours a day studying.

I spend about three hours a day playing or practicing volleyball. If we have a home game, probably four or five hours. Traveling is an all day event; we will usually leave about noon. Tomorrow we leave at 12:30 PM and we won't get back until 1:00 or 2:00 AM. Our game day is on Wednesdays mostly. Next coming weekend we have off, then we practice every weekend. We take Sundays off. When we get free weekends, we get Fridays off. That way if people want to go home they can leave whenever their classes are done and they have to be back by Sunday night for practice. During preseason, we practice every day, probably about seven or eight hours a day for two weeks. During the season, we only practice a certain number of hours a week and get one day out of seven off.

I am a sophomore. I will be here playing volleyball my last two years, as of now. I know a lot of people had to quit because of the nursing program, but I think it might be different for me because I don't have as many hours as they do. The nursing program has a set schedule for everybody. You have to take certain classes each semester. There are always one or two elective classes or core classes that aren't in the nursing program that I have already taken. So my schedule won't be as busy as others and I might be able to keep playing.

I came when I was a freshman with twenty-seven credit hours. So I was three hours away from being a sophomore. I took seventeen and sixteen hours last year, and I took three hours at home this summer. Our high school, Shawnee Mission Northwest, had honor classes, so you can do AP credit, but you have to take a test for it. I only got my psychology credit, three hours, that way. The rest of them I did through our community college. So I did that for a lot of my classes. You pay for however much the community college is, but it was a lot easier because you didn't have to pay for the books. You got them from the high school. All I had to pay was the $33 per credit hour. I am glad I did that because I took Composition I, Composition II, and history, classes I knew that I would do terrible in if I took them at a four-year college. I was going to take calculus but then I decided that my senior year I didn't want to have to take a math. I took Statistics, General Psychology, and Physics I. I got credit for Biology 100, but I really don't need it because I am in Biology 107 right now. So it doesn't matter, but I have a credit.

Most of the classes I took in high school I had to take because I was taking college-prep classes. I had to take History I and II in my junior year. I took those and got college credit at the same time. Everybody knows about it, so many people do that at my high school. History was the first class I did for college credit because I'm terrible with history. I knew the teacher. I knew that he taught it and I knew he was an easy teacher. I'm glad that I got Comp. I and Comp. II done. Last year my roommate took Comp. I and she had to write a paper, sometimes two or three a week. When I took Comp. I at high school, I wrote three or four papers the whole year. We read all the time in our English class, but we didn't write half as much. I told my roomate "I am so glad I took Comp. at home, because here it is just terrible."

I'm the secretary chair (assistant to the secretary) of CPO [Council of Prehealth Organizations]. I joined because I heard about it on our division day my freshman year. Then this girl and I went to the group informational meeting and talked about it. I talked to my parents about it—how good it would look on my resume. That is mostly why I joined it. It was also interesting and I learned a lot from it last year. I didn't know anything about applying to med school and I learned a lot even just from one year.

I haven't gone to a meeting yet this year because their meetings are on Monday nights and I have a class then. Our president and treasurer, who is one of my really good friends, lets me know what's going on. We have a big bulletin board so I can go by and pick up the stuff I need. The secretary is who I work with so she calls me and tells me what to do. I haven't decided what I am going to do about that. I don't know if I am going to stay a member.

We have to do a lot of stuff. Every semester to be considered an active member, we keep a strict file on everyone. If people want letters of recommendation, the science teachers can come and look them up and see what all they have done. I haven't done anything. We have dues, either $8 a semester or $12 a year. We have to do an hour of fundraising, which is the only thing I have done. You have to attend two different events. We bring speakers all the time, those can count. At the beginning of the year we have a picnic for freshman and during visit day we tell them all about it. So we do different things that are not mandatory. We have a social committee. Like last year we had scavenger hunts, picnics, and we had a little Christmas party. We went bowling one night. We can go to any of those or any of our speakers. We have to do an hour of community service, too. We have a street adopted for the Adopt-a-Highway program. We have to attend every meeting, or another member has to fill out an excuse form before we miss the meeting.

We also do school tours. We go to the medical school in town every week and we get to see their gross anatomy lab. Mostly the medical school does mock interviews for us, pretend interviews for juniors and seniors like for what you would go through to get into med school. To get into med school, you do first applications, second applications, and then you do interviews depending on the school. Interviews are weighted very heavy in the application process.

CPO brings a lot of speakers. Last year we had a doctor from Australia come who talked about the differences in med school today, and how to get into their med schools. We have one night when seniors talk. They tell everybody else what they have to do to get into med school, how to apply for med school and take the MCAT. It's all paperwork, like for MCAT you have to fill out two forms. Med school can get your scores at any time and you don't have to send it to each school. They just go through your file and find it. So you have to fill out these forms and take your MCAT and do whatever you have to do. Sometimes schools will send out for questionnaires for your interviews. Sometimes the seniors talk about everything they do; they talk about how much it costs them, like the MCAT costs about $50 and most people take it twice. Almost every application is about $50 and then if you have a second application it adds up pretty quickly. So you get an idea how much they are paying applying to schools. They also talk about different things that med schools offer. If you get accepted and you wanted to defer your admission for a year, you can take a year off and then go the year after that and you are still accepted. They talk about general stuff that underclassman usually don't know about.

We do MCAT reviews in groups. The MCAT is offered twice a year in August and April. Most people take it in April of their junior year and in August of their senior year because applications have to be in by January. So you shouldn't wait till April of your senior year but that is generally what people do. Right towards the beginning of the semester we start doing MCAT reviews and at first it is really basic. It is just a Sunday afternoon or something like that. People come in and at first it is not very organized, but when it starts coming around everyone starts talking about when the MCAT reviews are. MCATs are on a Saturday and it is an eight-hour, all-day thing. Either a week or two weeks before it we do a practice one for whoever is taking the real one. They come in at the same time. Usually we try to get the same room that the MCAT will be held in and do it the exact same way as you would be taking the test so they get a real view. CPO didn't take up a whole lot of time last year. It would take up more time this year if I would go to the meetings.

I've thought about either joining Tri Beta or AΞE, but I can't do either now. Tri Beta is the biology honor fraternity and AΞE is the chemistry honor fraternity. I was thinking about joining those but I don't think I will anymore. I don't have time to do it. I know there is one for nursing and I might join once I start taking nursing classes.

We don't go to church but we were going to. We have been twice this year. Mike and I said that we were going to go to church all the time this year but I'm not here that much on weekends, anyway. Usually volleyball tournaments are Fridays and Saturdays and so we are back late Saturday. But most of the time, we don't get back till five in the morning and I'm not getting up for church. We need to go more, I think. The church we went to was Catholic. I can't even remember what street it was on. The first time we went was when his parents were in town. We have always wanted to go to the Catholic Newman Center. But we didn't want to take his parents there so we took them to a real Catholic church. I think church is important but I never go. I'm not Catholic, though. I've been more to the Catholic church in the past couple years than I have been to my own.

My family is Presbyterian. My mom is very active but my dad doesn't go. When we lived in Ohio we went almost every Sunday. We lived there for four years and that was pretty much a rule. In 1991 when my sister graduated from high school my parents did a special graduation ceremony for all the seniors in our church. I've been to Catholic church more in the past three years of high school and college. It doesn't bother me. Sometimes I feel awkward, like when I don't take their communion. I can't take their communion because they won't let me. When I go to a Presbyterian church I take our communion, even though I'm not baptized. I shouldn't walk into a Catholic church, especially when they take communion because everybody kneels down and then they get up and walk up in their big lines. I sit there twiddling my thumbs. I know half the things they say now because I have been there several times. My best friend's ex-boyfriend was Catholic. He came from a big Catholic family. We used to go to the Lake of the Ozarks all the time with them. So when we went we had to go to church. His mom never made me go because I wasn't Catholic. I knew if I didn't go she would look down on me. She was a very strict Catholic. So I went every time they went. I know the Catholics pretty well now. I still feel pretty awkward a lot, especially since I am not baptized. I know nobody knows that except my best friends and a few other people. I guess I am ashamed of it. It didn't happen when I was little because we moved around so much and so we were gone all the time. When we lived in Ohio I was going to do it, and I had to take a membership class because you have to take it to get baptized. At the time I was in gymnastics and the classes were on Saturday mornings when we had practice. So I never did it. It will be done someday, I just don't know when.

The majority of my friends are Americans. There is one guy friend from my high school that is Korean. I don't find it hard to make friends. I consider myself to be both introverted and extroverted. Once I get to know people I am more outgoing but when I first meet people I won't talk that much. Mike said that the first time he met me I didn't talk much. He is a very verbal guy. Other words that describe me are competitive and self-conscious. What everybody else thinks about me is very important to me. I can't stand it when somebody is mad at me or somebody hates me.

I don't have any hobbies. That was a problem when I had to write for my media class. We were supposed to write about our hobbies and I don't have any. I like riding horses. I don't do it enough to make it a hobby but I would like to. I think my favorite movie is *The Outsiders*.

People don't think I am Korean. Most people think I am Hawaiian or Puerto Rican or Chinese or Indian. It doesn't bother me except when they are ignorant about it even after I tell them. There is a girl on the volleyball team and her parents thought I was Indian and when they found out I wasn't, they said, "Oh, we're so sorry." It's not a big deal; I don't care. My sister in New Zealand was nicknamed Pocahontas. They are all white over there and there aren't any black people. Their black people from the island have light complexions like me or like my sister. They have dark complexions and curly hair like our African Americans do. That is their so-called "black." I know that one of her softball coaches on her team was from the island. My sister is the pitcher. I remember her telling me one time she asked the umpire for the ball. The umpire said, "Your father has it," and he pointed to the first base coach, the islander. She said, "My dad? My dad is in Kansas, but that's okay." A lot of people thought she was an islander but other people on her team thought she was Indian.

14

Interracial Marriage

Su-Hee Sparks was born in Shape, Belgium, in 1973 to an interracial couple. Her father was a European American who met his wife in Korea while stationed there. Su-Hee Sparks was also married to a European American and worked as a psychological therapist while attending Truman State University as a senior majoring in psychology at the time of the interview in 1996.

I was born on 6 November 1973 in Shape, Belgium. My mother is from South Korea and my father is American, so I am half Korean and half American. My father was stationed in Belgium when I was born. He's still in the army. We were there for only a year. Then we came back to America, first to Maryland, then to Virginia, and last to Louisiana where I spent most of my life. After that we went to Korea.

My mother is forty-nine and my dad is forty-four. My mother didn't finish second grade in the equivalency of American schools. She says it is a lot stricter in Korea. Of course, she never stayed in school long enough. She was very liberal and strong-willed. She was the daughter of a government official and was very spoiled in a lot of ways. She didn't like school so she skipped all the time. There was no way of controlling her. Her father left her and her mom sometime in her teens and by that time they had given up on her. She always told me that when she was in school she would get in trouble. Since she was the daughter of a government official, she went to a special school that was very strict. They had to cut their hair like a boy and wear uniforms, and if they got into trouble they would get smacked with a ruler. She would get slapped on the knuckles with a ruler by the big ladies that were very mean to her. They went to school six days a week. I lived in Korea for a year and school was in session on Saturdays. I

A Korean bride and her American husband, Seoul, South Korea, December 1978.
Huping Ling Collection (Courtesy of Huang-Suk Harrington).

think it went until 5 PM on Saturdays. Their education is a lot harder than ours, and their senior year in high school would probably be equivalent to our senior year in college.

My mother didn't work until she was in her twenties. She was a waitress and she modeled, too. When I think of my mom as a model, I think of today's version of a model; it is totally different. She was a very popular hair model. She would be showcased and there would be some pictures of her. She was very free, very wild. She used to love going to the circus.

My father got his GED (General Education Degree) in the army, but he actually took it before he went into the army. The army was his career and he spent twenty years in it. My father is currently taking college courses, majoring in criminal justice. I'm not quite sure what he wants to do. He retired from the army in 1990. He's working as a prison guard and hoping to get promoted in that system. My mom used to own a cleaning business but it got too hard on her health, so she decided to retire and now she is a housewife.

My parents met through the army and they traveled all over the place. For the last ten years they have been in Missouri. My dad was in Korea in 1970, and was stationed in an American Sony post there. His brother was killed in the Vietnam War when he was twenty-one, so the army didn't want to send my dad to Vietnam because his mom already lost one son there. My mother was young when the Korean War happened. It was in the 1950s and she was born in 1947. She does remember that she was taking a trip somewhere in the mountains and there were a lot of North Koreans, and she remembers her best friend at that time getting killed on a bridge right in front of her. That's one of her deepest memories.

My mother had an arranged marriage [before she met my father]. She didn't want an arranged marriage so she knew she wasn't going to have one. She did whatever she wanted. The reason my grandma and other relatives wanted an arranged marriage for her was that she was pregnant. They would not allow her to keep it and she had to give up the child so that her arranged marriage partner would not know and that her family name wouldn't be blackened. The reason she could marry my father was because she got older and she could say no to her family. To this day she has no idea where her child is. I am supposed to look for her when I get older. That's my duty, although I don't know her name or anything.

Koreans still do arranged marriages here in the United States. There is a big Korean church where they have them, but not as much as they used to. Koreans are becoming more Americanized. But there are still people who live in the old ways. High-class society will marry other high-class society. They wouldn't go lower.

When my parents met in 1970 my dad was nineteen years old. He went to this restaurant where my mom was waitressing. Apparently, from their story, she was popular, and my dad liked her and said, "I'm a rich American." That trapped her into marrying him.

She wanted to come to the States, as a lot of Korean women had this fantasy of America. She was so used to being in a certain class. Her mother was still pretty well-off financially from her father. Even after her father left, my mother still expected to be treated a certain way, like a princess. She was very spoiled. That's probably why she rebelled as much as she did. She did modeling, she saw people in the circus, and she would watch people acting. She always dreamed of a certain way of life, the American way of being able to live in a big house, having all this money, doing whatever you want, and seeing something new. That's why she came over here.

She didn't come here out of love for my father. This is something she will freely admit and that my father realized. My mom then was twenty-five, six years older than my father. After she found out my father wasn't rich, she didn't really care because she would have had an arranged marriage with someone. She was going against the social norms by marrying my dad. My parents got married on 28 May 1971 at the U.S. Embassy. There was no fancy wedding, no Korean traditional wedding. After they were married they went to Belgium and then came to the States in 1974.

Because she was married to an American citizen, my mom was automatically guaranteed an American visa. But she did get her citizenship quite a few years later in 1981. We were living in Louisiana at the time. She went to New Orleans to get it and she was on TV because they had a news camera that day. You can see about twenty people, raising their hands in the pledge of allegiance. I was yelling, "That's my Mom. That's my Mom!" They gave her a book called *Our U.S. Government* and two other books. I remember helping my Mom read these books. She learned English from my father, from my sister and me, from the schoolbooks we brought home, and from watching TV. She took some English classes in the States. Some of what she learned she picked up from being a waitress. Basically her education derived from my sister, my dad, and me. She's still learning. She watches CNN twenty-four hours a day. She also learned from commercials. If there's a new product, she wants me to try it. If she sees a really cool commercial sometimes she'll reenact it for me. Her favorite is the plastic wrap commercial where the lady gets wrapped up by the plastic wrap.

After my parents got married, they went to Belgium. Then my sister and I were born. Later my father went to Korea and my mom came to the States by herself and then met my dad in Illinois, where his hometown is. It was rough because my grandparents on my dad's side really weren't open to her. My aunt, uncle, and grandmother all treated my mom very poorly. The whole town did. They spat on her and little kids threw stones at her. It was not a very minority-welcoming town. They would always put her down and make fun of her.

They made her almost like a servant. My mom, not knowing American ways, went along with that. She cleaned the house, cooked, and did whatever was needed. She thought that's just the way that Americans were, and throughout her life she has been treated like that. When we were living in Illinois, I was three and my sister was four, and a man tried to break into our house since my father had left. He knew that my father was gone and he tried to hurt us, or kill us probably. The police didn't come until hours later. My dad's family didn't come either.

I went to see my great-aunt this past weekend. She is the only one who actually respected my mother. I don't really keep in contact with my dad's mother's side. I only stopped by and saw them out of obligation. I rarely talk to them and they rarely talk to me. They talk to my sister more than me. They send her birthday cards, Christmas cards, but they will forget about me. It is probably because I look more Asian than my sister. That is how they have always treated my mom and me.

I lived in Korea for a year in 1984, when I was twelve. The very first day, I felt different from the Koreans because they were touching me and telling me how pretty I was. But after that I felt at home. I would walk in my *gi*, my Tae Kwon Do uniform in the village. I would interact with people, I would go to the store by myself, I would do anything. It felt like home to me and I didn't want to leave. I lived in a little village where people don't see a lot of Asian Americans. My sister and I could go into the store and get clothes and shoes for free. I don't know if it was like that for everyone or if it was because we were from overseas. They knew my mother for some reason. I know that my mother used to model a little bit. They could have known her from that or from her high status, which is kind or ironic since it was twenty years ago. They treated us with respect and my dad said it was because we were Asian American children.

I had a Korean friend. Her name was Sarah Lee and she was a high school student. She was in her freshman year in high school, which would be equivalent to our senior year in college in the United States. They went to school six days a week. It just amazed me, her level of knowledge. I didn't attend a Korean school. I took correspondence from Baltimore because we had to for our education. But I took Tae Kwon Do classes there and I played with a lot of the school kids. The school there was very hard. My friend was always studying and she said that there were only so many spots to get in and that she had to work hard.

I only speak and understand a little Korean. I grew to understand it more when I was living there. But as soon as I came to the States I forgot. My mom and dad always wanted my sister and me to be bilingual, but when they were a young couple, an American doctor told them that would only make us stupid. So they never taught us for fear of us being slow at school. I got cheated.

When I was in Korea, the one thing I noticed that was different is how their society is so family-oriented. Their grandmothers still live with them. I remember one day I was watching a woman play with her two little kids. When I think of her I think of how everyone is trying so hard to get somewhere and to provide a better life for their children and that some-times we forget that we have the basic necessities like happiness, love, and caring that we need to show to our child. I'm not saying that Americans don't do that but I don't know if that's a priority. I would say the whole community affects what a child does in Korea. I think because over there everything is about honor, you don't do anything in public that would dis-grace your family. So I think those are community restrictions. Here I think it's more mother- and father-based than anything else, although we like to say we're a community.

My parents' relationship is kind of stormy at times because of the communication breakdown. They fight a lot. As they get older, they seem to be calmer and they are still together. They have been together for twenty-five years. I guess it is a typical marriage, a little stormier than most just because my mother tends to be more violent. She is a little woman, but I think she picks fights. She is also very physical and my dad has to restrain her. That was hard for us growing up to watch. My mother would physi-cally fight and my dad will hold her back. But it is a lot better now. It was because of my mom missing her home and not understanding what was going on and my dad not being understanding of her confusion. She's like a baby every now and then, because to be married for twenty-five years and to have only been back home for one year during that whole time is really hard, especially not being able to see her own mom. I think she blames herself a lot for not being able to see her mother because she wanted to leave Korea so bad, and that's hard for her. But we're planning on taking her to Korea next year.

Now they have grown up together but they got married on a lot of false intentions. When I talked to other Asian Americans, it seems as though it is the same way with their families. I know a lot of Asian American friends who are Korean Americans, whose mother and father had the same relationship: fight, fight, fight.

I met a woman in Korea that my dad may have had an affair with. My father claims it wasn't an affair, he was just helping her. He witnessed her buying drugs so he tried to help her out. I really don't know what the relationship was. My mother claims it was an affair, so let's just leave it at that. And my father claims that my mother has done the same thing, too.

I want to say that it didn't make me feel any different towards my dad. But I can't help it, I look at him differently in that respect, always wondering whether or not it was true. But he is my dad and I love him and he will do anything for me, as I will for him. It made me grow up. I guess I can't look at him through rose-tinted glasses anymore. He is just my dad, a man who has problems. My parents aren't perfect, that's how I look at it.

One of the things that I learned by being a military brat was to adapt to different situations. If you were to take a city person to the country, they would probably be in shock. But I learned to adapt to many types of situations. I never had problems growing up in different places and being Asian. I think the biggest culture shock was to come back to the United States and to find out that ignorance about ethnicity still remained. My naiveté was blown to pieces when I came to college.

When I was growing up, I thought attitudes would be more favorable since I was going to schools for military children. But a lot of the kids would call me Sushi and pick on me. I had friends but there were people who were ignorant who did not know how to address me. My sister hardly got any of that but I did and that was partly because I looked more Korean. It stopped for a while and I thought it was over with and when they got older they got smarter. My relationship with my classmates was pretty good. In high school it was fairly decent. High school was pretty scary at times. We had a lot of race wars. People were just being ignorant. I guess when I was younger it was harder because younger children are mean and cruel.

When I started dating my husband, his ex-girlfriend decided to call him and she and her friends taunted him for dating an Oriental girl. This was a year and a half ago. It's just hard to believe. I'm twenty-some years old and I'm being ridiculed for being Oriental. That's basically what she did. He was on the phone and I heard her chanting, "You're dating an Oriental girl. You're dating a Chink." I was really shocked. I remember two or three years ago reading about people being called Orientals, Asians, yellow breeds, and I remember a girl being called half-breed. It was like we were animals. There is a lot of ignorance out there. People wouldn't think that I would get that kind of reaction because I am half white. Well, I do.

We lived in Bridgetown, Illinois. It is a small town on Illinois River, and it is about forty-five minutes away from Springfield, Illinois. You would think that they would be more accepting, but not that town. There are no minorities whatsoever. I remember when I was younger there was a black family. However, no one knows where that family went.

I grew up in the States, mostly in Louisiana for the early years, and then in Missouri for the later years. We moved to Waynesville, Missouri, in 1985. That's when my dad retired from the army. It was a smaller town but it wasn't a problem for me, being half Korean, because we still lived on an army base for the most part. It's hard now because I'm not an army dependent anymore and that lifestyle is gone for me. I'm not surrounded by soldiers or any of that stuff. In the army, one of the benefits is that you see a lot of different cultures because people are traveling all over the place. When you get on an army base, you have a conglomeration of African Americans, Asian Americans, and all kinds. I think that benefits people. The only Korean friends I had were in Korea, though. Not because I didn't want to have any but because I wasn't surrounded by a lot of them when I was growing up in the army base. I had some Korean friends in high school, there were a lot more in Waynesville. There were several Korean churches, Korean stores, and Korean restaurants.

When I was growing up my parents instilled a lot of Korean culture in me. My dad loves Korean culture. It wasn't as though I knew I was learning it, it was just a part of me growing up with the food and the custom of taking off your shoes before entering the house. My mother always told me that when I get married, I should act a certain way with men. She told me I had to understand that my husband was going to be tired when he came home from work and I had to be able to make him comfortable or serve him in some way. I also have my independence and that comes from my dad. But I always remember the Korean culture part of it. I see that coming out naturally. I think I know quite a bit about Korean culture and customs, not so much history, though.

I got a lot of my superstitions from my mother. She's very superstitious and I don't know if that's a Korean trait. I think in Korea there's an unlucky number, I believe it's three, like we have thirteen here. If my mother has a bad dream she will say, don't say anything or you're going to have a bad day.

My Korean heritage is intertwined with my American heritage. My dad pushed for Korean more than anything else. He was trying to encourage me to be Korean and my sister was the more American one. I would probably describe myself as an Asian. I would probably say Asian over American. I only say I am Asian American or Korean American when I fill out applications. Basically I call myself a minority or a person, because I personally don't like to label or pigeonhole myself. If anyone were to call me anything, I would rather they call me by my name or what I am, which is a person. But I will probably say I identify more with the Korean part of me.

That probably makes it harder for me since I live in the United States. It is also hard because I am more sensitive and more aware of the stereotypical views of Americans. I view Americans as being stronger, harsher, and more violent. I don't see Koreans as that way. Even though I have been raised here, I still hold on to the old-fashioned Korean outlook because my mother has told me I need to be kind to people. And I guess that's also the Buddhist way of thinking.

If my mom saw me right now she would faint because I look terrible. She always said women should look like women and should always look their best, every day, all the time. She gets up at 4:30 in the morning, puts on her makeup and cleans. And that makeup doesn't come off until nighttime. She doesn't leave the house unless she has her makeup and her hair done and is dressed up. It's just something she does. She always told me that Korean women have to look their best and Korean girls do not talk back to their mothers. It has to do with respect.

As a wife, I'm expected to do a lot. My mother is always telling me I have to make sure the man is happy. You don't yell, you don't argue. I've broken that rule a couple of times. He's not expected to clean when he works. She said, "Even though you work, when you come home, you make sure you have a nice clean home for him when he comes." So my mom is very big on providing a calm and relaxing environment for the man, cooking dinner, and making sure he's fed and healthy. The big thing is never to talk back, don't argue with him. I think that she was very rebellious at times, but I think she also "knew her place" at times. School was something that she just could not do, but the lack of a father didn't help. Her mom tried to instill those traditions as much as possible.

The Korea that we talk about is always going to be old-fashioned. In Korea, women didn't amount to much because men were always the workers. It's more important to have boys because girls can only have children. That's the Korea I know from my mother. She thinks American women are too wild and I think she's just very old-fashioned in a lot of ways, which is kind of ironic because when she was a kid she did so many things that she shouldn't have. But as she got older she became more traditional, and she thinks American women are very outspoken and very rude. It's hard for her to understand because Koreans don't do that.

Growing up, my sister and I tended to talk back. We were teenagers and it seemed like the norm. We just don't do that with my mother. It's hard, and I think I respect my mom's traditions. I probably understand it a lot more than my sister does, but that's because she was always so rebellious. So she never took the time to understand it. I love my mom and I love her culture. When I was in Korea, I felt that I had found a part of me that was missing. And that's where it was, I had found it. It was hard, and I find myself being traditional in a lot of ways, but I like it.

My parents didn't want me to marry anyone but a Caucasian American. My mother was very adamant about that, she didn't want me to marry a Korean. A lot of times she would tell me that a Korean is not as "good" as a typical blonde, blue-eyed American would be. I think a lot of that is because of the way she was treated when she came here. She thinks that I would have a better life if I didn't marry someone like her.

I think that being who I am has a lot to do with my mother's culture. In a kind of weird sense, I don't think I would be a strong and caring person if I wasn't Asian, because I am part of a minority and I have had to endure many things, name calling, a lot of discrimination that I felt and have seen my mother go through. That has taught me to respect everyone and to love everybody. I can never make anyone feel so low, so dumb, and so unworthy as I have felt myself and I've seen my mother feel. I think that if everyone could be put in a position where they go through so much pain and disgust and see that and actually feel it, then maybe we won't want to put off those feelings and push those feelings onto someone else. I think that's what I've gained from being an Asian American.

I met my husband, David, on the first day I started working. I was working with him on the nightshift. We ended up having the same Abnormal Psychology class. We also had a mutual friend, my next door neighbor. We don't understand how we had never met. He asked me out the second night we worked together and we had been dating ever since.

I think my Korean background does affect my relationship with my husband because I've realized my mother's teachings, even though it hasn't been outright teaching. It's what she's told me about her culture and also how I should act. It's like whenever he tells me to do something I jump up and do it. I find myself doing a lot of the things that I see my mom do, making sure he's well-fed, sometimes not even saying anything when he asks me to do something. I just jump up and do it. I always make sure his dinner is prepared. I cook a lot of different foods and David likes to eat Korean food. Tonight he was making chicken fried rice. That's a Chinese dish, but we like a Korean dish that I make. We cook a lot of different things. I'll do something and everything's for him. Sometimes I'm so confused and I think, "I need to do something for me." Sometimes I feel like I'm trapped and I'm going back and forth. I am not sure.

We've talked about how we want things to work in our marriage. He knows it's hard for me because I'm always trying to please him. If I go shopping, I say I'll go shopping for myself and I'll come back with bags for him and nothing for me. When I cook dinner, it's what he wants and to his specifications because he's very picky. He's always telling me, "If you want something, cook it for yourself. If you want it that way, you don't have to do it for me." I can't do it because I'll feel this extreme guilt, letting him down, or letting someone down. I don't know who, the Korean custom god!

We split household duties pretty equally. David is very good about that. That's one thing I have to say, there are those things that I probably do a little bit more, but that's because I want to. He'll tell me to sit down and relax, but I can't. I'll be wide awake at two o 'clock in the morning because I want to get up and clean and do something that needs to be done, like put the dishes away or something. He's telling me, "You're not doing that. You're going to lay down and relax." He is good at keeping the house clean because he likes to be clean also.

When we make family decisions we talk about it and we discuss it. Then we'll decide from there. There are a lot of times where he'll make a decision because I won't or I'll say it's up to him because I don't want to step on anyone's toes. Like dinner tonight, I didn't want to cause problem. I don't think it's my place to make the decisions sometimes. I think I get that from my mother. I'm very submissive in a lot of ways.

I get along great with David's parents. His family lives in Iowa. He asked his father if my being half Korean was going to be a problem, because his father was in the Vietnam War and he has some reservations about different minorities. He said, "No, it's not. I don't have a problem." In fact, I think I've added a lot to his family because they always ask me about my mother's culture. I'm always learning and I try to provide the answers for them. I think I've added more to their family than they probably counted on.

I am very close to my mom and my dad. If I had to choose between either one of them, I couldn't. I love them both too much. My whole family is very, very close. We would die for each other and we would die if anything ever happened to any one of us. We would probably not go on living because we wouldn't know how.

My mom and I were very close when I was growing up. We got into little fights but that is normal. I am her baby and we always call each other and talk. She knows it was her fault for leaving school and cutting classes. But she felt as though the way my sister and I talk to her was being condescending to her. She didn't understand that it wasn't. That is the only kind of glitch in our relationship when we were growing up. It was her thinking that we were purposefully trying to confuse her. And we weren't and it was a constant battle trying to explain to her. As we taught her more, she began to understand the way we talked wasn't to confuse her by any means. It's just that as we became more educated our vocabulary was going to grow and change. That was a problem for her. It is hard for her to talk to people because she thinks they would think she is ignorant. My mother is a very smart woman. She watches CNN twenty-four hours a day so she can gain more knowledge.

She reads the Bible, which is difficult for her because her mother is a Buddhist. But my great-aunt urged her toward Christianity and my dad did, too, so now she is a Christian. She was baptized last month. Since she came here she has tried to be American in different ways, and she thinks it's wrong if you don't believe in God because that's what she's been told. She respects her mom's religion. It's like she combines Christianity and Buddhism in a way. My grandmother is a very devout Buddhist and when you go to her house her main furniture is the shrine. I'm a Christian, and I don't really know a lot about Buddhism. But there are some things like meditation that I do that I think come from my grandmother's religion. In Buddhism you have enlightenment and a lot of the principles of enlightenment are to be kind to everyone and I try to do that as much as possible.

My mom doesn't go out much. She is not antisocial and she has friends, but she doesn't call them or hang out with them. She is content being at home. She had her own business. She was cleaning quarters for army bases. They contract so many people to clean the houses before new families come in, and she did that, but the chemicals got to her. That's why she had to stay home. But she doesn't go out and talk to anybody unless she goes out shopping and she sees her friends.

Education is emphasized very strongly in my family. It's kind of mixed; my parents had very high expectations but their education level wasn't college, so they expect me to go to graduate school. I've always been the responsible one in the family. I've always been the one that was headstrong. So they expect me to do everything right. They had high expectations for me because I always had really good grades in school. They always expected me to be a lawyer or a doctor and go very far in my education. My sister has a high school education. They don't expect as much from her at all because she's always been different. She's headstrong, too. She was always the rebel. I think my mom sees herself in my sister and that's why they don't get along. She doesn't think my sister is as bright and as good. She's more of a woman that needs to stay home. It's like I'm caught between two worlds, old and new. They were just happy that my sister finished high school. My dad is going to college right now. But I am the first one to graduate or to actually complete college even in my extended family.

Sometimes I had difficulty in school. I had to go through speech therapy because I couldn't make certain sounds, the *s*'s and the *t*'s, as clear as they should be. They don't know if it was because it was natural, or if because in Korea they only have certain letters of the alphabet. I don't think they say *l*. So that might have been it.

We're not quite sure where my mom's extended family is in the United States. My mom's aunt (my grandmother's sister) owns a car-part factory for Korea. Supposedly they move the parts here to the States, but my grandmother doesn't know exactly where she is. My mother's aunt has factories in the United States also. My mother wanted to make her daughters equal with her family, and to be equal with everybody, she really stressed education.

My mom views motherhood as very important. But my dad and she had rocky times. She would always say, "I would never divorce your dad because it is important to be a mom." She didn't see being divorced as a good way of being a mother. She felt as though kids need both parents at the same time, in the same house. As a wife, no matter how many problems they might have had, marriage still prevails. It is a commitment and she has to maintain that.

I see my role as a woman as the same thing. Marriage is a long–term commitment that should never be broken. If you are not sure of getting married or you have doubts as to who you are marrying, you shouldn't marry at all. Because once I get married I do not have any intention of ever getting a divorce. Even if my husband had an affair, I wouldn't. It would be more of a forgiveness thing, and hoping that he wouldn't do it again. I guess I get that from my mom.

I don't think there's any certain way for women and men to behave. I think for women there are certain roles that are necessary, especially as a mother and wife. That doesn't mean you wait hand and foot on a man, but to understand that a man isn't going to get that nurturing from male companionship. We all need nurturing in some way and I think a woman can provide that better than a man because a man hasn't learned, or doesn't have that innate quality. Although I do think there are some women who are so strong that it may not be a possibility. I'm not trying to be old-fashioned and I think there is some nurturing that can best be done by a woman. It is just something that adds to us to make us different from the male species.

I think that it would be nice if those qualities could be as valued as what men do and that's where I think, in order for men to see that as a quality, we should try not to hide it. There's a certain way that you can show yourself to be nurturing but also be a strong woman; I've had men tell me that I'm a very caring individual but I'm not a weak individual. I think you can show a man that you'll be there to take care of him if he needs it, but you can also take care of yourself. Sometimes women get so wrapped up in wanting to be treated like a man, to be equal to a man, that we forget there are certain things that make us different from men. There are certain qualities that a man has that we as women probably won't possess to a certain degree. I think a lot of men are very aggressive. So I think there are just so many different traits for men and women. They are equal but that doesn't mean they're the same. They're different in physical and emotional characteristics. We shouldn't deny it, and we should learn to respect it. That's what will bring us to being equal.

I feel the pressures of the stereotype that all Asians are smart because I know I don't fit that stereotype. I used to think I did when I was growing up because I did well. I always had a 4.0 GPA. In high school I went down to a 3.8. I came to college and my first semester I bombed with a 1.7. That was because I was not so used to having all the responsibility and not being at home. Because my mother did everything, we didn't have to do chores. So I felt the pressure that someone is going to look at me and say, "Well, you are not the typical smart Asian person." But I don't believe in stereotypes anyway.

I've always been really close to my teachers, and I've always had friends. There were some who didn't like my name, and who would make some racial slurs, calling me Sushi and Slant-eye, that happened when I was a little kid. I have never really had any problems with the teachers here, except for two. One would always make some comments about Asians in class and another teacher made a racial slur towards me because I answered a question wrong. She asked me if I had pickled my brain in *kimchi* before coming to class. *Kimchi* is a Korean dish. I didn't say anything about it. I'm sure that the other students did. I just walked out of her class and told her I wanted to find a real professor that I could learn something from.

I've always tried talking to people I have a conflict with. I really go a roundabout way sometimes, so they don't feel I'm on the attack. I try talking to them and try to make it a learning experience all the time because I think that's the best way. I think you learn a lot more if you put them at ease and you say, "You're not the first one to make that mistake" and "I've been there before." They know that they can change and that they can do better instead of just saying that, "You did this" and "You did wrong."

I'm a psychology major. I plan to counsel those with substance abuse problems, especially adolescents, and hopefully have my own treatment center. Eventually I plan to continue my education, but I need a break. I plan on getting my master's degree in counseling, having kids, visiting Korea next year, taking my mother there so she can have that final good-bye, and teaching my husband a little bit more about the culture. He's been open about it; when he and I first started dating, he checked out books from the library on the history and culture of of Korea, and he read a lot about it.

I don't really talk to any other Asians at school. It is not that I don't want to. I've never been one to limit myself to one sect of people. I've always been friends with African Americans and some Asian Americans, I've always been with a mixture of people. When I worked at Main Street Market, I had Asians come up to me and ask me what I was. There was one Korean student and he always wanted to have lunch with me. We would always have breakfast and lunch together and we would talk. That's about it. They say hi but they keep to themselves and I keep to myself. It's not that I ignore them. It is just that I hardly talk to my own friends right now. I am too busy.

I wouldn't know if I have a lot in common with Asian students here because I don't talk to them. My roommate last year was Chinese. We could talk and understand each other because I am so used to people with broken English. I can understand them better and I can understand their emotional feelings. I was able to tell that she was getting frustrated, that she wasn't doing well in her lessons. I am very sensitive to Asians and their emotions just by looking at how my mother looks when she is upset, when she is getting frustrated. I could see it. Once there was a graduate student here teaching English composition. He was tutoring four or five Asian students at Main Street Market and he was getting so mad at this one student for not understanding. He was basically browbeating her and putting her down. I was sitting right there next to the table and I finally couldn't take it anymore. I said, "Look, don't talk to them like that. Are you thinking they are going to understand if you yell at them? No. Obviously, she is upset and does not understand because you are not making it clear. And if you did, maybe she would learn." That was probably disrespectful on my part but that was very disrespectful for him to treat her like that. It is like when someone says, "I am deaf" and someone else will speak louder. It was the same concept with him. She was right there and he kept yelling at her. I didn't like that. I am sensitive to that need. I can understand. But I don't interact with a lot of Asian students.

I am a residential coordinator. I work with adolescents who are chemically dependent. I do fairly well but I think it sometimes hinders me in the field because I'm a woman. A lot of people don't like female authority. I had an employee six months ago who obviously couldn't handle that authority. Some of the kids are not used to it either. I have to be more assertive and stress my importance. My boss is a female and she makes sure that it's as equal of an opportunity as possible.

Otherwise, I get along pretty well with my coworkers. I don't really have a problem with them. My coworkers are very supportive of me. They know what the kids are doing wrong, and they don't want to encourage that. And I don't really think that anyone who would show any racial remarks would be working there just because that is not a positive role model for these kids. My husband and I are in the same field, so he's very supportive of my work. It's also easy because he works there. We try not to talk about work at home because we don't want to bring work home.

The kids that I work with are pretty harsh and a lot of them are white supremacists. They don't like to take any type of reprimands from me, not only because I am a female but because I am a minority. I don't know if it is because it's a fad for them, or if it's from their parents. I feel very stressed because of my job. My job is centered around stress. Everything I do is stressful. I am in danger of saying the wrong things because what I do really affects these kids as they are very young and impressionable. It's very important that I model positive behavior and that's what I want to teach them. I have to think about what I'm going to say beforehand and that's pretty hard because sometimes I get so angry at them that I fly off the handle and yell at them a little bit. I vent with coworkers, yell and scream, or we will go out to eat and just sit there, name off names, and keep yelling at each other.

We have to maintain confidentiality at all times and that's pretty difficult because we take the kids on campus and different places. I know a lot of people on campus and they would come up to me and ask me, "Who are these people?" and, "Why are you with them?" and I am just like, "These are my friends." It is really hard.

I like working with the kids. I like to see them smile when they accomplish something, and when they see that there's a better way of living than relying on substance abuse, even though it's short-lived most of the time. What I hate most about the job is that I know that the kids, especially these kids that want to quit and that say "Thank you," are going to go back to the same environment and use substances again. I don't have a good salary but I think I am making pretty good money for a college student. Now that I'm married, I wish I had more. But I have good benefits.

It is really hard to keep in contact with my Korean relatives. My mother calls her mom and when I am around I talk to her on the phone, even though my grandmother has very limited English. So I have to try to understand her. But that's about it. My grandmother does not want to leave Korea. She thinks that the Buddha will make her sick if she leaves. My relationship with her was very good when I was in Korea even though she couldn't speak a lot of English. It was not as though we needed to. It was an automatic love. And she was always so kind. We would use a lot of hand signals, take walks in the village. It is funny because she and my mom have the same relationship that my mom and I do. They tend to baby each other. My grandmother would treat my mom like she is two years old. When my friends here see my mom treating me like a little baby and I react like that, they think I am weird. They get so annoyed by it but they have to understand that it's the way I was raised.

I plan to raise my children the same way, the Korean way, probably more equal distribution between American and Korean ways since my husband is headstrong and he has a set way of doing things. Our kids will probably be equally American and Korean. I have more Korean upbringing than others. I want my kids just the same way I was, to be respectful to people, and to be ladylike. When you are in a relationship, you should be very respectful of your man but not give up your independence. You should also be more willing to give than take. In fact, if I have a daughter, my daughter's name will be the same as mine.

———— ◆ ————

Su-Yi Edwards was born in Seoul, South Korea, in 1967 and immigrated with her parents to Brazil and then to the United States. She graduated from the University of California-Riverside and married a European American biology professor. She was a research technician at Kirksville College of Osteopathic Medicine at the time of the interview in 1995.

I was born in Seoul, Korea, on 27 January 1967. My father had an engineering degree and a minor in law, and he was a mechanical engineer in Korea. We moved to Brazil when I was two, my father didn't get to do his engineering career because his command of the Portuguese language was very poor and his degree wasn't worth anything there. My mom finished her high school, because at the time women didn't go to college for degrees. She worked at a bank until her first child, my sister, was born, which was kind of unusual in Korea at the time.

My family decided to immigrate to Brazil after my mother's parents immigrated to Brazil. My grandfather decided he wanted to farm and he bought land sight unseen in Brazil. My grandparents and two or three uncles of the family immigrated to Brazil. My mom kept getting letters from my grandfather saying how wonderful everything was. She missed them because she and her sister were the only ones who stayed behind in Korea. She decided to go ahead and join them. She was married and all three of us were born already. They basically sold everything and went to Brazil. It turned out the land my grandfather had bought was swampland. They couldn't really farm it. Life was miserable. But he had a lot of pride so he couldn't admit to my mother that life was awful and he had to make all of those wonderful letters. My mother told me that for the first year after we moved there, she never unpacked. All the clothes were packed because she couldn't decide whether she wanted to stay or go. I don't think buying land that way was really popular. My grandfather was very impulsive, although he was saying at the time that Brazil was trying to get immigrants because it was such a big country.

After we immigrated to Brazil, my dad started working as a taxi driver, and eventually he and two of my uncles opened a furniture business. They had a pretty successful business. Then the economy in Brazil collapsed and they decided to immigrate to the United States in 1984. One of my uncles wanted to break the partnership and come to the States, so he removed the capital that he had invested. After losing that much, the whole company went bankrupt and my dad thought they didn't want to try again in Brazil since he didn't know what would happen with the economy. Since he didn't have a career, he was more like a businessperson; he would have to open up another business, and then they weren't sure whether things would work out again. In addition, my parents wanted us to go to college in the United States. Once they arrived in America, my parents bought a small Mom and Pop's convenience store in California and that is how they supported the family.

I was sixteen or seventeen when we came to the United States, a senior in high school. I hated it. I didn't want to come at all, but my brother and sister were excited about coming. They were older than me and were in college in Brazil. In Brazil, everyone goes to college, but it was not guaranteed that you were going to find a job after college, so they were kind of disillusioned with school there. I guess everybody at the time thought America was so great. So they really wanted to come. Some of their college credit transferred from Brazil to the United States. The only problem that they had was that the grading system is different in Brazil. It is hard to get an A in a class in the United States, but it's not impossible. In Brazil it is pretty much impossible. They don't make exams that you can actually do well on. They make it very, very difficult. Then if you try to convert the

GPA to American grades, it's against you, even though you may intellectually know more than a person here.

All the kids came to the United States with student visas but my parents came with tourist visas. The visas expired and they overstayed. They had their own business. It wasn't like they had to get their W-4 form from anybody. Once I got married I changed my status and I'm a citizen now. If you marry an American you can get a residential visa temporarily. Then after a certain amount of time, you become a permanent resident. When you are a citizen, you can sponsor immediate family members. So we basically sponsored my parents even though they were here. They were illegal pretty much for all that time. The only disadvantage is that they couldn't take advantage of any of the services offered. They couldn't use Medicare or Medicaid or any of that stuff. They pay taxes because they own a business and they have to pay taxes on it.

I think my parents had very high expectations of me. People say that Asians don't value women very much, or don't think that they should do much. My parents didn't make any distinction between boys and girls. I have a brother and a sister, but they made no difference at all between any of us. They wanted us all to have the same type of education and have professional careers.

My brother has a MBA in international finance, and my sister is in a doctoral program for health physics. I have a bachelor's degree. I am the big disappointment of the family. I didn't want to pursue anything beyond my bachelors' at that point. I was tired of school. I had chosen biology as a major because I wanted to go to optometry school after I finished, but by the end of it I just didn't like biology at all anymore.

I got married in 1989, right after graduating from college. I went to the University of California–Riverside. My mother doesn't like talking about the fact that they were illegal immigrants. It was very hard because she was embarrassed. She didn't want us to speak Portuguese because she thought that there were a lot of Koreans that came from Brazil illegally. So she thought that if we spoke Portuguese then people would know that we were illegal, which we really weren't. The only difference was as an international student I had to pay three to four times more than the average student was paying in tuition. You have to pay a lot more if you are not a resident. I did go to junior college for two years and I transferred to the University of California. People would pay maybe $100 a semester; I was paying $1,500 a semester for the same classes.

I didn't have any difficulty with school when I came here. I graduated with a 3.23 GPA at the university because everything I took at the junior college was transferable and they were not necessarily easier courses. In California, the educational system is set up in such a way that they have the junior college and then the university, like in Riverside. So they had some kind of arrangement. They had systems where if you took the right classes they were totally transferable. I did well but I don't remember learning very much. I guess I was very good at memorizing and spitting it back out. Of course I did very well in math, as of course you know all the immigrants do. Even in English and things that are more liberal arts I did okay, too.

My relationship with my classmates and teachers was normal. I didn't like approaching the professors very much because I always thought that you only came to the professor if you had problems. If you were doing okay in the class you didn't necessarily go see your professor.

I think in Korea education is really stressful. There are only so many spots at the university. There is a lot of competition. I just met a girl from Korea who is in high school here and she said she used to go to school from seven in the morning until about midnight. She would go to regular classes and then she would have all of these extra classes and she would actually not go to bed until one or two o'clock in the morning. She said she got four hours of sleep a night. It's really very stressful because there are a lot of people in Korea and there are not that many openings at colleges.

This is our [she and her husband's] first year in this town. For the last three and a half years we were in Georgia; we stayed at the post doctorate Emory University. I actually like it here better than Georgia. Everybody's surprised, but I like it. I guess I was ready for change. I didn't like Atlanta very much; it's different. Coming from California, it was very different going to Atlanta, even though it's supposed to be a very cosmopolitan city. It felt strange.

I'm a research technician at the microbiology department at the medical school here. I get along with my colleagues and coworkers very well and my boss is very nice. I get bored sometimes, but I don't feel job-related stress. Actually I wish there was stress, I work better under pressure. It's a very laid back atmosphere.

I don't think people treated or do treat me any differently because I'm Asian and female. I did have a conflict in Atlanta when I worked in a reference laboratory. I worked with somebody who was mentally imbalanced and none of us knew that until it came to a climax. I started work there three months after this girl had started. And a promotion came up that I got. After that she hated my guts because she felt that she deserved the promotion. It was a very tough time because everything that she accused me of was very much just what she perceived. It wasn't anything that I had done. It was like, "she looks at me funny" or, "her tone of voice was very bossy." How do you fight somebody else's perceptions when you are not trying to do those things? She had a nervous breakdown and that is how it was solved. When it came to the climax, she actually threatened to beat me up. She did not say this to me, but to my supervisor. That is how imbalanced she was that she could actually come to our supervisor and tell her that she wanted to beat me up.

The supervisor did take the threat seriously and several things had happened in the course of the year. She had already been in therapy a while and she had come back with an understanding that we were going to try to work on the problem. We all walked on eggshells to make sure that we didn't hurt her feelings. So when this finally happened again they called the doctor and tried to commit her again and that was it. My supervisor knew that I had not done anything to provoke her and that she was already in therapy and on drugs. It was bad.

Now I am a college graduate making about $7 per hour and even that is better than a lot of people make. In a small town, it's tough to find a good-paying job. I guess I feel lucky that I do have a lot of good benefits. We don't have any problems with money. The cost of living is lower.

The people I work with are very nice, including my boss. Sometimes I feel like my job is too slow. I wish there were more things to do. It is boring because I work in a microbiology lab and we do DNA sequencing. I always have to wait for my boss to tell me what we are doing that day or what the project is for the next couple of days. That is partly because I haven't been there long. I've only been there for two or three months so I don't have a project that I can come in and work on at my own pace. I work Monday through Friday from 8:30 AM to 5:00 PM. Sometimes I know what we're doing in advance, we go weeks at a time when I have things to do, but then we come to a halt when I've finished everything we had planned on doing. Then we have to wait until he thinks up another experiment.

I met my husband, Tom, in college; I think it was the summer before my senior year. Tom was getting his PhD in the laboratory and I volunteered to work in the lab for the summer. I wanted a recommendation letter from his advisor so that I could go to optometry school. That is how we met. I didn't get my letter, by the way, but I caught a husband so it's a trade-off.

Tom is really funny. You wouldn't know to look at him, but he is actually funny and very intelligent. I think that is the thing that struck me about him the first time we met. He seemed to know so much about so many different things. I call him the human sponge because he basically knows everything. He would be a good jeopardy contestant. He did try out for it, by the way. It was hard; he had one hundred of the one thousand dollar questions.

I have a good relationship with my husband. As far as sharing household responsibilities, it is about 50/50 or 40/60 and sometimes he does more than I do. Whoever has time, whoever feels like it, does it. We go through spells where I do most of the cooking or he'll do most of the cooking. It's pretty even. I don't do everything here.

He doesn't let me help with his grading (he's a professor at Northeast Missouri State). It depends on the test. If it was multiple choice it would be no problem at all, but most of his tests are essays, so I wouldn't know enough to get the meaning of the stuff because maybe they are a little bit off but maybe they are a little bit right.

We make decisions unilaterally. We talk about it. It's funny because I tend to be the impulsive one and he is the one that has to research everything about the topic. It works out well because I make him decide faster. If I waited around for him to say the final decision, we wouldn't get anything done. By then the sale price is gone or the deal is not there anymore. So we usually talk about it. I wouldn't buy something big without talking to him and I know that he wouldn't do that either without talking to me first. My husband also is supportive of my work.

I have a very good relationship with my parents. We get along really well. After I got married, we got along even better. As a matter of fact, my dad just sent me a coat this past weekend. It was a total surprise to me. He's never bought me clothes and he actually bought me something and mailed it. I was very shocked. My parents are in California. Both of my in-laws are deceased. But Tom's sister raised him, and she and her family are in Las Vegas. So when we go to visit my family, we usually drive up to Las Vegas. We try to see them once a year. It's either around Christmas time or during summer vacation. But now that we are in the Midwest, maybe we could do it more often.

I actually know some Korean. I can understand my parents really well, but I can't talk back to them in Korean very well and I usually respond in Portuguese. They know Portuguese, too. They speak in Korean and they respond in Portuguese. Tom doesn't speak any Portuguese, unless we are going on boring road trips and I try to teach him Portuguese by pointing at different things.

My parents had no problem with my marrying outside my ethnic origins, although they really wanted my brother to marry a Korean. He was the last one to get married and I think in Korea it is a tradition for the parents to live with the son and his family. If they were going to do that with my brother, it would be easier if he were to marry a Korean who could speak to my parents. But my brother married a Japanese girl. I have no idea whether my parents will live with them because she is an only child so her parents are probably going to live with her. I think once my parents got to know Tom, they were very happy. Even now they say that he is a better son-in-law than a lot of Koreans would be. I think Korean sons-in-law don't treat the in-laws as well as they expect to be treated by the in-laws. And that is just liberty. I think that Tom goes out of his way to treat them well and they appreciate that. My parents don't have any American friends. The only thing they know about Americans is what they read in the Korean papers, which is not always the best example. So they thought that Tom wasn't serious about me. They thought that Tom just wanted to take advantage of me and leave me. Tom met them pretty soon because I lived at home then. He did all sorts of things around the house trying to get on their good side. He ate all of my mother's cooking; he would eat all the Korean food and ask for more. My brother-in-law is a very picky eater and it took longer for him to win my parents over because of that.

Brazilian food is very different from American food. The meals are very different in the way they are arranged. Lunch is the biggest meal there. Dinner is very light; you have bread and eggs, like what you have for breakfast here. But everybody has a real lunch. You have rice, meat, and a salad for lunch. They eat lunch at eleven or twelve o'clock. Even the people that work still take their hot lunches to work; they don't eat sandwiches. They always made fun of Americans on how they always ate hamburgers and other fast food.

The cooking I do is mostly American. I don't know how to make Brazilian dishes; they are difficult to make. I think a lot of it is labor intensive. Sometimes I can cook, although my mother never taught me. I know how some things tastes and I try to imitate it. But we mostly eat American foods plus a lot of rice.

Portugal discovered Brazil and it was the only country in South America that was colonized by the Portuguese. But they also had a lot of influence from Indians and Africans. They had slaves at one time and there is a lot of African influence, so the cuisine is very different from Portugal. It's like a mix of stuff. They eat a lot of rice and beans but the beans are not like Mexican beans. They don't make refried beans. It is beans with a runny sauce. Rice and beans are staples of the diet.

I don't have any children. But if I did I think I would raise them as liberal Americans. When I was growing up, I don't remember my parents raising us as Koreans. They just wanted us to get immersed in the Brazilian culture as much as possible. I think that worked out really well for us. None of us have any self-esteem problems. I know I will get a lot of heat from other people. I wonder if sometimes by trying to be different you create more problems. It's almost like a wall when you expect people to treat you differently in a way. It makes a good point that you've got to prepare a kid for whatever they are going to encounter in real life. I don't remember running into anything where I felt awful because I didn't look like other people. Our kids are going to be half-Caucasian so why should I just emphasize my half? I think they would be raised as Americans. I don't think I would try to drub them, "Don't forget your Korean heritage," unless they ask. If they ask I would anwer, and I think I would send them to my parents to answer their questions.

What I like most about America is it's being a developed country where it is so easy to have so many things. People don't struggle as much. Even if you are poor you can still get a good education, which is not true in Korea and I'm sure it's not true in Brazil. There is a big class separation there. So it's the equality here that I like. However, I hate the politicians here. It's like the person who lies the most gets elected. If you tell the truth no one elects you. I guess it's our fault, the public's fault. It's not the politicians' fault. The abortion issue worries me and I think there are too many Republicans in Congress right now. We are Democrats, by the way.

During our spare time we go out for breakfast at Pancake City on the weekends. We like renting movies. Mostly I like socializing, getting together with other people. I don't have to have outside interests; I just like meeting other people. I would like to go to church but I haven't woken up early enough on Sundays. My mother's family is very religious. They are Christians.

What I like most about the town is the small-town feeling, not having to worry about crime. That is a big issue. Even though we never experienced violence or crime in Atlanta, it got tiring every time we turned on the TV to see that somebody else got killed, somebody else got shot. It was so random as well. You could be in the wrong place at the wrong time and get shot; things go on in the bad areas and you just stay away from it. But once the crime starts going on in places you don't expect, it's scary. So I like that here you don't have to worry about it. Tom was just saying that we have been here for three months and he hasn't been panhandled a single time yet. He used to walk to work every day, it was pretty nice. I would trade the cosmopolitan life any day for this because you can always go to a big town and go to the theater or a show. But it's your daily life that's going to add up at the end. So I like not having to worry about those things. There is another thing I like up here—not much traffic; you can get from one end of town to the other in five minutes. That is really nice. In Atlanta, we had to drive a lot; the roads are really narrow and really old. I don't think they accounted for all the cars there now. They have too many cars and they always run the yellow lights. They never stop. So that took a lot to get used to.

I wish there was a Target here, and maybe another movie theater that showed more recent movies. The choice of movies is very limited; sometimes the movie will be at the video store at HyVee and they will be playing it at the theater. Also the price of housing could be cheaper. Houses are kind of expensive for a rural area in a small town.

We never got interested in any professional teams in Atlanta. Tom actually hates the Braves; he doesn't care much for sports. In Atlanta I went to Six Flags over Georgia. It's not as good as the one in California, but it was good.

I don't get any newspapers from Brazil or Korea. When I was in college, my sister was getting *Asian American Magazine*. It was kind of interesting to see all the Asian people on the pages. Whatever comes out of the national American news is the only thing I follow.

Most of my friends are Americans. It was very hard for me to become close to Korean people, even in college. The school I went to did have a lot of Koreans, but I didn't speak Korean very well and I had a hard time relating to them. I belonged to the International Club, not the Korean American club. I didn't feel much like a Korean, maybe because I felt more like a Brazilian. So it was easier being with other international people rather than one particular race or nationality. To start with it was easier to get along with the international people than it was with Americans. The international people were in the same boat as me. Their English is not very good still. I think they are more accepting, maybe because they want to meet people and they are lonely, while most Americans have their own lives already and they don't particularly need another friend. Now I get along with anybody.

Yong-Mi Jones was born into a farmer's family in Chungiu, South Korea, in 1972 and immigrated to Springfield, Missouri, with her family in 1976. Her family history chronicles the struggle and success of Korean immigrants. Her interracial dating and marriage and her parents' reactions to them typify the experience of interracial marriage among American-born or American-grown Asian women. She was attending Southwest Missouri State University and lived in Nixa with her husband, a European American, at the time of the interview in 1996.

My full name was Yong-Mi Moon, now it's Jones. I was born in Chungiu, South Korea. It is located in the southern part of Korea. The story was that my sister went to Yonsei University. She checked our family genealogy to find out about our names. Yong means courageous, Mi is beautiful, and Moon is a scholar. What she found out was that, with the stories that my dad had told her, in China there was a king who had three sons. And one of the sons settled in my dad's old town. Their last name was Moon. My dad was in the second or third generation from the prince at that time. Because of the mixed blood, our family is beautiful. And my dad was educated by the best teachers in that town. My dad was taught by a Japanese man, probably up through the eighth grade, which was a lot back then. My dad can speak and read Korean and Japanese, and he can read and speak a lot of Chinese, too. His education stopped because they were sending all of the Japanese people back home when the Korean War started. Then he had to go and fight in the Korean War.

My mom was from a very poor family. She was the fourth daughter and she had a baby brother. In Korea, you have to have a son to carry on the family name. By the time my mom was born, my grandmother was devastated that she had another girl instead of a boy. My grandma left my mom outside on a cold night hoping that she would die in the middle of the night. Then my mom's grandma came and said, "What are you doing?

This child has done nothing wrong. Why are you doing this?" My mom is strong, she is alive right now.

The girls in my mom's family had to work really hard, harder than the boys, to keep the family going. My mom had no education at all, and everything she's learned, she learned on her own. I remember that when I was four or five years old, my mom would pick up my dad's newspapers after he read them and look through them to see what characters she knew, and she would just keep saying them over and over. Probably within the last ten years she could read enough characters to comprehend a lot of it. She's sixty-one now. Six years ago, she started to teach herself English. And then, of course, her hands don't want to write. But she would write her ABC's ten times every morning and when she came home she would spell things and pronounce her alphabet.

I always thought people back then all had matchmakers that set them up at birth. Then I talked to other people that are my parent's age who met each other through school. But for my parents it was the old way. My maternal grandma liked my dad's family. My paternal grandpa really liked my mom because she was a hard worker. My dad told me that he saw my mom's older sister and thought she was really pretty, so he thought my mom must be pretty, too. In the town that they lived in at the time all the guys wanted my mom and all the girls wanted my dad. So that's how it goes.

Back then the bride and groom didn't see each other until they got married. It was all set up. My maternal grandma interviewed the boys coming of age, each one of them with the other elder ladies in a room. In a five-by-five room with about seven gray-headed women saying, "Are you going to do this?" The decision was made and my dad was going to marry my mom. There was no courtship. The man's gift to the bride was some fabric to make a dress. My dad picked the best fabric and sent it to my mom. Of course my mom liked that colorful fabric. On the day they were supposed to get married my mom was deathly sick. My dad had to walk several hours to the nearest medicine person to get certain herbs and things that my grandma had requested, which was not cheap at all. My dad was telling himself, "I didn't even know this girl and she's sick on her wedding day and I've got to go buy this medicine." After about a week had passed my mother got better and they had their wedding.

When they were married, my dad was eighteen or nineteen and my mom was sixteen or seventeen. It was a traditional Korean wedding. The bride was in her traditional gown and the groom was, too. My mom was sent over to my dad's house and they gave gifts to her family. During the ceremony, neither one of them was supposed to smile because that means their first child will be a girl. That's why in a lot of pictures you won't see people smiling at weddings. They bowed to each other and bowed to his family and then they went off into their own room. They were by themselves for a couple of minutes. They had never met before the wedding and they've been married for about forty-five years.

My family immigrated to the United States in March of 1976 to Springfield, Missouri. We immigrated because my dad has two sisters. They are both younger than him. During the Korean War, they were all separated and the youngest one got married to an American military person and moved to the States. Both of them thought that she was dead for twenty years. They didn't hear anything from her. Then my dad got a letter from my aunt saying that if anyone knew my dad to let him know that she is in America. She had asked my dad to come to the States, the dream of the golden streets and stuff like that. So that's why we came.

My dad's parents both died when the Korean War had just begun. My dad's grandpa raised his grandchildren. With my dad being away fighting in the war, my aunt had to provide for the family. She did miscellaneous work here and there. She probably met her American husband that way. When my dad and my aunt finally met they were both adults with their own families. My dad had great respect for my uncle-in-law for taking care of her and being good to her. There is a stereotype of Asian women and American military men marrying. I can't say how they got together, but I don't think my aunt looks like a streetwalker or anything like that. A lot of people probably thought that she did it to get out of the country.

We had a farm of several hundred acres in Korea. My dad sold our land there and applied for a visa and then we moved to Seoul. We didn't think it was going to be a very long process. My dad was expecting us to leave immediately. We had to take health examinations and there were only one or two doctors that the country had doing the tests. They said my dad had something wrong, like hepatitis. The medication cost my dad something like a hundred to two hundred dollars a week. He would keep going back and the doctor would say, "Yeah, you still need to take the medicine." While they did that, we waited about a year and a half, and the doctor still said he needed to take the medication. My dad had asked for another doctor and they wouldn't let him see anybody. By that time, my dad had lost everything. All the money we had was gone. He told them, "I'm a bum. I have seven kids. We thought we could go to America right away. You're not letting us. We can't do anything." So another doctor that he had never seen came. He asked my dad what the matter was and my dad explained the situation to him. Then he examined my dad and said there was nothing wrong with him.

The doctors were keeping him there because they could make profit off patients. After that, my dad went to the Korean consulate. He had an interview with a Korean man. The Korean man asked my dad to write all the children's names in English. My dad said he couldn't speak English. The man said, "What are you going to do in America if you can't speak English?" There was nothing my dad could do. Then an American guy came in and spoke to my dad in Korean. He asked him what was going on so my dad explained the situation again. He asked my dad to come into his office and he did all the paperwork for my dad. All that was required for him was to go in and write down the birth dates of the children. We left immediately after that. My oldest brother stayed in Korea because he had just gotten married a couple of months before we moved to the States.

Springfield, Missouri, was the first place we went to in the States. We flew there and it was a two-day process. At that time I was four years old, the youngest in my family. My parents weren't used to hamburgers and whatever else they served on the plane so my mom didn't eat for two days. None of us really ate anything. When we flew into Kansas City, my dad called my aunt and said we couldn't fly anymore because being on the plane gave us motion sickness. I don't remember any of that, but my mom said it was so hard for her to see her little kids crying. My oldest sister was sixteen and she said it was so hard to travel with the six of us.

I have three older brothers and three older sisters. There is almost a ten year difference between me and my siblings because after my mom had my brother she didn't see my dad, who went to the army, for almost eight or nine years. When my brothers and sisters came here they were still school-aged. They went to public school. The two oldest were my sisters; one was sixteen and the other was fifteen. For them it was good that we came to the States because in Korea they were at the age when you started to have to pay for their education. It was very costly because right after them came my two brothers and another sister coming right up. When we came here, education was free and they went to the public schools. We stayed with my aunt for the first five months. They had a seventeen-year-old daughter, a twelve-year-old son, and another daughter who was probably eight at the time. At first it was fun that they had someone to play with. But they had the language barrier. When it came to buying stuff, there were six of us kids plus my parents now and they couldn't get as much, so there was a lot of competition between my brothers and sisters and my cousins.

My aunt had a trailer for us to live in when we first came. After we felt comfortable we went and lived in the trailer. My sisters went to Parkview High School. Then there was a conflict. My uncle had a veteran friend who was paralyzed. When he was on his deathbed he asked my uncle to help his wife and two daughters. My uncle promised that he would do what he could. There was a conflict with my uncle trying to spend time with his family while keeping his promise. That lady manipulated my uncle. My aunt had gone through too much and couldn't take it any more. That's why they ended up divorcing after twenty years of marriage. Of course, my uncle didn't want that but there was nothing he could do.

My aunt's oldest daughter was my sister's age. My sister was a cute little thing and didn't know anything about boys. She went to Parkview with that girl, her name was Cindy. She told the teachers evil things like my sister was smoking. My sister didn't know what to say whenever they accused her because she couldn't speak English. The girls didn't like her because she was cute and the boys liked her. So school was very difficult for my sisters. For my sisters it was hard also because they didn't want to go to school but they knew they needed the education. And my parents needed them around. It was a bigger strain for my second sister because she was responsible for taking care of the family so she ended up dropping out of school.

My brothers also had a very rough time. They were teased because we were the second Korean family to move into Springfield. The first didn't have any kids so we were the first Koreans around school. I don't think there were many other Asians, and there were very few blacks. A lot of people can't distinguish the differences in Asian people, so my brothers would get teased about being Vietnamese. They had a hard time. Once they started speaking English, they formed a familiarity with other people.

My parents were both farmers in Korea. When we came here no one wanted to hire a person who could not speak English and without any skills. My dad started out working at Diamond Head, working in the kitchen, sweeping, cleaning up, and doing whatever he was asked to do. He was getting about $300 a month. This was back in 1976 or 1977, supporting six kids and a wife with $300 a month. He wouldn't take any food stamps because he had too much pride. We bought a used ten-speed and I remember he would, even in the rain and snow, ride that out to Diamond Head every day, back and forth.

When we moved to Springfield, my dad would not let us speak Korean. We had to speak English. That's why it took me a while to speak Korean because everyone had to use English, except my mom and dad. We learned English by being around people who spoke it, like little kids in the trailer park or in school. I think they had one teacher at Parkview that worked with my sisters. We also went to SMS in the evening to take English classes. I remember doing that for a while. They took me, too, because my parents and my sisters had to go. They didn't know what babysitters were.

My parents did treat my brothers differently than my sisters. I was the exception. But the boys had more freedom. They didn't have to work as hard. My sisters had to sacrifice themselves to help support the family. My brothers were just ornery. They've had a lot more freedom.

Everybody in my family went to the same school, except for the two youngest. As far as education, I think it was more that if we want it we can go ahead and take it. My parents were not saying boys need it more than girls, or girls need it more than boys. My parents were the exception to the rule. That was pretty much put on by my aunt. She said the girls needed to help the family and the boys need to go to school. That was the same for higher education, too.

Most of my immediate family, brothers and sisters, are still in the Springfield area, because of Korean family values. My oldest sister worked at Zenith. That's how she learned a lot of her English. She married Roger who is from Taiwan. They have a restaurant in Springfield. My second oldest sister is a single parent and works in my first sister's restaurant. If it weren't for the family being close and being there she would have had a difficult time raising her kids. My third oldest sister graduated from the University of Missouri as pre med. She went to Korea to be an international student and got married to a Korean that she met there. Now she lives in Seattle and she is a housewife. She is kind of studying. I think her plan is to go back to Korea and be an English teacher.

My oldest brother came to the States about four or five years ago and he has his own restaurant now. In Korea, he was a fashion designer/seamstress. He worked in a company that specialized in leather, making jackets and things. He was one of the big people there. But when he came to the States, not speaking English or having the education, he had hard time. He went to school in Korea but most of his education was from working and he couldn't transfer all that back here. So he learned from my dad about how to run a restaurant. They live in Baxter Springs, Kansas, which is an hour and a half away.

My second oldest brother went to Drake University on a scholarship, both academic and athletic for soccer. He wanted to go into business first but then found his talent was computers. He worked in California with computers. Then he transferred over to Iowa State and graduated from there. He is now back in Springfield and has opened up his own computer store, the IBM clones. He does an awesome job; he does a lot of networking for companies and personal computers, too.

My third oldest brother graduated from Parkview High School, too. He and my second oldest brother graduated at the same time. They felt it would be easier if they were together in school since they were only a year apart in age. His talent was tennis. He got a scholarship for that. He went to Drake for a while. He came back after his second year to help my parents with the restaurant. Now he works with my second oldest brother as a technician.

A lot of my family have started their own businesses. That is something that my parents have instilled in us. I can't imagine working for somebody because you can't make money. I know you need employees as well as employers. My parents came here with absolutely nothing and within fifteen years or so they've managed to go from having nothing to having something.

I am married to an American man. His name is Chad. I met Chad when I was sixteen at a church youth camp. He grew up in Germany, and that's important. He graduated from high school at sixteen and then came back to the States because his dad was in the army. I had just moved back to this area and our churches, for the first time, went on this trip together out to Colorado. For some reason, we were up in the mountains; I knew who he was but that was it. We really didn't talk at all on that trip. I thought I liked him or I could like him. I was thinking, "Okay, Lord, maybe someday we will meet and something will come of it."

When I graduated something strange was going on with my church so I decided I would try visiting other churches and I knew that he was going to the church out in Wilson Creek. But I wasn't sure if he was still here or if they went back to Germany. I started going there but I didn't see him for a while because he was working. I just had an infatuation a long time ago and was afraid to see him face to face.

We met as friends there and at first we would just go out in groups and do stuff. At that time he went to Drury University as a theater major, so he had to go see plays for school. I thought that sounded like fun. So we would go to a show and maybe dinner, and then go home. It was very platonic. I had a boyfriend, he had a girlfriend, but they were in a different state. Once we were all supposed to go do something and everyone else backed out so it was Chad and me alone. We had decided that we were all going to go to the haunted houses. I asked him if he really wanted to do this and he said no, so we went bowling. This was around Thanksgiving. I had a boyfriend that lived in New Mexico. I was cold and Chad gave me his hand. I thought he was just holding my hand because I was cold. From there, I ended up breaking up with my old boyfriend because it was time to break up with him. He was just so serious and I wasn't ready for that. Chad started calling every other week and then every week. We went to Silver Dollar City together to go see the Christmas lights. I thought, "This is more than I want." I wanted to break up with him but I don't know why I didn't. I was kind of seeing someone else at the same time. Around April it was our first kiss, so I guess it was a while.

I think we both knew that we were going to get married. It was just a matter of time. I had told him that I didn't want a long engagement, six months was enough time to plan. Chad didn't want to talk about marriage until he was financially secure. He didn't want to have that problem, because the number one reason why marriages fail is finances.

I was always told that I couldn't date someone until I graduated from college. I changed that rule. My family didn't see Chad as my boyfriend. He was just a friend that I went out with. I don't think they ever thought anything of it because he didn't make any commitment to me and I didn't make any commitment to him. They never really saw him, either. I was always working so we would go out late at night.

In the beginning, my dad and my mom didn't want me to see anybody. Because Chad was an American, my dad didn't want me going out with him. The one time that I actually liked an Asian, my dad said I couldn't go out with him because he was Korean. It was pretty much no boys. When I was dating my old boyfriend, my dad told me to wait for graduation. My birthstone is opal and I liked this ring I saw in a store. I told my dad I liked this ring and he said he would buy it for me if I broke up with my boyfriend. To anyone that I was remotely friends with, my dad would say he didn't like them. But with Chad, he never said I couldn't date him. I think he was watching me because I was always outspoken. I told my dad everything. He was waiting. Whenever Chad would come over, he would not even acknowledge him. He would not say hi or anything. My mom, with Chad, never said, "No, you can't date him." She just wanted me to be happy and meet a good man and make sure our goals were the same. She was always pleasant to him. I think the reason my dad behaved like that is because I am the youngest.

I don't remember much about how they were towards my sisters when they were dating. My oldest sisters are married to Taiwanese and Chinese men. I think there was a thing with the different race, too. But when my third oldest sister was out of college and met a Korean guy my dad didn't want her to marry him because he was too Korean. He only went to college in the States. I think my dad really tried to see if I could stand up to him and say, "This is the man that I am going to marry." He was trying to get us to realize that this was what we wanted and not what someone was trying to talk us into.

I think my parents knew, just like Chad and I knew, that it was just a matter of when we would get married. My mom thought that I had to have a ring before I could decide. That's why Chad, instead of asking permission from my dad, went ahead and asked me and then we confronted my parents. We sat with them and discussed it. This was in August. I told my parents I was going to marry him in January. Chad would still come by and say hi. My dad at that time was kind of hateful in a way, but he realized that Chad was part of my future. He had always realized that his daughter was going to be gone in six months, because I had a ring and we sat with them. He was totally against the wedding. I told my mom that I was totally awestruck. What was I going to do? She told me to start planning to have the wedding in January.

My parents and Chad's parents had never met formally, had dinner or anything. Before Thanksgiving, I kept telling my dad that he had to meet Chad's parents. So when Thanksgiving came around my dad told them that they could come over to discuss the wedding. About a month before the wedding my dad actually said yes in front of Chad's mom and dad. But he was still denying the whole thing. On January first, New Years Day, we all bow to my parents and tell them, "Have good year" in Chinese. Then they give us red money packets. That year my dad said he was only going to give it to the boys. So I said I wasn't going to bow to him. Finally I decided that it was my last year to do it, so I went ahead. My dad started crying. He told me to live well and be happy and be prosperous. Normally my dad is not emotional at all. He just hugged me and was crying. I had never seen him cry before. I have made him cry twice in my life. It was hard for him to let me go.

After that he involved himself in the wedding. Most people have a dinner and serve alcohol at their weddings, but I didn't want alcohol to be served and that's why I had it at the church. I just wanted cake and punch and to say, "Thank you, bye." My dad thought he had so much to do to plan for the wedding. I told him, "I have everything taken care of." I don't know how I did it all by myself, but I did. My dad cooked everything that morning. He worked on some dishes that required a full week or a week and a half to cook.

It was weird because he was in a daze on our wedding day. I had gotten the tux, shoes, and everything for him. When my dad goes out in public he usually dresses very nicely. He came to the church with his tux on but he picked his oldest pair of brown shoes. He had his wide pinstriped navy suit with a darker navy diagonal tie and the old brown shoes. I was just ready to die when I saw him. I asked him what he was doing and he was like a little baby. I said, "Dad you can't do this." He said, "Oh I'm fine, I am more comfortable in this." He would not change. My dad has never been that way.

He likes Chad now. He's accepted him into the family. Chad, being raised in Germany, has always been around other cultures. He wasn't a little boy from a hick town who goes, "Ew, what's that?" He eats everything and he'll try everything. He doesn't drink but he'll do anything else that he needs to do. He has a very giving heart. He has taken a lot of crap from my parents. My dad has been vicious to him sometimes. For example, when Chad came over once, we hadn't seen each other all day and it was late. He wasn't feeling well so he was lying on my bed with the door open. My dad came home and told me that Chad needed to go home. Chad asked what my dad had said and I told him not to worry about it. My dad came back later and yelled, "You go home!" It was awful. It hurt Chad's pride, of course. He was angry and felt like my dad could have said it in a nicer way. In a way my dad did and I was a bad person because I didn't tell Chad. That's why communication is a very important thing. Chad could also put himself in my dad's shoes. Me, being his daughter, and Chad lying there on my bed looked bad. I don't think situations like that caused problems between Chad and I. For Chad, it didn't matter what other people thought. He knew he loved me.

Before I ever dated anyone, I always asked if his family would be okay with me. Unlike Chad, it matters to me what the family thinks. It was very important to me. I had asked him what his parents thought about him dating an Asian. His parents grew up in Jonesbourgh, Arkansas. He went and asked his parents. For Chad, his father's opinions matter a great deal. His Dad said, "It doesn't matter if you marry the darkest African woman as long as she is a Christian and she is saved." For a while I thought his parents didn't like me, but they did. I even asked them if they had problems. They felt like we were mature enough and we knew what we were getting into. I think I have a bigger problem with the interracial marriage than Chad does. I told his parents about the situation when my dad wasn't accepting us. I have very open communication with them. They understood and wanted to know if January was going to be the date. I said yes and I told them that my mom said it was okay. They said okay and they prayed for the situation. Everyone was telling me that my dad was going to turn around.

For me it didn't stop with his parents. He has a younger brother and sister. Their opinions matter to me, too, because when I think of a family unit I think of my experience. Of course my experience is my own and our family is very strong. I wondered what his aunt and uncle thought, and what his grandma and grandpa thought. Things like that were important to me. They weren't to Chad. I don't remember his brother, who is twenty-one now, until he was a senior in high school. It was always a "Hi, how are you" kind of thing. His sister is now seventeen and graduating from high school. I didn't really talk to her that much, either. When Chad and I were engaged, their attitudes were different to me. His sister and I always talked a little bit but there was always a level of discomfort. His brother and I never really talked. Once we were engaged, he told me everything about himself, some things I didn't want to know.

It was so cute because we got engaged on August 10, 1995. The year before, his immediate family and I had gone to Arkansas for a weekend. They had invited me to come and we went camping in a cabin. His brother and sister both had opportunities to bring a friend but they didn't want to. They wanted it to be family time, so even then they accepted me as part of the family. His brother had never been in a lake before. We had on our life-jackets, and he didn't ask anybody else this and this made me feel really special. He said, "Is this thing going to hold me up?" I said, "Yes." And he said, "Is it really?" I said, "Yes." It was just like a little kid asking. I jumped into the water first. Then I showed him how I was floating and he jumped in the water. This was when he was nineteen or twenty and he was just so cute.

Chad and I discussed having kids very early in our relationship. I think that as much as we can, we'll make my Asian heritage affect the raising of our children. My parents just came back from Korea. We sent them for three weeks; it is the second time they have gone since we first came here. The last time they went was in 1991. My mom wants me to go back to Korea this summer with her. Chad, if he can, will go with us. I told him that he isn't going unless he learns Korean. He said, "Okay." We discussed this because I was always told, "Don't date anyone you don't plan on marrying. If you don't have the same goals, it's not going to work, or it will be difficult." I would ask off-the-wall questions to everybody and if they didn't answer it right or didn't want to answer it, I said, "Okay, bye." We both decided that we want our children to learn Korean but also learn other languages.

My favorite thing about Chad is his determination or his ambition. When you come to America you think of the golden streets, the things you can accomplish, you go for your dream. Those are the things my parents have taught us. You can be whatever you want to be. A lot of people I met here are like, "I've got to go to school. I've got to go to work. I'm going to get a job." That, to me, is a poor person's mentality. Whatever the world wants to hand me, I'll accept it. For Chad, he doesn't accept it. He uses his challenges, struggles. He climbs over his struggles. He looks for what more he can do. He doesn't just let it stop wherever he is.

15

Generational Conflict

Christie Kim was born in Columbia, Missouri, in 1979. Her parents immigrated to the United States from South Korea in the 1950s and were both physicians. She was a high school student in Columbia, Missouri, at the time of the interview in 1995.

I was born on 22 May 1979 in Columbia, Missouri. I have never lived anywhere but in Columbia. My parents came here about twenty years ago. I am not really sure why they came here. I know my dad got a job here and my uncle on my mom's side lived here in Columbia. But I'm not really sure. I never really talked to them about this. My parents are both physicians and they went to medical school while they were in Korea. They are now citizens of the United States.

I think there are definitely different expectations in Korean families than in American ones. Most of my friends are Caucasian and there's a big difference between what their parents expect of them and what my parents expect of me. It varies a lot from family to family, but in general, they expect them to go to college, to try hard in school, but not to the degree that my parents expect me to try hard in school.

School is definitely what my parents put the most emphasis on. It wasn't something they threw at me one day, but they've always expected it of me from early age. Even in elementary school, they always expected me and my brother to get the best grades. They always told me to do my best, but I knew what they expected of me. I think what they tell me is not exactly what they're feeling. I think what they want to tell me is that I have to be the best. But obviously they can't tell me that so they tell me to try harder. I feel pressured from that.

247

I spend a lot of time studying. I don't spend as much time studying as my parents want me to, but I don't think I'd be able to deal with studying as much as they want me to. If I'm not studying and I know I should be studying, I feel guilty; whereas if my parents hadn't been telling me that I should be studying, I would be a little bit more relaxed about it. It seems like I always have this little voice inside my head.

I have one brother. I know from my relatives in Korea that there really is a difference between what's expected of male children and what's expected of female children. They expect so much out of him and I'm not sure that they know exactly what to expect from me because I'm younger and I'm a girl. But my parents expect at least as much out of me as they do of my brother because they have more of an idea of what I need to be doing. They know more what they're doing, too. They know what to emphasize if they want me to get into a good college, which is the goal right now, and they know the system better. I think that it would be the same even if we lived in Korea. Although I'm not really sure how things work in Korea, but basically my parents want me to get into a good college because they want to see me succeed when I'm older.

It varies how I feel about this pressure. While I feel like I have a definite advantage over people whose parents don't really stress their education very much, sometimes it gets to me and I resent it. I can't really help that, even though I know it's for the best, it's hard to take sometimes because it's hard to deal with seeing other people who don't have this pressure while I have to deal with it.

I think they'll tell me what college to go to. My dad has emphasized that anything I do is ultimately my choice, but my parents do actively express their opinions and so I have their perspective of what I should do. My dad talks to me a lot and he's really good about that. He seems to understand me and he can relate to me a lot better than my mom can. His English is a little better and he understands me and my brother a lot better. I'd say we have two-way communication.

I don't speak the Korean language. Any Koreans that I encounter, I feel they look down on me a little bit because they think I should be more cultured. But I'm not really sure how they view me because I can't really communicate very well with them. I don't know about my mom, but my dad definitely thinks that I'm being pulled away from Korean culture because of America. He really believes in the Korean way of doing things and sometimes I can tell that he thinks I'm too Americanized and that is a bad thing.

They tried to stress my learning Korean, my dad especially. When I was younger, he really tried to get me and my brother to learn to speak Korean because there was a Korean school in town. But I didn't understand why I had to learn Korean. I figured that I was always going to be living in the States, even though I think I've been to Korea five times, and I figured that my parents would always be there to help me out whenever I needed to talk to my relatives. I didn't understand that the language was a big part of the culture and by not knowing the language I would be missing a lot of the culture. I definitely regret not knowing it now. Now I want to learn but I really don't have enough time. I figure that when I get to college, or maybe even later, I'll learn it. But I'll definitely learn the language.

I went to the Korean school mainly for language. I was probably six years old. It was on Saturday mornings and that in itself was pretty bad. I really hated the whole thing. There were some kids there whose parents spoke to them in Korean at home and they could understand more Korean than I could, so I always felt like I was totally lost.

We have Korean food for most meals. I like it. I went to a summer camp and I was gone for six weeks. I didn't realize until then how much Korean food we ate and how much I would miss it. My parents get a Korean newspaper, but I don't know anything about what's going on in Korea. Obviously, when they talk to their family in Korea, they find out what's going on there.

I feel like there are differences between me and my Caucasian friends. I don't feel most of my Caucasian friends can relate to what it is like for me to be Korean and I don't think they understand that my parents really stress education. I know that there are some Caucasians whose parents do stress education, and their values and interests are similar to mine and so I don't think it's just Koreans. I think my values are the way they are because of what my parents have been telling me. But if they were Caucasian and they had been telling me the same thing, I don't think I'd be any different. My parents don't think that a friendship network is important for me. It's definitely not as important as school. I don't think it's because family is more important. I'm not sure if it's so much about being with family, because my brother is off at school and my dad's always on call. My parents have friends from work but their closest friends are Korean. I'm not sure if the differences are just personality or if it's about being Korean. I don't usually make spontaneous decisions, like some of my friends do.

Part of me really wants to be what my parents expect me to be. I see how hard my parents have worked and everything they have now is because of their hard work. But at the same time when I'm not at home I'm surrounded by people who have very different values and it makes it hard to keep my focus on what I should be doing. What I really want to do sometimes is just kick back and not listen to my parents. I don't do that because I'm scared. I'm scared that when it really comes down to where I go to college or what I become, I'm not going to, firstly, live up to what my parents expect me to be and, secondly, I'm not going to be happy, I'm not going to have what I want. I think even though people say money can't buy happiness, it's hard to live without it. It's not something you have to have, but I don't think you can live happily if you don't have it.

I think a lot of people, when seeing an Asian, automatically think that he/she is intelligent. And that's not true. It's not even a genetic thing. Also at school I think a lot of times guys will be more comfortable approaching somebody who fits the cheerleader stereotype. I think guys see me a bit differently than they see my Caucasian friends. I think they see me as harder to approach. I don't know, maybe I'm just being self-conscious.

In America there are a lot of kids who live for the moment and they really don't know where life is going. They don't know what they want and they don't know how to get what they want. I guess I don't understand them. And then there are whiz kids who are really into drugs or kids who drop out of school. They need to think.

I've seen discrimination with my parents. We walked into a Denny's once after my parents and I and another Korean family had gone on a float trip. We were driving back and were exhausted, and we had all been sleeping in the car. So we got out of the car, walked in, and there was a guy at the bar and he said, "Welcome to America!" I was like, "What are you thinking?" I didn't say anything to him but it made me mad.

When I was in kindergarten or first grade there was some discrimination because I was Korean. Kids don't know about that. I don't have a particular instance that I can speak of but I know people, still today, think that I'm Chinese and they're like "that Chinese girl." Last Saturday we had the girls' district tennis meet. My friend Emily, who's Caucasian, and I were playing doubles together and it was a changeover. Emily heard the two girls on the other team talking. One of them said, "Which one's better?" The other one said, "The Chinese one." I wish that people would take the time to ask or recognize that there are other Asians besides Chinese. But I can understand because I don't know the difference between an Argentinean and a Dominican. I can't really differentiate. I don't think that my teachers have treated me differently because I'm Korean.

I think that the movies, TV, and media are what create that stereotype of Asians. You don't see a lot of Asians in movies, but you'll rarely see an Asian that goes against that stereotype. It doesn't bother me that there aren't more Asians in movies. I saw the movie *The Joy Luck Club* and I thought it was pretty accurate. I cried a lot during that movie. I could relate to Waverly, whose mom was getting her hair done in a scene. They were in an argument and Waverly didn't feel like her mom ever respected her and her decisions, and her mom was always judging her. I feel like that a lot. I think that sometimes my mom's expectations of me get in the way of her seeing me as her daughter. Sometimes I wonder what would happen if I didn't do well in school and I didn't do what she wanted me to do. I wonder if she'd ever say, "That's okay because you're my daughter."

I wish there were more Korean people my age around here because they'd probably be going through the same thing as I am. Each summer I go to a program that's like a boarding school. There's usually a lot of Asians there. I feel like I can relate to them a lot better than I can to my friends here because they understand what I'm going through and I can understand what they're going through.

I plan on getting married. I think my parents, if they could have what they wanted, would have me marry a Korean. If I didn't marry a Korean, they'd want me to marry a Caucasian. I don't know what they would do if I didn't marry a Caucasian or a Korean. Even though they try to be very open-minded about things, they still have a hard time with it. Even when it comes to dating it makes them really uncomfortable. If I tell them that I'm interested in an African American, they would be scared, not because they view African Americans as a different kind of people. But they wouldn't want me to marry an African American for fear that I would be treated differently in society and that it would be hard on me and my kids. They want me to marry a Korean because they think it would be the easiest or maybe the most convenient. I think they'd probably be fine with other Asian groups, too.

My parents don't do the grounding thing; they're really subtle about things and that's almost worse than being grounded, because to be yelled at or to know that my parents have lost trust in me is awful. Being subtle is more effective for me.

My parents aren't the kind of people to be overly interested in how

I'm doing and how I'm feeling. I think they're more interested in what I'm doing rather than how I'm doing, as opposed to when I see my Caucasian friends and their families, it's more like, "How was your day today?" With my parents it's like, "How'd you do on that test?" I really don't like it. I've told my mom that it bothers me. I told her that it seems like our whole relationship is based on academic-related subjects that every conversation we have seems to be her asking about college and doing well in school, or the SAT. She never asks me how tennis is going or how my flute solo is going. It's always about grades or school. It makes me feel like that's all that matters in our relationship and that we don't have a strong relationship. And that bothers me. She knows it bothers me, but she's focusing on what she thinks is most important.

There's also a language barrier. A couple weeks ago I got in an argument with my mom and I was telling her that I feel like she's only concerned with my grades and performance. I asked her why she never asks me how I am doing, why everything she said to me was about school and why she couldn't ever talk to me about anything else. I was crying. She told me that part of it was that she couldn't communicate with me very well, because of the whole English issue. At that point that I felt weird because I didn't really see her as a person. Before I always assumed that she could understand me because I was her daughter, and I knew English so she should know English. I hope that once my parents feel like they're through pushing me to do things then we'll really have a chance to get to know each other without a purpose.

There's not a strong emphasis on chores or responsibilities. We have somebody come and clean our house, but my dad expects me not to make a mess. I think that's just his personality. But basically they won't ask me to do anything as long as I'm doing schoolwork. With cooking, it's pretty much if I'm hungry and nobody's cooking then I'll make my own dinner. If I need something washed, I'll do it myself.

I think that women's roles and men's roles in Korea are the same as here. My mom was definitely a bigger part of raising the children than my dad was. I don't think she encouraged me to be more Korean than American. But now she tells me that I'm different than my other friends and I shouldn't expect to try to be like them, because I'm not. I don't know if my parents have an accurate perception of what it is to be an American kid because they never grew up with them and they never were one. Basically, my mom wants me to be more prepared for the future.

On a typical day at school I have to go to marching band practice really early, six-thirty in the morning, and then I go to school. I have tennis in the afternoons, either meets or practice, and so I get home at six, or later if we have a meet. I eat dinner and then sometimes I'll go to the library and study. But sometimes I'll stay home and get all my homework done and I try to get to sleep as early as I can but it's usually not that early. I do not watch TV a lot. I listen to the radio whenever I'm in my room.

I don't work. I don't think my parents would let me because I don't have enough time. Basically they provide everything I need. They pay for everything and they got me a car and they don't say anything about spending money for that kind of thing as long as I'm holding up my end of the bargain.

My parents like the fact that I play the flute and tennis because it looks good on paper. They don't understand that I play tennis because I like it, because it's fun, and because I'm really close with the girls on the tennis team. They don't understand that I play the flute because of how it feels to make music. My mom will ask me how I'm doing in tennis to know that I'm playing varsity because she wants to get that on my transcript. My mom only pays for my flute lessons because she wants me to make all-state band and because she wants me to get one ratings at festivals. That's all it is to her, but I can't complain because as long as I get what I want out of it, I'm not going to argue just because her motives are wrong.

I don't have a religion. My mom is a Christian and she tried to influence me when I was little. I used to go to Sunday school and church services, but I accepted that there was a God because my mom went to church and I had to. But once I really thought about it, I'm not sure enough about the whole Christianity thing to be considered a believer. I'm not sure about my dad's parents' religion but my mom's mom is Buddhist. I think my grandmother wishes my mom was a Buddhist, but I don't know if she knows that I'm not of any religion.

I'm thinking about medicine as a career. It probably has a lot to do with my parents' influence and the fact that they're always going on about how there's always a need for doctors. I see how well they're living and I think it would be hard for me to lower my living standards after I've spent all my life living as comfortably as my parents do. I'm keeping my options open, though. I want to go to an Ivy League school, wherever I can get in. I hear about how great Stanford is from my brother.

When I have my own children I want to impart them with Korean culture. I can understand why my parents want me to be disciplined, I would want them to be disciplined. I would want my children to value their education. I don't want them to try hard in school for me. I would want them to do it for themselves and to understand why they're doing it. I think they'd be happier and more focused if it was their choice. I'd also continue having Korean food. I want them to have an interest in the Korean language, but if they don't, it's totally their choice. Nothing's going to be forced on them. I'd want their punishments to be more vocal. I'd want there to be more communication. I think they'd be more comfortable with that.

I don't want to stay in the Midwest. I would like to live someplace where I could learn a little bit about my culture. I think it'd be really good for me to go on a trip to Korea and learn more of the language and the culture. I bet if I went, at first I would feel out of place because I don't speak the language.

Part 5
Asian Indians
and Pakistanis

South Asian American women with Indian and Pakistani heritage had diverse experiences. The Indian Muslim women from upper-middle classes and the northern Indian region had a strong desire to preserve and uphold Muslim and traditional Indian values. Anjum Ahmed was a housewife from a well-off Muslim family from northern India, an area that holds conservative Muslim communities. Her efforts to preserve Muslim and Indian traditions not only reflected her individual socioeconomic background, but also represented the collective aspiration of many South Asian women to create and preserve South Asian cultures on American land. South Asian American women make deliberate and conscious efforts to create an ethnic cultural environment within American society. Would their efforts be eventually futile as the later generations would be more Americanized as predicted? The first-generation South Asian women saw a considerable percentage of the younger generation enthusiastically practicing Indian traditions.

Surya Gupta was a university professor specializing in nutrition. Raised in an Indian family that values education, she and most of her siblings received graduate education in India. She displayed a strong tendency of independence in her views of education, careers, marriage, and leisure. At the same time, she missed the traditional values in Indian culture and wished to raise her children with both American and Indian heritage.

Rekha Desai was a Hindu woman practicing medicine. She was born into a professional family, with her parents who expected her and her sisters to be professionals as well. In pursuing a medical career, she made the tough choice of living in a separate city from her husband, also a medical doctor, juggling work and child-rearing single-handedly. Like her Muslim counterparts, she also viewed it as important to preserve Indian traditions and encourage her children to be assimilated while remembering their Indian heritage.

South Asian women working in other fields seemed to have experienced subtle discrimination. Seeta Patel was managing a motel in a midwestern town. She entered into the business because she enjoyed meeting different people. At work, however, she encountered slight discrimination from some potential customers who walked away after knowing the motel owner's race. Seema Khotlay worked on assembly lines in a factory producing automobile parts. Although a fast and efficient worker, she was rejected when she applied for a new position at the factory.

The young women of Indian heritage are at the cultural crossroads. Munni Jameel and Mini Menon, born in Massachusetts and India, respectively, and attending American universities for undergraduate or graduate studies, both shared the dual identities as American and Indian. They were pressured to measure up to the standards set by their parents and perceived by the general public in their academic life, while hoping to incorporate both American and Indian values in their personal life.

The elaborate traditional weddings in India described in Anjum Ahmed and Seeta Patel's interviews and the wedding for American-born Indians in the United States as depicted in Mini Menon's interview offer interesting insights on how South Indian Americans have preserved their heritage in a different environment.

Interviewees in this section are Indians and Pakistanis rather than Bangladeshi, Sri Lankan, Nepalese, and Bhutanese women, who make up a significantly smaller percentage of the South Indian American population. Some of the Indian and Pakistani women came to the Unites States decades ago and thus the cities in India today might quite differ from the milieu they recall, given the rapid socioeconomic changes that have occurred in Indian urban centers in the past decades.[1]

[1]I thank Rajini Srikanth for her insightful comments on this section.

16

At Home and Preserving Traditions

Anjum Ahmed was born into a well-off Muslim family in Patna, Bihar, India, in 1961. She immigrated to the United States in 1980 after her arranged marriage to an Indian graduate student who was studying at Cornell University; he later became a chemist. She was a housewife and mother of three children living in suburban St. Louis, Missouri, at the time of the interview in 1998.

I was born in Patna, Bihar, India, on 2 July 1961. I have three sisters and three brothers. I am the middle one. My mother was a housewife and my father was an engineer. They both died in an airplane crash several years ago.

My childhood was a nice one. We lived in a joint family, with both sets of grandparents, aunts and uncles, and five cousins in the same house. It was a very big house, about twenty rooms. We had ten to twelve servants. They had special servant quarters. That type of lifestyle was very common in India for people who were well-off. My family was considered upper-middle class. Now having servants is also common, but not very much. Before, the servants usually came from villages; the children of servants who stayed with my great grandparents would automatically come to the family as servants. But now more and more people are sending their children to study in the towns. Not that many servants are available now. Education is getting to be the norm. Servants are also getting more expensive. When I go back, I see things are more expensive. To send children to good schools requires much more money now. People have to earn more to maintain their standard of living. Sometimes people's pay can't catch up with inflation. Although the living standard is somewhat raised, overpopulation, overcrowding, and pollution are all problems. When I was growing up, life seemed simpler. There were few wants. But now everybody is running after money. People are not happy. They just want to make more and more money to support their families.

My father had a post-graduate degree in engineering. He did his master's in England in the 1950s. It was very expensive to study in England. My mother had a master's in English. She wanted to become a doctor. But at that time, her parents didn't want her to do it. They said, "No, you are a girl, we don't want you to be with boys for too much time, and have too much going out of the house." It was a different culture. But now things are changing. Women are getting more education and they are working outside of the home.

My parents got married in 1953. After the marriage, my mother stayed at home. My brothers and sisters all have good educations, except me, because I got married at very early age and I didn't finish my college education. All my sisters have done their master's, and all of them have become housewives. They didn't pursue a career. It was common for a girl to get higher education and find a husband and then stay at home. Education was not necessarily preparation for a profession. Women got an education and then stayed at home. She has to decide whether she wants to or not. We come from a small city. But when you go to a big city, like Delhi or Bombay, most women work because life is more expensive. For example, an apartment costs much more there. Just like in the United States, both husband and wife have to work to support the family. It's much like here, getting an education for girls is not for a profession, but to make them more desirable for marriage.

My major was psychology when I was in college. I really liked children so I wanted to study child psychology and find out why children behave a certain way. I want to finish my degree someday, but I haven't decided. When I got married, I took a course at Cornell University. Then I had my first son, and I stopped taking class and stayed home. Then my kids grew up and went to school. I thought it was more important to stay home rather than sending them to a babysitter.

There is a public education system in India, from elementary school to university. It is free but it is not very good. There are private schools, mostly run by Christian missionaries. About 90 percent of people in middle class send their children to private schools. I went to private schools all through school. They used to have nuns coming from foreign countries. I was taught by nuns from Ireland. Missionary schools were very common and they used English as the medium of instruction. But now most of the missionaries have gone back. But they still have English taught by the local nuns. Like here in the United States, in parochial schools they don't force students to practice religion. I went to a girl's missionary school until the seventh grade. It was in Patna, and was quite an elite school. When I was in seventh grade, I went to boarding school in Darjeeling. Then I went to a Patna Women's College. It was a very famous Christian college. In college, I lived at home, because the college was about five minutes from my home. But my brothers and sisters lived in dormitories at their universities. Two of my brothers went to Delhi for college; my sisters went to Darjeeling. They had to stay in the dorms since it was far away. They all went to good universities.

I didn't date when I was in college. Dating was not common, but now it is becoming more so. When we were growing up, if we went on a date it was a bad stigma on the family. You had to uphold that and wait until your parents proposed a marriage for you. You had that much trust in your parents. You let them choose your life partner. You know that they will do what is best for you and you trust them. You are not supposed to date.

My husband was the first man who proposed to me. My mother and my husband's mother were classmates. They grew up together in the same town and they were together in school. When my husband's mother got married she moved away to another part of the country, in Calcutta. My mother stayed in Patna with her family. My husband's grandmother was also from Patna. She was the matchmaker. Matchmakers are not necessarily professionals; it can be anyone, a friend or member of the family. Basically, people say this is a good family. Not only the girl and boy, but also the families first have to get along. Otherwise there would be too much tension. They have to see the same standards, see if the families get along well, if they are nice families, how are the parents, how are the siblings, and whether there was a divorce in the family. All the family history is taken into consideration before the marriage. We do a family background check first. When my family and his family were arranging our marriage, I was aware of what was going on.

It took half a year from the engagement to the wedding. First my husband's grandmother called up my parents and told them that they were coming to see the girl and then the boy was also coming to see the girl. Then they were going to decide. So we knew when they were coming. They decided when the two sets of parents met. Before I got engaged, I saw my future husband both in a picture and in person. I first saw him when he came to India from the United States where he was working on his master's degree. The decision was between both sets of parents. They would let the boy see the girl and then they decide. But actually, we had so much pressure from our parents, we knew what they wanted. There was no point for the boy seeing the girl or for the girl seeing the boy. We knew what we had to do. We had to agree. We knew what they liked, and what they didn't. We spoke for an hour. Then our parents asked us separately. Do you like him? I said okay. We all said okay. Then the next day, we were engaged. There was an engagement party. We had a big feast; gifts were given to the boy and me. The boy would receive gifts from my side and I would receive gifts from his side. I received cloth and engagement rings and lots of sweets. After that they decided on the wedding date and wedding arrangements. They started planning when the wedding was going to take place. In my case, my husband came back from America, since he was a student then. After six months, he came back to get married. When he first came back to see me, it was winter. The wedding was in the summer of 1980. When we got married, I was nineteen and my husband was twenty-four. Then weddings mostly took place in the bride's house, but now it is mostly done in hotels because there are too many problems having a wedding at home. You have to arrange for the cooking. We had invited 1400 people to our wedding. You have to decide who could take care of what, and there were so many things to take care of.

The wedding ceremony, called the *henna* ceremony, went on for three or four days. During these days, you had to feed all of these people. It was very costly. I didn't really know the value of money because I wasn't spending it and my parents were. Your parents gave you a wedding; you really didn't have to worry. The average cost for a middle class wedding was probably two to three hundred thousand rupees at that time. If you convert that to U.S. dollars, it would be about twenty to thirty thousand dollars. You had to feed so many people and you have to give gifts for everybody. And you give jewelry to your daughter, lots and lots of pure gold jewelry. It's an incredible loss for the parents of the bride. That's why in India whenever a daughter is born, parents start saving. If you were not rich enough and couldn't afford a wedding for your daughter, the daughter would remain unmarried or be abused by her in-laws. That's what happened in India to Hindus for a long time. Now it's not like that. Because now education is coming, girls choose their own husbands. Boys and girls meet. It's

An Indian bride at her wedding prior to coming to America to join her student husband, Patna, Bihar, India, 1981. Huping Ling Collection (Courtesy of the bride).

An Indian American woman going to a cultural function as a performer, St. Louis, Missouri, 1993 (Courtesy of Ann Rynearson).

much more like here. Things are changing. Weddings are not so elaborate and costly any more, because no one has the money and time. It was the joint family so everybody would help. Now everything is breaking. It's the nuclear family. People are going to bigger cities to work for better jobs, or going abroad for more opportunities.

After my wedding, I came to the United States with my husband. I went to Cornell University, in Ithaca, New York. I liked it there, it was very nice. But I was also very lonely. Coming from a big family, I missed them. It was hard to adjust. My husband would go to school and I would be alone at home. My husband was completing his master's. I was also enrolled in a psychology class. I didn't have any language problems and I didn't really have culture shock.

There were many Indians there. We were friends with them. We lived in student housing. I cooked Indian food most of the time. I actually learned cooking here. I didn't know how to cook because in India we had servants. I didn't even know which spices for what dish. Cooking was a big shock to me. Life was hard. I also had to learn cleaning. It took a lot of time to learn. Sometimes I would get angry. But my husband did most of the cooking, because he was already here and he knew how to cook. He learned cooking when he came to the United States because he had to. He taught me how to cook and then I took over the cooking. Then my mother-in-law came from India and she stayed with us. I picked up more cooking from her. I wish we had a servant who would cook for me or do the cleaning for me. But labor is so expensive here.

During my seventeen years in the United States, I have returned to India five times. I went back to see my parents and stay there sometimes for two or three months. It was always very hard to leave India.

One year after our wedding, I had my first son. After I had my first son, I stayed at home, taking care of the kids. It is difficult to raise children here. You have to stand a lot more from kids. You want them to have your culture and learn things the way you were brought up. But things are different here. You don't have an environment here. If my parents didn't teach me something, I would pick it up from my cousins. It's good to be with grandparents. You see how they behave and you can learn from them. But here you have to constantly teach your children good manners, how to behave with elders, about art and religion and what our religion wants from us. Because it is different raising them in this country and they see different things, I have to keep teaching them, so when the time comes they know what is right.

I prefer to raise my children the Indian way. Some of the things are good here, but I don't want them to date when they grow up, or to smoke or drink. There are many things I don't want my kids to do. So I keep telling them. I teach them my religion because I want them to be good Muslims. I am not afraid that they will have trouble fitting in or that they would appear different from their American peers since they preserve Indian traditions. There are so many Muslims here. In high school and middle school they have a lot of friends. They have friends who go to school with them in the same grade. Most of my children's friends are Indians. My children don't want to become 100 percent American because I try to keep them in their own culture, and mix Americanism with their own. They know that others are like them and they are not singled out. When they see other friends doing that they feel they can do it. Not like they are the only ones. They should not feel like that. Maybe they were the only ones in their classes if we were living in a remote area where there are no other Indian families. Then I would feel bad. But we have all the Indian facilities, including a mosque, here.

My son didn't express that he wanted to be like other American children. But my daughter sometimes asks why she can't go for a sleepover in an American house. But I tell her, no, you know you can't. She is much more social than my son. He understands, he doesn't like sleepovers. You never get any sleep at sleepovers, kids are going here and there. I don't want them to do that. I have no problem with my son. My daughter has so many friends. I kept telling her that her friends can come to our house, she can invite them, but I don't want her spending the night in their houses. I want to see what's going on, and I want to see how her friends are. I have that problem with my daughter, because she is overly social. I have stopped her when she was going to wear different kinds of clothing. She is small now, nine years old. I keep telling her she has to dress properly. She can't wear revealing clothing. I tell them these small things.

I wear Indian dress all the time. When I go out with my Indian dress, I don't feel uncomfortable. Sometimes people stare at me but sometimes they don't. Sometimes they say they like my dress. Sometimes they comment on how pretty my dress is. I have never had anyone who said anything negative. Maybe they are looking at me, but here we have seen so many Indians who wear saris. I don't think it is strange. Maybe I have always stayed in places where there are a lot of Indians like us. I was in Los Angeles where there is a large Indian population. I was at Cornell, and there were also a lot of Indians there. I never felt the need to look like an American. My husband has never told me that I should wear a shirt and pants, like many husbands tell their wives. I have heard from friends that some husbands say they should dress up because they get embarrassed. But my husband never told me that. It was okay with me. In fact, once he said that he liked the way I dressed. I never had a problem with the way I dress.

We talked a lot about family affairs. Running a family is not an easy job. We discuss everything. Maybe I am the boss in the family, but I ask his opinion about the children, about the family. We discuss things together. If we purchase a major thing, we both make the decision. If we want to get a dining table, we both have to decide and we both have to like it. He gives me the checkbook. I manage the family finances. I don't have to ask him for money, he asks me for money. Maybe it is typical among Indian families in the United States that families operate this way. In India it was different; the husband would give money to his wife. But here the wives are doing most of the household work, like buying groceries, running errands, and most of the things to run a household. The husbands don't do all of that; the husband basically just takes care of his job. I think that actually it is the wife who is managing the house.

Most Indian husbands in the United States are very controlling, but not my husband. He agrees with whatever I say. Somehow I am lucky. Some husbands want to restrict their wives and dictate the way they dress. But it also depends on which type of family you have come from. Some husbands want their wives to be ultramodern, dressing in the typical American way because they feel shy about Indian dress. And the wives are not ready for that when they come straight from India. But they have to dress up just to please their husbands. Sometimes, the Muslim husbands force their wives to wear the scarf on their heads. I am not talking about all the husbands. There are all kinds of Indian people. Most of my friends are liberal. Their husbands don't force them; it's up to them.

There were not many divorces in India. Maybe there are divorces nowadays. When I was growing up, there was no such thing as divorce. Even if the wife was unhappy in the marriage, she would still stay with her husband. If she divorced her husband, it would be a stigma on the family, and her sister and brother wouldn't get married because she was a bad girl, so her family was bad. That's why during a marriage arrangement, they check the family history. It would be written of, and no one from her family would get married. But things are changing because women are getting more education, divorce is more common.

If there are extramarital affairs among Indian families in the United States, it is not good. We don't like that. People get divorced. Divorce is more common. Some of my friends' marriages didn't work out. But there are not many single mothers among Indians in the United States, maybe 5 to 10 percent.

Coming to America, many Indians have become more religious. I feel I have become more religious. Since the environment is not like that in India, I have to try hard to create that environment here. When we were growing up it was different. You were into religion because you see everyone doing the same things. But here you have to make sure that especially your children see you because they don't see it outside. If you don't do it, you won't have such an environment. That's why I became more religious. I have to consciously and voluntarily be religious. I take the children to the mosque, I take them to Sunday school where they have to learn traditions. In India, it was all part of growing up. You have to read the Quran. But here, since the wife does most of the cooking and cleaning, sometimes you don't have time to talk to your children about religion. I teach them the Quran. You have to make it very special for them, and find time for that.

Why do I want to preserve the religion since it is so hard? I want my children to have something to lean back on. Religion is a very strong point for me. When they grow up, they have a way to return. The religion is always there. They have God to turn to. That's the way I have been brought up. If you are under stress or if you need something, you pray to God. It gives you a great feeling. The spiritual dependence is important for my mind. I understand that people might think even though I have tried very hard, after several generations the religion will slowly fade. It is not true. Now I see these young Muslim girls wearing head scarves, which I don't. They are much more into religion. If you are going to the mosque, you see the younger generation is much more into religion. They do things for Muslims. It's amazing. I would like my children also to grow up like that. They have a strong sense of religion in their life. I am happy to see the new generation. Not all are like that; but about 50, 60 percent are very good Muslims. Will they have difficulty coping with mainstream society when they are so immersed in Muslim culture? This generation I have seen is growing up and getting married. They are doing very well. Hopefully, people are becoming more aware of Muslims. For our generation, if we tried to go to work wearing a scarf, it would be difficult. But now people seem to know much more about Muslims and their values. If I give my children a strong background, I don't think the religion will slowly disappear. If they have a strong background, they will pass it on to their children.

When my children grow up and date or get married, I have told them it has to be a Muslim. I have my preference. I don't know if they will rebel, not listening to me, but I have kept telling them, you have to marry a Muslim. If you like somebody, you tell me, but no dating, no kissing, or anything. My older son, who is sixteen, is not dating now. I know his whereabouts. He goes to school and comes back. I check on him. If he likes somebody, he should tell me, and maybe I can arrange a meeting, or maybe I can talk to the girl's parents. I told him it has to be a Muslim. I keep emphasizing, even to my youngest son, who is six years old, that no dating, or no kissing before marriage. They might rebel, I don't know. But I keep telling them and I hope it stays somewhere in their brain. I tell them that God does not like this decision, that it is our religion. I keep bringing up religion. I can just hope for the best. Most time I spend with my children, I would like to preserve Muslim culture.

I haven't given any thought about having a career. I haven't really decided if I want to have a job outside of the house or not. I don't know what I want to do. Now that my kids are growing up and they are all in school, I have to think what I want to do. But I haven't thought hard about it. When I was young, I never thought to become a professional woman. I just want to work if I want to. But it should not be that the household depends on my income. I don't want something like that. I don't want that pressure. If I want to work I will. My husband said, it's okay, I don't care if you work or not. He wants me to stay home and first take care of the kids and their needs. I didn't want the kids to go to babysitters. When they come back from school they want me to be there to take care of them. I like that. Although there are more and more Indian women who are working outside of the home, I don't feel pressure from them.

There are differences between Muslim women and Hindu women. Most Muslim women stay at home. Most working Indian women are Hindus. I have friends who are Indian Hindus, they are working. But most of my Muslim friends are staying at home. I have a Muslim friend who was teaching preschool. Her case was rare, because her husband was in Texas and her kids were all in school. She started working at a daycare because she was getting bored at home. But before that she would not want to work. Since her husband was not in town, he would come back once a month. Since she worked in a daycare, not in an office like a nine-to-five professional job, she had flexible hours there. She would be back by five or five-fifteen. I also wouldn't mind working like that when my kids are at school. I don't want to have a job that has a lot of pressure or is very demanding. I want to be home when my kids are home.

I prefer living in the United States to India. Life is better here and you have much more facilities. Since my marriage, I have lived here. In India, unless you have a servant, it is difficult to manage. Here I am able to manage it. Whatever I need, I can go and get it. I don't have to be dependent on others. But in India, you are dependent. You can't go out, you can't drive a car, you have to wait for the driver to take you, you have to depend on the servants to do this or do that. I like the freedom I have here in the United States. I enjoy the freedom that I don't have to be dependent for everything. In the beginning it was hard to learn how to drive. But now it's okay. I am an okay driver.

I have a brother in the United States who is looking for a residency. I have a sister in Washington. I have many cousins here; they are living in every part of the states. I have lots of relatives in America. I don't really feel lonely. I have a cousin, a third cousin as our grandparents are siblings, living in St. Louis.

I have lived in Los Angeles, Cornell, and St. Louis. In Los Angeles, life was too fast and there was too much crime. I didn't like it that much. It was good that there were a lot of Indians there, and the weather is good. But I was scared of earthquakes. You never know when you can have one and where your kids will be. That was one of the reasons we moved to St. Louis. In upstate New York, in Cornell, there was too much snow, and there was not a big Indian community. It was a moving population. You made friends with someone, and they finished their work and would move on. It was difficult. But most Indians in St. Louis are settled. The weather, compared to New York, is very nice. It is not too big, not too small. I have never thought of anything about St. Louis that I didn't like. I like where we live. There are lots of Indians; my kids have friends whenever they want and they don't have to go out of the neighborhood for friends. I like it and the kids are happy.

The Indian community here is very large. In the mosque, there are about five thousand people that come to worship. That's just Muslims. If you add Hindus, maybe there are more. I have never been to the Mahatma

Gandhi Center [a Hindu temple], so I don't know. There are many more Hindus.

I am not very involved in the Indian community. In the beginning I went to the mosque every weekend. Now I have stopped doing it because my son is very busy with band. They have activities every Sunday. I am home trying to help him with his work. Sunday I usually try to take my kids to the mosque unless something keeps me busy or my son has activities.

I am not really involved with any American community, except sometimes I go to school and help. Last year I would go to my son's class or my daughter's class to help out. Apart from that, I am not really involved because I am busy with the children and I like to be with them and do things for them.

My husband's company has some social functions like picnics and a Christmas party. I go to these functions, dressing in Indian dress. I always dress in Indian way. In winter, I sometimes wear pants, but there has to be a long Indian dress with it. I don't wear very short shirts. At these gatherings, there are all Americans. They always tell me that I have a nice dress, pretty dress. I really don't feel out of place. I have always stayed in universities so the people I am meeting are a different set of people. They are professors and they are more cosmopolitan. I never felt uncomfortable being around them because in India we are exposed to all the religions—Hinduism, Christianity, Buddhism. In India, there are so many different people. In fact most of my friends in India are Hindus. I don't mind other religions, but I want my children to be good Muslims. And to be good Muslims, we have to be tolerant towards other religions. Our religion doesn't teach intolerance or to be bad to people. It's contrary to my religion to be a bad person.

17

Foreign-born Women
in Professional Fields

Rajni Raman was born in southern India in 1950 and immigrated to America in 1979 with her two children to join her husband, who was already in the country. She worked for the Medical Arts Building in St. Louis, Missouri, as an insurance coordinator for managed care at the time of the interview in 1998.

I was born on 10 October 1950 in Vellore, Tamil Nadu, in the southern part of India, but I was pretty much raised in Bangalore, which is now called the Silicon Valley of India. My father was a businessman who owned a coffee shop. I have four older brothers: one is a police officer in Bangalore, one is a security officer, one is an accountant, and one is an office manager for an insurance company. They are all married and have kids, and they all live in India right now.

I was the youngest in the family, so I always had to look up to my brothers. They always pampered me and they would say okay, give her this, give her that, so I was never forced to do anything. I was not expected to do what my brothers did because we are all different. My parents left it open, whatever we wanted to do was fine. I was given a choice and not forced to do what my brothers did. My brothers were also the same way. They did not have to follow in the oldest brother's steps. They did what they wanted to do and my parents were okay with that. They treated me individually, and I enjoyed my childhood.

I went to a Catholic school during my high school years. It was a private school where I had to wear a uniform and two braids. That is how they disciplined the students. We had to wear a uniform—a skirt, blouse, and shoes. It was an all-girls' Catholic high school run by nuns and mothers and was a restricted private school. It was all taught in an English medium. The school was three miles from my house. I had to walk there because there was no bus or anything and the only transportation was to walk.

After graduating from high school, I went to an all-women's college, which was a little more lenient than my high school. It was a state college. I took two buses to get there. I did not stay in the dorm because it was in my hometown. Seldom did you see people staying in the dorms. If someone was from out town or in the military, like my father, they would live in the dorms. Dorms are not a big thing in India because every city has a university or a college in it and people just commute from home.

I graduated with a bachelor's degree when I was twenty years old and then I stayed at home for two years to learn household chores. Basically, a girl must know how to sew and cook. These things are expected from a girl when she gets married since women take care of the family. I used to enjoy cooking, but not anymore. Now I enjoy sewing, so I do it.

I got married in 1972 when I was twenty-two years old. It was an arranged marriage. My husband is from Gujarat in the western part of India. His sister is married to someone in my hometown and his whole family came for the wedding. After my marriage, I moved to his hometown in Baroda, Gujarat, and lived there for seven years. It was a joint family consisting of my in-laws, one unmarried brother-in-law, and one unmarried sister-in-law. There were differences among the family members, but that was just part of life. You cannot just get mad and leave. That is what family is about in India and family values are important. The mother-in-law and sister-in-law always dominate a family, but my in-laws were exceptions. They were nice people, so I was thankful for that.

I gave birth to both of my kids, a daughter and a son, in India. While I was in India, my husband's brother, who was already in America and had a green card, sponsored my husband to come to this country. My husband came and found a job and then he sponsored us. My daughter was five years old and my son was a year and a half when we came to this country in 1979.

We were in Muncie, Indiana, for one year because my husband had a job there. Then he found a job in St. Louis, Missouri. We have lived in St. Louis for sixteen years. My husband is a mechanical engineer at Flat River Glass in Park Hills. He has a master's degree in engineering from Baroda, India.

I have a bachelor's degree in economics from India. After I came to America, I took several courses and then worked in several places. When I came St. Louis in 1982, the first job I had was to deliver newspapers. After six months, I got a clerical job for the same newspaper company. I worked there for two years, then had to go to India because of a family illness, so I quit. When I came back, I did not go to work. I was involved with the children's school activities—being a room mother and a member of PTA. Then I decided that I needed to do something else, I needed money. So I went back to the same clerical job at the newspaper for a year. At the same time, I started going to school, taking computer and accounting classes, because I wanted to expand my career opportunities. Then I worked as a stocks and bonds broker for year and a half. In 1985, there was a stock market crash and I was laid off. Then all the accounting and computer classes I took came in handy. I got a job at a bank as a teller and worked there for almost seven years, and I started working towards my associate degree in banking. I have a couple more classes to take before I finish my associate degree. I thought the banking job was not going anywhere; it was a dead end. I wanted something that would let me move up. I did not like to stay in one job doing the same thing day in and day out and I did not see any opportunity at the bank to move anywhere.

In 1985, I became a U.S. citizen. I applied first because we had a green card when we came. I had applied for American citizenship even though there was no particular reason to because having a green card is as good as being an American citizen. I became a citizen first. Two years later, my husband and the kids also became citizens, so my family members are all citizens.

I have a job now at a medical arts clinic as an insurance coordinator for managed care. It is very challenging and I try to keep up with all of the insurance policies. There are many changes in the medical field and I have to attend several seminars and training sessions at work. I like the other employees. There is another woman in the managed care department, and there are the Medicare and Medicaid departments and insurance department, so there are seven or eight of us working there.

My oldest daughter went to school in the United States from kindergarten onward. She graduated from high school and now she is in a MD program in Kansas City, which is a six-year program. She is in her fifth year and she will graduate with her MD in two years. She wants to do either pediatrics or have a family practice. She got married in April of 1996 to a man in St. Louis. He is also of Indian origin. He came to this country to do his master's in engineering and he graduated from the University of North Carolina in Raleigh. He has a good job in St. Louis and he is taking night classes to get his MBA. My son also went to school from kindergarten to high school in St. Louis and now he is a pre-medical student at the University of Missouri–Columbia. He is a sophomore and lives in an all-male dorm. MU has such a big, beautiful campus.

Even though my children were brought up here, I always taught them the culture of India like the dancing and the music. Although I am not a great singer, I always played music for them, so at least they could hear how the Indian music sounds. At home, we speak the mother tongue, which is Tamil. I taught them to read and write the basic alphabets and the basic words and they have picked it up well. Even when we talk on the phone, we talk in Tamil. My daughter can read Tamil and my son attempts to speak it. I am proud of them. They always follow the Indian culture, food, and they participate in Indian programs. For six years my daughter has learned an Indian classical dance, which is called Bharatanatyam, from Mrs. Usha Singh in St. Louis. When she graduated from her dance school in 1992, she had her dance debut there. She is very much into Indian culture. She always talks in our mother tongue.

At the same time, my children are Americanized. Sometimes they like to get up late and do not like to go to bed until 2 AM, which is not the Indian way because we go to bed at 10 PM and get up at five or six. I do not know how much they are Americanized. I do not see anything wrong with being Americanized as long as they know where to draw a limit. They had a curfew when they were growing up. At the same time, I was liberal with their going out and having fun with their friends. I never restricted them to making friends of a certain race or color. I always taught them where to draw the line so they could stay out of trouble. I do not know how to distinguish between Indian and westernized, so they are both. Even though they have left home and gone on to college, I still see they are in touch with the family and me. I know that both of them are still participating in all the associations' functions like India Night, which they had in Columbia. When my son and his friends get together, he talks about Indian culture. My daughter is still participating in Indian dance even though she is in medical school. I know that even though they have left home, they have taken the culture with them and I am proud of them.

I do volunteer work for hospice care. I used to do a lot of volunteer work. I used to participate in many Indian community programs, coordinating the programs for different associations and temples. We have the Gandhi Center, the Hindu temple in St. Louis. I used to participate in fundraising or coordinating *puja* (prayer) and functions. We have several functions, so I used to coordinate the festivals for the temple, making phone calls. We used to go there as a family because they had a youth center. Now the children are gone and it is becoming too long of a drive for me with work. I just want to stay here and give an opportunity for someone else. But if they need me they always call and I go help them out.

There are many Indians in the St. Louis area. I met a friend in K-Mart the very first time I moved here; she had been here seven or eight years so she knew a lot of people. She had small kids so we used to get together every so often. The community grew bigger and bigger. There were activities that I wanted my kids to participate in and we went there. Then the Hindu temple, the Gandhi Center, came, so it just grew and grew. That is why so many people ended up at my daughter's wedding because I knew so many of them through so many different venues. That is how our friendship expanded. Now I do not go to temple as often as I did; I pass my time by helping others.

I like to read many books. We subscribe to an Indian newspaper, *India Abroad Indian News*. We get a couple of other Indian papers and I also subscribe to magazines from India.

I have visited India four times—in 1982, 1986, 1990, and 1993. In 1982 and 1986, I just went for a visit. In 1990, my mother-in-law died so we had to go for the funeral and in 1993, I went for my father's birthday. At one point, we thought we might want to move back to India but the kids were in school. Now the kids are in college and my daughter is married, so we say if we become grandparents then our ties are here. It is a questionable situation. We really do not know.

We came here with nothing, we did not have a job or money. We left everything in India and came to the United States. If we had gone back to India, there would be nothing there for us. We would have to start all over again. In India, everything is very expensive and there is too much inflation. It is very difficult to live there after living in this country. Here you have cars and easy access to groceries, schools, and so many things. In India, you have to struggle a little bit or you have a lot of money to live luxuriously.

Surya Gupta was born in Puri, Orissa, India, in 1963. She came to the United States as a graduate student and was a professor of nutrition at Truman State University at the time of the interview in 1996.

I was born on 1 July 1963 in Puri, Orissa, in India. My mom has a high school diploma and my dad has a bachelor's degree. He also has a law degree but he did not practice law, he was working for the federal government as an accountant. My mom was a housewife.

I have three sisters and two brothers. In fact, I have a twin brother. My parents have the same expectations for all of the children in our family. Most of them have post-graduate degrees. My elder sister has a post-graduate degree in physics. My brother has an engineering degree. My other sister is also a professor and she is working towards her doctorate in political science. My third sister is the only one in the family who doesn't have a post-graduate degree. She does have a bachelor's degree. Finally, the youngest children are my brother and I. He has his own business. He was working for his master's in commerce. He also has a law degree but he does not practice.

I went to an English medium school starting in kindergarten; the language of instruction was English. In India, math and science are exceptionally strong. I think that is lacking here. My bachelor's degree was in science with a focus in food and nutrition. I went to a university called the Orissa University of Agriculture and Technology. The educational system is very different in the two countries but each has its own advantage. In India, they have more of the traditional system where if you are getting a bachelor's degree, for example, you will study for three years and at the end of the third year, you take the comprehensive exam for all those semesters. So it's very difficult to score points. Some schools have the grading system, they give A, B, C, D grades, but some other schools have what they call the division. If you score 60 percent and above you get the first division; 50 to 60 percent is the second division; 40 to 50 percent is the third division and below 40 percent you fail. Getting a first division is as hard as getting an A.

After that, I went to another school in a different state, which is supposedly the best school in India. It was called the Banaras Hindu University. In fact, BHU is the biggest university in Asia. It has almost every department you can name. It had forty-eight dorms for men and about ten dorms for women—a huge university!

It was my dream to get my PhD. After I got my graduate degree in India, my professor wanted me to work with her for my PhD program, but

I said, "No way!" If I start there, I will probably end up finishing it. It was my dream to come to this country because I heard so much about the educational system. I think after I went through the traditional system in India I felt it was very easy to get A's here. I went to Old Dominion University in Norfolk, Virginia. ODU only has thirty to thirty-five thousand students and when I first went there I said, "This is it? It's so small." I got my PhD in health services, and my cognate was in healthcare management. For my PhD, I had an assistantship, and at Old Dominion, once you get an assistantship, the school pays your tuition.

I came to the United States with a student visa. The first couple of weeks, I could not understand everything because of the accents people had, but after a while I picked it up. I do not think there was a problem at all. The professors were very helpful. My friends were very helpful. I have spoken English since kindergarten. I am working on becoming a permanent resident.

Before I came to the United States, I was working for the state government in India, in the Department of Agriculture and Food as a training officer. Several counties together make a district, and I was in charge of a whole district. I was planning and conducting training programs in nutrition and other areas. That job was a mix of training programs and teaching. The last six months I went to a government project where I was teaching. I liked when people came and told me, "Oh, you did this well."

I am now a professor at Truman State University. Before I took this job, I was offered another research job in Tucson, Arizona, at the University of Arizona. My family members thought I was crazy to come here instead of going there, but that was a research-oriented job and I already have a strong research background. I wanted to build on my teaching skills. I think my job now gives me a good balance between teaching and research. In addition, mentoring students can be fun. On Mondays, Wednesdays, and Fridays I teach from 8:30 to 2:30, and after that I catch up and do other things. On Tuesdays and Thursdays basically I do other things. I have office hours and I prepare for my classes. I teach community health, nutrition, both higher and lower levels, and substance abuse prevention.

I have several research projects going on. I just finished writing a manuscript for the Nutrition Education Program. They have a program called NIP, Nutrition Intervention Project, in the state of Virginia. That is the subject of my dissertation. I evaluated that program and did a rural-urban comparison. I am sending that paper out to a journal soon.

I am a board member of the American Diabetes Association and I do a lot of work for them. Projects that I am involved with in general include the Christian Community Clinic, where our students go and teach. The clinic is for Medicare/Medicaid patients, those people who have no insurance. It is run strictly on a voluntary basis. Physicians, nurses, our students, they all volunteer their time. I help the students to prepare to teach nutrition there.

In my free time, I love to paint and sometimes I listen to music or do something that helps me relax. I listen to both Indian and American music. I like soft rock; I do not like jazz. I did one painting last summer and want to do some more. I was working with watercolor before and I have recently started with oil. I like oil painting and I love to do natural scenery.

When I first moved here, I was lonely because all of my friends and family are on the East Coast. I would call domestic and international, I did not care. My telephone bill was $800 the first month. Now, it is not as bad. My sister is in Virginia Beach, my aunt lives in Buffalo, New York, and I have cousins in New Jersey and Boston. Oftentimes I go and talk to or call my friends and colleagues. I go out with my friends and colleagues for dinner or lunch. Petite Three is a small theater that I have been to a few times. I will go out and watch movies or sometimes rent a movie and watch it.

I am not married and I have mixed feelings about arranged marriages where the parents look for a husband for their daughter. I think it's working well right now in India. It has both advantages and disadvantages. Sometimes the bride and groom have very different interests. However, the advantage is that one goes into the relationship without any expectations. They start with zero and work together. However, sometimes they cannot get along for whatever reason. Most of them, about 95 percent, work though, because people go in with the attitude that they have to make it work. Here, if you know someone you have a lot of expectations and if after marriage they are not met, you are very disappointed. In addition, when you are dating a guy before marriage he always tries to portray his best side so you never know the other side. Whereas in an arranged marriage, you see him as he is. You never see the good side or the bad side.

I do not think I could ever marry someone without knowing him first. I do not want to sleep with a man unless I have known him for a year so I know that we can get along well. American and Indian societies are two extremes. Arranged marriage in this country is not as common. No one raised in this country would settle for that. My aunt has been here for the last thirty years, and my eldest cousin recently got married to his class-mate. My younger cousin is the same; he will not marry someone who he does not know. So I doubt whether the second generation of Indians have any arranged marriages, but if they do—and I've known a few cases where the parents take their daughter or son back home—they do not have as much success. Many of those marriages have failed because the girl or the boy is not ready. When someone who was not raised in this country comes to America after twenty or thirty-five years, they have their own lifestyle set. It is very difficult to acclimatize and adapt to your spouse right away. That is probably one of the reasons it has not worked.

If I have children, I would like to teach them my language so that they will know their background and their heritage. I am from Orissa and my mother tongue is Oriya. In India, different states have different lan-guages. I can speak Hindi, Bengali, and Telgu. I think most people only know the one they grew up with and it is hard to understand everyone. If my children would go to India, they could understand and talk with other people and maintain our culture. I want to teach my children the language, the religion, to respect their elders, and values of that nature. I think taking them back home is the best method. If they would stay there for a month or a few weeks they would pick it up very fast. I plan to raise my children with both American and Indian methods; I believe a combination would be best. I see good and bad in both. I think that in India, they do not teach you to be independent as early as they do here because traditionally we stay with our parents and they take care of our education. After marriage or once we start working, we move out. But here, once you are eighteen you move out and are on your own so you have to be independent.

I cook all Indian food. Sometimes I do a mix of Indian and Ameri-can, depending on whom I invite. If I know that people like Indian food I will cook it. It is something different since they usually eat American food every day. I mostly cook Indian because it is very healthy. Macaroni and cheese tastes good but it is so high in fat! I became a vegetarian a couple of years ago, not strictly, but mostly. I will eat meat if I have no alternative. There are not many American recipes for vegetarian dishes. I get my spices whenever I go to Virginia Beach, Buffalo, or Chicago. However, Columbia, Missouri, has an Indian store now, which is great for me. I have been there a couple of times. It is not too bad. Sometimes, I get some stuff from Zim-merman's, which is approximately ten miles away.

*Devon Avenue, an Indian
American neighborhood
in Chicago, 2000. Huping
Ling Collection.*

I like the independence of living in America compared to India. Whatever you want, if you pay for it, it is yours. Good service is not common in India. This is a fast society, you go to the bank and things are done quickly. The same things in India take more time, which is frustrating once you are used to a better system. I think here, if you are educated and know what you are doing, it is easy to live alone. There is no one to point any fingers at you. Whereas back home, if you are not married at forty years of age, people would gossip.

The position of women in India is changing a lot. Feminism is catching up there. Thirty years back, my mom's generation, women were not educated as much. They were not working outside the home. Right now you find that almost all women who are college graduates prefer to work. Here, I think women are more advanced because they are taught to be more independent. I think if you are a woman you would be much better off in India because here you have to take care of everything. Back home there is a support system, which I think women here lack. If I needed anything my mom would be there. My sister, who is a professor, works. She does not leave her son with a babysitter; she takes him to my mom's place, which is very close. In America, you must support your whole family with no help. It's difficult. But if you have money you can buy everything here, so that's the difference. If you are hard-working and you're in a better paying position, then probably it's okay.

I wear American clothes. It does not make any difference to my parents or to my brothers or sisters. Some people may raise their eyebrows if I wear a skirt and blouse, but if I wear slacks and t-shirt or anything else it would be okay; pants are accepted. People wear jeans all the time. Even married girls wear traditional clothes, not sari, but maybe Punjabi salwar, something with pants and a top. However, if I wear skirts or something else it would be considered a little modern but it would be okay. I usually wear Punjabi salwar, or jeans, or slacks.

I miss the festivals in India the most. We have thirteen festivals in twelve months and each is different. People cook good food and get together, listen to music, it is just like Christmas here. I miss it a lot! I like the Festival of Color. On that day, everyone has colored powders. Everyone will go out to the streets and play with those powders. They put it on your hair or cheeks. Some other people play with colored water; they will sprinkle it on you. After that, people get together for parties. They go to each other's house and they distribute sweets and wear new clothes.

I still follow the international news. I talk to my parents almost every week and I get some news from them. Sometimes my friends will send me e-mails and say this is happening or that is happening. You can always get news on the Internet. Indians have a lot more access to computers now than before. People used to be more concerned with properties like houses but now they have more electronics like TVs, VCRs, telephones, and computers. I think most people have a TV and a VCR. I think middle class families have telephones, but not the poor. However, I do not think the middle class family has computers, probably because of the access. If you go to South India, they have more computers than they do in North India because the South India constitutes the Silicon Valley of India. A lot of multinational companies in the United States are going to India and hiring people because it's much cheaper. Two thousand dollars here is like sixty-five thousand rupees in India. People get thirty-five, forty thousand rupees there in salary, and companies can hire computer engineers, computer scientists, and pay them only two thousand dollars, which is a lot to them. The rupee has devaluated a lot. When I first came here, six years back, it was like seventeen rupees to a dollar, now it is like thirty-two or thirty-three.

I think it would be much better for the United States to have a national health care system. The United States is the only country that does not have a national health care system. It works as a free market and health care can never work as a free market. For example, you want to buy a sweater, you go to different stores, look at the quality and the product, the price, and then, make a decision. For health care, you can never do that. When you go to a physician, you don't ask what degree the doctor has, or if they provide the services, if they have the license to do that, or if they are qualified to provide those services.

Rekha Desai was born in Palakkad, Kerala State, India, in 1967. She was trained as an ophthalmologist in India and came to America to join her husband, an Indian resident physician in Chicago, in 1995. She was doing her residency and was a mother of two living in suburban St. Louis at the time of the interview in 1998.

I was born in Palakkad, Kerala State, India, on 8 January 1967. I have a sister who is four years younger than me. My father had a master's degree in electrical engineering. My mom had a bachelor of art degree in fine arts. Then she got married and she had us; she never worked. She never wanted to work outside house; she just wanted to be a housewife. Most Indian women of her time went to college only to better prepare themselves for marriage. We were happy and she was happy with the arrangement.

We had to travel a lot because my father worked for the railways. We moved quite often; about every three years, we moved to a different place. It gave us opportunity to make friends very easily, since we changed schools so often. It was very fun, meeting new people and getting used to new schools.

My parents were strict about rules and that children understood them and did their studies. Most parents in our region, which is Hindu, are quite strict as far as girls are concerned. Initially, my parents were thinking that they would be happy if they had a son. But then my father saw both of us as doctors, he said you couldn't have done better than any son would have done. Because we made them happy and both of us have gotten very good educations. They don't need sons. They didn't continuously keep trying to have sons when they were young. They said two was good enough, as long as we were able to raise them well.

We had servants because in railway service you get servants and other benefits. We used to have a nanny and gardeners. We followed a kind of old British tradition. We had clubs. Wherever we went, there were always railway clubs. Every Friday, Saturday, or Sunday we had games and movies in the club. We got together with friends. It was very fun once a week. Our life was westernized. Even the houses we lived in were huge bungalows built by British people, with fireplaces.

Until the twelfth grade, I did my schooling in Central School, which was a central government school. We joined that school because of transferable jobs. These schools were such that all of India would use the same syllabus, and when you transferred anywhere they would take you to the same class and you would do more or less the same studies. They were very good schools.

I took my entrance examination for medical school. It was hard to get into medical school because you are competing with so many students. If you get good marks you get in, otherwise you are turned down. I enrolled in Calcutta National Medical College. That was four and a half years of training and a one-year rotation of internships in all different subjects like medicine, pediatrics, gynecology, surgery, and things like that. We had to do two or three months rotations on each of them. After I finished my medicine, during my internship I got married. Then I came to Nagpur where my husband was. Nagpur is near Bombay. I took an entrance exam for all Indian medical post-graduate and I got to do ophthalmology. I have finished my ophthalmology training. The percentage of women in medical school was 60 to 65 percent. I heard that the percentage of women at engineering school was 30 percent or less. A lot of women went to medicine. Most of them stay in India. A few of my friends went to England. Very few have come to the United States.

The percentage of women who get higher education was very high in Kerala, the state where I came from. Even the literacy percentage was very high. I would say 60 to 70 percent of women would get higher education in urban areas. But when you take a comparison between the urban and rural areas, the rural areas are very bad. When you take the overall average, the percentage for women to get higher education is much less.

Right now most of the women college graduates try to find jobs after they graduate from college. The society is becoming more open towards working women because of the rising cost of living. So nobody minds that his wife goes to work; on the contrary, I think it's quite welcome that she gets a job.

How did I choose medicine as my field? A lot of my family members are doctors, both my grandfathers are doctors, my two uncles are doctors, and my cousins are doctors. Before I went to medical school, I knew I wanted to be a doctor. When I became a doctor, my sister wanted to join medicine. Although my father said one of us should become an engineer like him, and one of us should be a doctor. My sister said she wanted to be a doctor and she went to medical school. I like my decision to become a doctor. I guess I was a good student at medical school. All my education from elementary school to college was in English. When I came to the United States, I didn't have problem with English at all. I understand that a lot of Asians have problems with English.

I got married in India in 1990 and had a son in 1991. I did my post-graduate work after I had him. I also worked for a year as an ophthalmologist consultant. Five years after my marriage, I came to the United States. One of my motivations to come to the United States was to join my husband. Because he was here, I was having difficulty setting up a private practice of ophthalmology as it was very expensive. There was no good hospital that I could join and work. Secondly, my husband was very interested in neonatology and he got a chance to do that here. So he said we should move. The moving was very hard because my husband had set up a private practice in India. We had our own children's hospital there. It was very hard closing it down and selling it off. My parents were supportive of my decision to come to the United States. They said whatever I feel is good for me, I should do it; don't worry about them and just go.

I plan to stay in the United States. We have to do our residency and we have to get a job. But I think my children would like to stay because they have been here so long. I don't think they would like to go back to India. A visit probably would be okay, but I don't think they would go back to live there.

How do I compare the medical fields in the United States and in India? I don't work in the clinical field, I work as a research assistant in ophthalmology. I found that some subjects and some topics are very advanced here, but we were not exposed to them in India when we were doing genetics and immunology. But I think when it comes to the clinical methods and day-to-day physicals, we are better because that's the main way we diagnose in India. Here, everybody I have seen is depending on x-rays and tests. But over there, we have been trained to listen to the patient's heart and find what kind of problem it is. That's the difference. In India, it is not so easily available for a patient to have x-rays. It is also very expensive, so you have to rely more on what you heard, what you saw, and what you felt rather than what tests are coming out. So that is the advantage in America. I have not had any contact with American patients yet because I have not started my residency.

I was not employed to be a research fellow. I was doing research for someone, and my salary was coming out of a grant that they had. That income was not much. I was doing that so I got to interact with them, and I got to go to the hospital to see the clinical side. Even when it comes to residency, although compared to rupees the salary is a lot, when you compare dollars it is not very much. But after you finish residency the income is good. When they are doing residency, generally the income is $30,000. You do three years, and it may go up to $32,000 and $33,000 at the end of third year. That's it. Once you finish your residency and get a job, your income is up to $120,000 as your beginning salary. There is a big difference. But in fact you have to be a resident before you start working in your private practice or in a hospital. So in residency you don't do it for income's sake, you do it for what you can get after the residency. Your degree, your license, everything depends on your residency.

Income was one of the reasons I chose to be a doctor. I felt that in India, ladies go either for medicine, banking, or teaching. Now they are going into civil service. It all depends. You get through your entrance examinations, you get admitted to a medical school, and you get to be a doctor. Otherwise, you go into banking, or teaching, or whatever. I was fortunate to get through it.

What is the disadvantage of being a doctor? I think dealing with the terminally ill patients and families and telling them bad news was the worst part of being a doctor. In addition, I would do something and the patient's family would not want to understand what I was doing is for their good. Otherwise, every part is good being a doctor, other than the fact that you have less time to spend at home with your kids. I am concerned about this aspect, but I will choose a subject for my residency in which I wouldn't be called in too much. My husband wants to be in emergency medicine, and he will be called. We have to compromise, otherwise the kids will go wild. We have to decide that one of us will take a less intense job. So one of us will be with the kids. What will be the less intense job? It depends, if I do endo-crinology or gastroenterology, I will be called for certain procedures. I know that to be a doctor, I will be on call for eight hours, or I may be on call for the day, but the rest of the time I don't need to be on call. Something so that both of us don't have to work, at least one of us stays at home. I don't want to wait till my children grow a little bit older and then go to work. Because it's getting tougher for foreigners to get admitted as residents. If I wait, I don't know if I will get it. The rule will come because the rule changes so fast. And the seats for residency have been reduced. I don't want to wait any longer.

What is the procedure of obtaining a residency? You have to come here and take a U.S. examination that has three parts and you have to score well in these examinations. I scored 82, 83, and 82 in parts 1, 2, and 3, respectively. The maximum scores you can go up to are 90th, 97th, and 98th percentile. On the average, people score around 80, 85, and 86. Around the 75th percentile is passing. Some hospitals only look at applica-tion forms if you score an 80. For those who have scores below 80, they don't even look at your forms. They want your experience. If you have worked in America, they want to have a good reference letter, preferably from an American officer. They say it is easier for them to call upon and verify whether you have truly worked with them and how your work was. They want to know not only your work behavior, but also how you get along with other people. It depends on whether they want you or not. And you choose a certain number of colleges and they choose you. Then there is a matching process. If you like a college and they like you, you are matched. So you get there.

The board examination is quite expensive. It's $500 per exam. There are three exams, each costs $500. Now a fourth exam is coming; starting this June there is another practical exam. It's $1300 and it is held only in United States; you can't take it outside the United States. That is a big amount for someone who is not from the United States and for someone who has been in the United States. It is very expensive, so that gives you the motivation to pass.

I had a baby only six months ago. When I was taking my exams two years ago I had my son without any help, because my husband was a resi-dent at that time. Since he was so busy, I don't blame him. It was his first year of residency. I was preparing for the exams. I would give my son to the babysitters and go study in the library. Now I have a nanny to take care of my baby daughter. It is not easy to find a nanny. That's why some female doctors have to stay at home after they finish their medical training, either they can't afford a nanny or they can't find one. And you hear so many scary stories about child abuse. Maybe that kept some of us from leaving our children with other people. When you are away, you feel like you don't know what's going to happen when you go back home.

Starting from Monday, September 28, I will be working on my residency at Barnes-Jewish Hospital. It takes forty-five minutes from my home to get there. For the first month, it is call-free and I won't be called. After that, each month I will have a different rotation; depending on what rotation I have, I might get called. When you are in residency, you don't get paid when you are called. My husband is paid by hour when he is called.

I don't feel I have any difficulty in my workplace. Actually where I am going to start my work, there is a mixture of Americans and other people. Actually there are hardly any Americans, two of the professors and the attending physicians are Americans. But the residents are mostly Indians, Chinese, Iraqis, and Pakistanis. It is very international. At the same time, I get to interact with all the American patients, American professors, and attending physicians. It's a good mixture.

I have an arranged marriage. We had some family friends in Calcutta who had common friends with my husband's mother and father. So they knew both of us. My parents were looking for a doctor for me, and his parents were looking for a doctor for him. So they said we have a matching of horoscopes. When you are born, according to the star positions, your horoscope is written down. We had that. We have to see that the horoscopes are matched of the bride and groom before they can get married. Although it is a superstitious belief, our parents followed it. In an arranged marriage, they usually see the horoscopes. If they match, a marriage will happen. It matched for me and my husband. We sent photographs to each other, and we liked each other. After that he and his family came to Calcutta to meet me. Then we went out, and we saw that we could really get along. If it is a marriage for love, that is different. Love marriage is quite common now. There is no need to see horoscopes in a love marriage.

My husband is three years older than I am. Usually Indian women prefer to have a husband who is a bit older. Now age differences between husbands and wives are decreasing. Initially, in India you would find husbands that were ten or fifteen years older than their wives. That was common. My father was ten years older than my mother. That practice came from the belief that if the husband was older, he could take care of his wife. The older the husband was, the more stable he was financially. But when we got married, my husband was a medical student. He was doing his third-year residency. But I knew he would be financially secure. We already had our own hospital and everything.

How long does it take from engagement to marriage? In my case, we got engaged on 24 November 1989, and we got married on 5 May 1990. During that half year between our engagement and marriage, we were quite far away from each other. I was in Calcutta, he was in Nagpur. He came to visit us five or six times, because it was a twenty-four-hour journey by train. He was working on his medical degree, so he couldn't get off much. I was doing my internship and I couldn't get off much, either. We talked over the telephone and we wrote to each other. I went to his home once before my wedding. Usually, a girl or a boy doesn't go to the in-laws by herself or himself before marriage. My mother came with me to his house. And we didn't stay in his house. We stayed at the mutual friend's house. I could go out with him alone, but I couldn't go from Calcutta to his house in Nagpur and stay in his house alone. We used to go out for movies and things like that. People prefer to be a virgin when they get married. Now in many cities in India, it is very common to have premarital sex.

I knew him very well before the marriage. Five days after we got engaged, my father had a very bad heart attack. He and his father came over to help us. That way we got very close to each other, because he was so supportive. By the time we got married, we knew each other quite well. It was like a love marriage. It was an arranged love marriage.

We have been getting along very well. He goes out of his way to see everything is fine for our family and for me. He is quite protective. Though he says that here in the United States, you have to do everything on your own, he is always watching what I am doing. He wants me to be independent, but at the same time he is quite worried about me. So every night, he calls to see that everything is okay. He would say, you know you have to do it by yourself. And next day, he calls up to ask how it went. It is not that he is possessive. He is just very concerned about me. We have been married for seven years, we know each other very well and we are comfortable with each other. He is not a controlling husband, either. We always talk about what we want to do. I always ask him, and he always asks me before we make any major decisions. Our relationship is very equal. He never wanted me to stay at home. He said that even though we have children, I will do

my residency and I will have my job, because I have done the same studying as he has done. Both of us are doctors, so it's not that I want to work
and him to stay at home. We should both work outside the home. So that
way it is very equal. I don't know if this type of equal relationship is typical
among Indians. But I think before the Indian husband was always the controlling one in the household. Now the wives are getting more educated
and are working outside home, so naturally they want to be equal with
husbands. Maybe among modern couples, this kind of relation is quite
common.

Life in America is pretty busy and pretty tough, because you are all
alone. You have your kids, you have your work. Sometimes Indians who
have done medicine in India come to America and would not join residency, and stay home and look after their kids because there are so many
problems. I have done medicine, I don't want to stay home and forget
everything that I have learned. I should go on even though I have two kids.
It doesn't matter. I can do it.

In India, we get a lot of help from family members. Although we
lived alone, relatives and a lot of friends were nearby. Family friends of my
husband's were close. They would come running for anything. The most
difficulty I feel is the lack of support, in terms of human power, not financially. Of course, financially it is much better here than it is in India. The
feeling that I am alone, that if something happens I don't have anybody to
call upon, is difficult.

After both of us become stable, we will buy a house. Actually we have
to find a place to stay, because he is in Chicago and I am in St. Louis. I don't
know where we are going to be three years or four years from now. Until
we are sure that we are going to get a job somewhere, there is no point in
buying a house there.

I do want my children to preserve Indian heritage and culture, but at
the same time, I want them to be assimilated into American society. Even
though my son knows English, I still want him to know our mother tongue.
We do go to the temple, so he is aware of this culture. With whatever I have
and whatever I can get here in the United States, I try to do the festivals as
we used to do in India. So my son is very much aware of Indian culture. As
my children grow older, they will have American influence, I can't stop
them from being Americanized. I think if they don't get Americanized, they
will stand out and they will have difficulty mixing with their classmates. But
still I would like them to know that they are Indian, even though they have

become Americanized. I don't know how it is going to be in the future, but I really would like them to know a lot of Indian culture. I am not sure if my children will go back to India. We want to stay and it will be another five to ten years before we can go back. But my son will be fifteen then. I don't think he would want to have any major change at that time.

I want my son to marry an Indian woman, but I don't know whether or not he will. I don't think I will mind if my son marries an Indian or not, but I would like my children to have family values and not just American ways. I don't know whom they are going to meet and like. Anything would be fine. I am very open. My husband is more open than I am. I told him I would like them to get married doing Indian things. He said you have to have an open mind, you don't know what is going to happen. I said okay.

When we are in the United States, we mostly associate with Indians. I feel more at home if I am among Indians. We talk about things back home. I still remember so much about India. I enjoy being with Indians. I haven't had many American families as friends. For one thing, we have been too busy with our studies and residency. When we were staying in an apartment, it was mostly residents from India or Pakistan. We never had a chance to make a lot of American friends. We are colleagues and we are okay. I don't think I will know American society very well until I mix with them properly.

I do have some cultural concerns about being accepted, mostly about my kids being accepted into mainstream. I don't want them being pointed at because they are Indians. Of course, I am concerned about drugs, there isn't much in India. That's one major concern about raising your children here. I don't want them to get into any bad company.

I like oil painting. I did not learn painting professionally. I went to one painting class and learned how to mix the paints and how to use the canvas, then I started painting. I like artifacts and I like making things. I have an interest in art. I read books, I watch some things on TV, and I like to make things. I did ten paintings when I was pregnant with my daughter. It was a way of releasing tension. I felt good after painting or knitting. I knit all of my daughter's sweaters and caps. I don't want to be immersed in medicine, medicine, and medicine. That makes you feel very bad. Painting is quite an expensive hobby. The canvas is not so expensive, but the paints and frames are. I used to play Hawaiian guitar, but it has been long since I have left it. I want to teach my son some of the fine arts, either painting or music.

I also like to write books. When I was in medical school, we had a literary club. I was the editor of the magazine. I wrote poetry. My English is better than my Hindi. I can read and write in Hindi, but my thoughts flow better in English. I feel better in English when writing poems, essays, or other kinds of creative writing. I want to write a novel about something, maybe my experiences with my patients. Maybe my coming to the U.S. and how I coped with everything. I want to do something rather than medicine. I like to decorate my house and keep it very neat. I think I try to keep everything so neat that I waste too much time on trying to keep everything clean.

My main purpose to come to St. Louis was to do my residency. If I had gotten a residency anywhere else, I would have gone there because it is so difficult to get a residency. And with my visa status (H-2), I did not choose to come to St. Louis. I would have loved to stay in Chicago, but I didn't match there, and I matched with St. Louis so I came here. St. Louis was the only place where I got my residency. I have been given options in many places, like Chicago and New York, but I didn't want to go there. I matched here, so I came here. It is a difficult life, I feel. My husband is in Chicago; the kids and I are here.

If I had choice, which city do I prefer in the United States? We came to the United States and stayed in Chicago for the past three years. I love Chicago. If I were given any chance, I would really go back and settle down there. I like Chicago because you can stay in the suburbs, you are quite out of the city. But you have the city, which is so mobile. There are so many things to do in the city. Another thing is that there is a large Indian population there. There is a whole street of Indian shops. You don't miss home too much if you are there. If you feel homesick, you can go there and you see lots of people in saris. Then you think: okay, there are a lot of people like me, so you feel good about it. I like Chicago in that way.

I have never been to California, so I don't know if I want to live there, but certainly not New York. It's too busy and too congested for me. Chicago is not too busy. It is more open than New York is. There are areas where you can go that are not congested. You can always live in the suburbs and still go to the heart of the city and enjoy the city life, and have the things you have when living in suburbs. We just moved to this apartment two months ago. For the first two years, we were living opposite of where my husband's hospitals were, because it was so much easier for him to just cross the street to go to work. There were a lot of Indians there, so I never felt I was in America. It's like Bombay or something. I enjoyed my time there.

I am a Hindu. In Hinduism, you don't have to be like Christians, having to go to church and something like that. You can go to the temple anytime. There is no obligation that you have to go this day or that day. But we like to go when we have a lot of festivals and pray to the God. I do my daily prayer at home. I don't have to do the daily prayer at a certain time, I can do it at anytime I feel like, either when I am going to bed or when I wake up. Whichever time, there is no set rule that I have to go there and say it. I just think of God once or twice a day. We do have a lot of things like prayers, they're called *slokas* (it means sentences). But I don't say those prayers, I just think of God.

18

Factory Work and the Hotel Business

Seeta Patel was born into a farmer's family in Veluk, Gujarat, India, in 1950. Unlike most Indian women, she married her husband by her own choice. She and her daughter came to Canada to join her husband in 1974, who had been working in Canada for two years; they later became Canadian citizens. Her family immigrated to America in 1982. She was the manager of Wilmar Motel in Fairfield, Illinois, at the time of the interview in 1996.

I was born on 30 March 1950 in the small town of Veluk in the state of Gujarat, India. I do not remember my mother. I was only about six or seven years old when she died and my aunt raised me. We have friends and family members who talk about it so I know how it happened, but I don't remember it. I have two older sisters and two younger sisters, but one of them died. My mother had a baby boy, but he died after three days. I do not have any memories other than those of my aunt, grandmother, and my sisters. I have two sisters in India and one in the United States. Another sister came in 1974, but she died three years later. In total, there are four living sisters. My father remarried and I have a stepsister and a stepbrother. I had an aunt who was the wife of my father's brother. She was a very nice person. I felt like she was my mother because she was always helping us. She only had one son. She treated my sisters and me like her own daughters. This fills the absence of my biological mother.

I remember my father very well. He was a good man. He was a farmer and he studied up to the seventh grade. He had a higher education than most people in our town and he was respected. He was the mayor of our small town of about five hundred people. When we had our Independence Day celebration or some special events going on in school, he would come down and open the ceremony. When people finished high school they would receive a certificate and have a ceremony and my father would come down for this also. He was always interested in his kids and work. He always checked on how we were doing in school.

Once a month, he would take us to the city. We saw movies and ate out, which was a really big deal for us. When he said, "This Sunday we are going to go," we would talk about it with our friends for the whole week. We were happy and then we did not want to do our homework. However, we knew that if we did not do our homework, we could not go. When we went, we wore our nice clothing and jewelry. We went shopping or to the park. That is an example of a fun day for us.

Growing up, I remember a lot of discrimination against girls. Girls nowadays go to school, but in 1950, not many girls went to high school and not many attended college. In the whole area, I knew of only one or two girls who attended college, but numerous boys attended college despite their lackadaisical study habits. Most girls finished elementary school up to the seventh grade, and any further study was considered a very big deal because it required moving or commuting to the city. When I went to high school I stayed in a dorm.

Girls usually don't leave the home. They stay with the family because they are not allowed to go out. Parents are not as strict with boys, but girls always had to do housework—cook, clean, take care of the younger siblings, and learn to be a typical housewife. People don't notice when a girl grows up because all her time is spent in the house. Maybe right now it is a little different and they treat the girls better and allow them to excel in school. But girls are still expected to get married.

However, my dad was a different man. I never remember him treating my sisters and me badly. He always did the best he could. He told us to study and to make our own lives. We were very happy and it makes me feel like going home.

I studied at a school with many girls and we wore uniforms. They had certain rules for my dorm. The boys and girls dorms had different rules. It was a really big deal by that time. We had separate buildings, but we shared a prayer room and did certain activities together. Every morning we had to pray. Then we had to exercise and in the evening we had to pray again. We had to wake up by six-thirty and somebody would come wake you up if you were still asleep. Someone would notice your absence from the prayer so you always had to go. In the evenings after dinner, we could go and walk around. Then we could go to the prayer room and do our homework. However, if we walked outside and thought, "The weather is nice, I do not want to go and study," and did not go to the prayer room, someone would find out that we were not there.

We had no choice but to follow the rules. We did have a choice in food, though, because they would make us whatever we wanted. We couldn't waste the food; somebody at the door watches to make sure that all the food was eaten, and if not they would say, "Go back and eat your food." We had to drink milk every day and everybody had to take a shower every morning and wear clean clothes. In addition, nobody was allowed to lie because if you said something deceitful or if you stole something, there was a harsh punishment. If you did something, everybody knew it. No one was going to say anything, but if everybody knew it, it was embarrassing.

In India, parents usually arrange the marriages of their children. They look at the boys and their families and then they think, this one is suitable for my family. I never thought I could marry someone from another caste because my father was born into a certain caste. He was a somewhat religious man, too, so he did not say anything, but we grew up knowing that was how it would be. I knew that my husband would be from my caste. But my marriage was not arranged. I was in high school while my future husband was in college. I had heard his name because he studied in the LLB; he was going to be a lawyer. The year he finished his bachelor's degree, I was in high school. Very few girls were living in the dorms then and were allowed to get married. One of his friends and his sister studied with me and we met through them. I was in the tenth grade when I met him. We were living in separate dorms that were close so we met in the city. We went on dates and he took me out to eat at restaurants. Sometimes at noon, we had a break and we would eat together and then walk to the park. Sometimes on the weekend, we would go see a movie.

Bringing my future husband home to meet my dad was very scary. I prayed every day because I did not know how I was going to tell my father. If he said no, we would not be able to see each other or be allowed to date, which was very scary. Then one day, my father came and talked with me about my boyfriend. I told him about his town, his father, and his studies and concluded that he was a good boy. It worked out very well but it was so scary because this was not normal. If the parents did not approve and did not get along, then they would not allow you to get married.

My two older sisters had arranged marriages because my father was stricter with them. He tended to believe that no matter what the problem was, you had to face it yourself. He said to me, "I'm not going to be around so I want you to know this is the person, this is the family." If I had any problems, I would tell him and he would try to solve it.

I got married in 1968 after I had known my husband for three or four years. After I finished high school, I knew nothing about housework or cooking because I had grown up in a big family on my father's farm. My aunt and older sister did all the work. In India, a girl is supposed to know how to cook before she gets married so my father said, "You have to stay home for one year, learn about cooking, and help out your sister and aunt." So after high school, I stayed home for one year and then got married.

My younger sister got married directly after high school. We had a double wedding. It was a long ceremony. My father was popular in our area and he knew many people. We made plans to get food and had it prepared. In India, if a father does not give a gift at a wedding it is fine. However, if he can afford it, he can give the girls clothes and jewelry. When I got married, my father gave me a sari. It was a new brand and a different style. He also gave me some gold jewelry. At the wedding, he gave my husband and my sister's husband a watch as their gifts. After I was married, I could not wear dresses at my husband's house because I had to respect the family—my husband, his father, and his brother. I was still allowed to wear dresses and skirts at my own father's house.

The ceremony lasted for two days. The ceremony always starts in the morning with the girls. The morning of the first day we started doing the *puja* (prayers) while the priest came. Then we invited our family, friends, and the townspeople to come, stay, play music, and wear nice clothes. Then we had a small dinner. In the evening, they came around again and they sang a song. They gave us sweets like brownies and cookies. The next day was the wedding day and the whole family and the priest did some *puja*, and then we took a good shower. Then everybody had lunch together. At about 3 o'clock my husband's family rented buses and brought their friends and family, because my town and my husband's town are thirty-five to forty miles apart. My husband had four buses and four cars of people. My sister's husband also had his friends and family come and they built a tent and decorated it for the wedding. There were a lot of people. The wedding was in the evening. It was a big celebration. Our wedding was at 9 o'clock at night. We had a dinner with everybody together. Everybody ate and then went back to the house we had chosen as the relative's house during the wedding. When the time came for the ceremony, they came back. We had a special stage and the priest came and started the ceremony. It lasted for about an hour and then we ate cake. The husband's family gave gifts to the brides—a sari and some jewelry.

After the wedding, I went to my husband's house, which is the traditional thing to do. We stayed there and after two or three days we came back to my house. If the husband works and has a house of his own, after two or three months the bride would go and visit the entire husband's family. Then his family comes and visits the girl's family. I did a lot of cooking for my husband's family. We had a helper to clean the dishes and the house, but I usually did the cooking.

In 1972 our first daughter was born. Then three months after she was born, my husband went abroad. He visited England, America, Canada, and Brazil; I think he got four or five visas. He stayed in Canada for a while. It was hard, but I knew his father would take care of my daughter, Nipa, and me. If I needed help, I could also go to my father. We lived in a small town, so it was not too difficult.

I moved to Canada in 1974 and I liked it. My husband had a job when I arrived. He liked it so much there so he applied for immigration. When he got immigration, he sponsored Nipa and me. We got our visas and moved. Before I left India, my husband was living with four or five men in one house. When I arrived, we rented one room and a kitchen with another Indian family from Africa. They lived downstairs and we lived on the second floor. They had three kids and the mother worked so I took care of her children. I was in a new country so I did not start working right away. Then I decided I had better work and when I got a job the other family took care of Nipa. We later moved to an apartment and I became pregnant with my second daughter, Hina. My husband worked at the airport. After we had two children, we decided I should stay home. I took care of the children, cooking, and cleaning. Nipa started kindergarten and Hina was still very young. I stayed at home until 1982.

In 1982, we decided to leave Canada. We had been living in a big city, but we both had grown up in small towns where everybody knew everyone. We were thinking that our kids were not going to experience the way we grew up, so we thought about moving to a smaller town. We were looking for a town with nice people, less crime, and a good place to start a business. We also wanted better weather. My younger sister and her husband came to America to study and she became a citizen. So we asked her to sponsor us and she agreed. When we got our immigration papers we moved to Colorado Springs. My husband had a friend in Atlanta and some friends had a business in Illinois.

My husband came to Fairfield, Illinois, to see if he liked the town, community, people, and schools. We later moved there and started our business. We decided to open a motel. I enjoy working there. I like talking to and meeting the different customers. It is a small historical town so people like to come and talk. I like the people there; there is not too much rushing, and they are easygoing. They take the time to talk and I like that.

When I came to the United States, I had two daughters. I had never been a mother before and I did not have a mother. However, my childhood was one of the best parts of my life. I tried to remember and I did the best I could, but this was a different life. We were away from our family; it was just my husband, my two kids, and me. I had my sister, but she was thousands of miles away and we hardly saw each other. I think that was the bad part, missing my family, but we found good people here. When I first came, I thought I was never going to find people that I could trust. Our friends were nice and they treated us as if we were family after a while.

I occasionally noticed discrimination against me. People would come to the motel and ask the price of a room, and then they said they would come back but they did not. Some people would leave after they saw my race. I saw some good people, too, though. In this business, I have had a chance to see all different kinds of people.

Once we moved to the United States, I made my children learn English so they would do well in American schools. I did not make them learn how to write Gujarati. When I first came to Canada, I was afraid to speak English. I knew only a little bit, but I thought if I spoke Gujarati and taught it to my children, they would not do well in school because of the language problems. I wanted my children to do really well in school. That is the way I thought and I had control. Now that my children are grown, they have the control. Now I can speak in Gujarati, but before I did not want my children to mix up the two languages. Hina and Nipa even got an award in English, and then I said they had been doing well.

Sometimes I think when I get older I do not want to live alone. Maybe I want to live with my family and move back to India. Other times I think my kids are going to be here, so I have not definitely decided to go back. When my children finish studying and settle down I would like to travel. However, I have not made any serious plans to go back to India.

I noticed that there are some differences between India and America. There are no nursing homes in India. My uncle and aunt are older, but they do not take any medicine. They do not have any serious diseases. Like most older people, they get sick, but not enough to take medicine every day. They also take care of the children. Right now the aunt who raised me is taking care of my brother's sons and daughter. They do not have babysitters. I had never even heard that word before I came here.

After twenty years, I still do not like American food. I went back to India three years ago and since we have a big family, food is always around. Someone always prepared the meals, so we ate at home almost all the time. Here we eat out or order food so much because I don't have time to cook.

———————◆◆◆———————

Seema Khotlay was born in New Delhi, India, in the 1950s. She came to America at the age of 25 to get married to her husband, who was then living in Canada. They moved to a midwestern town in 1970, where her husband got a job at a local factory. They had two sons. She was employed at a local factory at the time of the interview in 1996.

I was born in New Delhi, India. My father was a college graduate and my mother had only three or four years of education because she came from a village where they did not tell women to go to school. My father was a manager for a company in India. My mother stayed at home to take care of the kids. I have seven sisters and I used to have three brothers, but they all died when they were younger than seven. I am the youngest of the seven girls, and we are one to three years apart.

My eldest sister got a graduate degree. One of my other sisters got her PhD. One of my sisters got a degree in Sanskrit and another got one in economics and fine arts. I have a master's degree in fine arts. My father expected a lot in education. Some of our relatives were thinking, "Why are his daughters going to college?" or "He is paying so much money," and "When they get married, he needs to pay money, too." My other family members, like aunts and uncles, were against education, but my father didn't listen to them. He made everybody study and he had a good life.

My marriage is an arranged marriage. It was a traditional way of getting married in India and still is to a large extent. Before I came to the United States, I was already engaged to my husband, who was then living in Canada. His parents saw me in India and they decided to take me as his wife. I needed to come here to get married. I first arrived in Chicago when I was twenty-five. My wedding was a traditional ceremony held in the garage of my sister's house. There was a fire in the middle. We needed to walk around the fire seven times and make promises to a fire god or holy spirit, promising each other service, love throughout life, and giving life to the fire. We put flower necklaces around each other's neck. Then we had many things to eat.

When I first met my husband, I thought "I don't know him," but so many things were going on. I thought we needed to get to know each other. He got to learn what my feelings were and what I liked and I learned what he liked. We needed to compromise for each other and get on with our life together.

When I first came to the United States, I was not nervous because I was thinking of my father. He and my mother were already in America with my eldest sister in Chicago, so when I came here I was happy to see them. It is the Indian way that every sister gets married and has her own life. The bad part was I did not drive at that time, so I was dependent on my sister and I was at her mercy. She was taking me to work and choosing my clothes. I only spoke a little English then, even through I knew English. In India we spoke Hindi. We still speak Hindi at home, but outside we speak English.

In 1970 we moved to this town because my husband got a job here at a local factory. I didn't have any choice but to move here, and I was pregnant at the time. I like it here. I like living in a small town better than a big city. It's very peaceful and it's not hectic. It is more comfortable, as long as I have job.

I never worked in India. Since I came to America, I started working. I first worked in a telephone company as an operator. Then I took some classes on child-care at the vocational training center. Now I have a job in a factory that makes auto parts and I have been working there for three years. I am making brake switches called universal switches. I also make emergency brakes. It is so nice. I like everyone there. They are wonderful to me. On weekends, it is hard for me to stay home because I do not get to see my coworkers. I like to work, even on Saturdays and Sundays. I like to see people. At my job I usually do not feel stress. If I feel like I am working too hard I can tell my boss and they will understand. If I have something on my mind, I will go and talk to them about it. A few days ago, they had a new job opening and I applied for it. I do not understand why another person was hired; I am curious. I am going to ask the personnel manager when she comes back from her vacation. I am going to talk to her, and she will explain to me why I was not hired for the job. I feel like they did not do anything wrong. I like to talk, but I do not like to tell another person and then another person the same story.

During a typical day, I work on an assembly line. I am fast. My boss was surprised to see how fast I work. Normally employees make 100 percent of their quota. I always make 130 to 140 percent, and that is hard to do. 100 percent is what they think one person can make.

At home I cook all kinds of dishes. I am a vegetarian so I cook spaghetti without meat. I cook spaghetti, macaroni and cheese, pizza, and tacos. My favorite things are *chapati* and *dal*. *Chapati* has chopped potatoes in it. If I do not feel like cooking, we make something very fast or order a pizza. I do most of the household chores; my husband washes the dishes once in a while.

We have two sons, one is sixteen and the other is thirteen. We want the kids to be like us, but they are not doing their part. I think it is just their age. We do not have many relatives like uncles and aunts here. The children do not have much love from the other side of the family. I am working so I can't pay attention to them. I cannot stay at home and take care of their stuff. Maybe I am not giving them everything they need or something is missing. I want them to be good people, not telling lies or hurting people. If they get married, I hope they love that person dearly and do not cheat on her. One should have a good family life and education first and other things come next. Therefore, I try to teach my children Indian culture. My sons understand Hindi, but they do not speak it. I took them to India once when they were very small. I want to take them to India again.

One thing I do not like is that my coworkers are always asking: "Has your son started dating?" He is not thinking about dating yet and I don't want him to unless he is grown up and has a job. My son likes to study and I want him to pay more attention to studying. If he finds a girl and dates her then we need to talk to him about it. I am not particular if he finds an Indian girl or other girl as long as he loves her, and the love is pure. That is the most important.

I like living here and I like how people think differently here than in India. I like freedom. Kids should have freedom so they can grow up to be a complete person. They do not need to be scared of anybody or anything. There is not much pressure. I do miss some things in India, like my family, and how they get together on certain days. In India, children go to their relatives' houses. During summer vacation they stay with relatives as long as they want and they get all the love from uncles and aunts. We can send our kids on holidays to have time alone. I miss that part, because we do not have anybody here to support us. Here we cannot send the kids anywhere else.

I love seeing my friends, talking, or going to play tennis for fun. I like to watch tennis. Sometimes I go to the YMCA and walk with my friend. I would like to make more friends so I can play tennis with them. I like swimming, too. I do not like to read. I have so much work, I do not have time to sit down and read. If I am reading, I will think, "I better vacuum this place," or "I should clean this house." My husband reads many books. He always watches the news, so there is no choice. If I am sitting here, the TV is on the news channel. I am not interested in American political issues because I just think about my work, my home, my kids, and my friends. I do not have time to think about anything else.

I am a Hindu. We practice it here, although not many people do. However, I am not very religious. I do not pray. To believe it is more about how you act in everyday life. You do not say words to hurt other people's feelings or tell lies. I think that is more important than prayer, although I like prayer, too. But I like ways that are more peaceful. First, I need to improve myself, and then I can pray.

19

Attaining Education

Munni Jameel was born in Southampton, Massachusetts, in 1973. Her parents came to America from India to study at the University of Massachusetts in the early 1970s. She was a student at a medical school in Kirksville, Missouri, at the time of the interview in 1996.

I was born in Southampton, Massachusetts, in 1973. I have one sister and one brother. My parents did all their schooling in India. They went to a high school run by Jesuits and they both went to a university in India. They got married there and then traveled to America to study at the University of Massachusetts. Education was the biggest factor for them to immigrate to America. They wanted to be in the United States because at the time it was the general feeling among the young people who wanted to leave India and come to America where there were more opportunities. It is a wealthier nation. I think education was what made them come here, but they saw beyond that toward long-term plans. They came with student visas. My mom has become a citizen since then. My dad is currently working to become a citizen.

My dad received a scholarship from the University of Massachusetts so that was where they decided to go. Then my mom entered a program over there. My dad got his PhD in chemical engineering, my mom got her master's degree in education, and then they moved to California. My father is a chemical engineer, but he does financing and auditing in the company that he works for back in California. My mom is a travel consultant.

They both acquired a good education. When they see kids here, they always talk about how hard they had to work. When they saw my siblings and me in high school, they said, "Compared to what we did in India at

301

your age, you are slacking." However, when they saw the subject matter we were studying, they said, "Wow, we didn't study that until we were in college." I worked hard in high school, but I did not stay up until two or three in the morning as I do now.

My sister just started her freshmen year at University of California–San Diego. She does not want anything to do with medicine, like me; she is more into the political field. She likes to be involved with politicians—not so much in law. I do not think she wants to be a lawyer. She likes to read and write. My brother has shown interest in the medical field, but he is still too young. One day he wants to be a doctor or a detective. He's not really sure what he wants to do as far as careers go.

My parents were a lot more protective of me because they did not know what growing up in America would be like. Being their first child, my curfew, studying, and every move I made was monitored. I am thankful that I was pushed to do well. They did not neglect my brother and sister, but they are more relaxed with rules with them because they understand more now. They have seen that I have gone through the system and turned out okay and nothing went wrong.

They did not think they should have lower expectations of me because of my gender. I think it was the reverse. They pushed me to do well because I had so many opportunities as a woman in America. The simplest things like riding a bike and skiing, my Mom said "You know, women don't do stuff like that in India, so it's good that you have a chance to do it here." When I expressed an interest in medicine they really encouraged me.

I got my undergraduate degree in molecular and cell biology at UC Berkeley in 1995; it was tough for me. I did very well in high school, but I do not feel like I really worked for my grades. I think that things came easier to me. When I got to Berkeley, I was thrown for a loop because it was a huge school and I had gone to a small high school with small classes. The classes at Berkeley were huge. I was left on my own with little guidance. I had a tough time there. I went up and down, back and forth, but by my junior year, I figured out what to do and how to handle the system. I did not have any relationships with my professors because it was such a big school. I had to make special effort to get the recommendations I needed for medical school. However, in Kirksville I feel like the professors really try to get to know you. I feel like reciprocating and I feel free to approach them before or after lecture. Here I have a large group of close friends and the whole class is somewhat close. At Berkeley, I had a smaller group of close friends and that was who I was always with. I was always meeting with people, but my core group of friends was smaller.

When I came to the medical school in Kirksville for my interview, everyone was so nice and welcoming; they would bend over backwards to help the students. And not just at the school; I noticed as soon as I got to the Kansas City Airport that everything was different from Berkeley where nobody knows who you are; you are a number at the school, and no one would notice your absence. You are on your own, doing your thing, and obtaining your degree. However, I felt like the people at Kirksville College of Osteopathic Medicine truly cared. That was important to me because I feel like in training to be a doctor, there has to be personal relation skills in your education; there has to be a personal touch. Therefore, I chose to come to Kirksville for medical school.

I really like living in a small town. Kirksville is the smallest town I have ever lived in. I like not worrying about my safety all the time. I like the quietness around me, which is good for studying. What I like most about Kirksville is the friendliness. I know if I ever needed help it is there for me. I just wish it were closer to a big city; sometimes I need to go to a city. Nevertheless, I really like living in a small town compared to somewhere like Berkeley, which was crazy after a while and I could not take it. I do not think I would ever want to live in a big city.

Everything I do locally and in the community is through the SOMA (Students Osteopathic Medical Association). I am the SOMA president. We try to organize our activities to integrate with the community; we do things like working with Special Olympics and blood pressure clinics. We are in the community, but work through the medical school.

I feel like the sheer numbers in my class discourage me. There are only 28 women in my class and 120 men. I know that is partially because more men than women accepted the spots. However, I think in many medical schools, you see that there are more men than women in the field. Moreover, I know that the numbers of women in medical school are increasing, but it still seems to be low. In that sense, it is a little discouraging. But it is encouraging that the numbers are growing. At first, I was in shock when I saw the numbers in my class. But right now, it makes absolutely no difference to me because everyone became friends and I am not treated on the basis of being a woman. I am treated as a medical student. In addition, I think both sexes are equally encouraged and there is equal opportunity for both. The competition is still there, a little bit. But it's not as if the men are necessarily running the show in our classes.

I have noticed lately that I do not look at anything in terms of race anymore. Even when I am choosing friends, race does not matter. I have always had friends of many different racial backgrounds. I used to be a lot more conscious of what race a person was, but for some reason the older I have become the less I pay attention. It is strange because many of my good friends here are of Indian background. I didn't go and purposely seek out these people and say, "I am going to be friends with the Indian people here." It just happened that way.

I do not know where I will end up in the future. I am hoping to go to Michigan for my third and fourth year of school, and then I will have my degree. I do not know where I want to go for my residency. I am probably going to do internal medicine or family practice for my specialty because I want to stay general, maybe something in the primary care field.

I do not think I have been discriminated against. Sometimes I picked up on it a little bit in high school, not because of race but because of my sex, which surprised me. I was strong in science and math, as were other girls, but there were boys who were strong in science and math as well. It always seemed to me that the teachers were more encouraging of the boys in science and math classes. If I did well, or if my friend who was a girl did well, that is great. But they seemed extremely supportive of the boys. That is the only time I noticed discrimination based on gender.

I have a boyfriend who is also Indian. I have known him since I was nine years old; we are family friends. We did not start dating until the end of my junior year of college. I like most how comfortable I feel with him because I know him so well. There is nothing that made me decide whether I liked him or not; it was a gradual thing over the years. He is my best friend; I can tell him anything and he can tell me anything. Right now it is tough because we are apart. He is in England working because he was transferred on a project. He has been there for most of the year. At first, it was hard for me to be in Missouri and have him to be in California. That was a strain on the relationship. Now he is in England and it is even harder because it is difficult to coordinate when we can call each other. Right now, the relationship is hard on both of us, but we try not to let it weigh things down because there is really nothing we can do about it at this point. It is based on understanding and trust.

What I like most about living in America is the freedom to choose whatever I want to do. There are no limits. If I need help it is there for me.

Women have amazing opportunities here compared to what I have heard my mom say about India. I feel lucky to have that, and I guess I take it for granted a lot.

I do not take part in the politics, especially now with the elections going on. I really hate seeing that stuff on TV. However, I know it is all part of what America is about and I am sure most democratic countries go through the same thing. I do not think there is anything I really dislike about America.

At home my parents speak Gujarati. I understand everything in Gujarati. I can speak if I have to, but I am not very good at it. My mom makes Indian food about half the time and the other half it's a variety of foods.

If I have a family, I think I would have a combination of Indian and American parenting. In comparison with my American friends, I think I appreciate the fact that my parents were involved in my education. At the time I hated it because they were always on my back pushing me to do things. Now I look back and I am so thankful for their encouragement. I know that I want to be involved in my children's education. I want to be protective of my children. There has to be certain rules and a certain element of strictness. On the other hand, I will have to trust my children. There will be so many opportunities for them and they will have to be able to take advantage of whatever they want to without having to worry about an overprotective parent.

I want my children to learn all about India. I want them to learn about our religion, Zoroastrianism. There is one god in our religion and it is similar to many religions. It is basically "Do good and don't do evil." I pray every morning and evening. There are many fire temples in India. In these temples, a flame continuously burns. We do not worship the fire, but we pray in front of the fire because that is the symbol of our religion—the fire, the light, and your way of talking to the god. Back home there is one temple near my house that I go to for social functions. They usually have prayers and ceremonies in the fire temple, then they have the social gathering outside. If there is one happening when I am home, I go. However, there is nothing here for me to attend. It is more of a personal practice. I pray once in the morning, and I think that helps me during the day. I do not really know how.

I am not very religious. However, I am religious to a certain extent, and I would like my children to learn about that. I think learning about religion brings in not only Indian culture, but some Persian/Iranian culture also, which I think is important. I would like my children to speak another language, but that is not going to happen if I do not teach them. I want them to know a lot, and they do not necessarily have to make it a part of their life, but I want them to be aware of it.

I like to exercise, play basketball, and go running. If I ever have a free evening, I like to hang out with my friends, having dinner at home or going to eat somewhere, or just doing nothing. I love to talk on the phone with my family and friends or write letters to my grandparents in India. It is more like trying to catch up with myself because I feel swamped all the time here. I read *USA Today* in the library. I used to subscribe to *U.S. News* but I do not have time to read it anymore, so I get *Life* magazine now. I try to follow the daily news, but sometimes I find myself out of touch with the world. I do not want to sound like I do not care about what is going on. I do, but I do not like the way that the politicians handle certain issues. I think that is my problem. The backstabbing, making promises, and lying and cheating always get to me and I say, "Blah! I want no part of that." However, I do care about certain issues. For that reason, I try to read the paper and vote on the issues. I try to stay involved and I do care, it is just the system itself that gets on my nerves.

Mini Menon was a 1.5 generation Indian American from Chicago, Illinois. She was born in Bangalore, India, in 1975 and came to America with her mother and sister to join her father, who was working on his doctoral degree at Columbia University, in 1977. She was a biology major at Truman State University at the time of the interview in 1996.

I was born in Bangalore in southern India on 27 June 1975. My parents were working in South India, but they are not South Indian. I was born a month early and I only weighed four pounds. My parents did not have a name ready, but they were going to nickname me Mini for sure. Then it stuck so they named me Mini. It is actually a common name. When I visited India a few years ago, everyone was named Mini. I was surprised.

When my parents were growing up there was a lot of bartering going on. My mom tutored, and the father of the student would help my mom with math, or something like that. There was no job for money that my parents participated in when they were in school. India is all about social activities—that is life. Social life never ends there; that is the biggest problem. My mom said she used to have to go hide to study. There were people around all the time. There was always a relative around; there were always people from the neighborhood around. My mom had three brothers so there was always someone coming over to play. My mom was a tomboy. Badminton is a really big thing. It is a British sport that has a very big influence in India. They play a lot of cricket, which is like Indian or British baseball. My mom used to play a lot of that, but they also had their Indian version of hopscotch when they were younger. My mom told me about the games she used to play when I was in India a few years ago. They are all very fun and very basic.

My mom grew up playing music or singing for four or five hours a day in addition to her studies. She was a big nerd. My grandfather is a classical Indian music fanatic and he named my mom Veena, which is an Indian stringed instrument. She sang, played the sitar, harmonium, and Indian drums. My mom's grandparents were very wealthy, her grandfather was a lawyer. He had a big family, and they had a huge bungalow with large amounts of land. During the summer, they would spend months at grandma's house, and my mom remembers their childhood days hanging out at that palace of a place, and running through the floral gardens.

My dad did almost the same thing, except with male versions of the sports. He also did the things people do here—ride bikes, play around the neighborhood, and socialize. As long as the children are well balanced, they can do whatever they want. Summer is just as fun as it is here.

My parents had been living in South India for a couple years before I was born. We are from North India, near New Delhi. My mom has her master's degrees in English and classical Indian music. It is classical Indian music/ Sanskrit, which is a Latin version of Hindi. It was not common for women her age to have much education past high school. Both of her parents are English professors. That is why she had the English background, but she is an exception. If there were women that were educated, it was often in the arts or humanities or English. She was the stereotypical female liberal arts person. She had only brothers but she was smarter than them. She had scholarships because she was a National Merit Finalist; she had top scores in her state.

My mother became a teacher in India. She was allowed to teach at the college level because English was not a common skill to have and they needed professors. She taught English to students at the higher grammatical level. Because she passed boards, she was allowed to teach. In the arts, humanities, and English, there were female professors. Not often would you find a female math or science professor. She did have a few friends that went into math and science, though. Since we moved to the United States, my mom has done a lot of post-graduate work, like library studies.

My dad has his PhD minus thesis. It is called a professional degree. Basically, he did his doctorate but not his thesis. He has it in metallurgical engineering. He got his PD from Columbia University in New York. They paid for him to come here for school and then got him a job. That is how we moved to America, we followed him here. He was going to finish his degree and go back to India, but then he decided to work here.

My immediate family all moved to the United States. I have one sister who is seven years older than me. I was two when we moved to the United States. My sister, mother, and I stayed back in India for almost a year with my grandma after my father left. We did not know how long it would take, but he got some job offers while he was getting his degree. He was alone here for about nine months. He actually followed his younger brother who was the first to come to the United States and suggested my dad pursue studies here. Everyone on my dad's side of the family is here. On my mom's side, there is still one brother in India. He has a steady job there and he takes care of my grandparents because everyone else is gone. They live together, which I think is why he decided to stay. We talk often to them and the phone bill is expensive. My mother's two brothers are in Washington DC and California.

My dad had a student visa, F-1, when he came here. My mom got the visa for spouses, F-2. We first arrived in New York City. My uncle lived in New Jersey so he was really close. My mom stayed at home while we were young. My uncle was a physician so my mom helped him out. He had a practice out of his house and people used to come to the clinic in the basement. We stayed upstairs and got to see the people coming in and out. It was a sad time in my mom's life because it was a big change. She adapted well, and now she does not think she could live in India again.

My dad works in the steel industry. He works in a plant and does quality control on their inner-castings. He worked for several years as an engineer in India, but he pursued a different variation of engineering when he came here.

My mom does everything around the house. My dad contributes when he is asked. He would not mind helping, but it does not occur to him. My mom gets tired of asking him so she would rather do it on her own. If there is a car problem or the vacuum cleaner is broken, he will fix it. He also does all the paperwork. My mom told him if he will do those things, then she will do the rest. I think it works out well. He works longer hours than she does and he has the final say in financial and safety matters. Otherwise, my dad is not too concerned that my mom would make the wrong decisions, so she has free rein on other choices. My dad encourages my mom to do even more at her job.

The typical middle-class Indian family would probably approach decision-making the same way as my family does. The husband is usually the main breadwinner, so he makes a lot of the bigger financial and other decisions. The wife makes the general "bringing up the family" decisions.

I learned English when I was a baby, from day one. I also speak Hindi. I learned them simultaneously. In India, a person has two options: you can go to English-based schools, in which all of your subjects are taught in English; or you can go to a school where English is taught as a subject and the rest of classes are taught in Hindi. Both of my parents went to English-based schools so all of their learning was in English. It is not surprising because the British ruled India so long. My grandparents went to English-based schools too. They have British accents.

I have U.S. citizenship; I got it in the summer of 1995. I had to apply because my parents are not naturalized. If they were while I was under the age of eighteen, then I would have been automatically naturalized. My mom wanted to keep her Indian citizenship because she has no desire to vote and she is not into politics. My dad is crazy about politics. He got his citizenship a long time ago. But my mom wanted to keep her Indian citizenship for heart-rending reasons. Also, it is a lot easier to travel back and forth to India if you are an Indian citizen, you do not have to get a visa.

My parents expected a lot from me because I was generally a good kid. I never felt pressured because my parents were laid back and always wanted me to do my best. In fact, I am always the one who feels like I do not do well enough and they tell me to calm down. My mom is always telling me to go to sleep. She wants me to think about my decision to study medicine. She doesn't think I would want to continue it if I had a family. That is not really sexist because she knows I could handle it, but I think she thinks of it that way because in her generation it was not done that way. Expectations of females in India as a whole are less than expectations of males, though it is changing a lot. It is hard to generalize because my parents are both from cities. I am talking from the perspective of a middle-class, city-oriented family with an education, which is not typical in India. Where I am from, it depends on the family background and the attitude because even some educated people are still very traditional in their thoughts. Some of my friends' parents will not let them date or have boys call them. When I went to India, I got that perception in most places. I visited when I was five and again when I was a sophomore in college.

In Indian families, there is a high level of respect for parents. There are some conservative American friends that I have, completely Caucasian, that have the same thing. I think in general you can stereotype that. It's a big part of tradition that you respect your elders in anything they say, even if it is irrational. In my family, it is a little different because my parents are both from "forward families." But in general, I think I respect my parents. I never give them a tough time, but I am allowed to say things that I know kids in India are not allowed to say to their parents, such as, "I don't think so, Mom!" People who came here from India would think I am very disrespectful.

My parents are very liberal. I think we have a mutual respect for each other. My parents do not ask much of me regarding rules, so I try to respect them as long as they are reasonable. Otherwise, I try to talk them out of things. They never grounded me, but they did give a lot of lectures, and they were usually right. I was a good kid. I have never felt the need to go through a rebellious stage. I have been through the teenager "I hate everyone" stage, but I did not want to escape to college only to get away from home. They gave me all the freedom in the world, and I did not abuse it.

My sister is seven years older than me. She got married my freshman year of college; I miss her a lot. She does not have any children yet. She and her husband plan to relax and travel until they decide they are ready. My brother-in-law is a physician and he recently got a job after his thirty-first birthday. They both moved to the United States when they were nine so they have similar backgrounds. They got married in a traditional Indian wedding. The Americanized Indian wedding is a shorter version, only a couple hours long, of what happens in India for a week. In the actual weddings, there are eight or nine hours of taking vows. My mom said, "I was ready to pass out and die." The couple sits down for periods at a time; they sit under a canopy that is decorated with flowers, usually marigolds. Banana leaves are very symbolic and so are coconut trees. Setting it up is a pain.

We had three hundred people at my sister's wedding in October. The hardest thing to find was a place that would let us have Indian cuisine and set up the canopy. We ended up having it at a Unitarian Church that would allow a ceremony from another religion. We had all kinds of American and Indian friends there; people came from the coasts and from India. Although we made it very modern, it was still done in red, a holy color that symbolizes love. It was also very relaxed. A person can get up and walk out during the ceremony, and it is not rude. A person can get a snack while the groom recites his vows.

During the ceremony the bride and groom must sit very poised. The family is very involved. The parents on both sides sit under the canopy with the couple and they all hold hands for a second. They do a ring exchange. They also do a garland exchange, which is the final vow. The bride puts a garland of flowers around her husband's neck and the husband puts one around her neck. There are other parts like circling the pyre, the holy fire, in the middle of the canopy. The bride ties her sari to the groom's and they walk around seven times and say vows. Those are very symbolic vows. The ceremony is done in Sanskrit but they usually translate it so you know what is going on.

A real important part of the wedding is the woman becoming a part of the husband's family. It is almost as if the bride's mom is completely giving up her daughter. The woman used to leave her family and stay with her husband's family. Things have changed now, but it is still a concept that the husband's is her first family. After the wedding ceremony is done, the bride comes back wearing clothes presented to her from the groom's side of the family, usually picked out by the groom's mom and sisters.

There are all kinds of activities for girls the week before the ceremony. We had a girl's luncheon where we danced and sang in our basement, and the bridesmaids teased the bride before she got married. It is our version of a bachelorette party. The groom has his own party. There are all kinds of teasers that go on during the wedding as well. The bride's sisters and cousins steal the groom's shoes because he cannot wear them in an Indian ceremony. It is not holy to wear them into the temple. Then the girls negotiate and he gives them money. The girls say, "No, no, my sister is worth more than that!" It is fun. I kept raising the price when I did it. There are all kinds of fun parts, but there are also some serious parts when people watch them walk around the fire and take the host with them. We see that they have taken this seriously.

My mom and dad have a wedding album. They got married on horses which is traditional for our caste, the warrior caste. My parents rode in to their ceremony on horses. They also have a lot of pictures of the garland exchange.

I want the Hindu festivities at my wedding. I think it is more fun than the Catholic wedding I have been to, but I do think that the Catholic wedding is beautiful. If I end up marrying someone who is not Hindu, I would like to do both types of ceremonies. That is what a lot of mixed couples do these days; they have both on the same day. It makes it more fun and interesting.

It would be very nice if I married someone with the same ethnic background. For lack of a better word, it would be convenient. If it does not happen, it would not matter. I think there are people in my culture that know less Indian culture than people who have studied Hinduism and Indian culture. I would rather have someone who is knowledgeable and open-minded rather than someone who happens to be Indian. I do not think I am looking for someone Indian, but if I found someone it would be a bonus. I would love to meet someone who would be willing to travel to India and see my family there. It is very important to me to have that.

I think the way I will raise my children will depend on whom I marry. I would like them to know about Hinduism. I was brought up Hindu, but my parents were very open-minded about religion, and the Hindu religion itself is very open-minded. It is important that you do believe in a God and that you are open to other people as a whole. We are so polytheistic that we celebrate Christmas at our house, because God is God. My parents, when they were growing up, had vacation for Christmas. I believed in Santa Claus when I was younger. My parents are very accepting of other religions, and it is condoned to try to convince someone to convert. Different religions believe in different things, but Hinduism is almost a philosophy. It has never been taught to me as a religion but my parents have given me the morals.

Divorce is not very common in India. The rates are hardly measurable. It is starting to happen a little more now. You would think with arranged marriages there would be divorces left and right, but it is hardly heard of. Even in the big cities you hardly hear about divorce. It is considered taboo. It puts a mark on the woman, but probably does not mark the man. It is a very sexist and male-driven society in India, although it is different in cities. Sometimes women are allowed to remarry and it is accepted, but it depends on the situation. The cases of divorce are usually regarding arranged marriages that were not within the proper socioeconomic status.

The two people were married because of money or security, and then the woman hates the man. She runs off and gets divorced. If it is abuse or something extreme, that is acceptable.

When my grandma visits, she stays in the United States for about two years at a time. She has a visiting visa. She stays with my uncles and my family and everyone across the country for a couple months. She stayed with my family in the summer of 1996 and I got to spend a lot of time with her. We are having a family reunion in California soon because my grandma is here again. It is the first time she is visiting as a widow. It is nice because she can be with her kids.

I am getting my bachelor's of science in biology and psychology in May. It has been challenging. I would not say that I had any real problems but it was a tough pre-med core. I would like to be a psychiatrist. I want to go to medical school or pursue a program in psychology.

I think there are stereotypes of Indian students. People assume we are really smart especially in math and science, but I have never felt that professors or students expect more from me because of my background. I work ten hours a week for my scholarship job. I work for a professor. I usually do errands, run copies, tutor, and help with labs. We have an agreement that I will work the hours but I work them at different times. It is just her and me; there is no real relationship within the office. I like the fact that she understands that I will get stuff done for her. I like the respect I get from her. She knows I am busy and that I do not have to come in physically, but she knows that when she gives me work I will get it done. Sometimes I do not like when she needs help and I am completely swamped with work. It seems that it comes up at different intervals when I have strings of exams. She comes up to me and asks, "Could you grade this stack of biology exams?" And I am like, "Ughhhh! Yeah, I'll have them for you tomorrow."

I like this town because it is very convenient, I don't have to wait in lines. It is small so I can get around quickly. There is a low crime rate, and I feel relatively safe. The people are very friendly. It has the necessities, like banking, volunteer services, and community help. On the other hand, I do not like it because it has some conservative people who don't care too much for the university students and see us more as a nuisance in the town. There is a lot I like about the university. I am glad I came to school here because the people are very down-to-earth.

During the summers, I have a paying job. I work at the YMCA as a swim teacher, and I worked in telecommunications. Last summer I did not have a job because I came back in the middle of it. I went to Europe on a study-abroad program through the biology department. We went on a marine biology trip to Ireland and France. We learned a lot about biology and we were able to take advantage of the historic sights and the tourist sites. It was three weeks long and compact, but it was fun.

My mom cooks Indian food three or four times a week. There is usually something Indian left over in the fridge. She sends it up to me with other people who are coming from my hometown. Indian food has a lot of breads, starches, rice, and spicy flavoring. Curried foods are saucy foods. There is very little meat. More than anything, I think I miss the spicy flavor. I do not think American food has any flavor at all. It is very bland, like raw vegetables.

It is easy to tell that we are Indian by our house. My mom burns all kinds of incense. It is a big part of our religion, so it is around every day. Also, there are a lot of pictures—especially in our basement right now. I do not know if it happens to go with the decor or that we have made a lot of recent trips to India, but there are a lot of peacock feathers and Indian-looking things. There are little cut-outs of Indian instruments pasted all over the walls. My mom gives a lot of her lessons there. There are a lot of elephant statues on our side tables. I have been in Indian homes where everything is carved ivory, so I don't think my house is that bad. We have a bindi, which is a symbol of marriage. We wear special attire whenever we go to Indian functions. When we go to temple, we wear Indian clothes.

I would not want to move to India. I don't think I could survive there, it is too different. My parents told me even they could not survive there. They told me how things have changed, how corrupt things are, and besides, we are used to the conveniences of life here. That does not happen there. The power goes out all the time, the water supply is low, there is bribery going on left and right to get things done. It is very different in India than what my parents would want me to see. I would get sick because I am not used to the bacteria there. But I would not mind studying there for a year or two, maybe to pursue medicine for a while. I know that I would be putting myself at a big risk because I get ill around people.

In my free time, I am not being very productive these days. After I have done my homework, I like to sit because it is nice to savor the moment. At home when I have free time I like to paint, listen to music, and make tapes. I like to sing. I talk on the phone a lot. I like to swim, so if I have a lot of time I like to go to the YMCA and do laps and work out. I swam in high school. I also like to go running and play outside. I like to spend time talking to my parents and friends. I like to shop and travel. If I had all the money in the world, I would travel all the time.

My dad is the president of the Indian Association in my hometown. There are three hundred families associated with it. He is always doing something for the festivities that are going on. This past weekend was our Indian Christmas. In India, it is a religious gift exchange and the Festival of Lights. We have our lights on all the time. They are in the window because we put them out for different occasions, like weddings. With the Indian Association, there are different types of Indian dances.

Part 6
Vietnamese,
Laotians, Hmong,
and Thai

Many refugees from Indochina took dangerous routes to escape their Communist-controlled homelands, and their adaptation to American life was difficult. Dung Nguyen was a teenager in 1975 when she escaped Vietnam by boat and journeyed to her new life in America. Ha Che, a Vietnamese social worker and wife of a South Vietnamese army officer, was lucky enough to flee the country with her children by airplane. Beth Pham's family, however, risked their lives to take a boat that first sailed to Malaysia and then to America. Dara Phannarath, a Lao woman, sailed across the Mekong River to reach Thailand and stayed at a refugee camp for a year.

Once matched with their sponsors, these women came to America to start a new life. Both Ha and Dara lived in the south part of inner-city St. Louis where apartment rents were cheap and the public transit system was accessible, but the apartments were plagued by crime and drug abuse. Nevertheless, Ha, Dara, and most of their countrymen were able to move out of the inner city and own houses in the better neighborhoods of the suburbs once they obtained gainful employment and saved enough money. Although they gradually assimilated into American society, the dreadful nightmares of escaping their homelands continued to haunt them.

Although coming from the same country, Vietnamese adoptees had different experiences in America than the refugees. Most were adopted by American Vietnam War veterans who witnessed the plight of the Vietnamese orphans and felt a sense of responsibility. The Vietnamese adoptees came to America as infants and had little knowledge of their birth parents and few ties to Vietnamese culture. Growing up in a predominantly white culture, they perceived themselves as whites as well until they encountered prejudice against them because of their physical differences, as evidenced in the stories of Amy McKee and Jessica Littlewood. The prejudice and discrimination reminded them of their Vietnamese origin, yet they continued to identify themselves as Americans while developing an appreciation of their ethnic distinctiveness.

The interracial marriages of a Lao woman and a Thai woman in this chapter depict equal and supportive relationships within the marriages. Pinmany Danson, a Lao American woman, married a European American she met in Laos, and enjoyed full support from her husband of her undertaking in compiling a directory of Lao in America. Cantana Lopez, daughter of a Thai woman and a former American serviceman stationed in Thailand, testified to her parents' successful marriage.

Like other second-generation or American-grown Asian American women, young Laotian American women often conflicted with the values of their Laotian parents and the ethnic community. Noi Yang, a Hmong American, who was born in Laos but came to America when she was one year old, disagreed with her ethnic Laotian-Chinese mother's values and customs. She felt it was difficult to preserve these traditions while she lived in America.

20

The Refugee Experience

Dung Nguyen was a Vietnamese refugee who fled the country with her cousins by boat in 1975 when she was fourteen. The rest of her family remained in Vietnam. She lived in Florida, Kentucky, Chicago, and Missouri and was married to a Vietnamese American. She and her husband and children lived in a city in Missouri at the time of the interview in 2003.

In Vietnam, where I am from, there are basically two religions—Buddhism and Catholicism. I was born a Catholic. My father worked for the government in forestry. He checked people who cut down trees and shipped them. He checked paperwork. He was a civil servant. His office was closed down because it was overrun with Vietcong. My mother stayed at home with the children; they had four boys and four girls. Only my brother and I got out. We had a house in Diem Van, outside of Saigon. There was an American army base nearby in Lam Bien, about a ten-minute walk away. For a while, my father and sisters and I lived in Ca Mau, at the far south point of Vietnam. We came back in April when the war really started getting worse.

On April 29, 1975, it was decided that I should flee. It was about five o'clock in the afternoon the day before Saigon fell. I was fourteen then. There was an American ship in international waters outside Vietnam that my parents instructed me to go to if I got the chance and they would meet me later. I wasn't worried because I was never by myself; I was always with someone else.

My four cousins and I went to a small Chinese merchant ship in Saigon. It only held a couple hundred people. Most were getting ready to move their families back to China or Hong Kong, out of the war. We jumped on. I thought we were going to one of the islands of Vietnam to get out of harm's way because there was fighting everywhere. I never thought we were going to America. If I did, I never would have gone. I would have been too afraid to do that. That was the day before we found out we had lost the war.

The Chinese weren't really helping us, they were trying to get themselves out; everybody was trying to get away from the North Vietnamese. We just happened to jump on the ship and there was space for us. We were all packed on very tight. I slept standing up. A couple days later, after we gave them all of our Vietnamese money, the Chinese dropped us off on a pontoon, like the ones the American army travels in from their big ships to land. The Chinese ship couldn't dock with an American ship because the American ships were so huge and would smash it. The Chinese didn't want to take us to Hong Kong, and we didn't want to go with them either. We were left there and waited until an American ship came and transferred half of the people; women, the elderly, and the sick went first. Later, during the night, another ship came, a merchant ship, which took the rest of us. We hadn't had water for over twenty-four hours. We scrounged for rice on the floor of the pontoon because we were so hungry.

We had to walk on a gangplank up onto the American ship. It was really high and scary. As soon as we got on, they gave us water, because we hadn't had any, and a C ration, what the American armies eat, I think. I think that the American government might have prepared them because they were carrying all kinds of C rations, so we all got a box. We went down two or three levels to stay wherever we could find a little space to lay our blankets out.

This ship went to the Philippines. It was such a long trip that some of the elderly, women, and children got sick. They had to restock their supplies because there were so many of us. They left the sick people in the Philippines. Then we went to Guam or Wake Island; I stopped at Guam Island. We got off and the Red Cross helped us register. We didn't speak English, so there was no way to communicate with the Americans. The army gave us hot food—rice, Spam, and fruit cocktail. I remember because I didn't know how to eat those things yet. We don't usually eat sweet and salty on the same plate. We would run away after they gave us the Spam and rice before they could scoop out the fruit cocktail. They thought it was funny.

They put each family in tents where we slept. They brought our things to us in shopping carts. We wanted to carry our own things, but a soldier

Above, Guam tent city in the early stages of the emergency parole program for Vietnamese refugees, 1975 (Courtesy of INS).
Below, Vietnamese refugees wait in tent shelter outside service's processing center, Fort Indiantown Gap, Pennsylvania, 1975 (Courtesy of INS).

would not let us. He carried them and put them in the tent we chose. The next morning, we had breakfast and then they put us on airplanes and we flew to Wake Island where we got to stay in a little house. It was also a barracks for the American army. That night we got a cot and a sheet—a white sheet. We took it and made pajamas out of it. We had a bucket with soap, shampoo, and personal items in it. We had to register again. We were checked for tuberculosis and lice. Then we got shots.

When we first came to America, we were flown to Fort Chaffee in Arkansas, another army base. There we were matched up with sponsors who had signed up in their churches or with the Red Cross, and then we got to go wherever they were. We didn't need proof of residency because we all came in as refugees. When I registered myself, I also registered my family, my parents and my brothers and sisters, so they could contact me if they came. They knew where my brother was living, and they gave me an envelope with his address on it. He was living in Pendleton, Pennsylvania. I wrote to him and told him our cousin and I were going to Florida and gave him our address. He wrote back and we kept in touch.

Our sponsor lived in Tallahassee, Florida. We stayed with a man who owned a music shop for two months. He sold pianos and guitars. I think they had a daughter that was two years younger than me. There, only one cousin and I stayed together. My other cousins stayed somewhere else. After a while, they rented us an apartment and found jobs for my cousins while I went to school.

I first went to eighth grade four days a week. Half the day was spent with the other children, and the other half with the GIs learning English. The first day I went to school, I met two other Vietnamese girls who went there. There was also an American who spoke Vietnamese that helped us learn English, which we didn't know at all. I think he was in the army. Every day I rode the bus with the sponsor family's daughter. Every day at lunch all the girls would surround the three of us; I think the teacher told them to. They would teach us English. They would point to their nose and say "nose," and point to their ears and say "ears," and we would repeat what they said or else they would keep repeating it until we did. The next thing I knew, I could understand and speak English. I guess it is because I listened to it and absorbed it; I had no formal training. But to this day, I still do not know grammar.

Sometimes I would be harassed by kids at school. Some children would call me Chink, but they didn't really understand what it meant. I believe that once you go into a small town where there's less of a cultural mix, there is more discrimination. When I first went to Lexington, Kentucky, there were not a lot of Vietnamese there besides my brother. I would be called names all the time and one time I got in a fight on the bus because a boy touched my bottom. I slapped him on the face. I think he got expelled. My husband has a stutter and people always left the water cooler when he stopped by to talk with them because it made them so uncomfortable. This went on for a year, but now his coworkers know my husband and they get along better.

When we lived in Chicago, there were all kinds of nationalities there and everyone had their own area. But there were so many different people there, you could turn around and see a German, or a Chinese, or a Vietnamese, and it would be no big deal; people grew up that way, so they treated everyone the same. There were more opportunities there. A manager could promote you simply for doing a good job. But here in Missouri, it is so American that there's a certain ceiling I can't cross because I don't have the support of my friends and family. It's harder when I stick out like a sore thumb. I am tall for a Vietnamese woman, almost five feet four inches. People usually mistake me for being either Spanish or Korean, but they never guess right. If people ask me where I'm from, I tell them I am originally from Vietnam. But if they ask in a discriminating way, I tell them Kentucky.

After a while I wrote to my brother and told him I wanted to come live with him because my cousin wasn't treating me very well. Finally my cousin gave me a one-way ticket to Kentucky, so I went there to live with my brother who was with a bunch of friends at the University of Kentucky Newman Center. They didn't like a girl living with so many boys, so they found a family for me to live with who had a daughter my age. These were the Galiskis. The father was the president of a big company and they were really rich. I had my own room and everything.

My life in America was easier in some ways. In Vietnam, every time I came home from school, I had to do the shopping and housework and watch my brothers and sisters. At first we had a maid to do all that, but after my sister got older my mother said she had to start learning to be a good wife. So my mother let go of the maid and had us do all the work. That's when I was twelve. We were shy. We would always hide when company came over. My mother would have to ask us to come out so we could serve drinks. It was always the girls who were supposed to bring drinks and I was always the one who had to do it. When I came to America, I always wanted to help out, but the family said they didn't want me to do that. They didn't want me to feel like a maid, they already had one. I only had to vacuum. In Vietnam, because of all the dust, we had to sweep two or three times a day and mop twice a day. So vacuuming once a week was easy.

At first I didn't have any chores to do when I lived with the family and neither did their children. But after they saw me always clearing the table after dinner, they gave each of us a job to do around the house. They also gave us an allowance. I was raised to help out at home and not to complain about the food I was given. Sometimes I would not know what I was eating, but I would never ask for anything else. I still would not do that. I learned to happily accept what I was given instead of asking for something else. Sometimes I would just not eat certain food and go hungry.

When I was in Vietnam, I was expected to finish high school, then marry, have children, and stay at home. I was expected to know how to make soap, to sew, to cook, to do the shopping; there were not a lot of options for women. I never planned on becoming anything. I always dreamed of becoming a teacher, but I didn't want to go to college. When I came to America, I realized I could become anything I wanted and could go to school as long as I wanted. I was able to finish college, which made my parents really proud. Then I got married. I did marry a Vietnamese man. My mother didn't think it would last because I had become so Americanized. My husband and I are equals, but I still have a traditional inclination. He works now and I don't; I take care of everything at home. When we both had jobs in Chicago, we both had chores, but I still did most of the housework because I felt it was my duty as a woman.

Being from Vietnam, I always think of the Japanese as being an older group of immigrants. It seems like more of them head big companies or are managers; they seem more advanced than us, at the top of the ladder. I feel like Vietnamese are on the lower half of the ladder because the newer immigrants move slower. But in other ways, it is easier for us because the doors have already been opened.

In Vietnam, children are supposed to be seen and not heard. They always do what their parents tell them. I raised my children in a Vietnamese and American way. I think they are a little confused because I expect them to be respectful and to obey me, but I also want them to be independent. I have taught them to clean the tables and bring water when guests come over. I think they also confide in me, which does not happen between parents and children in Vietnam. The parents tell the children what to do and they listen. They don't ask about school or their friends or their feelings. But I ask them about that stuff all the time. We have a good bond. I don't want my children to have the same feeling of obligation that I do towards my parents, having to always make them happy and take care of them.

I do miss Vietnam a lot. I miss my family and the chance to get to know them. When I left, one of my brothers was only a year or two old and I never knew him. I went back about four years ago and I knew he was my brother, but we had no connection. It is the same with my mother. I don't know if I would say that I love her. I think I missed something. Between the ages of fourteen and twenty, a child really blossoms, and I wasn't there with her. I think I lost my childhood during the war. I can't remember being happy and carefree. The war divided my family. I don't think my mother loves me as much as my sister who stayed with her. I send my mother money and talk to her every once in a while, but I don't have the same feelings that I have for my American mother. I talk to her on the phone once or twice a week; I know everything she's doing.

If I stayed in Vietnam, I don't think I would be the same person I am today. I have had a better life here in terms of happiness. My husband and I have a relationship where we can talk, we can share, we can laugh. I don't think it would have been like that in Vietnam. I don't think I would be with someone who really knows who I am. I know that because I am here, my children have a chance at a better future.

Ha Che was born in Cambodia in 1932 to ethnic Chinese parents and moved to Vietnam with her parents in 1952. She and her children came to America in 1975 as Vietnamese refugees. She lived in St. Louis, Missouri, and worked for the International Institute of Metro St. Louis at the time of the interview in 1999. Her recollections of life in Vietnam and adjustments to life in America provide a vivid account of Vietnamese American experiences.

I was born in Cambodia in 1932 and my parents moved us to Saigon, Vietnam, when I was twenty years old. My father worked for the Vietnamese government and my mom was a housewife. I have four sisters—two are in the United States and two are in Vietnam. I acquired a college education in Vietnam, receiving a degree in social work and nursing. After 1981, I began working towards my master's degree in social work. I did not finish it because I had to take care of my children.

Life was peaceful in Cambodia. Our ethnic group was the majority so it was easy to live. Everyone knew everyone else and we had a lot of friends in Cambodia. I lived there until 1952, when we moved to Vietnam. We felt lost in Saigon, but the living situations were similar. Life was good in the 1950s and 1960s; but I found out life was different there from what I was used to.

In 1954, Vietnam was divided into two parts. Communists from North Vietnam came in—we had not been exposed to them before. People were running away from the Vietcong with the help of Americans. Old people stayed in the North because they did not want to go. They let young people leave. Most Catholics left because they no longer had their freedom of religion. Most rich people and intellectuals left as well because they were not liked either. This rush of people made South Vietnam more crowded. I do not think the South Vietnamese complained about it; in fact, they were trying to help. We helped each other.

Life in Saigon was prosperous in the 1960s and early 1970s. People moved from the countryside to big cities where it was safer. Communists, known as Vietcong, moved into the country; they were spread all over. The Vietcong would come and terrorize people during the night. Vietnamese people were caught between two political parties. One party was the Communists and the other, the Nationalists—they came and looked for the Communists. Consequently, people started to leave in fear. They went to the city to look for jobs. It was hard to get jobs; there were a lot of unemployed people. Saigon was crowded as a result. I felt the impact of the war when I lived there. For a while, we had to live in shelters because the Communists could attack at any time. You never knew when you would be hit.

There were many United States servicemen in Saigon and other big cities. People liked them because they created more jobs for us. They employed Vietnamese in their stores to serve them. Most girls worked in bars. It is hard to say exactly how they treated Vietnamese because everyone was different. Many girls got involved with American soldiers. Some married them, some did not. Some even became prostitutes, but most did not.

I got married in 1956. I continued to work after I got married. Because of the war, the social situation in Vietnam changed. Men went to war and women worked. Life changed especially for those who were educated because they were able to leave the home to go to work. Most of them did not want to stay at home anyway.

It was common practice that once a girl got married, she stopped going to school. About 30 percent of girls went to college. The rest of the girls married wealthy men guaranteeing that they would not have to work. Some people went to college to meet other people. Most of those who got married had arranged marriages. I met my husband on my own and he was serious about marriage, so we got married. In our country, we do not date. If you have a friend, he or she would commonly act as a matchmaker.

Even though I did not find my husband through the help of a friend, I did find my job through one. I had a friend who worked for a volunteer agency; there was an opening and she asked me to join. I had a nursing degree at the time. With a nursing education, they let you work for six months and after that you can become a registered nurse. After another six months, you can become a social worker. Nursing and social work are very closely related. I graduated in 1954 with a nursing degree and I later got training in social work. I worked as a social worker until 1975 (when the whole country fell to Communism). I worked to help the poor.

We were middle class and were well respected. Some middle-class people stayed after the Communists took over but rich people left. Many left because of the lack of freedom. They feared for their lives from the Communist Northern army. We never thought of leaving Vietnam to go somewhere else. If the Communists had never come, we would never had left.

In 1975, boat people started coming to America and everyone had a terrible story. I have heard stories of people escaping on boats because living conditions were so bad. It was a secret in the beginning. People who organize the trip only took ounces of gold. On the boat there is danger, especially while going through Thailand, because pirates would come and steal anything valuable, including clothes. There were also terrible storms. I have heard stories about people who drank urine when there was no water on the boats. People would rather risk their lives than live under Communist rule.

We flew out of Saigon three days before it fell. Saigon was in chaos when we left. We did not know anything about the future; we were lost. I left with my four children. My husband was an officer in the army and because of that, we were upper class. He helped to provide transportation for our family. We first went to the island of Guam and then to the United States.

We left Vietnam with a twenty-four-hour notice. We could not bring everything. I had only a small bag for each person and a change of clothes.

I didn't have any makeup. We lived in a camp on Guam Island for two weeks for security clearance purposes. After that, they moved us to another camp in California. Then we went to Arkansas to wait for a sponsor. I stayed in that camp for six weeks.

I did not like the conditions in the camps. You have to get in line for food. It was humiliating; I did not want to be in line. I had just one meal a day. I talked with people and looked for friends inside the camp. There was a bus that brought in newcomers every once in a while and I found friends there. You do not know what your future holds while you are in the camps. Many people were depressed.

Finally we were allowed to leave the camp because someone had agreed to sponsor us. When I met my sponsor, I had a lot of questions to ask her. I asked her: How would people receive me? Were there jobs for me and schools for my children? Most Asian women wanted to live off men. But I was there on my own, supporting my children. My sponsor lived in Bay, Missouri (near Hermann, which is a farming area). We stayed with her for one year. She was responsible for our living expenses that year. The government gave her $500 per person one time to help with our costs. I still keep in contact with my sponsor.

During my first year in the United States, I worried a lot, especially about money. I did not have any money. I did not know how to find a job or how to survive. Many of my friends had the same feelings. I went to a psychologist for a few sessions, but did not continue because I did not have money. Financially and culturally, you have to start over again as a refugee; like a child, you have to relearn everything. You suffer from mistakes you make and learn from them.

My sponsor provided everything for us for the first year because I did not have a job. I did not like just receiving things; it was not balanced (though I appreciate my sponsor very much for everything she did). I do not like depending on anyone; it is especially not good for the children. Everyone has the right to raise their children and if you let others provide for them, it is not good.

I told my son I wanted to be his parent and friend. My son said I could not be a friend; I could only be a parent. I cried a lot at night, but I never cried in front of my children because I wanted them to be free of worry. Many of my friends are the same way. Many Vietnamese kids are motivated because for them nothing is easy. It helps them to succeed. You appreciate what you have. If you are rich, you do not need anything and therefore lack the motivation.

I have spoken English since high school. I worked for an American volunteer agency in Vietnam where I learned to speak English. But when I came to the United States, I still had a language problem. I could read and speak, but it took time for people to understand my accent, even though I could understand theirs. The first few years I was here, I regretted leaving Vietnam, but I do not think I had any other choice. It took me a long time to adjust.

My sponsor is a Christian so she had humanitarian reasons for taking me in. She has sponsored two other families. One of them came for a short while and then moved because there were no jobs available for them. Because we lived in a rural area, there were not a lot of jobs that I could do so I spent time writing my resume. My sponsor had a housekeeper so I followed her throughout the day to learn how to use the household machines such as a vacuum cleaner and a washer and dryer. I even tried to learn to cook American food. Her family was very wealthy—her husband had a turkey business.

I did not have a job for a year because I did not have a car and could not drive. When I got a car, I began working for the University of Missouri–Columbia doing social work. I worked there for three months. In 1976, we moved to St. Louis and lived near South Grand. I got a job with Lutheran Family Services. In 1977, I began working for the International Institute in Columbia where I stayed for three years switching between it and Lutheran Family Services. I began working as a caseworker for International Institute and then became a case management coordinator. In 1980, I began working for the International Institute in Columbia. I worked in Columbia from 1980 to 1986. The reason I went to Columbia was because my eldest son attended the University of Missouri–Columbia. I also went to California for three months in 1980. I left my children here because they were all in school. When the program in Columbia phased out, I came back to St. Louis in 1986.

There are 10,000 Vietnamese people living in St. Louis. Most of them live in South St. Louis, but they are starting to move to West County and North County. Vietnamese were overcrowded south of Grand and therefore businesses began booming. When I came to St. Louis, I lived in South County where the housing was cheaper. Being a single woman living in the city is scary. I live in Bridgeton now, a middle-class neighborhood with a lot of senior citizens; it is not that noisy. The houses are not fancy, but are

*Ha Che, former Vietnamese refugee and case management coordinator at
International Institute of Metro St. Louis, interviewed by Huping Ling, 1999.
Huping Ling Collection.*

affordable and comfortable.

In Vietnam, we owned our own house but here we rent. We liked
owning our own house. That is why many Vietnamese like to own a house
rather than living in an apartment. They start in apartments when they get
their first jobs and move up to owning their own houses. In apartments,
there are many restrictions and I do not even want to hang up a picture for
fear that the owner would charge me for it later.

From my observations, I think that the United States is an insecure
country. If you do not have a job, you cannot afford insurance. In Vietnam,
this is not something to worry about because your relatives will take care of
you. We did not have nursing homes or psychiatrists in Vietnam; Catholic
nuns had free shelters for the elderly. A nursing home was just another
place to go to have someone help take care of you. People accept nursing
homes easier now than when I was younger. Older Vietnamese do not

want to be a burden to their children, so they go to nursing homes. It is hard to plan for retirement for my generation. You still have to provide for your children and establish yourselves in this country. The next generation will be able to plan better for their elderly.

Now I have worked at my job for over a year in which I serve the elderly in the community. I am the coordinator of the program. I try to coordinate projects where I help seniors pass their citizenship test so they can receive Social Security benefits. I also work for senior resource links, like their senior centers. I do have contact with other Vietnamese in St. Louis through my job. I get to know them. I am serving the community through the institute.

When I first came here, I felt I could do a lot of things. But as time passed, I lowered my expectations and have tried to cope with new ways of life. A lot of people cannot cope with the new ways. When I began working here, I saw a lot of situations. I try to help the people, not with material things, but how to cope, especially with old people. I see more problems than before.

A common problem among Vietnamese elderly is that they are lonely and cannot communicate with each other. Transportation is a problem because they cannot drive—it is too expensive. Most do not own cars and cannot maintain them, therefore they are homebound. Even doing simple tasks like laundry is difficult for them. They can get rides from their children if they have any, or from their neighbors, or they take the bus. They come to the International Institute by bus. Another common problem Vietnamese have in the United States is their everyday interaction with people and their difficulty with that.

No one has committed suicide because of depression. Younger people have had to deal with crises in their lives. Overall, when people come to the United States, they enjoy their freedom. They have found that the more they work, the more money they get and no one controls them. In Vietnam, the Communist government controlled everything. It was a regime for poor people and rich people had to hide their money.

My older clients in general are not demanding. They try to cope with all kinds of situations. They are quiet. We Asians are more peaceful than vocal. I have some concerns because most do not speak English. I try to help them assimilate, but I do not think I can serve them in that way. The best example is their food. In the community, they have all kinds of help in centers. They have a senior center where they can go and socialize. They can have food there, but my people do not want to go because of the transportation. They do not like American food; the elderly eat Vietnamese food. They do not want to try. I am trying to provide some information and comfort for them so they can accept their situation. Even if you are not happy living here, you still have to make the effort. Senior people do not feel very happy, but at least here, you have freedom, and living conditions are much better.

I have four children. They are aged thirty-six to forty-two years. I raised them single-handedly. They are all married, all have college degrees, and are all employed. One of my children is a chemical engineer, the second is an electrical engineer, the third has a bachelor of arts in fine arts, and the fourth is a computer specialist. They all graduated with their BA from the University of Missouri–Columbia. All of my children can speak and read Vietnamese. They came to the United States as teenagers, so they had already learned their ethnic language. They are concerned about their children and keeping them bilingual, but they all married Vietnamese spouses. My children now live in Maryland, Indiana, and Texas.

I have been alone since 1975. I never thought about remarrying, I just think about my children. Once I got past the age of fifty, I never really considered it again. My children appreciate my sacrifice. They are now Americanized. What I like most about living in the United States is the freedom and the opportunities we have to become what we want. We have choices here. My children say you should do whatever you feel, and whatever makes you happy. But if I were to choose to do anything, they probably would not like it. Another thing that I like about this country is that your future is in your hands. You can become what you want to.

Many of my friends can speak Vietnamese and all of their children do as well. Eighty percent of others who came over with me have children who have gone on to be successful. Education is important to Asians.

There are a few Vietnamese social organizations. One or two put on social events for the most important holidays such as New Years. We have a Buddhist temple at North Grand and I-70. I am a Buddhist. I go to temple once in a while, but not very often because we do not have a monk there. We have a master every other week. One of my children is a Catholic. Once born, you are supposed to be Buddhist but mostly we worship our ancestors. On the death anniversary, I burn incense at the altar in my home. I prepare a meal to offer people. I invite friends to celebrate and to remember the dead and what they did for us. It gives us an occasion to get together. In my family, we like to talk about what our parents did for us. It is part of our culture.

We still have extended family in Vietnam, but my nuclear family is here in the United States. I am close to my children. I talk to them a lot; my telephone bill is high. I talk to them in Vietnamese, but my grandchildren do not speak Vietnamese. When I first came here I tried to talk to my children in Vietnamese but my sponsor said, "You should talk to them in English so they learn the language." I said, "I don't worry about English. They will learn that at school." If we do not speak it at home, they will lose it.

This country is very materialistic. In my country, life was slower. We had time with our families and children. I have not gone back to visit. It is not hard to go back now; I do not want to because my parents passed away and my sisters have their own lives—they have never come here. I have invited them to come but it is hard. I have kept a good memory of my country, but now things have changed a lot and I do not want to see that. Vietnam is different.

I want to retire here. I do not think I could cope with the regime. The reason we came was because of freedom. I have plenty to do when I retire. I plan to travel, visit my kids and my friends. I feel you need to be busy so you do not get rusty. To avoid that, I am trying to write my family history. When I first came here I wanted to maintain my language and culture. But I cannot because it is difficult and it is not practical. I asked my grandchildren to call me grandma in Vietnamese *Ba noi* or *Ba Ngoai*.

I combine both Vietnamese culture and American culture. I try not to go against the mainstream. My children and grandchildren will be a part of the melting pot. I let them do things they feel comfortable doing, but I tell them not to let other people affect what they do, for example, by giving them a strange look. I do not want them to forget their roots.

Beth Pham was born in Qui Nhan, Vietnam, in 1975. Her recollections of her family's escape from Vietnam by boat in 1981 and the subsequent hardships and adjustments to new life in America are compelling and captivating. She was attending Truman State University at the time of the interview in 1996.

I was born on 9 October 1975 in Qui Nhan, Vietnam. I moved from there to Iowa when I was six years old. My whole family, including four brothers and three sisters, came to the United States. In Vietnam, my parents were farmers. At one time, my father worked for the government, I am not exactly sure what he did, except that he did paperwork. My mother was a housewife. Both sets of my grandparents were doctors and they were both rich, so we lived in a mansion.

My father was put in jail after the war because he had worked for the southern government. Since the North won the war my dad was put in prison because anyone affiliated with the southern government before the war was sentenced to certain prison term. My father was sentenced to only two years because his level of involvement was minimal.

During this time, my mother had eight kids to support. She knew she could not support all of us on her own, so she kept my youngest brother who was nine months old and everyone else was separated. I was sent to live with my mom's sister. They gave me what they could, which was not much. We did not eat a lot. The main food was rice and it was not very good rice, but we always had leafy vegetables in our diet. They saved the best for me—each day I got corn or an egg, and that was a big deal. My mother visited me once when I was about three or four. I remember she promised me she would go to the store and get me a dress. I said, "Okay." She never came back. At this time, everyone was suffering from post-war depression and everyone was poor. The next time my mother came to visit me she promised me shoes and I said, "No!" She had promised me everything, but I knew she was not coming back. I hung onto her as she was leaving and she did not know what to do. She knew she could not leave me there so she took me home with her. She still could not support me, so after a couple days she sent me to stay with different relatives.

This time I was to stay with my uncle on my dad's side. I was not as homesick because I was able to be with one sister and two brothers who were also staying with my uncle. It worked out but they were very poor and my brothers and sister worked a lot. We stayed there for about two years until my father got out of jail. I was five years old then. It took us a while to get together and then my dad planned an escape.

I think my dad had been working on this plan for a very long time. He and my uncle had been saving money for a while. My uncle was the captain of a ship or a fishing boat. They, along with other people in the village, put money together and bought another boat—we had all agreed to escape together. One night, I remember it was very foggy, they woke us up in the middle of the night and told us to be quiet. It was really, really late.

One by one my dad gathered us. All the relatives were aware of this and they had their children ready too. We went to the harbor where we met with a lot of people.

The captain of the other boat had to go get more supplies and we went onboard our boat. When the other captain came back he heard a commotion outside—the Communists had discovered the boats, but by then our boat was under my uncle's control. We were able to sail away under the commotion; but two of my brothers were on the other boat. The 130 people onboard their boat hid deeper in the thresholds and did not leave the same time we did. We worked for a long time to save up money to pay back the relatives who bailed them out. It took us seven years to reunite with my brothers.

My uncle knew where he was going and remained confident. We hid at the bottom where they put the fish and crabs. It was very stuffy and crowded. I remember feeling suffocated. A lot of babies were put to sleep with special sleeping pills, but my mother did not want to do that. She gave my brother some milk to make him sleep. She is lucky because when we reached the United States, the mothers who used the pill realized their babies had mental defects as a result.

We first sailed to Malaysia. From there we came to America. Because my dad worked for the United States government, our family had immediate access to the country. We were actually allowed to go to any democratic country, that way the U.S. government could assure our safety wherever we went; it was just up to us to get to these places.

I finally arrived in the United States in October of 1981. I think that the hardships we went through to come to America fueled us with the desire and the drive to get an education. If you go through the trouble of leaving your country and all the hardships that go with it, you are going to be more determined and make the most of every situation. Overall, it depends on what your values are and what they stem from.

After we arrived, my mother and father got into the sewing business. This was very menial work. They sewed for a book bag company called Balance. My siblings and I worked there, too. We tore apart mistakes the sewers made. It paid very low wages, low enough that my family's income was unable to support six kids and to send money back home; therefore, we worked for a very long time.

We moved to Mobile, Alabama, and my dad got a job painting houses but the fumes gave him headaches and he was not able to do that for very long. We had a relative who owned a Chinese restaurant so my oldest sister went to work there. She was the one who took care of everything. She knew English from the school she attended in Vietnam. We sent her to see what the conditions were like. She checked it out and said they were workable, so my parents joined her. They worked there for about five years before my family opened our own restaurant, which we have owned for eight years. It is called Old Lee Chop Suey. My brothers and sisters and I would work there after school.

When I first arrived in America, I started attending school. I was sent back to kindergarten because I did not know my alphabet and I did not speak English very well. I was a year older than those in the class, but I learned the language and adapted well. At first it was difficult growing up with American kids because of the language barrier. I felt like I did not know what was going on. I always felt confused and scared. But as I caught on, I became more and more determined. I built up confidence. I felt like I could fit in if I could become one of the best. I thought this because I thought people looked up to you when you were better then them and showed that you had a talent or something special to distinguish you from the rest.

The living conditions were pretty bad when we first arrived in America. Our clothes came from Goodwill and that is why to this day I always sponsor Goodwill and help out. I believe in charity organizations also because a church sponsored my family. Through them we were able to have a Thanksgiving dinner. When we lived in Kansas City, before we really established ourselves, we lived in a two bedroom home. Four boys slept in one room and four girls in another. The funny thing was that we did not think that there was anything wrong with that. I had friends with whom I went to visit and they had their own room and things like Cabbage Patch dolls and Strawberry Shortcake. I had only one doll, but I was happy. I had more than other people did and my mother always reminded me of that.

I know that a lot of people in Vietnam wish that they had the chance we had in coming here and an opportunity to establish themselves in America. Several of our relatives have asked us if we could sponsor them, but it is not easy. There is a limited number of immigrants that can come to America and those who are fortunate enough to come here work hard. Sometimes I see people sitting around and think of what an incredible country they are living in and the chances they are missing out on to make something out of themselves.

When kids were prejudiced against me it hurt. Kids were cruel in junior high school. They always made fun of everyone else's differences. Sometimes I was hurt by it and sometimes I would keep a positive attitude and think, "One of these days you will see who is better." I have always had a positive mindset and I think that helps in achieving my goals. It is a driving force behind what I do—not to be better, but to prove that I am not stupid. A lot of people look down on minorities and think that they do not have talents, but they do not realize that the only reason we may seem stupid is because of the language barrier. We just need to be given a chance.

I remember in junior high I was called Egg Roll and things like that. One time a kid told my brother that he could not sit next to him. I got so mad that I pulled the kid aside and said, "Don't you dare touch my brother. If you do, I will come after you." He said, "No, I didn't do anything." And I said, "Next time, if he wants to sit there, you are going to let him sit there." I am very protective of my family.

In the eighth grade, we were the new kids in the neighborhood and we had to go through it all again. Every time we were put into new crowds we had to establish ourselves all over again and we had to go through the same kind of prejudicial ordeal. I thought that kids were being prejudiced, but they did not realize the differences and when they made fun they were just acting young and naïve. I kept thinking, "One of these days, you'll see." That day came when I was in high school.

While I was in high school, I was involved in a lot of leadership roles and I won the Coca-Cola scholarship. It was a $20,000 scholarship and the television and press came. Everyone wanted to be my friend—they approached me. One of the guys who discriminated against me when I was in junior high came up and asked if I wanted to go out. I said no because I remembered how he used to be. I am not resentful, I just knew what type of person he was and I do not respect that. I talked to him, but I would never date him.

It was tough being an Americanized child of Vietnamese parents. Everything was okay at first, but when I got to junior high and high school it was really difficult because my parents did not always want us to be influenced by outside things. They would tell us, "Don't think about a boyfriend (or girlfriend)" because the more you go out the more you will be influenced. We were encouraged to hang out with our family and to go to work. But that did not work. My parents believe in honor and status—the biggest one being status. They believe that you should always establish yourself because that way no one can say you are stupid and no one can look down on you. Not only do you represent your family, but you represent your race as well. In my family, race was never a big issue. I do feel prejudices sometimes, but growing up it did not matter because I knew who I was and what my talents were.

My family always told me that they did not want me to date because they thought I would get into trouble. It was hard. My mother is a very traditional lady. She is one who is always saying, "A lady sits like this," and "Girls don't laugh too loud." I always got in trouble for that because I am rebellious. She raised her girls with a lot of manners. She never went into detail about how you should hold your teacup or anything like that, but promoted things like "You don't always go for the best thing first" and "Be considerate." If you are at a dinner, you should try everything at the table because people will think bad things about you if you do not.

There were definite differences between how my brothers were raised compared to my sisters and myself. During the war, they were in Vietnam. I only spent about six years in Vietnam and that was enough to influence me, but I am still not as strong in the culture as they are. They grew up there. My youngest brother is Americanized now, but he still understands the language. I can speak the language and read and write very little. I wish I could read or write more. When I was in Vietnam, I only made it to the kindergarten level—very elementary.

My parents have an intermediate understanding of English. My family and I always did the paperwork for the bills for the restaurant in Vietnamese. We had to speak it back in order for my father to understand us. This has helped me to keep the language; so has talking to my brother.

A couple years ago, my parents went back to Vietnam to see their culture because they knew it would be a while before they would be able to get back again. I was going to go with them, but it was pretty risky. They videotaped some of the things they saw while they revisited Vietnam. I liked the people I saw. They seemed very gentle and very genuine. Outside it seemed very disorganized and rushed. I think a lot of that is in my personality. I think who I am today is not because of the influences of one country or the other, but it is the best of both worlds. I can see what I like of both and put them together.

There are other ways my parents keep us informed about our culture though. I always watch movies about the Vietnam War, the reasons and the causes. I ask my dad questions about it. He gives me the political view of the South and about what he did. He teaches me some things while we watch these movies.

I believe I have a strong connection with my Asian heritage, but I have been very Americanized. On a scale of one to ten, I would say I am about a five and a half. When I am with a Vietnamese person, I can talk to them and feel comfortable. I do not believe it when people say if I were to go back to Vietnam, I would not be a true Vietnamese and here in America, I am not a true American. I do not think it is important to call yourself one thing or another. I have the best of both worlds.

My parents went to high school in Vietnam. There are not a lot of colleges in Vietnam and they are very difficult to get into. Not many women go to college. You can always get a job when you are in high school or with a high school level education. The level of education a high school graduate receives is more intense and students learn more and faster. I knew my multiplication tables when I was in kindergarten. When I came here, teachers thought I was smart, but it was because of what I had learned in Vietnam. It was so funny how the teachers looked at me because I knew my multiplication and division tables. They have yearly exams, whereas we have them every semester in America. They also get tested over four years of studying and they get tested in college. Vietnamese schools focus more on the analytical subjects such as mathematics and chemistry.

One of the culture shocks that has struck me while being here at school is how the students do not respect their teachers. In Vietnam, we always have the utmost respect for teachers. What they say goes, even if you do not agree with them. Teachers are allowed to hit students in Vietnam. I was discouraged from becoming a teacher by my parents when we came here because they told me I had more talents than that and I did not need that kind of disrespect.

At college I do not have much contact with other Asian students. I do not know why, but I feel a little different. I do not know how to talk to them; I do not know the language of people from Taiwan or China. There is only one boy I know who is Vietnamese and I talk to him. I feel like I am making polite conversation. I would say hi but I could never become really good friends with him.

My relationship with my classmates is very good. I love and enjoy all of my science classes and my classmates and we help each other accomplish a lot. I feel very comfortable at this school because my teachers and professors help me a lot.

I can really appreciate the United States after my parents visited Vietnam. There are so many things that are available for you. In other countries, especially Vietnam, there is nothing there for you to grasp. Here, there are so many opportunities. People say we are beginning to lose that and even if you are hardworking you cannot find a job. I do not believe that. In Vietnam, there really are no jobs available.

Almost all of my family members are engineers. My oldest sister is a chemical engineer, two of my brothers are electrical, and my third brother is mechanical. My sister is majoring in business. The sixth child is a pharmaceutical student at UMKC (University of Missouri–Kansas City). My younger brother, who is still in high school, is looking into being a veterinarian. I am looking into pre-med but I am also interested in international business. I would like to stay in the Midwest when attending medical school. I am thinking about going into pediatrics and family-oriented areas. I would settle for becoming a family physician. Money is not the motivating factor. Medicine is a highly respected profession in my country and my dad wants us to fulfill that aspect with our careers.

I think that college experiences in America are better in the respect that there is so much financial aid available to help students, whereas in Vietnam, if you do not have money you do not have any options. The country only requires education up through the fifth grade and if you want to go on, you have to compete for positions and take entrance exams. Their schools are more intense and grueling. Of all educational systems that I know of, I have to say that America's is the most lenient and the government is very supportive of its students.

I suppose I belong to an intellectual family. I think we are all hard workers because we all know that my parents are not able to afford to send eight kids to college and so we all shoot for full-ride scholarships. I believe you only live once and so I try to do what I can. I love to read. I think it has helped my English considerably. I also like shopping, sailing, and traveling. I love crafty and creative stuff, too.

I work a couple places on campus for my scholarship hours. I work at Time Out (To give Interest in Multi-cultural Environment, with Outreach and Unity in Thought) and I am a teacher's assistant for an ecology class for one of my professors. My Time Out coworkers and I are always debating over issues, but we get along very well because we respect each other's opinions. The organization helps me experience what other races feel, what they go through and what they experience. I like working as a TA because it is a good resume builder, it keeps me occupied and around people, and I am glad that I have a chance to influence students. I do not get a lot of stress from working as a TA, but I do with my classes and grades. Those are the things that take up a lot of time and emotion because I put a lot of pressure on myself to do well.

I always call my boyfriend when I am stressed. He thinks I am brilliant and he always builds me up. My family helps, too. If I do not think I can do something, they are there to comfort me and tell me it will all be okay. My sorority sisters are also there to help me release most of my stress.

As in any group, in my sorority I have found my own group that fits with my personality. Although I am friends with most people, there are a few with whom I am best friends. If I was not in a sorority, I would be a lot lonelier. It allows me to be involved and be a part of things.

I do not feel that being a woman has much bearing on me as a person and what I choose to do; at least not as much as my Asian background does. I am not so much influenced by society as I am from my family. I believe you have to establish yourself firmly as a person and that a good education is extremely important to have so that if you have to take care of yourself in the future, you are able to. Things like affirmative action bother me. If people are fighting for equal rights, then why do we provide special privileges for people? Even though programs like that are designed to help people like me, I do not feel that we are establishing justice. I think that it is up to each individual person to help make the change because when the government forces people to be accepted against their will, then there will be resentment. Sometimes people get carried away in using the color of their skin to get what they cannot accomplish themselves.

My parents would not let my sisters date while they were in college. I am a junior now and I have a boyfriend. I do admit, though, that dating does take time away from my studies. I got two Bs and I was freaking out because I thought my parents would not let me have a boyfriend anymore. Now I am getting three Bs. It is always in the back of our minds and we know that we should always do our best. All of my brothers and sisters graduated with honors and I want to be a part of that, too, because I do not want to break the mold. Although I want to be like them, I have never been in competition with my brothers and sisters. We have always been helpful toward each other. They are good role models for me.

I am dating a Phi Kappa Pi guy and have been lavaliered. The reason that I love him is because he accepted me from the very beginning for who

I am. He loves my culture even though he does not know much about it, because it is a part of me. He is trying to learn my language—that is cute. That impressed my parents. I get along with his mom very well. Both our parents have met each other and they really, really love each other. He really supports me in everything I do. The most important thing is that he puts my happiness above all else. We have very good communication. Because I am more fluent in English than in Vietnamese, I prefer American men. I also like the features of American men and bigger built guys. Asian guys are smaller.

When I get older, I definitely plan to have children. I plan to instill a part of my culture into them. Mixing cultures in children is something my sister is going through right now because she is pregnant and her husband is American. I plan on trying to teach my language to my own children.

I think family is very important. The differences between Vietnamese and American families were also a source of culture shock to me. We have so much here in America and kids growing up here take it all for granted. They do not use the abundance of resources offered to explore their potential and consequently there are broken families because they grow up to be irresponsible adults. In Vietnam, we have irresponsible adults, too, but everyone knows what their values and morals are. We are losing that because the family unit is not strong.

Our family was really close because of our living conditions—we were always bumping into each other. When we got a bigger house, we were still close, but it allowed everyone to do his or her own thing. We have come a long way, as everyone has their own television in his or her own room. But we are still reminded not to take things for granted.

My own relationship with my parents is a very good one. I am very close to them. I do not tell them everything, like American kids do, because there are certain boundaries you do not cross and it is established that parents and children are not friends. The reason that the family unit is strong in Vietnam is because of the respect children hold for their parents. I would never call my mom names because that would make me feel bad. Not only would it make her look bad, but it would make me look bad for having such disrespect toward my family. You do not bring your family name down. We also respect our older siblings. It is different for my youngest brother because he is Americanized. My older sister could ground me if she wanted to and I would have to obey her.

An aspect of our lives that has changed because of coming to America is that of religion. When we were in Vietnam, we were Buddhists, but because the Christian church sponsored us we changed our religion; we are now Christians. Our Sundays were completely taken by church activities. In the mornings, we went to a Christian church—not that we understood a word of the sermon, but we felt holy—and after that we crossed the street and went to a Vietnamese church because their services did not start until noon. Afterwards, we went home for dinner. It was like that in Iowa and Alabama. Now everyone is gone and my parents go to a church that is bigger and everyone is not as close. I go when I can, but I do not go as often as I used to. I am still close to God, but it is just between him and me and does not involve so much worshipping at a church.

———————◆◆◆———————

Dara Phannarath was born in Vientiane, Laos, in the 1950s. She, her husband, and their three-year-old son escaped Laos in 1979. They stayed in a refugee camp in Thailand for a year and finally joined their sponsor in St. Louis, Missouri, in 1981. She worked for the Lao Mutual Aid Association and lived in St. Louis at the time of the interview in 1999.

I was born in Vientiane, Laos, in the 1950s. My dad had a college education in France that was enabled by a government grant. My dad worked for the Lao customs service; it was a good government job. My mom had middle-school education and was a housewife with old skills of weaving and looming. Her life was affected by the war; she escaped from highland to lowland (she is a Hmong). We had a good life as middle class in Laos. There are three children in my family and I am the middle one. My brother is three years older than me and my sister is two years younger than me. My brother went to a university and later became a teacher. My parents escaped Laos in 1975 and are now in Paris.

During the war, I was ten. I remembered when I escaped from the city to the countryside. After the war, I came back to our house. We started over again and my dad still worked for the customs.

I went to kindergarten, high school, and college in Laos. I first worked at a private school, then at a Lao travel agency. From 1976 to 1979, I worked for the United Nations as a secretary of the Food Organization (FO). The FO helps the Lao with medicine to fight mosquitoes, to improve fish, and to save children. My boss at the FO was an expert from France. To be a secretary, one has to know two foreign languages. I learned French at high school. The second language was English or Russian and I picked English. French was popular in Laos. If you speak French, it means you are educated and you can get a job easily.

I got married in 1976. My husband worked for the government. He was a professor in Laos, teaching electricity and math. My husband told me we should leave since the Communists were taking over and life was getting worse. The government controlled everything. Everything imported from the outside was stopped. Everything started new. People worked in the fields and dug ditches. If you did not work, you could be sent to the labor camp. No one trusted each other. If you talked about politics, they could come to arrest you.

I left Laos in November 1979 with my son when he was three years old. My husband came from work and couldn't find us, so he was very sad. One week later, he followed and found us. He walked across the border.

We went to Mekong River, where the soldiers were stationed. There were four families in a canoe, including seven adults and three children. We were all shivering. I didn't bring much with us, just a few shirts. Water entered the boat. We then crossed a tomato field. We stayed in a temple. I paid $100 to a guy who helped smuggle us to Thailand. Later we were caught by a truck driver. He said, "You are escaping and you are illegal." He took us to jail. One side of the jail was for women and the other side for men. We were detained there for two or three days. They asked about our backgrounds and took our pictures. Then we were sent to a camp in Nong Khai, Thailand, and my husband came to join me.

At camp, I went to school. It had sewing and cooking classes; it also had an English class. People from outside came to sell goods. We could go outside with permission. The Thai government ran the camp and Thai Catholic nuns helped the refugees. Conditions in the camp were not good; it was not safe and you were on your own. There were smugglers and robbers there, and you could get killed for $5 or $10. If you died, no one cared. Thai people did what they wanted to do. You had no way to fight back. No matter how upset you were, you had to keep it inside. It was tough. Once a week, we could get chicken and rice. Only one tenth of the money from UN reached us, the rest went to the corrupted Thai government.

We stayed at the camp for a year. We first applied to go to Canada, but it didn't work. Then we applied for the United States. They came to do physical exams. We got a sponsor in St. Louis. Six of us—myself, my son, my husband, and three of his nieces—came to St. Louis in January of 1981. We

Dara Phannarath, Project Director, Lao Mutual Aid Association, St. Louis, Missouri, interviewed by Huping Ling, 14 June 1999. Huping Ling Collection.

were not properly dressed for the season and it was first time we saw snow.

Our sponsor was very nice and we had a four-bedroom apartment. Three months later, I started to work for Lutheran Family Service as an interpreter. My husband worked part time for the International Institute. Later on, there were budget cuts at the Lutheran Family Service and I lost my job there. Then I worked for the International Institute. I also worked for a tailor and other odd jobs. In 1986, I started working full time for the Laotian community and served the Lao Mutual Aid Association (Lao MAA) as an interpreter. Later on I found a full-time job at the South Technical High School translating and helping Laotian students. I want to help Laotian students to become engineers and I see them with potential in engineering careers. I hope to send my children there some day.

Life was strange to me, since we had our old tradition. When we went grocery shopping, I bought a lot. I also cook a lot. I didn't know how to budget money. In our country, I didn't pay rent. Driving was not easy for me either. We bought a used Volkswagen since the grocery store was far away in South Grand. We didn't worry about driving since my husband knew how to drive; he learned this skill while he was studying in France. The ways people looked at you were different. Some welcomed you, some didn't. Church people were kind. We didn't know how to speak English. That was good; otherwise, there would be a big fight. Our grass was high and we didn't know how to cut it. Students made a shortcut in our back-yard and we didn't know what to say. We had a lot of problems and we had to learn everything. My son liked McDonald's. We watched TV and learned from news. We listened to American music. In Laos, I watched American movies and listened to American music. We attended English class at the International Institute.

My daughter was born in 1983. She is active and loves sports. My daughter is good at math and she is planning to go to a university and become a pediatrician. Both my son and daughter are good at soccer. My son now works for an international company. I speak Lao and English mixed with my children, but I speak Lao with my husband.

My husband works as an instructor for English as a Second Language at a high school and he has worked there for fifteen years. His English is very good now. He is also very good in French. He had a master's degree in electrical engineering in France and he could get a PhD there. He is very bright.

It was not safe to be in Laos. We are lucky to be alive. Coming to the United States, you have more opportunities to be what you want to be. You learn from your mistakes and you adopt good ways. I know my own ways and my own roots. No matter how long we have lived here, we know our tradition. When they see we are hard working people, they should treat us as human beings. We should respect each other.

When I first came, I was criticized for taking the U.S. tax money. I said, you will see. We proved what we can do. People accepted us more and more. You give me respect and I will give you respect, too. We always learn. The more we learn, the better we live. I like to laugh. We don't mean any harm. We are very warm and friendly to anyone. We don't know the word stranger. We talk to strangers in our country.

Initially, we were discriminated against. We went to a restaurant and they didn't serve us. I have been in this situation several times. I forgive them since they didn't know who you were. They looked at your dress and knew you were foreigners because we didn't know how to dress and when to dress formal or casual. I told my clients what they should dress and told them that they had to learn American ways.

One time, my son played soccer and our neighbor called the police and complained. But the neighbor played their radio loudly. If we drive a nice car, they would say you sell drugs to get a nice car.

Initially we rented an apartment or duplex. We had a lot of problems with neighbors. We needed to sleep at night. They smoked drugs; they were high and couldn't sleep. Some neighbors left at three or four in the morning.

Now we live in a house in North County that we bought three years ago. It is twenty minutes from my job here. We have our own garden. We grow beans, cabbage, and flowers. When I come home from work, I am tired and I get relaxed from gardening. We also have our own parking. When we lived in the apartment, we used to fight for a parking space with neighbors.

We are Buddhists. We went to a Buddhist church and met a lot of Lao. There is a Lao Buddhist Association. I am the first woman to direct the Association. If we don't have a grant, I work for free.

I have never gone back to Laos since I came to America. I never had time. Also my children are at school and they would have a hard time adjusting to life in Laos. We just escaped because of hard life there. Now the Communist government in Laos has changed and life is better. It is not as scary as twenty years ago and it is safe to go back as a U.S. citizen. We still have nightmares, but we still miss our country. The past is the past.

I am proud of what I am. You still have to think about your own roots. We cook rice, we cook our own food and we use a lot gingers. I brought some sticky rice to work and people love it. My son loves rice and so does my daughter. That makes life easy. I have learned to cook American food from a cookbook. Sometimes I cook food with cheese.

Lao children are better adjusted. They are more outgoing. They go to school and spend six to nine hours there. They do their own stuff. I brought them to our culture and teach them to respect elderly. The grown-ups are more conservative in our culture. Some are not adapted at all.

I am a community leader and I work for Lao MAA. Lao MAA was established in 1976. We rent a room from the International Institute. If we don't get a grant, the International Institute does not charge us. We help the

Lao with employment, school, and immigration. Many Lao immigrants don't know how to speak English. I do all kind of things for them: go to the hospital, apply for social aid for them to go to school, go to the police, go to jail, do green card and citizenship, sponsor their relatives, file papers of every kind, help write a resume, find a job.... All these services are free for Lao refugees. I get paid by the state's Social Service Department.

I serve about one thousand families or 1,500 Laotians in St. Louis. Some live south of Highway 44 and some in Bridgeton. The majority of them live south of the city, as a grocery store is nearby. Many of them work in factories, such as marble company, light company, and coffee company. Some work in railroad. Some do sewing alteration. Some work in bakery. Thirteen Lao own Chinese restaurants and one owns a bakery. However, the majority are laborers. My husband and I are the only teachers. I teach my knowledge to my people. When I go to the store, people ask me for information and I provide it. Wherever we go, people respect us and we are role models. Helping my people makes me feel good.

Most Lao were from the farming area and don't have any education. They don't speak English, they have to use hand gestures. It will take a long time for them to adjust to their new life in the United States. When I see them happy, I am happy. I can train my clients and feed my knowledge back to my people.

I am thinking I want to be a counselor. I have four years of college education from Laos in English and French. I was also educated in counseling. I also want to become a computer programmer, but I will have to take classes.

We don't have a Lao language school. Some of the Lao MAA Board members would like to have a Lao language school once a week at the International Institute, but their dream has not yet materialized. I can type on my keyboard in both English and Lao. I got my Lao computer program from California.

Most Lao are in California. The majority of the Hmong in the United States are in California, Minnesota, Wisconsin, and North Carolina. I am not familiar with them. Hmong are highland people, and we are lowland people. We have different cultures. We speak a different language and we dress differently. But no matter highland or lowland, we are all from Laos. Usually we are separated. When the Hmong moved out, they adopted our language.

I am an individual agent and I am the only one to work for Lao

MAA. I hired some young workers, but they needed insurance and I couldn't afford it. So I have to work by myself. I have a lot of volunteers, all Lao. When I need help, they will come to the Lao MAA to help me out. We have a community and we have a board. We work together and we fight together. Once a year, we have a party. We have our own musical band and a singer. They work hard for six to seven days to prepare for the party and they have fun. When International Institute has its annual international folk festival, I send my group there to do Lao dance and craft. We don't have picnics. We invite people to our house and share information.

Most Lao in St. Louis live in apartments near South Grand Avenue. There are a lot of apartments here. However, South Grand is not safe and there is too much robbery, burglary, and stealing. Once people save enough money, they move to safer places. Now 50 percent of the Lao own their houses.

Many Lao, about 20 percent, are divorced. The main reason for divorce is gambling. Gambling is an old habit and it is getting worse here. A few committed adultery. I have done a lot of counseling with the divorced families. The kids are jeopardized; they turn to drugs, watch violent TV programs, and lie to their teachers and parents. Many parents come to me for help. This is a major problem of the community.

21

Vietnamese Adoptees

Amy McKee was born in 1975 and was a Vietnamese orphan. She was adopted by an American family, and her adoptive father was a Vietnam War veteran. Growing up, she had been struggling with the problem of her identity. She was studying international marketing at Iowa State University at the time of the interview in 1995.

I was born on 8 January 1975. An American family adopted me when I was five months old. I do not know anything about my birth parents. I have no way of finding out anything about them. I have no real records of who I am because I was born in a tent in a jungle in the middle of nowhere and everyone from there has the same last name. My parents wanted a little Vietnamese girl because my dad was in the Vietnam War and he thought I was so cute. He saw all the needy children when he was there. My parents were put on a waiting list for a Vietnamese child, and one day they got a call that told them to meet me in the Chicago airport in two hours. There I was and there they were; we have been connected ever since.

I have eleven brothers and sisters; seven are adopted and four are biological. My brothers and sisters range in age from ten to twenty-three years old. Seven of us are in college now, the rest are being home schooled. My family is Catholic. I used to go to church every week; I was very devoted to my religion when I was a freshman in college, but now I am not. I have not been to church in about six months.

I have some problems with my identity and how others perceive me. I think being an Oriental in a white family contributes to that. My other brothers and sisters who are adopted and are white have some similar issues. However, it is easier for them to be thought of as my parents' natural kids. I feel as if they are treated differently.

When I was eight years old, my mom put me in Vietnamese classes, but I flunked out. They taught me the alphabet and a few words. I was a total rebel at that age. I hated my parents and I wanted to find out everything I could about Vietnam. I would say, "I'm going back." So they said, "Well, first you have to learn the language," so they took me to the class. It was not really a class; it was just this girl from Vietnam that came over on the same plane as me, who knew a bunch of Vietnamese. When I was in the second grade, we learned about the Vietnam War. I also did a 4-H project on Vietnam last year, but that is the extent of my studying on Vietnam.

I cannot say that I have made the extra effort, recently, to look into the news about Vietnam. I am not really caught up in their culture right now. That attitude might change in a couple years. I used to read all about the wars, but it is too depressing. Now I like America. I am not interested in going back to Vietnam. Well, I suppose I am a little, but I do not think it will be as interesting as going to Europe or somewhere like that.

I went to a public junior high school. My parents were really mad because some of my brothers and sisters screwed up. So my parents put me in a Christian school where I would be protected. The school I moved to was a small Baptist school, and I was Catholic. I got along with the people there okay, but our religions clashed. They did not believe in what I believed in and they tried to make me believe in what they believed in—it was not going to happen. They were white, too. My brother Dan and I were the first minorities to go there.

While I was there, my school put on a production of *Helen Keller*. I had problems with the play director. They wanted to paint my face white because I played the part of Helen. They also wanted to take the little white girls who played the roles of slaves and put black paint or oil on their faces. My dad threw a fit. In the end, no one had to wear any makeup. I was an Oriental Helen Keller! The part of Helen Keller actually went to another girl first, a white girl with blond hair, but she did not have the grades for it, so I got to play the role because I was the only other person to try out for it.

When I went to school there, I dated the pastor's son. The pastor did not like me because I was Oriental and teaching his son things that he should not have been taught. I got suspended from school for three days because we were caught holding hands during lunch. I had to pray for the next four days to God to be forgiven and I had to apologize to everyone in the school.

Now I am attending a state university. I am majoring in international marketing. I want to advertise and market products. I plan on taking a product across the world and distributing it. Several languages are required for my major. I am taking Spanish now and have taken French and Latin in high school. There is a large Oriental population here; I am just one in the crowd. At my previous college, St. Ambrose, I was one of the few Oriental students. Here white is a minority.

I did not get any scholarships here, but I got a lot at Ambrose. They were basically all academic scholarships. I probably got accepted because I am a minority, but I do not think I got any scholarships for that reason. I am paying for the rest of my college education through financial aid because there are so many of my brothers and sisters currently in college.

I do not like the affirmative action laws. I think there is a lot of prejudice out there, but I do not believe that there should be a quota for Asians hired. That is just as stereotypical as anything else. I would not expect to be hired just because I am a minority, just like I knew that I got accepted to Ambrose because I am a minority, along with my being female. I think it is stupid that some people complain "Oh, I was not hired because I am black" or "because I am Oriental." I think the job was not for you then. Why would you want to work there anyway when the people have that attitude and hire you just because they have to meet a quota?

I think people also treated me differently because I am female. I wonder sometimes if I get hired at some places because I am a minority and they have to keep their quotas. I did notice a difference when I worked for President Riverboat Casino, how the Asians got treated compared to everyone else. They had one African American person working on the boat, maybe two, and they got treated very well.

Right now I am unemployed. I am a student. I have worked at HyVee [a local grocery store] in the deli. I have also worked for the St. Ambrose library because I was studious. I worked on the riverboat when I was younger, it was right before they changed the gambling age to twenty-one. I was never teased there because I was Oriental, but I was teased because I was short. There was a lady in particular that came up to me and said, "Oh! Are you Irish?" because of my name on our name badges. I am Vietnamese, and they would ask me if I was Irish! So I cannot say I was never teased.

I have recently been hired to work at Walt Disney World next semester. I will be there from January through May. I will be working for the merchandising department and taking marketing seminars while I am there.

Growing up, there was a time when I was discriminated against for being different. I went on a Catholic retreat in a small town. There was this girl who was in my so-called family and she wrote on my folder, which I still have, "I'm sorry I'm not allowed to like your kind. I wasn't raised to do that." It was really sad and made me mad, it hurt my feelings a lot. I guess there were a lot of people at that retreat that would not talk to me because I was Oriental. I think that was my only real experience with discrimination.

In grade school, I had two Asian American friends. I had a lot at St. Ambrose. People always called us the "Asian Invasions" because we would always stick together. A high school friend of my brother's gave us that nickname. He had gotten it from his football coach, then I just picked it up; it is kind of funny.

I used to complain about my run-ins with racism all the time. Other incidents that were similar to the retreat incident happened, but I cannot recall any now. If people never saw an Oriental person before in their life, it is probably because they have not been exposed to it and then they did not know how to handle it.

Since I have been here, I have been approached by the minority organizations often. When I first came here for orientation, I had to go to a separate meeting than everyone else, and I could not register unless I went to it. This guy who was Japanese talked for forty-five minutes; I could not understand him very well. I had to sit in this room with all these minorities; no one wanted to be there. We were all mad because we had to go to this meeting and no one else did. All they said was welcome to the campus, you are a minority and we are here for you. Then every day they would call. I do not want to be a part of their group. It is not that I hate minorities, but I do not have time for the groups. If I want to be in their group, I will let them know.

At Ambrose, it was the cultural groups that acted differently. The African Americans would sit here, the Orientals sit there, and the white people sit somewhere else in the cafeteria. It was always segregated and very seldom did we mix or mingle. There was such a diversity problem at Ambrose. It was really bad. It was always blacks against the whites and the Orientals against the blacks. Because it was a private college, everyone who went there was rich, except for me. There was so much tension. There were separate student unions for the blacks and Orientals that only they could go into. I sometimes think the school tried to create tension. There were always fights and problems. I hung out with the whites because my roommates were white. I actually got along with all three groups. I did not hang out with the Orientals until my sophomore year, which is when I started working with them. I did not find it harder to make friends with other Asian Americans because I get along with everyone.

I am not dating anyone right now, but the last guy I dated was white. I never met his family, but I talked to them on the phone, and they did not have a problem with their son dating an Asian. But there was a guy that did have a problem. I cannot remember his name, but he would not date me because he said his parents would not approve. We did date for a while, but he said he could not continue it because of his parents.

I have gone places and all the Oriental guys there thought that because I am Oriental, I would like Oriental guys, but I have never dated one. That is really weird. I danced with one in eighth grade, but I have never been attracted to any. I think that minorities assume you like them because you are a minority.

I like living here better because you can say "hi" to anybody and anybody will say "hi" back to you. There is more diversity here; everyone is a friend with everyone, no matter what race you are. The college makes this town because it is so big and the city itself is smaller.

I think I will run into problems wherever I go because I am not white. I rented a room in a sorority house at a small college last summer. I could not go over to my roommate's house frequently because I was a minority. I went over there once and her father was nice to my face but I had a feeling that after I left he was not. He does not like any religion besides Christianity, and he does not like minorities. He teaches his kids to hate everyone, but my roommate and her sister know better. Their younger brother, on the other hand, follows his father in some ways.

I think blacks get more media focus. I do not think there is such a big deal about Asians as there are about blacks. Like the Rodney King beating, if that would have been an Asian American it would not have been made into such a big deal because Orientals are not as outspoken. We do not have the Million Man Oriental March. There used to be a show on TV called *American Girl*, that was about a second-generation Asian American living in America; it did not last very long or go over very well. I do not think they should make us an exception and say there should be more Oriental shows. I think whatever the population wants is what they should watch. We have the Spanish channel, but nobody watches it. That is just like saying there should be more shows with Mexicans. I guess there are mostly shows with white people, but then again there is *Bill Cosby*. There are a lot of movies though, like *the Joy Luck Club*, and we have enough Kung Fu movies to last a lifetime. In most shows, Asians are portrayed as being quiet, laid-back, and smart.

I think I act more American than anything. I was raised American with white parents. I think of myself as being white on the inside and Oriental on the outside. I think that if I were in an Asian family, it would be different and I would look out for more Orientals. I think I am aware of it because three of my brothers and sisters are black and my brother and I are Oriental.

I think that all the Orientals I have met do not follow the perception whites have of us as being "model minorities." We are all outgoing, loud-mouths, and totally sarcastic. When I was younger, the "model minority" was the stereotype. In school, there were two black guys who sat behind me and they would say things like, "Amy, she's so smart, she's an Oriental, she's super smart." My brother Alan is my role model and he is white. He is kind and compassionate and good at everything he does.

Jessica Littlewood was born in 1975 in South Vietnam. A war orphan, she was airlifted by a helicopter out of Vietnam on the eve of the Communist takeover and adopted by an American family. She grew up in Kansas City, Missouri, and was studying English at Truman State University at the time of the interview in 1996.

I was born in South Vietnam and came to the United States on 3 April 1975. I am not sure of my exact birth date because my birth certificate was destroyed on its way here, so I am actually older than the date I celebrate my birthday on. I was in an orphanage for the first couple months of my life in Vietnam. The orphanage was one that participated in a baby lift. A baby lift is where planes and helicopters are sent over and as many babies as possible were taken out of the country. The plane I was supposed to be on was called the *Galaxy*. My birth certificate got on the plane but they ran out of room for me so I was taken away on another airplane or a helicopter. The *Galaxy* crashed with all those babies on board, and with my papers. It is really sad what happened because so many people died, and I was supposed to be on that plane. All I had on me was my wrist bracelet that had my name on it.

I have worked with a lady recently who actually worked at an orphanage in Vietnam. She told me that there were a lot of babies in Vietnam who were children of American soldiers and Vietnamese prostitutes. She said that the orphanages were really dirty places and there were lice everywhere. There were a lot of orphanages, I do not know how many, but the nuns who were killed in the plane crash ran a lot of them. There has been a book written on it—my brother is in the book. He is so cute; under his picture it says "Shawn USA." Most of the babies either went to the United States or France.

I have two older brothers, both are adopted. The older one is from America and the middle one is from Vietnam. My parents wanted one boy and one girl; they got my older brother first. Then they adopted my second brother because there was a surplus of boys in the orphanages. They asked my mom if she still wanted to be on the waiting list for a girl and she said, "Well, sure." So they left her on the list and eleven months later they called and asked if she still wanted a girl. She still did, and asked those who called her, "What do we have to do and when do you want us to pick her up?" They answered, "Can you pick her up tomorrow?" So my mom had a one-day notice before she got me. They flew me up to Colorado and that is where I met my parents.

I have a good relationship with my parents. They still live in Kansas City, which is where I grew up. I remember my parents taking me to Jefferson City, Missouri, to be naturalized. I remember being in a courthouse in my dad's arms and watching a bunch of people taking oaths around me. I was worried because I did not know what they were saying, but my dad said, "Oh, the little kids don't have to repeat the oath." I was relieved, and then they gave us little American flag pins.

I am close with my brothers, although I am closer with my older one. I do not know why, I do not think it is because my other brother is from Asia; I think the middle brother and I are too close in age and so we fight a lot.

I do not feel that I have learned a lot about my culture. Sometimes I am embarrassed about it because it is where I am from. But on the other hand, I have been in the United States since I was two months old. If I wanted to go back and try to trace my roots, there would be no ties to connect me to anything over there. I consider myself American. I have wanted to go back to visit, though. I have heard it is a beautiful country. But my dad was kind of worried when I told him. He was afraid that I would get stuck over there or that something political would happen. My mom thinks that it was a really good idea.

Every once in a while, I feel guilty about not wanting to know my real parents, but then I think that God put me here for a reason and he put me in this circumstance. I have wonderful parents here, so I should not feel guilty. I think that my parents have told me all that they can. My dad fought in the war, but he keeps closed up about it. I do not want to press him on the subject because I have no idea what it was like and what happened to him.

Even though I have lived here all but two months of my life, I am still discriminated against sometimes. Not so much now because people have an awareness of it, but when I was little, kids would make fun of me. It took me a while at first to figure out that I was different. I remember one day my best friend and I looked into a mirror and could not see a difference. I said, "I don't see how we look different," and she responded, "I don't think you look different either." There was a time on the bus when a guy turned around and started calling me Suzi Wong. Suzi Wong was a rice product, and I did not catch on at first. When I finally did, I told him to grow up. Since I have always been here, it was no big deal, but as I have grown up, I have realized that being different is good.

I have always thought that my brother, who is from Vietnam, has had a really hard time dealing with the way he looks. Boys can be so cruel. I remember one time when we were on the school bus and a kid would not let him sit with him, or they would make fun of him and then he would get really upset. I remember this one time we were at the bus stop and this boy brought his Doberman with him. This was the meanest dog and the owner let it bite my brother.

I do not feel that I have ever been stereotyped as being smart because I am Asian. Students at school have sometimes thought I was an exchange student. Sometimes they are shocked when I speak perfect English with no accent. Then they will ask how long I have lived here and I will answer, all but two months of my life, and then they will ask if I still remember any Vietnamese. The fact that people will ask me that, knowing I was only in Vietnam for two months, is surprising.

I have gone to public school my whole life. Now I am planning on graduating with a degree in English. In high school, I had a problem with guys not wanting to date me because I am Vietnamese. Here in college, it is different. As guys get older, they realize that there is more than one kind of beauty. In my free time, I like to read. I also like sports, but not competitively. I am also involved in Campus Christian Fellowship.

22
Interracial Marriage

Pinmany Danson was born in Laos and married a European American who had been her high school English teacher in Laos. She was living in a small town in Missouri and working on compiling a directory of all the Lao in the United States at the time of the interview in 1995.

I was born in Laos. My father graduated from high school and my mother did not have a formal education and was a housewife. After high school, my father joined the army and moved up to the rank of major. I did not feel like they had any preset expectations for me. I was treated the same as my brothers and sisters.

I have four brothers and four sisters. My youngest brother received his bachelor of arts from Northeast Missouri State University (NMSU). Another brother has a master's in engineering and my other two brothers did not finish high school because of the war. One of my sisters has an eighth grade diploma, another spent a year at NMSU, another sister received her BA from NMSU, and the last one is in Laos now. She did not finish high school; she quit in the tenth grade.

I met my husband in the classroom. He was my high school English teacher in Laos. Here in America, that is something that is looked down upon. Over there, it is not a problem. I was a good student and that was what caught his attention. There were no problems with us dating. He had a system for his students that got As. If you got As, you got tickets to movies and stuff like that. They were not to the local movies but the ones at the American compound. He had to accompany us to the movie theater. This encourages kids to do well. We offend no one in Laos by dating because we did not hug and kiss in public. I think that is why our relationship was acceptable. People do not do in Laos as they do here. I was really shocked when I came here to see how everyone acted with each other. I am still reluctant to hug my husband in public.

I got married to an American, therefore I was an immigrant to the United States in 1976. My husband and I were married in Laos and six days later we left the country. The only way for me to leave the country was if I were to marry him and I received a visa on the spot in Chicago, where I first arrived. Chicago was the closest destination point to Ohio, which was where we were heading.

We left the country to go to Saudi Arabia in 1982. We had been overseas for three and a half years before we came back. My husband worked at the school at this time while training for the Saudi air force. While we were there, we did not worry about trying to keep our faces covered, but we did wear hats, scarves, and black *abaya* over our clothes. I was not required to wear these things, but it was recommended for my protection. If you do not cover your face, the men will say you are not a good woman. There is a lot of social pressure. This is especially true when you leave the compound, but that does not happen very often because the compound has everything that you would need—food and a basketball court. We left again in 1990 to go to Laos.

My husband is a very kind, sweet, and good-hearted person. He is different from other husbands. We share the household responsibilities, half and half. I cook and he cleans. Since I am working at home, he cleans up the house, vacuums, does the laundry, and takes care of the cars. In the morning, he fixes breakfast for our son while I pack our son's lunch. We make decisions on family matters together.

My husband is planning on getting his master's in education eventually, but we are adjusting now since we just got back from Laos. We were there for five years, so we are trying to get over the culture shock. We have to do this every time that we move.

I get along wonderfully with my in-laws. We celebrate holidays with each other. My mother died eight years ago and my father-in-law died four or five years before that. So we celebrate with his mother.

I cook a mixture of Lao and American food that mostly anyone can eat. I make it so the food is not too spicy. I usually broil or bake things. I prepare things like pasta. If I fix Asian food, I will fix it in a big pot, and my husband will not eat a lot of it, so I freeze it one serving at a time over a two week period.

Our son has been raised with both American and Lao cultures. He cannot be raised completely American because I am not fully American-ized and I still bring with me some Lao traditions, and he cannot be raised completely in the Lao tradition because we live in America. Our child is very well behaved. He is very kind and not rude.

I got married right out of high school, so I did not have time to work. When I moved here, I received my bachelor of science in accounting at Northwest Missouri State in 1982. I got along wonderfully with my class-mates and my teachers. I still talk to them, even though they are retired now.

In my home country, we do not have universities. The only upper-level education opportunities are law school or medical school. One would have to go to another country to study anything else. I would like to start a school in Laos with former teachers from my old school because the edu-cation in Laos right now is not good. Since I was there and went through the programs myself, I know what needs improvement. I have also had experience working with kids at the international school, and they were wild. I want my son to be raised right. Both my husband and I agree that this is the best way. If you do not teach children, they will be wild.

Even though my son is not being raised with full Lao instruction, he has learned some of the culture. Since we lived there for five years, he can speak the language now. It took him a year of being in the country before he learned the language well. It does not matter to me if my son marries a Lao or not. The important thing is love.

I have never had a problem with discrimination in America, but in Laos, where I was an administrator at an international school, I had a boss who was from Australia. Since I was there before he came, I was supposed to show him around, but he did not like being told what to do by me, he felt threatened. He was really rude about it.

Right now I am working at home on my own research. Earlier this year, I registered my own business where I compile names of the Lao peo-ple who live in America. When I have all my information, I am going to make a community directory, print it, and sell it. It is a lot of work. I have almost 50,000 names now. Because I am the only Lao person in town, I am working on this by myself. I would like some help, but I cannot find any-one here. All I am doing now, and would like help in doing, is recognizing the Lao names. You can differentiate what is a Lao name by looking at it.

This job is stressful because there is so much to think about. I have to think of all the possible ways to do it. I have to contact all of the people that are in organizations I get contacts through. I have even checked how much bulk mail costs because 50,000 is a large number of people to send things to. The book will be about 800 pages and cost at least fifteen dollars each. Of course, all of the contacted people will get a discount so that they can distribute it and make a profit.

The job is very flexible because I can work when I want to. I usually do not work at night, especially when good TV shows are on. There is no pressure for me to have this done by a certain date, although I do plan on having it finished by January or February of next year.

I plan on telling the people when the books are in, but they practically already know because I advertise when I talk to them. I also advertise in papers and magazines in big cities. There are big gatherings where I have been introduced in order to get my name out. I also plan on sending out newsletters when it is almost finished. I wanted to compile my book in 1987 or 1988 but I could not because the computers did not have Lao letters. I had ordered a Lao typewriter from Mexico because I know how to type Lao. By the time the typewriter broke, my husband and I got a call to work in Laos. We went down there and I did not work on the book, and still no one had done it by the time we came back to the United States, so I pursued it. I thought, "I will be the first to do it." A lot of people were really happy that I was doing this. It was a way that they could find lost family and friends.

I plan on doing this every year for a couple years because people move a lot and I want to make sure that I get everyone. It will be like a telephone book; a directory for people that also list their services in the area. I have also listed related businesses for Lao people and Buddhist temples. I do not have the businesses pay me to put them in my book. If someone wanted their ad to be bigger I would not do that, either. It is much easier on me to list the businesses rather than make customer ads. I will possibly change that in the second edition, though. I will have to pay for publishing all on my own. I will only distribute 10,000 at first.

It is a fulfilling job because I am being conservative and doing something good. It is something that the community needs. This is definitely a big part of what I find out every time I go out and talk to different people in the community. They commend me for it, especially the people in the different associations I talk to. Many had thought about doing this themselves, but have never had the time to do it.

The part I like least about it is being on the phone all the time. I get tired of it, and I get a pretty expensive phone bill as well. I used to talk every day, all the time. Now I have cut it down to weekends and evenings, when I am working within cheaper rates. The thing I like best about owning my own business is being my own boss. There really is not anything I do not like. As long as the money is there and holds out long enough to support what I do, I will be fine.

A typical working day for me is working from eight AM to noon, and then from two PM to five PM. If there is nothing good on TV or nothing else to do that night, I will work from seven PM to ten PM. About 90 percent of the time is spent entering data about the families such as their names, address, and phone number. I type about three hundred names per day.

So far my investment includes computers, a fax machine, printers, and about $6,000 or $7,000 to cover the price of hardware. My working capital includes the phone bill as well. I update my money situation about once a month. It was very expensive to get started. My husband is behind my work 100 percent. If he did not agree to it, I would not do it because our money is together; therefore we both must agree on how it is spent. He helps me when he is free, that is why we have two computers.

When I am not working on my book, I like to spend my spare time reading. I do not have much, but I try to read things that I like or things that I want to know more about. I also try to get out of the day-to-day situation and do something that opens my eyes and helps me contact other people. I do volunteer work now, once a week, every Wednesday. I volunteer three hours a week, selling used books in the local public library. I have been doing it for almost a year now.

I also started reading a Lao magazine I subscribed to for keeping up with current events. My husband is more interested in it than I am. I am more interested in participating in local community activities, like ones at the library. I also take some classes. We do not attend a church regularly. We have been approached to join a church here, but we have not made a decision. I have also worked in the business office here at the university.

Most of my friends are Americans. In this town, though, I have found it easier to make friends with other Asians. I try and go to international events that the university sponsors, such as the international dinner. We went last year, it was delicious, and there was a good show that went along with it.

The thing I like best about living in America is the freedom of traveling and doing things. There is also a convenience in doing things here, especially in the government. In Laos, it is different. Even though people have jobs and a salary, if you want something done, especially paperwork, it will not get done unless you pay them an extra fee under the table. It is very bad.

There is not anything bad about living in America. Living in a small town may be bad, but not America. This town is too far from everything, although I like the quietness here. Everything is easy to get to and it is easy to get everything done, but traveling is very hard because it is not convenient. Our home is here; it is our base. We have friends and neighbors who are very nice. It would be hard at this point in my life to have to move again. I would have to make new friends, which is hard enough. We have been here for fifteen years, living in a decent neighborhood. We bought our house when we moved here and we rent it out when we leave. I think we are planning on staying here until we go back to Laos. We will probably go back when my son finishes college. I might go back earlier because my husband will be here to support our son. I could travel back and forth.

Cantana Lopez was born in Illinois in 1976. Her mother came from Thailand and her father was an American serviceman stationed in Bangkok. She lived in a small town in Illinois with her parents at the time of the interview in 1995.

I was born in a small town in Illinois on 21 November 1976. My mother is from Bangkok, Thailand, and my father is an American. They met when my dad was in the U.S. Army stationed there. My mother was a waitress when they met. I have two older half-sisters who are Thai like my mom; they are twenty-seven and twenty-eight years old. My mom never married their father, and my sisters do not have any contact with him. My dad brought my mom and my sisters back to America with him when my mom was twenty years old and my sisters were really little, around two and three. America has more opportunities; I think that's why they came. My mom is a United States citizen. I don't think she had any difficulty living here. She's been a U.S. citizen since before I was born.

My mom didn't have a very good childhood. They were poor, like many people were. I think it was a lot better for her to live here because of what she has told me she had to go through. My mom had a mean babysitter once who would take the money my grandmother gave her to feed my mother and keep it. My mom always complained that she never had toys like me. She said she had to play with mud and sticks. She had a brother and a sister and she doesn't even know where the brother is right now. My mother was very close to her parents, though. They both died when I was seven or eight years old. I didn't ever get a chance to see them. My mother was there when they both died. She was informed that her mom had a stroke and then got on a plane and flew there to be with her mom. Her mom died a few days later and then within a couple of days, her father had a heart attack and also died. I think it's painful for her to talk about her family too much. She doesn't talk about any of this except when I ask her about it. I think she is happy that I was born in America and my sisters were raised here because of all the things that had happened in her own childhood.

My mom went to beauty school in Thailand and became a hairdresser here. She owns her own shop. I remember once we were looking at pictures of her school. It was different from the schools here and they had to wear uniforms. My dad graduated from a four-year college in Florida. Now he works at Sprint Center and has been there for as long as I can remember. My parents really emphasized education and good grades. If I did really well, they would reward me with money for each A. I didn't feel a lot of pressure at first to get good grades because when I started getting them, I was expected to keep them. The pressure came to keep them up because I didn't want to make my parents disappointed. Sometimes Asian kids are stereotyped as being the smart kids with the camera, but I've never thought anyone saw me as such.

My parents are big on responsibility. My mom is strict and both my parents expect a lot out of me. They thought the job I had in high school was good for me because it was supposed to teach me responsibility. I think that when I have children I will push them to learn responsibility, too. When my sisters and I were all at home, I had the small chores, like dusting, to do. After they moved away and I grew up, I had to rinse the dishes after dinner and vacuum and dust on Saturday mornings.

My parents and I get along pretty well. When I am fighting with them, we usually talk it out calmly. I'll yell a little bit and that'll be the end of it. When my mom and I fight, my dad usually stays out of it because when my mom gets mad she is really mad. Usually, when we have something to fight about we talk it out.

The food is about the only Thai culture that my mom has brought to the household. My mom is the primary cook in my family and she cooks a

Thai New Year Celebration, St. Louis, Missouri, 25 April 1999. Huping Ling Collection.

lot of Thai food. Occasionally she throws Thai food parties where she invites between thirty and fifty people. She's done it for two years now. She'll get up early in the morning and cook all day, at least ten or eleven or twelve different dishes. Everyone will come over and eat. It's like a normal party except that only Thai food is served. Many people come because they want to try the food, and lots of people really like it. The people who come are all Caucasians; she doesn't really have any Thai friends. I would like to learn to cook Thai food so that I could pass it on to my children someday. Otherwise we eat normal foods like everyone else. Sometimes if we want something like lasagna, my dad will cook because it is something that he makes best.

Sometimes my mom talks in Thai to her sister over the phone. I don't know many Thai words. It would be neat to know the language but it wouldn't be very useful. If I had the opportunity, I would probably learn the language. Sometimes I ask my mom how to say things in Thai. She taught me bad words when I was younger, but I don't remember them anymore. She writes little notes in Thai all over the place and no one knows what they say. My dad never learned the language. He knew a few words but I don't think he ever really spoke it. My mom said she knew English when she came to America because they had to learn it in Thailand. She still has a really strong accent and sounds funny, but she does know English. My friends sometimes have a hard time understanding her, but she says a lot of words pretty well. At first she might have felt a barrier with other Americans, but not anymore.

We don't have lots of Buddha statues and stuff like that. My mom is Lutheran now, she was even married in a Lutheran church. She said that she was Buddhist in Thailand because that's what everyone is over there.

When I get married, I don't really think my parents would have a problem with me marrying a Caucasian man. My dad is Caucasian and one of my sisters is married to a Caucasian, so I don't think it would be an issue.

I don't consider myself very Asian because I do not have any Asian culture in me. It is not a big part of me. I never feel ashamed or bad when people ask about my ethnicity. Sometimes people I just met know that I am Asian but they don't know what, so they'll ask. I don't feel that I was raised differently than any other American children or my Caucasian friends. I would like to know more about Thai culture, but there is not much I could do about that. Someday I would like to go over there. I don't know if I would do serious research, but I think the trip would tell me a lot about that part of my heritage. I would like to see the places that my mom talks about and see how they have changed.

23

Generational and Cultural Conflict

Noi Yang was born into a Hmong family in Beng Jun, Laos, in 1974. Her family escaped Laos, stayed in a refugee camp in Thailand, and then came to the United States in 1975. They had been living in Centerville, Iowa, since that time. She was studying early elementary education at the university there at the time of the interview in 1995.

I was born in 1974 in Beng Jun, Laos. I came to the United States with my parents and siblings when I was a year old. My brother is now twenty-two and my sister is twenty-three. I know that before my family came to America, my father received some education because he learned how to write a bit in Chinese and English. My mother took care of us so she did not get much of an education. They owned a store where they sold watches and repaired clocks until the Communists came in and closed the store down.

My parents decided to come to the United States because they wanted an opportunity to learn and to work. I am not sure of the process we took to get here because I was so young. I think we had to secretly sail in a boat at midnight and then we went to a refugee camp in Thailand. I do know that the United Methodist Church sponsored us and Centerville, Iowa, was the first place we came to, so we stayed here.

I felt like a minority here because our family was the only Asian family in the school system. I was affected only partially. Our friends did not treat us any differently. There would be days when I would ask my best friend if I act differently. She would say no. My eyes have been opened now that I am in college. I have met more Asian Americans here. I have a friend who I met through an ethnic minority organization on campus. She was born in Laos, too, so we have a lot of similarities. It is nice to be able to relate to others now that I am in college and to find people that I can talk to and relate to.

My relationship with my mom is something that is hard to talk about because we are so different. I have written a ten-page paper on this topic. It is very hard because she wants a relationship but there are cultural differences that get in the way. She did totally different things than I did growing up. When I was younger I wanted to go to the movies, hang out with my friends, and spend the night with friends, but those are things that my mom never did and she never got used to. I felt deprived for not being able to do these things and I was really frustrated. When I finally reached high school I did it anyway. My mom would always ask, "Where are you going, when will you be back?" It was like twenty questions, she would always ask why, why, why. I would get so aggravated and say, "Mom, you have to understand, I need to do American things because I am growing up here. I am sorry I can't cook or sew like you probably did back then."

I was not supposed to date until I was twenty or at least out of high school. It was not right to date and I wanted to please my mom, so I did not date much. But I also wanted to rebel against her, too. It was hard, and now there are times when I want to talk with her but I cannot speak Chinese so it is getting harder for her to understand. She only speaks broken English, I get so frustrated and impatient, and that is where the arguments come in.

Another thing we disagree on is customs. Sometimes it is not proper to do certain things according to her standards, but my point of view is that "I'm an American, let me do it." For example, we are not supposed to show affection. Right now I am going through a stage with my boyfriends where it is kind of weird because of that. It is also weird because I never had a father figure. We cannot have our male partners spend the night or make out. There is a line to be drawn because I have certain values set in my head from my Laotian background, but I am trying to live a normal life as an American.

Though there are certain things that I am trying to get away from doing, there are some things from my culture that I still incorporate in my life. We still do the typical customs like lighting the incense and we have a little tray of food and an altar with my dad's picture. My dad died of liver cancer a year after we got here, and my mother had to raise three children by herself in a foreign country.

My father was really into education. His words were that he wanted us to get an education and have a good future. That is an aspect of him that is instilled in all of us. My uncle who lives in Boston continually checks up on us and asks us what our grades are.

Another custom we still hold to is our Buddhist religion. That is a confusing topic because we burn incense but I do not know if we worship Buddha. The Chinese New Year is a big thing for us. We thoroughly clean our house, wash the sheets and curtains, clean, and scrub, just like it is spring cleaning. It is to get the old out and bring in the new. We make a big deal out of it. We have people who travel for miles to join our family dinner, just to be merry. We still celebrate traditional American holidays like Halloween and Thanksgiving, but we might have a combination of foods. We celebrate Christmas but it is not as big for us as for other Americans, and it is not as big as the Chinese New Year.

My family strongly believes in superstitions. For example, if you drop a chopstick while you are eating, it is bad luck and something bad will happen. If you are going to travel, then you should not do it. My sister dropped her chopstick one night and I made fun of her, but then she split a nail in half and had to go to the hospital. If I had not made such a big deal about it, it would have not been so bad. It just goes to show that you should obey the rules.

My sister and I are close, but my brother and I are not. My sister and I have always been good, but sometimes she is hard for me to deal with. I do not know if my relationship with my brother is the way it is because he is shy or if it is because he is a developing guy. When we were younger we used to goof off, but now he is more serious. Sometimes it is hard to deal with because I always wanted that father figure. Maybe it is harder for me to be open with men because I had a self-esteem problem.

Relationships have gotten a little better since I have been at college, but it is still frustrating to try to make my mom understand things from an American point of view. She does not understand the details involved in some things, but otherwise she is really smart and knowledgeable, and she knows when she is right. If I were to carry on a conversation with her about a friend of mine it would be frustrating. She is going through a really tough time now because I am the last of her children to go off to college, so she is by herself now. She works at a group home and the hospital so she has a lot of friends now. I have helped her improve her communication skills a lot and I am proud of her for that. We will be moving in May when my brother gets out of college and begins looking for a house; we will move up there with him.

My mom could not speak English when we first arrived here, so she had to do some odd jobs and minuscule work, like clean corn and stuff like that. We had to do a lot of growing up quickly. It was frustrating for us because we could not understand a lot of what was going on. When my mom went to sporting events or conferences, we felt the need to go with her to be a translator, but as kids we were not allowed to go to some things. When she went to banquets, I always felt different because my mom would not have anyone to talk to; therefore she was not involved and that made me self-conscious. Right now, I think she is doing a good job.

My mom cooks real Chinese food for herself, but it is awful for us. I do not have the taste for the food, like the stir-fry she makes with green vegetables. We like to butcher our own chickens but I will not eat it because the FDA does not check it. There is fish and pigskin, which she does not eat. I will eat rice and soup. Other than these foods, she can cook American food and that is what she makes for us. Sometimes it is hard for her to read recipes, but she throws things in and gets it right. In Lao tradition, there is this one really gross thing—when the butcher kills the chickens, they drain the blood out of the neck, boil the blood and eat it. That disgusts me and makes me sick. Sometimes I would go in the kitchen and say, "Yuck, what stinks in here?" My mom would get mad and say, "It's my food!"

When I was younger, the question for all us kids was, "Are you going to marry a Chinese person or an American?" There is so much pressure involved. Our mother would prefer that I marry a Chinese person to be able to carry on the culture with her grandkids, for them to look like they are Chinese, and to be able to communicate with them. Right now she fusses about "my kids marry Americans." I have one cousin who is engaged to a Chinese. I do not know how they met—she is from China. My cousin Su is dating an American. Another cousin, Sommal, is engaged to a white American and my older sister is with one as well.

It is really hard for my boyfriend to understand our culture. When it comes down to it, it does not matter. As long as I find someone who will treat me with respect, who cares for me and who is loving, I will marry him. My boyfriend and I are planning on continuing this relationship fore a while and then we will get engaged and get married. This is really hard because he is a Christian and it is important for my family to practice Chinese customs. It is hard for him to understand and participate in them.

There are little things that we do in our customs that are different from what he is used to. For example, when you get married relatives give

A Laotian woman weaving, Laos, 1992 (Courtesy of Ann Rynearson).

you 24 carat gold rings; we kneel on certain occasions; when couples are sitting in front of you, you give them a cup of tea and bow to them. My sister's wedding is coming up in August, so I will see how they handle the differences in their wedding. My brother will have to go through the traditions because he carries on our name.

Another thing that I am into are fortunes, although it is not right as a Christian to believe in them. My fortune said that I am a go-getter and very ambitious, which is funny because I am that way. I really see that trait in myself. The fortuneteller has also told me when I am supposed to get married, or find a man, who is not twenty or twenty-one years old. I will be successful and rich. My sister was told that she is mouthy and one of these days her mouth is going to get her into trouble. She is very smart and has high goals but she does not pursue anything. She has a lot of money, but she spends it all. At the age of sixty she will get very, very ill. Knowing this will help me because I will have to help our family prepare. By then my mom will probably be dead, so I will have to do some calling or find a Chinese shrink or somebody that is really holy to perform ceremonial things. All of this helps, it is called Bai Sri. People come and you wrap a string around each person there.

The fortuneteller knew that I was really sick when I was twelve years old. We did the same thing I will have to do for my sister. My mom called a fortuneteller to ask why I was so sick. He told her that my dad missed us kids so much that he touched me, and you are not supposed to do that. There are a lot of spiritual things in this reasoning and that is what happened. I recovered after a while. I had to stay in one of the balloons in the hospital.

Another tradition we have is on Memorial Day, we go out to the cemetery and bring a tray of food. We worship there. It is kind of embarrassing. We would have our incense and flowers there and we would pray. My mom would have to say something in Chinese and we just go along with it because we cannot talk. The other day, my mom lit incense and I asked her how she knew she was supposed to do that. She says you look at the Chinese calendar. During the New Year and Memorial Day, my mom cuts paper clothes as part of our tradition and burns them so that my dad can have the clothes.

I would like to incorporate and instill a lot of the morals and values my mom taught me in my kids. I believe all of us are good kids, and I think basically it is knowing the Chinese ways, knowing right from wrong, and having common sense. It is these things that she has always instilled in us so now it comes naturally. I will probably try to do that for my kids and tell them stories and explain it all to them.

My mom and my brother visited Laos last May. They stayed about two or three weeks. We still have a grandfather there. He is very, very old. That is why they went. They did not like it, though. The sanitation was awful and it was hot. My brother said the humidity was at 80 and it was crazy. My mom enjoyed the family aspect of it. Of course, things were very cheap there. There was a higher class of business people and then the village people that were very, very poor. There was nothing in between. There were water buffalo and no bathrooms. I would like to go there myself just to see how it is.

The Asian American Mosaic

Despite their differences in ethnicity, culture, education, religion, and personal character and temperament, Asian American women confront similar problems in immigration and settlement, employment patterns, marriage, and cultural and generational conflicts. At the same time, their disparate backgrounds also produce variations and diversities in their lives. On the issue of immigration and settlement, most Asian American women, either from the earlier and larger groups of Chinese, Filipino, Japanese, Korean, and Asian Indian, or from the later or smaller groups[1] regardless of their cultural, educational, socioeconomic, and religious backgrounds, have experienced initial linguistic, financial, and emotional difficulties and the subsequent adjustments. They later enjoyed different degrees of assimilation, acculturation, and Americanization in both legal and cultural terms, and their differences in birthplace, culture, ethnicity, religion, and socioeconomic conditions prior to and after immigration have created a mosaic of Asian American life. While the native-born Asian American women have enjoyed better educational, occupational, and socioeconomic conditions and opportunities, the foreign-born Asian American women and international students often experience more linguistic, financial, and cultural difficulties in education, employment, and daily life, and are more likely to be subject to blatant or subtle racial discrimination and cultural prejudice.

The lives of the Asian American women examined also demonstrate certain employment patterns across ethnic groups. In urban communities, many immigrant women, regardless of their ethnicity and educational background, have supplemented family income by taking sewing work at

---

[1] According to the 2000 U.S. Census, there are 2,314,537 people of Chinese descent living in the United States. According to the 2000 U.S. Census, there were 1,850,314 Filipinos, 796,700 Japanese, 1,076,872 Koreans, 1,678,765 Asian Indians, and 1,122,528 Vietnamese.

home (Beth Low and Lisa Wang's mothers), or have worked as manual laborers at assembly lines (Amihan Perez and Seema Khotlay), as laborers/ proprietors in family-operated ethnic restaurants (Liz Sing and her mother, Masako Smith, and Anna Crosslin's mother), beauty supply stores (Jin-Hee Cho's mother), laundries (Katherine Larson's mother), and motels (Seeta Patel). While in rural areas, immigrant women have worked on family farms (Kazuko Miller). Meanwhile, immigrant women with higher educational attainments and better occupational opportunities have found employment in professional fields.

Among the foreign-born professional women, Chinese and Japanese American women have worked in professional fields as a public school counselor (Ling Ng), university professor (Erin Zeng), piano teacher (Gena Chen), and researcher (Mina Yoshida), while Filipino and Asian Indian American women are employed in the health service industry as a hospital clerk (Bituin Perez), insurance coordinator (Rajni Raman), registered nurses (Diwata Lopez and Marie Bornales), and physician (Rekha Desai), or as university professors in nursing (Maria Herman) and nutrition (Surya Gupta). At the same time, many native-born Asian American women and international students are at the stage of attaining higher education to prepare for future careers. On university campuses, while the native-born women are dealing with issues of ethnic identity and generational and cultural conflicts with their parents, the international students have to cope with linguistic, emotional, and financial problems.

As cross-cultural and racial interactions and activities take place, interracial romantic relationships have developed within every group of Asian American women. In the realm of interracial dating, love, and marriage, there are different patterns between the foreign-born and native-born Asian American women. For foreign-born women, interracial romances occurred as result of multiple factors of American foreign policies in Asia and the Pacific Rim, the expansion of capitalism, globalization of the world economy, and transnationalism in Asian countries. American occupation of Japan from 1945 to 1952 and the close diplomatic and socioeconomic relations between the two countries produced many unions between American servicemen and Japanese women, as illustrated in the marriages of Anna Crosslin's mother and Kazuko Miller. Similarly, America's close ties with the non-Communist countries in Asia also brought many Asian women to the United States as military brides, as reflected in Su-Hee Spark's mother's marriage. Consequently, stereotypes of the military bride arise and many interracial marriages that do not involve American military men are often mistaken as such, as revealed in the story of Maria Herman. Cross-cultural and transnational activities in Asian countries as result of a rapidly expanding global economy have also given rise to interracial romantic relationships, as reflected in Pinmany Danson's and Martha Reeves's marriages. Many of these women encounter difficulties of language and unfamiliar cultural milieus. Compared to the foreign-born women, native-born Asian American women are more compatible with their partners in the interracial romantic relationships where they share common language, values, and educational and occupational experiences. Nevertheless, the native-born Asian American women still have to deal with the same issues of multiracial and multicultural heritage in marriage and in childrearing as their foreign-born counterparts. These similarities and dissimilarities indicate that Asian American women's lives are kaleidoscopic and multifaceted. One cannot and should not simply portray Asian American women's experiences as a stereotypical "model" of one kind or another that neglects the individual variables and divergences.

About the Author

Huping Ling is author of five books, *Chinese St. Louis: 1857–2007*, *Chinese St. Louis: From Enclave to Cultural Community*, *Ping Piao Mei Guo: New Immigrants in America*, *Jinshan Yao: A History of Chinese American Women* which won a 1999 Ford Foundation Award, and *Surviving on the Gold Mountain: A History of Chinese American Women and Their Lives*. She has edited four volumes and has contributed to scholarly books and journals. Ling is professor of history at Truman State University and holds a doctorate from Miami University.

Works Cited

Agbayani-Siewert, Pauline, and Linda Revilla. "Filipino Americans." In *Asian Americans: Contemporary Trends and Issues*, edited by Pyong Gap Min, 134–168. Thousand Oaks, CA: Sage, 1995.

Armstrong, Karen. *Islam: A Short History.* New York: Modern Library, 2002.

Asian Women United of California, ed. *American Women.* Boston: Beacon Press, 1989.

Asian Women United of California, ed. *Making Waves: An Anthology of Writings by and about Asian American Women.* Boston: Beacon Press, 1989.

Austin, Allen W. *From Concentration Camp to Campus: Japanese American Students and World War II.* Urbana: University of Illinois Press, 2005.

Bang, See Heeduk. "The Self-Help/Mutual Aid Component in Small Business within the Korean-American Community." PhD dissertation, University of Pennsylvania, 1983.

Barringer, Herbert, and Sung-Nam Cho. *Koreans in the United States: A Fact Book.* Honolulu: East-West Center, 1989.

Bernstein, Gail Lee. *Recreating Japanese Women, 1600–1945.* Berkeley: University of California Press, 1991.

Chan, Sucheng, ed. *Hmong Means Free: Life in Laos and America.* Philadelphia: Temple University Press, 1994.

Chan, Sucheng. *Asian Americans: An Interpretive History.* Boston: Twayne Publishers, 1991.

Chan, Sucheng. *Survivors: Cambodian Refugees in the United States.* Urbana: University of Illinois Press, 2004.

China Institute in America. *A Survey of Chinese Students in American Colleges and Universities in the Past Hundred Years.* New York: China Institute in America, 1954.

Daniels, Roger. "Incarceration of the Japanese Americans: A Sixty Year Perspective." *History Teacher* 35 (2002): 297–310.

Daniels, Roger. *Concentration Camps USA: Japanese Americans and World War II.* New York: Holt, Rinehart and Winston, 1972.

Daniels, Roger. *Prisoners without Trial: Japanese Americans in World War II.* New York: Hill and Wang, 1993.

Dasgupta, Shamita Das, ed. *A Patchwork Shawl: Chronicles of South Asian Women in America.* New Brunswick: Rutgers University Press, 1998.

Davis, Kingsley. "Intermarriage in Caste Societies." *American Anthropologist* 43, no. 3 (July–Sept. 1941): 376–95.

Espiritu, Yen Le. *Filipino American Lives.* Philadelphia: Temple University Press, 1995.

Espiritu, Yen Le. *Home Bound: Filipino American Lives across Cultures, Communities, and Countries.* Berkeley: University of California Press, 2003.

Fairbank, John King. *East Asia: Tradition and Transformation*. Boston: Houghton Mifflin, 1973.

Freeman, James A. *Hearts of Sorrow: Vietnamese-Americans Lives*. Stanford: Stanford University Press, 1989.

Gardner, Robert W., Bryant Robey, and Peter C. Smith. *Asian Americans: Growth, Change, and Diversity*. Washington DC: Population Reference Bureau, 1985.

Gillman, Ian, and Hans-Joachim Klimkeit. *Christians in Asia Before 1500*. London: Routledge Curzon, 1999.

Glenn, Evelyn Nakano. *Issei, Nisei, War Bride: Three Generations of Japanese American Women in Domestic Service*. Philadelphia: Temple University Press, 1986.

Gordon, Milton. *Assimilation in American Life*. New York: Oxford University Press, 1964.

Greenwald, John. "Finding Niches in a New Land." *Time*, 8 July 1995, 32–33.

Gregorian, Vartan. *Islam: A Mosaic Not a Monolith*. Washington: Brookings Institute, 2003.

Hefner, Robert. "Islam and Asian Security." In *Strategic Asia 2002–03: Asian Aftershocks*, edited by Richard J. Ellings and Aaron L. Friedberg. Seattle: National Bureau of Asian Research, 2002.

Hendry, Joy. *Understanding Japanese*. London: Routledge, 1995.

Houston, Jeanne Wakatsuki and James D. Houston. *Farewell to Manzanar*. New York: Bantam Books, 1973.

Humphreys, Christmas. *Buddhism: An Introduction and Guide*. Harmondsworth, Middlesex: Penguin Books, 1951.

Ichihashi, Yamato. *Japanese in the United States*. Stanford: Stanford University Press, 1932.

"Islam." BBC World Service, 2 July 2004.

Jensen, Joan M. *Passage from India: Asian Indian Immigrants in North America*. New Haven: Yale University Press, 1988.

Kitano, Harry H. L., and Roger Daniels. *Asian Americans: Emerging Minorities*. Upper Saddle River, NJ: Prentice Hall, 2001.

Kitano, Harry, Wai-Tssang Yeung, Lynn Chai, and Herbert Hatanaka. "Asian-American Interracial Marriage." *Journal of Marriage and the Family* 46, no.1 (Feb. 1984): 179–90.

Ko, Dorothy. *Cinderella's Sisters: A Revisionist History of Footbinding*. Berkeley: University of California Press, 2005.

Labov, Teresa, and Jerry A. Jacobs. "Intermarriage in Hawaii, 1950–1983." *Journal of Marriage and the Family* 48:79–88.

Lai, Him Mark. "Historical Development of the Chinese Consolidated Benevolent Association/Huiguan System." In *Chinese America: History and Perspectives, 1987*, 13–51. San Francisco: Chinese Historical Society of America, 1987.

Lee, Mary Paik. *Quiet Odyssey: A Pioneer Korean Woman in America*. Seattle: University of Washington Press, 1990.

Lee, S. M., and K. Yamanaka. "Patterns of Asian American Intermarriages and Marital Assimilation." *Journal of Comparative Family Studies* 21:287–305.

Leonard, Karen I. *Making Ethnic Choices: California's Punjabi Mexican Americans*. Philadelphia: Temple University Press, 1992.

Leonard, Karen Isaksen. *The South Asian Americans*. Westport, CT: Greenwood Press, 1997.

Li, Peter S. "Chinese Investment and Business in Canada: Ethnic Entrepreneurship Reconsidered." *Pacific Affairs* 66, no. 2 (Summer 1993): 219–43.

Lim, Linda Y. C. "Chinese Economic activity in Southeast Asia." In *The Chinese in Southeast Asia*. Vol. 1, *Ethnicity and Economic Activity*, edited by Linda Y. C. Lim and L. A. Peter Goaling. Singapore: Maruzen Asia, 1983.

Ling, Huping. "A History of Chinese Female Students in the United States, 1880s-1990s." *Journal of American Ethnic History* 16, no. 3 (Spring 1997): 81–109.

Ling, Huping. "Chinese Female Students and the Sino-US Relations." In *New Studies on Chinese Overseas and China*, edited by Cen Huang, Zhuang Gutu, and Tanaka Kyoko, 103–37. Leiden, Holland: IIAS, 2000.

Ling, Huping. "Family and Marriage of Late-Nineteenth and Early-Twentieth Century Chinese Immigrant Women." *Journal of American Ethnic History* 19, no. 2 (Winter 2000): 43–63.

Ling, Huping. "Governing Hop Alley: On Leong Chinese Merchants and Laborers Association, 1906–1966." *Journal of American Ethnic History* (Winter 2004): 50–84.

Ling, Huping. "The Changing Patterns of Taiwanese Students in America and the Modernization in Taiwan." In *Modernity and Cultural Identity in Taiwan*, edited by Hanchao Lu, 179–207. River Edge, NJ: Global Publishing, 2001.

Ling, Huping. *Chinese St. Louis: From Enclave to Cultural Community*. Philadephia: Temple University Press, 2004.

Ling, Huping. *Surviving on the Gold Mountain: Chinese American Women and Their Lives*. Albany: State University of New York Press, 1998.

Min, Pyong Gap. "Korean Immigrant Entrepreneurship: A Comprehensive Explanation." In *Koreans in America: New Perspectives*, edited by Seong Hyong Lee and Tae-Hwan Kwak. Seoul: Kyungnam University Press, 1988.

Min, Pyong Gap. "Patterns of Korean Immigrant Businesses in New York." In *The Korean American Community and Economy*, edited by Edi-Young Yu, Keyyoung Park, and Hyo Jung Kim. Los Angeles: The Korean American Economic Development Center, forthcoming.

Molly, Michael. *Experiencing the World's Religions: Tradition, Challenge, and Change*. Boston: McGraw-Hill Higher Education, 2005.

Noland, Marcus. "The Impact of Korean Immigration on the U.S. Economy." Blue Bell, PA: Institute for Korean-American Studies, Inc., 2002.

Osajima, Keith. "Asian Americans as the Model Minority: An Analysis of the Popular Press Image of the 1960s and 1980s." In *Reflections on Shattered Windows*, edited by Gary Y. Okihiro et al., 165–74. Pullman: Washington State University Press, 1988.

Park, Kyeyoung. *The Korean American Dream: Immigrants and Small Business in New York City*. Ithaca: Cornell University Press, 1997.

Peterson, William. "Success Story, Japanese-American Style." *New York Times Magazine*, 9 January 1966.

Root, Maria P. P., ed. *Racially Mixed People in America*. Thousand Oaks, CA: Sage, 1992.

Rumbaut, Rubén G. "The Structure of Refugee: Southeast Asian Refugees in the United States, 1975–1985." *International Review of Comparative Public Policy* 1 (1989): 97–129.

Rumbaut, Rubén G. "Vietnamese, Laotian, and Cambodian Americans." In *Asian Americans: Contemporary Trends and Issues*, edited by Pyong Gap Min, 232–270. Thousand Oaks, CA: Sage, 1995.

Shinagawa, Larry Hajime, and Gin Yong Pang. "Intraethnic, Interethnic, and Interracial Marriages among Asian Americans in California, 1980." *Berkeley Journal of Sociology* 33 (1988): 95–114.

Singh, Khushwant. *The Illustrated History of the Sikhs*. Oxford University Press, 2006.

Spickard, Paul R. *Mixed Blood: Intermarriage and Ethnic Identity in Twentieth-Century America*. Madison: University of Wisconsin Press, 1989.

Stephen, C., and Stephan W. "After Intermarriage: Ethnic Identity Among Mixed Heritage Japanese Americans and Hispanics." *Journal of Marriage and Family* 51:507–19.

Sung, Betty Lee. *Chinese American Intermarriage*. New York: Center for Migration Studies, 1990.

Suzuki, Bob H. "Education and the Socialization of Asian Americans: A Revisionist Analysis of the 'Model Minority' Thesis." *Amerisia Journal* 4 (1977): 23–51.

Tinker, John N. "Intermarriage and Assimilation in a Plural Society: Japanese Americans in the U.S." In *Intermarriage in the United States*, edited by Gary A. Cretser and Joseph J. Leon, 61–74. New York: Hayworth Press, 1982.

U.S. Immigration and Naturalization Service. *Annual Report*, 1995. Washington DC: U.S. Government Printing Office, 1995.

Walsh, Joan. "Asian Women, Caucasian Men." *Image*, 2 December 1990, 11–16.

Wang, Y.C. *Chinese Intellectuals and the West, 1872–1949*. Chapel Hill: University of North Carolina Press, 1966.

Waters, Marh. *Ethnic Options: Choosing Identities in America*. Berkeley: University of California Press, 1990.

Wong, Berhard P. *Patronage, Brokerage, Entrepreneurship and the Chinese Community of New York*. New York: AMS Press, 1988.

Wong, Morrison G. "A Look at Intermarriage Among the Chinese in the United States." *Sociological Perspective* 21 (1): 87–107.

Xu Xishan. "Sancun LinLian" [Bound Feet]. *The World Journal*, 8–10 March 1997.

Yang, Eun Sik. "Korean Women in America, 1903–1930." In *Korean Women in Transition, at Home and Abroad*, edited by Eui-Young Yu and Earl H. Phillips, 167–81. Los Angeles: Center for Korean American and Korean Studies, 1987.

Index

Korean adoptees, *continued*
identity crisis, 183–84, 192–93
Korean women, xxix–xxx, 175–254
difference of Korean immigration, xxix
generational conflict, 247–54
Hawaiian sugar plantation, xxix
interracial marriage, xxx, 176, 209–46
life in America, 194–208
post-war Korean immigration, xxx
the 1965 Immigration Act, xxx

L
Laotian women
higher education, 360
immigration, xxxii–xxxiv
interracial marriage, 318, 358–63
Lao Mutual Aid Association, 345, 347–49
Laotian community, 345, 347–48
refugees, 343–49
Lord, Bette Bao, xxxvi

M
marriage
age of, 6, 10–11, 18–19, 34, 79, 86, 262, 270, 282, 294, 297, 326, 344
attitudes about arranged marriage, 276
educations/professional status of spouse, 6, 10–11, 18–19, 34, 79, 86, 262, 270, 282, 294, 297, 326, 344, 346
relation with spouse, 81, 90, 264, 286–87
marriage in Japan, 154
See also interracial marriage
Meiji period (1868–1912), xx
Meiji Civil Code of 1898, xx
model minority, 2, 98, 129, 193, 223, 251, 355
See also stereopypes of Asians

O
one child policy in China, 46, 50
1.5 generation, 194, 306
Opium War, xxv

P
parental expectations, 247–50, 252, 302, 309–10, 364
parents, 24–25, 30, 45–47, 50, 52, 54–55, 57, 60–62, 64, 73–74, 78, 83, 88, 93–94, 99–100, 102, 103, 133–38, 146–47, 150, 153–54, 157, 162–63, 169, 194–95, 202, 220–21, 235–37, 247, 258, 269, 274, 280, 291–93, 297, 301–2, 306–8, 310, 319, 325, 334, 339, 343, 358, 367
preference for residence, 8, 23–24, 267, 289, 299–300, 303, 314, 363
professionals
Asian Indian, xxxii, 269–190
Chinese, 13–44
foreign-born, 374
Filipinas, xxvii
Japanese, 133–49
Korean, xxx
push and pull paradigm, xxiv

R
race, 341, 352, 353–54
refugees
camps, 320–22, 328, 344–45
criticism of, 346
elderly, from Vietnam, 331–32
escape Laos, 344, 367
escape Vietnam, 319–20, 327–28, 334–35
Indochinese, 317, 319–49
Laotian, and problems, 348–49
psychological trauma, 328, 331–32
Vietnamese, xxxiii–xxxiv, 317, 319–49
religion,
attitudes about, 39, 207–8, 300, 305–6, 343
maintaining religious traditions, 265–67
religious traditions, xx–xxiv, 319, 347, 369
role models, 188–89

S
San Francisco Chinatown, 4–6
second-generation
Chinese, 1, 4–12